4-14

2

ILLINOIS CENTRAL COLLEGE

A12902 039338

W9-CCV-370

Twitter

WITHDRAWN

Digital Media and Society

Twitter

Social Communication in the Twitter Age

Dhiraj Murthy

I.C.C. LIBRARY

polity

Hm
743
.T95
m87
2013

Copyright © Dhiraj Murthy 2013

The right of Dhiraj Murthy to be identified as Author of this Work has been
asserted in accordance with the UK Copyright, Designs and Patents Act 1988.

First published in 2013 by Polity Press

Polity Press
65 Bridge Street
Cambridge CB2 1UR, UK

Polity Press
350 Main Street
Malden, MA 02148, USA

All rights reserved. Except for the quotation of short passages for the purpose
of criticism and review, no part of this publication may be reproduced, stored
in a retrieval system, or transmitted, in any form or by any means, electronic,
mechanical, photocopying, recording or otherwise, without the prior
permission of the publisher.

ISBN-13: 978-0-7456-5238-2
ISBN-13: 978-0-7456-5239-9(pb)

A catalogue record for this book is available from the British Library.

Typeset in 10.25 on 13 pt Scala
by Servis Filmsetting Ltd, Stockport, Cheshire
Printed and bound in Great Britain by TJ International Ltd, Padstow, Cornwall

The publisher has used its best endeavours to ensure that the URLs for
external websites referred to in this book are correct and active at the time of
going to press. However, the publisher has no responsibility for the websites
and can make no guarantee that a site will remain live or that the content is or
will remain appropriate.

Every effort has been made to trace all copyright holders, but if any have been
inadvertently overlooked the publisher will be pleased to include any necessary
credits in any subsequent reprint or edition.

For further information on Polity, visit our website: www.politybooks.com

4/14 B&T 22.95

For Kalpana, Deya Anjali, and Akash
Dedicated in loving memory of Nagavenamma
and Venkatachala Shetty

You're not reducing face-to-face time . . . You don't choose to stay in and do Twitter. It's like those spare moments on the Web when I'm doing another task I switch over to Twitter for literally 15 seconds. There is no fewer face-to-face, no fewer phone calls, there's more awareness of other people in my life and maybe that even leads to further conversation with some people.

Evan Williams, co-founder of Twitter
(cited in Niedzviecki 2009: 132)

Contents

Figures and Tables

Preface and Acknowledgments

"What Hath God Wrought" – Samuel Morse's first message, on May 24, 1844, on the newly completed telegraph wire linking Baltimore and Washington – was a mere 21 characters long. Alexander Graham Bell's first message on the telephone to his lab assistant on March 10, 1876, "Mr. Watson – come here – I want to see you," was more liberal: 42 characters long. And 95 years later, Ray Tomlinson sent the first email, with the message "QWERTYUIOP," from one computer in Cambridge, Massachusetts, to another computer sitting beside it. Tomlinson's message: a spartan 10 characters.

In the past, technology determined the length and duration of the message. In the Internet age of today, our ability to communicate is seemingly limitless. But the computer has ushered in a new era of brevity. Twitter is a digital throwback to the analog succinctness of telegrams. Yet what is the significance of this electronically diminished turn to terseness? Does it signal the dumbing down of society, the victory of short attention spans, or the rise of new virtual "me" cultures? Are we saying more with less, or just saying less? Or perhaps we are saying more about less. This position is well illustrated by "status updates," short one- or two-line messages on the popular social networking website Facebook. Though these short messages are often trivially banal (e.g., "mustard dripping out of my bagel sandwich"), they are elevated to "news," which Facebook automatically distributes to your group of "friends," selected individuals who have access to your Facebook "profile," that is, your personalized web page on the site. Once the update percolates to your friends, they have the opportunity to comment on your update, generating a rash of discussion about dripping mustard, and so on.

This form of curt social exchange has become the norm with messages on Twitter, the popular social media website where individuals respond to the question "What's happening?" with a maximum of 140 characters. These messages, known as "tweets," can be sent through the Internet, mobile devices such as Internet-enabled phones and iPads, and text messages. But, unlike status updates, their strict limit of 140 characters produces at best eloquently terse responses and at worst heavily truncated speech. Tweets such as *"gonna* see *flm* tonite!" or "jimmy *wil* be fired *l8r 2day*" are reflective of the latter. The first tweet on the site, "just setting up my twttr" (24 characters), by Jack Dorsey, the creator of Twitter, on March 21, 2006, perhaps led by example. This book emphasizes that Dorsey's message, like that of Morse, was brief and, like that of Bell, was unremarkable – setting up one's Twitter and asking the recipient to return.

By drawing this line between the telegraph and telephone to Twitter, this book makes its central argument – that the rise of these messages does not signal the death of meaningful communication. Rather, Twitter has the potential to increase our awareness of others and to augment our spheres of knowledge, tapping us into a global network of individuals who are passionately giving us instant updates on topics and areas in which they are knowledgeable or participating in real-time. In doing so, however, the depth of our engagements with this global network of people and ideas can also, sometimes, become more superficial. Many of us would be worried if Twitter replaced "traditional" media or the longer-length media of blogs, message boards, and email lists. The likelihood of this is, of course, minimal and this book concludes with the suggestion that there is something profoundly remarkable in us being able to follow minute-by-minute commentary in the aftermath of an earthquake, or even the break-up of a celebrity couple. This book is distinctive in not only having Twitter as its main subject, but also its approach of theorizing the site as a collection of communities of knowledge, ad hoc groups where individual voices are aggregated into flows of dialog and information (whether it be Michael Jackson's death or the release of the Lockerbie bomber). Ultimately, Twitter affords a unique opportunity to re-evaluate how communication and culture can be individualistic and communal simultaneously.

I also describe how these changes in communication are not restricted exclusively to the West, as any mobile phone, even the most basic model, is compatible with Twitter. Tweets can be quickly and easily sent, a fact that has led to the exponential growth of its base to over 140 million users worldwide (Wasserman 2012). This has been useful in communicating information about disasters (e.g., the 2011 Tōhoku earthquake in Japan) and social movements (e.g., the 2011 "Arab Spring" movements). At an individual level, tweets have reported everything from someone's cancer diagnosis to unlawful arrests. For example, in April 2008, James Karl Buck, a graduate student at the University of California, Berkeley, was arrested photographing an anti-government labor protest in Mahalla, Egypt. He quickly sent a one-word tweet from his phone, "arrested," which caught the attention of Buck's Twitter "followers," those who subscribe to his tweets. His one-word tweet led to Berkeley hiring a lawyer and Buck's eventual release. There are, of course, many distinctions to be made between the tweets sent by Buck, or those sent during the Mumbai bomb blasts, and the more unremarkable, everyday tweets. Contrast the tweet Prasad Naik sent moments after the Mumbai bomb blasts, "Firing happening at the Oberoi hotel where my sister works. Faaak!" with Jack Dorsey's third tweet, "wishing I had another sammich." Though an intentionally striking and loaded comparison, it is just this absurdity that happens daily, hourly, and by the minute on Twitter. This combination of banal/profound, combined with the one-to-many – explicitly – public broadcasting of tweets, differentiates Twitter from Facebook and text messages.

Rather than selectively condemning Twitter as dumbed down or, on the other hand, praising its profundity, the book poses important questions to explore the possibilities and pitfalls of this new communications medium. Although I examine the practice of social media through specific Twitter-mediated events, this book's emphasis is both explanatory and theoretical. Specifically, my prime aim is to better understand the meanings behind Twitter and similar social media through concise yet sophisticated interpretations of theories of media and communication, drawing upon a diverse array of scholars, from Marshall McLuhan to Erving Goffman and Gilles Deleuze to Martin Heidegger. Though this network of thinkers and scholars crosses several disciplines, their work sheds light on a problem of communication faced since the dawn of the modern age: unraveling the connections, to paraphrase McLuhan, between the medium and the message.

The chapters present analyses of the shifts in which we communicate by exploring the role of Twitter in discourses of new media forms, communication, social formations, and digitally mediated communities. Early chapters introduce Twitter, historically contextualize it, and present theoretical frames to analyze the medium. Comparisons between historical media forms are made to highlight the fact that new media forms are not all that "new" in many of the ways in which they organize our social lives. For example, when the telephone began to get a critical mass in U.S. households, there were similar feelings of anxiety that the "public" would erode the "private," as anyone could call your house as you were having an intimate family dinner or in deep conversation with a visiting friend. The middle chapters include specific discussions of Twitter and its relationship to journalism, disasters, social activism, and health. The book then brings together theory and practice to make conclusions on the medium itself and its role in social communication within an "update culture," a culture in which society has placed importance on updating friends, family, peers, colleagues, and the general public. The question of whether this pattern signifies "me-centric" rather than "society-centric" cultures is explored in the conclusion. Between chapters, I single out an individual tweet to frame the forthcoming chapter.

My work on this book has been shaped by generous input and encouragement from family, friends, colleagues, and scholars. I am very grateful for their involvement in the development of this book. Students in my "In the Facebook Age" and "Critical Theory and New Media" classes have been taught material from early versions of chapters, and offered engaging and highly useful feedback. I am also indebted to my students for providing me with a treasure trove of examples of interesting Twitter users and tweets. Thank you to my undergraduate research fellow, Macgill Eldredge, who imported the data sources in chapter 7 into a standardized format and produced the spike data histogram. The reference librarians at the British Library patiently helped me navigate archives regarding the telegraph, material which fundamentally shaped the historical context of the book. I have greatly benefited from input from my colleagues at Bowdoin College. I would like to single out Susan Bell, Pamela Ballinger, Craig McEwen, Matthew Klingle, and Wendy Christensen for their input on early versions of chapters. I would also like to thank Andrea Drugan and the rest of the Polity team for their invaluable support in making this project a reality.

TEXT ACKNOWLEDGMENTS

Parts of chapter 3 are due to appear in "Towards a sociological understanding of social media: theorizing Twitter," *Sociology* (forthcoming, 2012), and parts of chapter 4 have previously appeared in "Twitter: microphone for the masses?," *Media, Culture & Society* 33(5) (2011).

CHAPTER ONE

What is Twitter?

> Facebook is composed of my photos. MySpace is
> composed of my favorite music. Twitter is composed
> of everything inside my heart.
>
> @GirlsProverbs

The tweet above compares three popular online social spaces.
For those unfamiliar with Twitter, the following chapter
explores what the medium is, how it is structured, and how
people use it. Twitter may not be a reflection of "everything
inside [one's] heart," but it is seen that way by some. Others
see the medium as facilitating support communities and
some have used it for speed dating. The following chapter
provides a basic introduction to Twitter as a communications
medium.

> It's funny because I actually started drinking late in life, at
> like twenty-two or so. So my parents who live in St. Louis
> never really knew that I started drinking. I was with Ev and
> we were drinking whiskey and I decided to Twitter about it.
> And my mom was like, "I knew you drink cider sometimes,
> but whiskey?" (Jack Dorsey, talking with Evan Williams,
> Twitter co-founder, cited in Niedzviecki 2009: 130)

Blair (1915) in his popular twentieth-century stage song, "I
hear a little Twitter and a Song," was, of course, referring to
birdsong. However, so ubiquitous the website has become,
that for most Internet-using adults, to hear a twitter today
refers to one of the largest and most popular social media
websites.[1] Twitter allows users to maintain a public web-based

asynchronous "conversation" through the use of 140-character messages (the length of text messages) sent from mobile phones, mobile Internet devices, or through various websites. Twitter's aim is for users to respond to the question "What's happening?" in 140 characters or less.[2] These messages on Twitter (termed "tweets") are automatically posted and are publicly accessible on the user's profile page on the Twitter website. Tweets are a public version of Facebook's now well-known status update function, but provide public awareness of all users on the medium rather than being restricted to one's friends. The dialogue between Twitter users occurs through the at-sign (e.g., a user can direct tweets to another user by prefixing a post with an at-sign before the target user's name). Anyone can post a tweet directed to @BarackObama or @CharlieSheen, and many do. Additionally, anyone can instantly see a tweet and respond to it.[3] One does not even need to "know" the other user or have their permission to direct a tweet at them.

There are 40 world leaders with verified accounts on Twitter, including Hugo Chávez (The Christian Science Monitor 2011), and it is estimated that more than 200 million tweets are sent every day (Schonfeld 2011). Though it is unclear as to how many of these tweets ever get read, the fact of the matter is that people are sending tweets and consider them to be meaningful. Twitter co-founders, Jack Dorsey and Evan Williams,[4] believe that the medium's appeal is due to "its ease of use, its instant accessibility, [and] its short bursts of seemingly unimportant chatter" (Niedzviecki 2009: 129). As these founders of Twitter highlight, one factor that has facilitated the popularity of the medium is its ease of use. Anyone with a mobile phone (and most people in the world now have one (International Telecommunications Union 2011)) can quickly fire off a text message to Twitter's mobile phone number. And because sending a text message has become a banal activity in scores of countries around the world (Ewalt 2003), the learning curve for using Twitter is relatively low for individuals familiar with "texting." As even the most basic mobile phone can be used, the technology is potentially accessible even in impoverished countries. This is an important distinction of the medium to Facebook and other emergent social technologies. One does not need broadband Internet access or, for that matter, a PC to regularly use Twitter (this is not to say that Twitter's uptake crosses traditional social boundaries and inequalities). Additionally, the time commitment required to post a tweet is minimal in comparison to posting a blog or publishing other material on the Internet. As Twitter creator and co-founder Dorsey (cited in Niedzviecki 2009: 129) puts it, Twitter's attraction is premised on "connection with very low expectation." Indeed, the contribution itself can be of "low expectation."

Though restricted to 140 characters, Twitter has simple yet powerful methods of connecting tweets to larger themes, specific people, and groups. This is a unique aspect of the medium. Specifically, tweets can be categorized by a "hashtag." Any word(s) preceded by a hash sign "#" are used in Twitter to note a subject, event, or association. Hashtags are an integral part of Twitter's ability to link the conversations of strangers together. For example, people during the 2010 soccer World Cup tweeted with both the #worldcup hash tag as well as tags to indicate teams (e.g., #eng for England and #ned for the Netherlands). Similarly, tweets pertaining to the 2011 Occupy Wall Street movement used #occupywallstreet and #ows. By including a hashtag in one's tweet, it becomes included into a larger "conversation" consisting of all tweets with the hashtag. The structure of communication via hashtags facilitates impromptu interactions of individuals (often strangers) into these conversations. It is for this reason that Twitter has been considered useful in social movements like Occupy Wall Street (see chapter 6 for more detail). Because hashtags represent an aggregation of tagged tweets, conversations are created more organically. Just because people are tweeting under the same hashtag, this does not mean they are conversing with each other in the traditional sense. Rather, the discourse is not structured around directed communication between identified interactants. It is more of a stream, which is composed of a polyphony of voices all chiming in. The technologies that most parallel Twitter in this way are Internet chat rooms and telephone party lines. In the case of the "ows" hashtag, it was a confluence of diverse Occupy Wall Street tweets that contributed to engagement by individuals. Either serendipitously or by reading through scores of tweets appearing second by second, individuals and groups interacted with each other after seeing relevant tweets.

Because tweets can also be directed to specific individual(s), even if she/he is a stranger or a celebrity, Twitter is unique in facilitating interactions across discrete social networks. For example, individuals can and do tweet @KatyPerry, the American pop singer. This form of directed interaction is powerful in that all discourse is public and its audience is not limited to the explicitly specified interactants. Often, individuals tweeting are putting on a show for others to see (see figure 1.1). Or there is no show at all. Rather, the ease of interaction offers a platform to voice a concern. For example, in this tweet, a user wants to convey his political opinions to Barack Obama and tweets: "@BarackObama. I know other countries need help. We have homeless and people in USA that we should help first, don't you thank [sic.]."

A user's profile page, known on Twitter as a timeline (see figure 1.1), includes all tweets (whether or not they are directed to another user). This shapes Twitter because anyone can "lurk" (i.e., observe profiles without their target knowing of this lurking). Not only does this encourage the theatrical aspect of profiles, but it also presents a different picture of consumers of a profile. Specifically, it facilitates new forms of consumption of a user's feed. Because one can see your tweeting history (from music to the fact that one forgot to do the laundry), it not only presents a different view of users, but also allows consumers of a profile to follow "leads" they find to be

Figure 1.1 *Runner's Strip* © Cait Chock www.caitchock.com

interesting (e.g., a tweet about a charitable event or a band). On the other hand, this also presents issues of privacy. The barriers between public and private become extremely blurred as one can see very specific conversations between individuals which are many times intended to be private, but are tweeted nonetheless (given the medium's ability to foster this (see chapter 3)).

The function of following users in some ways mimics a TV guide, where you can see a list of channels with some limited information of what is being broadcast on the channel at that moment. If the channel piques your attention, you can stay tuned in. On Twitter, one can tune into the timelines of particular Twitter users who can be people you are interested in (from A-list celebrities to your neighbor), a professional organization, a magazine/journal, a company, etc. The relationship of following and followed within Twitter shapes the consumption of tweets and user profiles. It has become commonplace to be "friends" with others on various websites. "Friendship" tends to indicate some level of familiarity with that person. However, on Twitter, one does not need to be on a first-name basis or even "know" the user to follow them. This relational structure leads to Twitter users following popular users (often celebrities or news organizations). Recall the television channel analogy; these popular Twitter users are followed because people would like to tune into these channels (regularly or at least once in a while).

This structure of channels and consumers of channels of information draws from notions of broadcasting (Allen 1992). Specifically, Twitter has been designed to facilitate interactive multicasting (i.e., the broadcasting of many to many). Television and radio are both one-to-many models where a station broadcasts to many consumers. Twitter encourages a many-to-many model through both hashtags and retweets. A "retweet" (commonly abbreviated as "RT") allows people to "forward" tweets to their followers and is a key way in which Twitter attempts to facilitate the (re)distribution of tweets outside of one's immediate, more "bounded" network to broader, more unknown audiences. It is also one of the central mechanisms by which tweets become noticed by others on Twitter. Specifically, if a tweet is retweeted often enough or by the right person(s), it gathers momentum that can emulate a snowball effect. This is all part of interactive multicasting, wherein many users are vying for the eyes and ears of many users. Again, this is in distinction from the more limited set of broadcasters in traditional broadcast media. Additionally, interactive multicasting blurs the role of consumers on Twitter as these consumers simultaneously become producers when they add a phrase and retweet a news story they find interesting. Even if they do not modify the original tweets, a retweet rebroadcasts the tweets to their many followers – though not production, it is broadcasting. Hashtags themselves are emblematic of interactive multicasting in that many users are broadcasting to many users on the topic. The "interactive" part refers to the multimedia content embedded in tweets (including hyperlinks, photographs, and videos). Recipients do not inherently passively consume these tweets. Rather, they can actively navigate this content or they can cross the blurred boundary and become content producers if they comment on the original content or tweet back to the original tweeting user (i.e., the original broadcaster).

Is Twitter a Public Version of Facebook?

Twitter is often compared to Facebook and sometimes considered as a public version of the popular social networking site. This comparison has some truth to it. Both mediums are social, tend to elicit regular contributions that are not verbose, and are highly interactive. However, the two mediums are unique in many important ways. First, the distinction should be made between "social network" and "social media" technologies. The former, which encompasses Facebook and LinkedIn amongst others, is defined by boyd and Ellison (2008: 211) as providing web services which facilitate users maintaining a "public or semi-public profile within a bounded system" and through which they can "articulate a list of other users with whom they share a connection."

Social media has been broadly defined to refer to "the many relatively inexpensive and widely accessible electronic tools that enable anyone to publish and access information,

collaborate on a common effort, or build relationships"
(Jue et al. 2010: 4). Some elide social networking and social
media together. The two are not mutually exclusive and social
networks are important distribution venues for content produced in social media. Though there is overlap, it is more
useful to make clear that social media is mainly conceived
of as a medium wherein "ordinary" people in ordinary social
networks (as opposed to professional journalists) can *publish* user-generated "news"/"updates" (in a broadly defined
sense).[5] Additionally, social media's emphasis is not as
"bounded" to communities of friends as social network sites
are. Rather, social media is a publishing-oriented medium
and the "social" part of social media refers to its distinction
from "traditional" media (Murthy 2011b). Though Facebook
and other social networking sites do multicast, this is not their
emphasis per se. It is to foster friend connections through
social sharing that is designed to keep ties between users
active and vibrant. Social media's emphasis is broadcast-based
and encourages the accumulation of more and more followers
who are *aware* of a user's published content (e.g., tweets).

In other words, Twitter is markedly distinct from Facebook's
friend-centered social network model. Twitter, in many ways,
shares similarities with blogs, albeit the posts on Twitter are
considerably shorter. However, once one's tweets are aggregated, a new structure emerges. This is not merely a technical
consideration, but rather the organization of communication
as a series of short communiqués is qualitatively different
from examining tweets individually. As a corpus, they begin
to resemble a more coherent text. Granted, the corpus is disjointed, but narratives can and do emerge. For this reason,
Twitter is best considered as a "microblog," a "blog" that
consists of short messages rather than long ones (Java et al.
2007). It is considered the most popular microblogging service, though others such as friendfeed,[6] Jaiku, Tumblr, Plurk,
and Squeelr (an anonymous microblogging service) have also
experienced exponential growth. Microblogs differ from blogs

in terms of the length of posts (a factor which also influences the frequency of posts in the two media). Ebner and Schiefner (2008) usefully compare this relationship between blogs and microblogs to that between email and text messages. In their study of blogs and microblogs, respondents saw the former as a tool for "knowledge saving, coherent statements and discourse," while the latter was most used for "writing about their thoughts and quick reflections" (Ebner and Schiefner 2008). However, the length of microblog posts should not be viewed as inherently deterministic of their communicative function. A key difference between blogs and microblogs is their social organization. Twitter, for example, implements a complex social structure which tweets support and foster. Tweets as "quick reflections" help keep social networks active on Twitter, whereas blogs are inherently more egocentric in focus.

The ways in which microblogs organize social communication may feel new. However, Twitter uses technology developed from earlier Internet media such as text-based gaming in Multi-User Dungeons (MUDs), Instant Messenger (IM), and Internet Relay Chat (IRC). IRC and MUDs were early synchronous precursors to Twitter. A difference between these earlier technologies and Twitter is that the latter is almost always in the public domain, whereas many MUDs and some chat rooms had restricted access.[7] This is an important distinction. Twitter has similarities to both blogs and chat rooms,[8] but its emphasis on accessible dialogic communication in the public domain is unique.

Understandably, one may find the differences between microblogging, social networks, and social media difficult to discern. Indeed, the boundaries are often blurry. However, it is important to draw some lines between these categories. At the simplest level, social networks are friend-based networks where maintaining and developing friendship ties are critical (Facebook is a prime example of this). Social media are designated as broadcast media, whose intention is to publish content to networks known and unknown to the author (Twitter is the most prominent example of this). There are different types of social media such as image-and-video-oriented social media. Twitter is one example of a microblogging-based social medium. For the sake of clarity, I define microblogging as an Internet-based service in which: (1) users have a public profile where they broadcast short public messages/updates whether they are directed to specific user(s) or not; (2) messages become publicly aggregated together across users; and (3) users can decide whose messages they wish to receive, but not necessarily who can receive their messages; this is in distinction from most social networks where following each other is bidirectional (i.e., mutual). The boundaries of public and private are critical to understanding microblogging as well as its predecessor technologies. Rosenthal (2008: 159) helps make this distinction by observing that "[n]ewsletters by e-mail are still newsletters, but blogs bring personalized and interpersonal communication into the public domain." Microblogs like Twitter follow a similar logic in that they consist of very short updates that can be read at the individual update level (i.e., at the level of the tweet) or as an aggregation of tweets.

Like blogs, microblog entries can be on anything of interest to the author (from interpreting current events to daily trivialities). Microblogs, as a medium, depend on the regularity of content contribution. Niedzviecki (2009: 130) argues that Twitter "works because of its constancy and consistency, [factors which lead you to . . .] stop thinking about what you're revealing and who's on the other end, reading about your mundane life." Microblog services group lists of users together based on interests, and their microblogs throughout the day are able to sustain discernible conversations. As DeVoe (2009) succinctly argues, "successful microblogging depends on having an audience." And tweets have an audience – whether followers of the tweet's author, or strangers. Dorsey (cited in Niedzviecki 2009: 130) believes that

Twitter users feel as if they are "writing to a wall" and they feel that "there's not much of an audience with Twitter." However, as Niedzviecki (2009: 130–1) highlights, this is purely a perception and, even if the audience is not "obvious or apparent," that does not translate to an absence of an audience with tweets disappearing into the ether. Rather, like any response-based medium, users would discontinue using the medium if they felt that they were not receiving the level of response they deemed important to them. Additionally, exceptional tweets are regularly highlighted in the media.[9]

On social network sites such as Facebook, users often interact with people they know offline (boyd 2007; Ellison et al. 2007). Users of social media often consume media produced by people they are not acquainted with, but have found of interest. This is especially true of retweets and trending topics on Twitter. This can lead to interactions with strangers and, albeit more rarely, celebrities. In my research on new media and a Muslim youth subculture (Murthy 2010), a respondent of mine recounted how he posted a tweet disparaging Deepak Chopra only to find that Chopra himself responded and invited my respondent to have a meal with him (an offer which was taken up).[10] Facebook and other SNS are structured to leverage stronger ties within a more proximal network, rather than maximizing audience reach.

Though instances like this one involving Chopra are the exception rather than the rule, they appear side by side with the hordes of more "normal" tweets. Of course, social network sites can include the banal and profound together (e.g., a Facebook user posts about their breakfast and later announces they are pregnant). However, a key difference here between social media and social network sites is the design of the former to be explicitly public and geared towards interactive multicasting. Combine the two – as Twitter does – and you have real-time public, many-to-many broadcasting to as wide a network as the content is propagated by its users. Though the tweets are aggregated into a microblog stream and constitute a corpus as a whole, they are still individual units. Tweets are analogous to bees in that they exist both as individuals and as part of a collectively built whole (i.e., the hive). And, like bees, a single tweet is a self-functioning unit in and of itself. Indeed, a single tweet can also pack a powerful sting! Ultimately, if an individual tweet is perceived as important to other users, it can travel far and wide, crossing many networks in the process. This is particularly true of tweets in social activism (see chapter 6).

Conclusion

This chapter has introduced what Twitter is and how it functions as a type of social media. A key aspect of this chapter has been to define differences between social network sites such as Facebook and social media such as Twitter. Additionally, Twitter has been explained as a microblogging technology which is specifically designed to broadcast short but regular bursts of content to particularly large audiences well beyond a user's direct social network. This chapter has highlighted how Twitter is structured to increase awareness of others (whether they are "friends" of yours or not). This awareness has been highlighted by Twitter's ability to broadcast the experiences of ordinary people during social movements and natural disasters.

Twitter has not just made the headlines through news of activism or disasters. Rather, Twitter often pervades both the professional and personal lives of its users. For example, Twitter speed-dating, when singles go to a bar armed with a mobile phone and send tweets to potential suitors, has gained a following in New York (Snow 2009). And, in Los Angeles, the Kogi Korean BBQ-To-Go van, which sells Korean-Mexican fusion tacos, sends tweets to its followers letting them know when and where the van will next be stopping (Oh 2009). Twitter has also become an increasingly popular medium for support networks. For example, Hawn (2009: 364–5) highlights the case of Rachel Baumgartel, a woman with type 2 diabetes who uses Twitter to inform her support network of her diet, exercise regime, and hemoglobin Alc levels. For Baumgartel and many others like her, Twitter functions as a medium for a network to keep someone "in line" on a daily basis in terms of following a treatment regime (see chapter 7 for a fuller discussion).

Additionally, Twitter has, in some ways, redefined existing cultural practices such as diary keeping, news consumption, and job searching, to name a few. Indeed as Clapperton (2009) remarks, it has redefined the way in which consumers complain. As he observes, big companies such as Jaguar trawl social media websites, looking for complaints, and then publicly respond to upset customers, offering help. This chapter has not sought to singularly reduce the diversity or complexities of Twitter, but rather to outline some of its functions and uses for those with little or no background of the medium. The following chapters will build upon the structural and definitional frameworks developed in this chapter. However, before doing so, the next chapter will specifically contextualize Twitter within "modern" forms of communications technology.

CHAPTER TWO

Contextualizing Twitter

The first twitter of Spring, How melodious its ring
The first twitter of Spring, How melodious its ring,
   its ring,
[. . .]
O'er the down and the dell [. . .]
song birds that flit, Singing cheerily twit, twitter
   twit, tra la la, tra la.

(Callcott 1863: 1–7)

In his late eighteenth-century play titled *The Telegraph, or, A New Way of Knowing Things* (1795), John Dent satirizes the effect of the telegraph at the time. As performed at the Theatre Royal in London, its protagonist, Sir Peter Curious, is dead set on getting a telegraph of his own so he can spy on his family and check if his wife, Lady Curious, is being unfaithful. Sir Peter describes the telegraph by saying it is "an apparatus, by which you may find out what's doing in one's family, let it be ever so far off" (Dent 1795: 9). The telegraph's ability to combine the immediacy of messages with interlocutors at great distances fascinates Sir Peter, leading him to add, "if you say in Basinghall Street, 'How d'ye do?' they'll answer you in five minutes, 'Pretty well I thank you' in the blue mountains" (Dent 1795: 9). Sir Peter, particularly keen to spy on his family, claims that the arrival of a telegraph of his own means that "I [Sir Peter] shall know to a certainty, what my Lady is about at Sydenham, and be convinced, whether I have any cause, or not, to suspect her of infidelity" (Dent 1795: 9–10). This notion that the telegraph will blur the boundaries of public and private culminates in a scene in which the coachman, gardener, butler, and housekeeper begin confessing improprieties (including the butler's theft of over a dozen bottles of champagne). They know that the days of raiding their boss's liquor cabinet are numbered as Sir Peter will, of course, find out about *everything* in the future through the telegraph (Dent 1795: 20–21).

Though Dent's play was written over 200 years ago, it is striking just how resonant it is with the contemporary reception to new media technologies which seek to similarly compress time/space (Harvey 1989) as well as shrink/blur the boundaries between private and public. Modern-day Sir Peters snoop on loved ones or children through new web-based technologies, including social networking sites (such as Facebook and Google+) and social media (such as Twitter). Dent's play also highlights the issues of privacy and time/space compression (i.e., shrinking the limits of geography and time). The relevance of his play is, however, much deeper in that the telegraph, his object of interest, has many parallels to Twitter. Like the telegraph, it is used to send short messages quickly and, like the telegraph, it is a controversial technology. In the eighteenth and indeed nineteenth centuries, most lauded the telegraph (with *The Times* (1796) calling it an "ingenious and useful contrivance" and *Scientific American* heralding it as the bringer of a "kinship of humanity" (cited in Fischer 1992: 2). Others at the time viewed it as a means to dumb down society and the harbinger of letter writing's death. Indeed, even in the early twentieth century, discussions of the telegraph's impact on letter writing continued (e.g., *The Times* 1900). Although these early critics saw the telegraph's immediacy and brevity as a threat to letter writing, ironically, the telegraph highlighted the permanence of letter writing in that it remained an important medium. Similarly, when the telephone was seen as potentially replacing telegrams, the permanence of the telegram became highlighted; as Peggy Olson in her ad campaign during an episode of the television series *Mad Men* remarks, "You can't frame a phone call. A telegram is forever." Indeed, the Queen of England continues to send telegrams to Britons who become centenarians. Critics of Twitter such as Keen (2010) view social media as threatening blogging and other longer-length electronic media. But will the efficiency, immediacy, and brevity of Twitter, on the other hand, give permanence to earlier, less efficient, and longer-length electronic media? Additionally, as tweets are being archived by the American Library of Congress, will the next communicative technology give permanence to tweets?

Though these broad historical arguments reveal similarities between Twitter and older communication technologies, what makes the medium distinct is also the result of its departures from the telegraph. Specifically, it is free to use, public (or perhaps semi-public), multicast (i.e., many to many), interactive, and networked. A multitude of tweets also instantaneously go "down the wire" rather than the one-by-one output of the telegraph messages. The power of Twitter and other social media is also that they are designed to provoke and call forth regular updates from their users. Telegraph messages were often unidirectional dicta or updates. Twitter's interactions are not only more interactive than the telegraph, but the more important point is that these interactions all occur publicly. Highlighting these differences is key to a critical yet balanced understanding of the potential uniqueness of Twitter.

Contextualizing Twitter

Sir Peter, the character in the play mentioned at the start of this chapter, believes that once he gets hold of a telegraph, he "shall then be acquainted with every thing, and find [his] Lady Curious out in all her tricks, and [his] servants too" (Dent 1795: 10–11). Though not "tricks," Twitter has enabled its users to become more aware of certain everyday aspects of fellow users' lives. For example, when someone follows the tweets of people met at conferences, she/he will most likely be exposed to some combination of their daily music listening habits, sports interests, current location, and shopping wish lists, amongst other things. Many see this as a means to get to know people at a more multidimensional level. Additionally, they see aspects of people's lives which are normally not in public view, what Erving Goffman (1959) refers to as the "backstage" of people's lives (see chapter 3 for a fuller discussion). Granted, the boundaries of public and private communication have shifted remarkably in modernity (Murdock 1993). However, speaking in the context of the telegraph and telephone, various emergent communication technologies have had the same effect historically. The question is to what extent Twitter has further shifted these boundaries? Rather than view Twitter as "the fate of our age," another potential approach is to consider the power of Twitter to democratize media consumption. Does Twitter enable consumers greater choice through more inclusive broadcasting? From this standpoint, Twitter users are individual consumers who make reflective decisions on what information they desire in their Twitter feeds. They can choose from a variety of sources: traditional media, individual commentators, friends, leaders in an occupational field, and so on. The hegemony of traditional media sources may be eroded in this case, as whoever is considered to be an expert or simply worthy of being listened to is potentially determined by consumers rather than producers. Or from Durant's (2010) perspective, it becomes more "demotic" (i.e., democratized).

The transistor radio presents a parallel case. Bliven (1924) made the argument that the "new" medium of the transistor radio would give choice to listeners, enabling them to tune into a variety of stations, rather than being forced to consume the viewpoint of one station. He argued that this would enable listeners to be more democratic in their listening as well as more reflective of content. We can think of Twitter as a new media radio in which the Twitter feed of any user is like a station. One can choose to tune into particular tweets or user timelines and tune out of others. Following Bliven's

Figure 2.1   The Notificator; photograph copyright *Modern Mechanix and Inventions* magazine (1935)

logic, this may be facilitating more democratic and reflective consumption.

Twitter can be traced to a long line of innovations in communication technologies. Besides the telegraph and radio, Twitter resembles early social sharing technologies. For example, Benedictus (2010) compares a 1930s message board, The Notificator, to Twitter. The Notificator, as described by *Modern Mechanix and Inventions* (1935) was a "robot messenger" designed to "aid persons who wish to make or cancel appointments or to inform friends of their whereabouts." It had a "continuous strip of paper" on which passers-by (at railway stations and other public places) could write a brief message after inserting two pennies (see figure 2.1). The passer-by's message stays behind a glass panel for two hours. The parallels to Twitter are numerous. Not only are all the messages on The Notificator readable to any interested passer-by, but any passer-by could also direct a message to anyone they wished. Furthermore, Twitter's timeline is a digital equivalent of The Notificator's scroll of paper. And, like The Notificator, whether that message gets read or not is not always guaranteed. Benedictus (2010) also points out that, "[as] with Twitter, the size of [The Notificator's] messages was limited, but what they might say was not."

Of course, Twitter has an exponentially further reach than The Notificator, is public at a global scale, and facilitates interactions between unknown individuals rather than intended recipients. Twitter's ability to broadcast tweets to far-reaching unintended audiences – with the exceptional case being a celebrity seeing one's tweet – marks a major shift from the locality of The Notificator's audience. Twitter's audience can be thought of as networked "global publics" (Delanty 2006), through which divergent groups and individuals from around the world are publicly connected. Nonetheless, it is useful to make the argument that public forms of social media are nothing new and that previous generations had already shifted the public/private boundary through the technological mediation of everyday messages. Furthermore, like The Notificator's messages, the terseness of Twitter does not limit its potential meaningfulness. In other words, Twitter is not as "revolutionary" as one might initially think. Rather, it follows a historical line of communicative shifts in public short-messaging services.

Twitter and the "Global Village"

The global aspect of Twitter's reach is important and can be easily understood through Marshall McLuhan's (1968) notion of the "global village."[1] McLuhan (1962: 31) argued that the process of "new electronic interdependence recreates the world in the image of a global village." McLuhan was referring to his prediction that globalized electronically mediated communications infrastructure was creating a level of interdependence which would enable all parts of the world to be connected in a sort of "global village." A year after he forwarded this theory, John F. Kennedy was assassinated and television coverage of the event provided ample evidence of the global reach of this broadcast medium (Bianculli 1992: 86).

Twitter has been similarly associated with an amplification of the global village; Morris (2009) believes that "Twitter, is closer to the Global Village that the Internet was envisioned to be." If something happens somewhere in the world – regardless of whether it is banal or profound – someone will tweet about it. Human rights activists can keep tabs on potential human rights violations in distant places, and fashion enthusiasts can interact with fashionistas in London and Paris, regardless of where they live. Twitter can be viewed as accelerating the reach of McLuhan's global village not just in terms of connectedness, but, importantly, in terms of awareness of others in the village. However, the global village is not without faults and limitations. Ayoo (2009) evaluates the possibility of information communication technology as enabling African universities to gain access to journals and other scholarly materials, thus connecting them to a "global village of higher education." However, Ayoo concludes that not all African universities have equal access, leading to an unequal participation in this global village. Taken within a context of Twitter, students at universities in affluent countries can send tweets to authors of books and follow researchers at non-profit organizations, leveraging the power of the global village to educate them. Their counterparts at less well-off African universities may remain disconnected from this village. Ultimately, cases like this demonstrate that the global village – like "local" villages – remains highly stratified and the idea of being able to be connected with anyone in the world through a 140-character tweet is an ideal rather than a reality. That said, we do seem more "connected," an argument made by Castells (1996) in his conceptualization of the "Network Society." Watts (2003) and Barabási (2003) also argue that computer networks are increasing our connectedness.

However, this perceived connectedness is economically

mediated. Facebook, Google, and Twitter are all corporate entities, whose ultimate allegiance is to investors and shareholders. From this perspective, Shah (2008) argues that applying the term "global marketplace" rather than global village is perhaps more apt. In this vein, Twitter is perhaps also a global marketplace for ideas, commodities, and ourselves. This notion of Twitter as a global marketplace is also useful in understanding the power that influential Twitter users have within the medium's global publics. Specifically, a tweet from an African university student has differential "success" in Twitter's global marketplace than tweets from users who have more Twitter clout. However, at the same time, if that student tweets something profound (e.g., about an imminent labor strike), that tweet could potentially be widely consumed in the marketplace. There is an interesting tension here. Though Twitter as a global marketplace has unequally distributed influence, it has some resemblances to McLuhan's global village in that even far-flung individuals are not only connected to an immense global network, but their voices can potentially be amplified exponentially. Though this is an interesting paradox of the structure of Twitter, it is a paradox that other communications technologies before it have also experienced.

Conclusion

John Dent's play, introduced at the start of this chapter, reveals many of the similarities between the telegraph and Twitter. Sir Peter Curious saw the telegraph as compressing space and time (sending messages quickly across great distances) and bringing the private more into the public (discovering the private actions of Lady Curious and his servants). Twitter follows these historical shifts. But, aided by technological and social change, it has amplified these processes. Just as the telegraph did not determine the erosion of privacy, neither has Twitter. Rather, the private has been becoming more public over time. Indeed, The Notificator displayed many "private" interactions between people to any railway station passer-by. Like the telephone, Twitter has not determined social sharing across great distances, but has facilitated already emergent shifts in social behaviors.

This chapter has also explored how Twitter has potentially extended Marshall McLuhan's notion of the "global village," an idea that everyone in the world is connected in the image of a village. However, it is important to emphasize that Twitter follows an already well-trodden path in which the telegraph, telegram, radio, television, telephone, and email have already been before it. Additionally, like these previous technologies, Twitter's access is not universal throughout the "global village" and, as such, there are disjunctures and differences in terms of who is actually connected to the village.

Additionally, this chapter has contextualized the succinctness of tweets. In the past, technology determined the length and duration of the message. In the Internet age of today, our ability to communicate is seemingly limitless. However, mediated communication (as opposed to face-to-face communication) has, in many countries, been marked by a new era of brevity (or a perceived era of brevity). In this vein, Twitter is a digital throwback to the analogue succinctness of telegraphs and telegrams – a comparison analogous to Standage's (1998) reference to the telegraph as the "Victorian Internet." Yet what is the significance of this electronically diminished turn to terseness? Does it signal the dumbing down of society, the victory of short attention spans, or the rise of new virtual "me" cultures where – as Marshall Berman (1982: 22) puts it – "the individual dares to individuate himself"? Are we saying more with less, or just saying less? These questions are intentionally sweeping. However, they are indicative of questions asked when communication technologies of the past became popular. This chapter has explored some of these questions and subsequent chapters will build upon these answers.

It is tempting to focus on the newness of Twitter. However, this is at the expense of gaining a richer understanding through historical context of the medium. Ultimately, Twitter, like the telegraph, has gained significant public attention. And like the telegraph, a new, revolutionary technology in its time, Twitter is experiencing both immense growth as well as harsh criticisms. Despite the centuries of separation, the users of both technologies share a common motive: the desire to communicate. James Boaz (1802: 2), in his patent application, talks about one ship vessel approaching another and using an optical telegraph to say: "I wish to speak with you." Though far less cumbersome than the 25 lamps of Boaz's telegraph signaling system, perhaps Twitter's millions of users are just trying to do the same: "I wish to speak with you." This time around, users do not have to even wait five minutes to hear from the blue mountains. "@SirPeter Pretty well I thank you" would be tweeted back right away. Also, unlike the telegraph, anyone in the world could be reading @SirPeter's messages, replying to him, or circulating his thoughts to their friends, family, and colleagues.

CHAPTER THREE

Theorizing Twitter

Lying in bed . . . Checking twitter and thinking . . .
Maybe I'll nap and study later.

@NatashaT_R

This chapter begins with Kierkegaard's critique of modernity as fantastical in its dreams, but ultimately lazy. The tweet above would be perfect Kierkegaardian fodder. But, rather than view Twitter as redolent of a lazy culture unable to converse in lengths greater than 140 characters, a set of theoretical frames is provided here to better understand the complexities of how Twitter and social media more generally are part of our social lives. Larger questions of whether Twitter exposes us to different worldviews or whether it reinforces existing isomorphic social structures are specifically explored.

> [F]or indications are the only thing the present age achieves, and its skill and virtuosity entirely consist in building magical illusions; its momentary enthusiasms which use some projected change in the forms of things as an escape for actually changing the forms of things [and, eventually] this present age tires of its chimerical attempts until it declines back into indolence. Its condition is like one who has just fallen asleep in the morning: first, great dreams, then laziness, and then a witty or clever reason for staying in bed. (Kierkegaard and Dru 1962)

Twitter is not merely a communicative technology. Rather, as Heidegger (1977: 4) warns, regarding technology as "neutral [. . .] makes us utterly blind to the essence of technology." Ultimately, computers and other technology form the medium, but are not divorced from the social. In his essay "The Question Concerning Technology," Heidegger forwards two statements regarding technology: "Technology is a means to an end" and "Technology is a human activity." He argues that the two definitional statements are not mutually exclusive and actually belong together. From this vantage point, technology is "a man-made means to an end established by man" (Heidegger 1977: 5). It is also, from his perspective, a "way of revealing" (Heidegger 1977: 12). This is where Heidegger is particularly useful for understanding the complexities of technology in relation to social media. Specifically, Heidegger conceptualizes this "revealing" through the concept of *Herausfordern*, which can be translated as "to call forth or summon to action, to demand positively, to provoke" (Heidegger 1977: 14). Rather than being neutral, the power of Twitter and other social media is also that they are designed to provoke and call forth regular updates from their users.

This chapter presents the first steps toward a theoretical understanding of Twitter. Rather than rush to breathlessly describe its novel role in contemporary economic, political, and social life, the points put forward in the previous chapter are built on by taking a step back and considering Twitter in broad theoretical terms. This chapter is intended to provide a selected literature review and a set of directions for scholars, students, and practitioners by making connections to scholarship in communications, sociology, and philosophy. A broad array of theoretical perspectives is purposely explored to both explain the nuances of understanding Twitter and provide a framework for understanding later chapters that focus on particular applications of Twitter. In this chapter, particular emphasis is placed on Erving Goffman's interdisciplinary work in order to provide a solid theoretical framework to critically explore Twitter's role in social communication. Other areas explored are democratization, self-identity, community, and the modern "event society." I will start with Lev Manovich's (2001) concept of the digital object as it is useful in understanding how the various components of tweets and Twitter itself come together.

Twitter as a Digital "Object"

Manovich (2001: 13) makes an argument for the theorization of "new media objects" rather than viewing new media as "products" or forms of "interactive media." For him, a new media object "may be a digital still, digital composited film, virtual 3-D environment, computer game, self-contained hypermedia DVD, hypermedia website, or the Web as a whole" (Manovich 2001: 14). Viewing from the perspective of the object in Manovich's invocation allows us to fluidly group together spaces of new media and to explore their cultural significance.

Following Manovich, it is useful to consider the environment of Twitter as a digital object containing further digital objects. Specifically, tweets (individually or actively) can be thought of as digital objects, as can the retweeting of sets of tweets, and so forth. Interactions (e.g., a set of at-mentions) can also be thought of as digital objects. We can then see the emergence in Twitter of discursive objects that have no set configuration. They can be composed of tweets with photographs, hyperlinks to blogs, hyperlinks to articles, and conversations with other Twitter users. A utility of the concept of object in this case is that it lends itself to an exploration of the parts that make the object, leading Manovich (2001: 15) to observe that the object helps us "instead focus on determining the new-media equivalent of a shot, sentence, word, or even letter." In the case of Twitter, we can examine interactions as objects or parts of objects. For example, a set of tweets with photographs of a natural disaster could be thought of as the "new media" equivalent of a photographic essay, all the tweets together forming a visual digital object. Include text from other tweets and a new object emerges. Though this fluidity itself can cause problems, it also highlights the fact that changing these configurations reveals certain social meaning that can be discovered from Twitter (and similar social media).

In this case, the object is useful in understanding social representation, refiguration, and reproduction. As Manovich (2001: 15) emphasizes, "new media objects are cultural objects; thus, any new media object [. . .] can be said to represent, as well as help construct, some outside referent: a physically existing object, historical information presented in other documents, a system of categories currently employed by culture as a whole or by particular groups." In other words, the digital objects that emerge from Twitter represent cultural objects that can be meaningful and even potentially evocative in the way physical objects are. Though this sounds quite abstract, computer-mediated communication has been doing this for some time. Just as emoticons (e.g., smileys) are imbued with meaning as digital objects (Derks et al. 2008), Twitter can give birth to similarly meaningful digital objects configured in many different ways (e.g., a highly retweeted tweet can become a digital object in its own right).

I Tweet, Therefore I Am

Self-presentation is an important aspect of Twitter. Though not reductively Cartesian (i.e., "I think therefore I am"), the act of tweeting is born from individual contributions and is about self-production. Indeed, microblogging services depend on regular posting by users. Without this regularity, the utility of social media such as Twitter diminishes significantly. As for status updates on Facebook, users of social media continue to regularly post as the status-updating practice becomes a meaningful part of their identities (Boon and Sinclair 2009; Nosko et al. 2010). Daily tweets that indicate what one had for breakfast or what one is wearing can easily be relegated to the merely banal. Indeed, "good morning twitter" and "goodnight twitter" are not uncommon. But, from Bourdieu's (1984) perspective, the daily, sometimes "banal" is pregnant with meaning. Indeed, Bourdieu (1984) was interested in the banal minutiae, which included what one had for breakfast. Reading the banal historically can also give it new meanings. Dayan (1998: 106–7) gives the example of how everyday, originally personal, discourses of emigrants can then be collectively understood historically to give insights into momentous decisions such as migration. In other words, documentation of the banal can be of direct historical value. Diary entries are another important example. They have traditionally documented everyday events, the "little experiences of everyday life that fill most of our working time and occupy the vast majority of our conscious attention" (Wheeler and Reis, cited in Bolger et al. 2003: 580). Mediated documentation of the banal is also nothing new. Indeed, nineteenth-century cultural critics such as Baudelaire lamented the ubiquity and banality of photography (Baudelaire 1965). Burgess and Green (2009: 25) discuss how the posting of everyday videos on YouTube is a digital version of activities including scrapbooking, family photography, and VHS home movies. The role of the banal and Twitter is best understood within this broader historical context.

In the case of Twitter, "banal" tweets serve as an important vehicle of self-affirmation. We can read tweets such as "had too many espresso shots today" as a means by which individuals affirm their identities in a constantly shifting environment, one that Bauman (2000) terms a "liquid modern" world. The seemingly banal tweet becomes a means for them to say "look at me" or "I exist." This need to affirm their identities keeps regular users invested in the act of tweeting (sometimes daily or hourly). This is part of what Ellerman (2007) extends into the psychological concept of "inventing the self," a cognizant, explicit self-awareness and affirmation of self. Goffman (1981: 21) also notes how our daily communicative rituals have considerations of "ego" and "personal feelings."

It is also useful to draw a comparison between mobile phone text messages and Twitter. Though the former is a private bilateral communicative act, its length and content is often similar to that of Twitter. As Licoppe (2004: 143) found, mobile phone-mediated communication helps people tell each other about their days, which brings the communicating individuals "closer." And this feeling of "closeness" is in no way lessened by its mediated state. Rather, as Putnam (2000: 27) argues, Internet-mediated communication presents a counterexample to the "decline of connectedness" we see in many aspects of American community life. Shirky (2010) extends this argument by noting that in recent years the hours of television American youths watch has declined (a first, given its always upward trajectory), a fact he attributes to an increase in hours spent using social media and other Internet applications.

Regardless, it is not difficult to make the argument that these forms of self-confirmation are redolent of the nihilism Heidegger associates with aspects of modernity. However, it is critical that we recognize the importance of these posts to the identities of the posters. We can understand this through "*Bildung,*" which Herder (cited in Gadamer et al. 2004: 8) refers to as "cultivating the human." And Gadamer (2004: 8) explains *Bildung* as the "concept of self-formation." From the perspective of identity, Gadamer (2004: 10) sees *Bildung* as describing "the result of the process of becoming," which, as such, "constantly remains in a state of continual *Bildung.*" Though it is easy to view tweets merely as a crude mode of communication, doing so misses the impact that tweets have on one's *Bildung.* For active users of Twitter, posting tweets is part of their identity maintenance and the constancy of active Twitter users confirms this relationship or, as a Cartesian aphorism: I tweet, therefore I am.[1] Though tweeting is part of becoming for its users, it departs from Cartesian dualism in that the former is contingent on a community of interactants, whereas the latter makes the argument that the individual mind is thinking and, as such, stands apart from community and, indeed, the body. Examining Twitter alongside Cartesian thought reveals that the former complicates the autonomous individuality of the latter. Specifically, Twitter seems to provide ways for individuals to assert and construct the self which are contingent on a larger community of discourse.[2]

Twitter as Democratizing?

One shortcoming of understanding social media through *Bildung* is that it does not capture the shift that media have experienced from being exclusively elite forms to more accessible ones. In other words, has the medium of Twitter opened up access to the production of selves by tweeting? Turner (2010: 2) argues that contemporary media forms have experienced a "demotic turn," which refers "to the increasing visibility of the 'ordinary person' as they have turned themselves into media content through celebrity culture, reality TV, DIY websites, talk radio and the like." Turner (2010: 3) makes the key point that the media has perhaps experienced a shift from "broadcaster of cultural identities" to "a translator or even an author of identities." George Gilder (1994), a dot-com cyber evangelist, extended this idea much further, arguing that new media would be "moving authority from elites and establishments [and that these . . .] new technologies [would] drastically change the cultural balance of power." However, Turner is more cautious, pointing out that the "demotic turn" seen in contemporary media should not be conflated with democratization and the end of the digital divide. Specifically, he argues against Hartley's (1999) notion of "democratainment," arguing that in neologisms such as this, the democratic is most always secondary (Turner 2010: 16). He argues that no "amount of public participation in game shows, reality TV or DIY celebrity web-sites will alter the fact that, overall, the media industries still remain in control of the symbolic economy" (ibid.).[3] The natural question that arises is whether Twitter is different in any meaningful way. An argument can be made that, within Western society itself, Twitter does represent a significant "demotic turn" (i.e., ordinary people are able to break "news," produce media content, or voice their opinions publicly). Katz et al. (1955: 219–33) argue that "opinion leaders," the "transmitters" of influence, play a key role in the "flow" of influence. They can have relative status in particular settings such as a workplace or interest community. If Twitter helps promote ordinary people into well-known "opinion leaders" (from citizen scientists to citizen fashionistas), the medium may be challenging traditional media hierarchies or, at a minimum, generating new forms of influence and new types of "influencers." However, if most tweeting "opinion leaders" reflect influence already present in traditional broadcast media, Twitter does not represent a significant redress in systems of communicative power. Twitter may be exposing us to a selection of new viewpoints and voices, but the actual influence of these voices may be relatively limited.

Even if the influence of ordinary people on Twitter is minimal, the medium can potentially be democratizing in that it can be thought of as a megaphone that makes public the voices/conversations of any individual or entity (with the requisite level of technological competence). However, Durant (2010: 5) cautions against "treating media communication as being like an ordinary conversation that has simply been amplified and made public." With Twitter, Durant's advice is particularly applicable in that discourse on Twitter becomes transformed by the medium rather than merely being amplified. Specifically, the ways in which we communicate via social media in general are qualitatively different from traditional face-to-face communication (though not in every respect, of course). Because the medium encourages association, users are already thinking of what hashtags to include in their messages, or who should be at-sign mentioned. Additionally, each communicative act has an element of self-advertising, so tweets as a mode of communication inherently involve methods to promote the propagator of a tweet to a larger audience. For example, if someone includes a trending topic hashtag in a tweet, it is many more times likely to be read by others through trending topic searches or through retweets (boyd et al. 2010; Kwak et al. 2010).

Another reason why it is important to think of Twitter as not being simply amplified is that the meanings of messages on Twitter are a product of different circumstances than, for example, a face-to-face muttering to a friend. The same muttering posted on Twitter can take on different meanings not just in its initial tweeting, but if it gets retweeted. A useful way to think of this is through semiotics, the sociolinguistic practice of understanding signification in communication. Every word we speak or write, argues Saussure (1916), is part of a structure of meaning. Simplified, this meaning can be represented by symbols (or "signs" in his terminology) which signify (i.e., stand for) something. What they stand for is not self-evident or, as Guattari (1995: 52) puts it, "signifying semiotic figures don't simply secrete significations." Similarly, if tweets are read in this way, they do not "secrete significations," but rather need to be interpreted. (Menchik and Tian (2008) do this in their semiotic study of email.) Technological spaces or, as Guattari refers to them, "mecanospheres" do not merely amplify meaning; rather, the mecanosphere "draws out and actualises configurations" (Guattari 1995: 49). Though predating current interactive Web technologies, Guattari is interested in deterritorialized "ontological universes" (ibid.), spaces where we (re)produce our identities. What is particularly significant is that technological spaces can mediate the connecting together of actors from an infinity-like set of combinations. When one is searching for tweets, whose tweet you may stumble upon and where that will lead you remain unknown variables. This has real impact on the significations individuals intend when they tweet. Ironically, as Enteen (2010: 9) argues, this is a "seductive" aspect of the Internet in that it "seduces its users into believing that the entire world can be reached by clicking a mouse [while,] the majority of users traverse only a fraction of available pathways."

Though we can think of infinite possible configurations, we still only traverse certain paths on the Internet (e.g., Amazon, Wikipedia, eBay, major news sites, and Google). Similarly, Twitter "seduces" its users into thinking tweets will traverse more pathways than they do in practice.

Twitter and the Event-driven Society

Microblogging, more than many web spaces, is event-driven. Indeed, part of Twitter's "seductive" power is the perceived ability of users to be important contributors to an event. Specifically, organizing social life by events presents opportunities for everyday people and traditional media industries to tweet side by side. One way to render this visible is through Twitter's "trending topics" function, a list of the most popular subjects people are tweeting about. Interestingly, there are always "populist" trending topics, such as what people are listening to, celebrities one hates, or the "#ToMyUnbornChild" trending topic which elicited tweets from soon-to-be parents to their unborn children. Simultaneously, a significant number are based around breaking news events (e.g., the death of Michael Jackson or the 2011 Japan earthquake). Though traditional media industries usually determine what events become considered important, some trending topics come into being through a single tweet or a small group of individuals.

The importance of trending topics on Twitter can be understood as part of what Therborn (2000: 42) calls the "event society (*Erlebnisgesellschaft*)." Huyssen (2000: 25) helpfully translates this as a "society of experience," which is event-based. Seen as part of the larger cosmology of Twitter, this reflects a particular aspect of modernity in which events, however transient or superficial, are of importance to society. Huyssen's explanation of *Erlebnisgesellschaft* captures these elements well. He writes that the term "refers to a society that privileges intense but superficial experiences oriented toward instant happening in the present and consumption of goods, cultural events, and mass-marketed lifestyles" (2000: 25). Through this reading of *Erlebnisgesellschaft*, the intriguing question of what constitutes an "event" itself emerges (e.g., does Charlie Sheen mouthing off to a reporter constitute an "event"?)

Erlebnisgesellschaft seems to draw from Kierkegaard's (1962) argument that "the present age is an age of advertisement, or an age of publicity: nothing happens, but there is instant publicity about it." Tempting as it is for some, applying Kierkegaard's "nothing happens" argument to Twitter is a potentially dangerous path. Rather, as argued previously, our interpersonal interactions on Twitter, as well as other new media such as Facebook and LinkedIn, are part of our daily happenings. And, following Adorno (1991), our daily interactions with these media are very much a part of our larger socioeconomic life. For Adorno, our interactions with any media are routed through what he calls the "culture industry," institutions which control the production and consumption of culture. What we listen to or what we read are all mediated by the culture industries and, from his perspective, its "commercial character" (Adorno and Bernstein 1991: 61). Ultimately, relegating Twitter to a space where "nothing happens" not only ignores the fact that the interactions we have on Twitter are a product of larger social, political, and economic process, but it also smacks of elitism (a charge which Waldman (1977) argues was, ironically, often leveled at Adorno).

In their work on YouTube, Burgess and Green (2009: 13) observe that there has been an "exponential growth of more mundane and formerly private forms of 'vernacular creativity'." Ultimately, viewing Twitter as mere web chatter ignores this vernacular creativity that Burgess and Green refer to. Instead, there is more analytical purchase in understanding the consumption of perceived "superficial" and "transient" viral videos or tweets, which become constituted as a cultural "event." As people retweet or forward videos to others, and discussions ensue offline and online, the media event is born. Television has been highly successful in constructing media events (especially in the years that people collectively tuned in on a particular day and time for the next installment of a show). For example, the episode "Who shot J.R.?" in *Dallas* and the series finale of *Magnum PI* are considered to be prominent "media events" in television history (Butler 2010: 139). These events were discussed for days and months afterwards and became part of the cultural memory for a generation of American television watchers (Austin 2011: 66). Through viral levels of retweeting and trending topics, Twitter has this ability to construct memorable media events as well.

However, Kierkegaard's argument remains critically important to understanding Twitter. The latter part of his argument is particularly useful. There is definitely an "instant publicity about it" in that everything from one's daily happenings or musings becomes part of a publicity-driven culture. In a sense, Twitter markets us through our tweets and, as such, shifts us more toward "an age of advertisement," where we are not necessarily advertising products, but rather ourselves (and our self-commodification). As research has shown (e.g., Livingstone 2008), the amount of followers/friends one has on social media websites factors into how we perceive ourselves. And, following the inverse trajectory, cyber-bullying has the real potential to harm or even destroy one's self-image (Li 2006).

Twitter and Homophily

By nature, events are inclusive for certain groups of individuals. For instance, the trending of the World Cup unsurprisingly includes global soccer fans. One important question is whether Twitter is able to bring together dissimilar individuals to events. This is particularly relevant because theorists of "cross-talk," a field of sociolinguistics which studies "intercultural communication" (Connor-Linton 1999), argue that coming into contact with differing or antagonistic perspectives can play a beneficial role in developing an energetic civic culture (Liebmann 1996). What role does Twitter play in cross-talk? Most users do not elect to follow the tweets of people/institutions widely dissimilar to themselves. Rather, as the new media literature has shown, people online, as they do offline, tend to associate with like-minded people (boyd and Ellison 2008; Livingstone 2008). This pattern is known as "homophily" or, more colloquially put, "birds of a feather stick together" (McPherson et al. 2001). In the case of many Internet applications, this homophily is combined with an elite bias, making for an even greater digital divide versus email and other more "basic" Internet functions (Witte and Mannon 2010). There is no doubt that heterogeneous interactions would increase the diversification of "circles of followers" on Twitter. However, the question is whether Twitter is exposing us to birds of a different feather. This is potentially relevant because heterogeneous interactions within associations/ organizations are directly correlated with increased tolerance and social integration (Coleman 1988). In other words, these groups are positively affected and become more cohesive. The literature on homophily (especially McPherson et al. (2001) and Yuan and Gay (2006)) demonstrates its effect on limiting group heterogeneity offline. McPherson et al. (2001: 415) put this simply: "similarity breeds connection."

Some have argued that Twitter has broken homophily's grip. The usually tempered *Christian Science Monitor* suggests that Twitter should receive the Nobel Peace Prize for exposing us to divergent viewpoints from ordinary people (Pfeifle 2009). However, as McPherson (2001: 415) observes, "people generally only have significant contact with others like themselves." And, unsurprisingly, the "people like us" (McPherson et al. 2001: 416) paradigm of compatibility is self-reinforcing. No significant research has been done to counter homophily on Twitter. Indeed, research has shown that homophily is positively correlated with information diffusion (De Choudhury et al. 2010). However, it is useful to make the hypothesis that it is potentially easier to break homophilic boundaries on Twitter. This, of course, involves willful action by individual users. That being said, many individuals have decided to follow tweets from users very different from them after reading a tweet they posted on a subject of interest. Say someone in Finland is following tweets with the hashtag #oilspill (referring to the 2010 BP Deepwater Horizon oil spill), they most likely will stumble upon tweets by ordinary people in the U.S. Gulf Coast. When they visit the Twitter profiles of these individuals, they are exposed to tweets that convey everyday things that are not necessarily related to the oil spill. The million-dollar question is whether this has any significant effect on the worldview of the Finnish user or whether it disappears in the web of *Erlebnisgesellschaft*.

Telepresence and Immediacy

The importance of tweeting to homophily and self-production explain some of the reasons people tweet regularly and with conviction. However, this only tells part of the story. That is, tweets, when aggregated in particular combinations, become important digital objects to their interlocutors. One of the ways in which they become particularly important is through their transformation into objects which are no longer perceived as digitally mediated.

In a class I teach on sociological understandings of the Internet, the first reading I assign to students is "The Machine Stops" by E. M. Forster ([1909] 1997), a dystopia which sees an earth devoid of oxygen in which all our interactions with the world take place from our own rooms (mediated by "the machine"). A key section of the story tells of a woman, Vashti, who is engaged in a primitive video chat with her son, Kuno, "who lived on the other side of the earth." Kuno asks her to come visit her in person ("I want you to come and see me"), but Vashti replies, "But I can see you! What more do you want?") (Forster [1909] 1997). The philosopher Hubert Dreyfus (2009: 49) sees Forster's vision as quite prophetic, arguing that we "have almost arrived at this stage of our culture" in that "our bodies seem irrelevant and our minds seem to be present wherever our interest takes us." Dreyfus considers emergent "Web 2.0" technologies as the bringers of a sort of "disembodied telepresence" (2009: 49–71) in which, like Vashti, people do not see computer-mediated communication as mediated communication.

Computer-mediated communication in general often makes us feel as if we're in a non-technological space, which has the immediacy of face-to-face communication. This occurs through the process of "telepresence," which is defined as the "perceptual illusion of nonmediation" (Lombard and Ditton, cited in Bracken and Skalski 2009: 3). The term is often associated with Minsky (1980), the founder of MIT's artificial intelligence laboratory, and has been used to understand immersive technologies such as Skype or virtual reality (VR) in which three-dimensional goggles or other technologies are worn (Bracken and Skalski 2009). Ultimately, telepresence is useful for understanding the perception of users that they are "there" and are not experiencing mediated interactions. However, telepresence is not restricted to immersive graphical technology and this is important to understanding our use of Twitter. Licoppe (2004: 152), for example, argues that the "mostly short and frequent communicative gestures" of mobile phone calls and mobile text messages create a "frequency and continuity" through which "a presence is guaranteed." He adds that it is not so much what is said, but rather the act of calling/texting that facilitates telepresence (ibid.), Twitter resembles texting in that it is not only limited to under 140 characters in length, but the social use of the technology is built upon a high frequency of contributions regardless of where the individual is physically located (on a bus, in a club, or with one's children).

One of Ebner and Schiefner's (2008) respondents adds

that microblogging can facilitate virtual communities because users feel a "continuous partial presence" of other users. In this vein, Rosen (cited in Crawford 2009) compares aspects of Twitter to a radio. Even if someone does not post on a particular day, they feel an aura of other users through the feed of microblog posts on their PCs. Licoppe (2004) has usefully theorized this as a "connected presence" in which mediated communication (in this case, Twitter) facilitates the construction of social bonds. Specifically, Licoppe (2004: 135) concludes that physically absent parties "[gain] presence through the multiplication of mediated communication gestures on both sides." In other words, a constancy of presence is felt through multiplied interactions – a process Twitter is inherently designed for.

Because of Twitter's ability to inform followers of the daily happenings of another user (e.g., "had espresso and croissant," "slept on bus," "laptop stolen," "at police station," etc.), there is a similar perceptual illusion of non-mediation in which a face-to-face interaction has occurred with that person. This not only follows Licoppe's (2004) arguments regarding text messages and telepresence, but also Wajcman's (2008: 68) argument that mobile technology has facilitated an "always on," "persistent connection." This is not a coincidence. Rather, Twitter has adopted elements from the successes of early synchronous Internet chat technologies, such as Internet Relay Chat (IRC) and ICQ, which also sought to create an "always on" state. What is interesting about Twitter (and other microblogging sites) in juxtaposition to immersive graphically-based technologies, such as the virtual world Second Life, is that simple textual updates throughout the day are what generate telepresence (such as text messages on mobile phones). In the case of individuals following the tweets of people caught in disasters, for instance, there is a sense of "being there" while one hears about the specificity of experiences from an "ordinary person" (e.g., "a bomb went off one block away from my office"). Similarly, if one is following the tweets of celebrities and reads about what they are reading, eating, who they are seeing, and so on, telepresence can also occur. One can perceive physical proximity to Justin Bieber or Lady Gaga, for example. Another interesting distinction between textual-based social media and immersive visual technologies is that individuals explicitly choose to enter the latter for their ability to generate telepresence. Social media, on the other hand, are conceived by most users as merely communications media. This illusion of non-mediation is critical to understanding the "unintended" (McAulay 2007) pervasiveness of social media into the lives of everyday users. Gigliotti (1999: 56) emphasizes that this "pervasiveness [is . . .] throughout disparate forms of contemporary human activity." Similarly, if one is tweeting from the bus (or even speaking on a cell phone), that person generally perceives a deterritorialized state where they are no longer on the bus, but rather in a liminal space of telepresence (which is why people can speak so loudly on their phones in a public space and not be aware of the dozens of eyes pointed at them). Bull's (2005) work on iPods and MP3 players reveals similar findings of liminality where the mobile music listener inhabits a distinct space which is there, but not there.

This ultimately speaks to shifts in our rituals of social communication. Part of this change involves less of a boundary between our bodies and our technologies. Clark (2003) argues that "carried devices" have become embedded into our daily lives, making us more "cyborg." More broadly, however, it seems that the embedding of our carried devices (e.g., iPhones, Androids, iPads, and other mobile computing devices) has led to us perceiving interactions mediated by carried devices to be part of our unmediated lives. The perception of non-mediation powerfully shapes our experience of mediated forms. Though communication is ultimately socially embedded, it does not always feel that way. Sometimes this perception of non-mediation becomes highlighted. A recent ad campaign in the UK run by BMI (British Midland Airways) has billboards proclaiming "Skype is good, but it can't give you a hug." BMI's billboards, albeit purely for marketing purposes, serve as a direct challenge to telepresence and a call for users to privilege physical face-to-face contact over mediated communication. In BMI's case, they are encouraging people to hop on a flight rather than turn on their webcams.[4] Stratification aside, such privileging also ignores the fact that mediated telepresence is extremely meaningful to people in a network society where families, workplaces, and circles of friends span continents. Given the importance of mediated communication in globalized modernity, understanding Twitter is an important task and one in which interactionist theory is particularly valuable.

A Theoretical Framework to Understanding Twitter

Any successful communication technology shapes our social world. However, as Raymond Williams (1990) famously cautioned, technology shaping our social world is different from determining it. Or, as Claude Fischer (1992: 5) puts it, "fundamental" change in communication technology "alters the conditions of daily life, [but they . . .] do not determine the basic character of that life." Fischer's (1992: 5) work on the telephone sees the medium as not "radically alter[ing] American ways of life," but rather the ways in which "Americans used it to more vigorously pursue their characteristic ways of life." In other words, the telephone facilitated the intensification of pre-existing characteristics of social life. In the case of Twitter, it may be intensifying pre-existing characteristics of an erosion of the private in which more quotidian aspects of our lives are publicly shared. These are some of the new messages made possible by the new medium. We learn about other people's daily rituals, habits, happenings, and the places they visit. Not only do we potentially get a certain level of richness that we do not get in other mediated communication, but we also are exposed to a certain candor. We are perhaps getting more truthful portrayals of some sides of people, which were previously kept in the private sphere or what Goffman (1959: 119) calls the "backstage," which refers to "places where the camera is not focused at the moment." Or, most likely, we are getting a posed view of the backstage: we see what people want us to/let us see. Twitter can be thought of as a sanitized backstage pass (especially in the case of celebrity Tweeters).

Given that the dramaturgical work of Goffman has been successfully extended to include mediated communication (e.g., Rettie 2009), it can also be extended to better understanding Twitter. Specifically, recent work like that of Knorr Cetina (2009) has argued that Goffman's work can be useful for understanding mediated interactions. In the case of Twitter, the work of Goffman and his interactionist followers is helpful in understanding the concepts relating to self-production discussed earlier. For the benefit of those unfamiliar with his work, I will first introduce some basics of Goffman in terms of face-to-face dialogic interaction before delving into Twitter. Goffman's (1981) approach places primacy on interaction and views our face-to-face social situations as critical. From one vantage point, to understand Twitter is to understand how we "talk." Goffman conceptualizes "talk" through three themes – "ritualization," "participation framework," and "embedding." The first refers to his argument that the "movements, looks, and vocal sounds we make as an unintended byproduct of speaking and listening never seem to remain innocent" (Goffman 1981: 2). A key aspect of ritualization is that we acquire gestural conventions over our lifetime and that these gestures cannot be captured by the term "expression" (ibid.: 3). Second, "participation framework" refers to Goffman's theory that "those who happen to be in perceptual range of the event will have some sort of participation status relative to it" and that these positions can be analyzed (ibid.). Lastly, "embedding" refers to the "insufficiently appreciated fact that words we speak are often not our own, at least our current "own" and that "who can speak is restricted to the parties present" (ibid.). He adds that "although who speaks is situationally circumscribed, in whose name words are spoken is certainly not." Goffman emphasizes that "[u]ttered words have utterers," but utterances "have subjects (implied or explicit)." He concludes that the subjects may ultimately point to the utterer, but "there is nothing in the syntax of utterances to require this coincidence" (ibid.).

I have intentionally outlined Goffman's three key themes surrounding "talk," although he is referring to unmediated rather than mediated talk. The literature extending Goffman's ideas of talk to mediated communication is now established (Adkins and Nasarczyk 2009; Bryant and Miron 2004; Riva and Galimberti 1998; Spitzberg 2006; Walther 1996). For example, Rettie (2009) successfully extends Goffman's ideas to mobile phone communication. Knorr Cetina's (2009) work is particularly innovative in extending Goffman's theories to interactive new media. Her work, which studied European stock-market traders, makes the argument that their inter-actions with other traders can be thought of as "synthetic situations," which are "entirely constituted by on-screen pro-jections" (Knorr Cetina 2009: 65). Knorr Cetina begins the process of extending the idea of "synthetic" to Goffman's con-cept of "situation," but stops at the "synthetic situation." To understand Twitter and other emerging media, we would be well served by extending Knorr Cetina's idea of the synthetic to Goffman's concepts of "embedding" and "encounters." Building from this literature, I will use Goffman's three key themes surrounding "talk" (ritualization, participation frame-work, and embedding) to make some initial extensions of his work to the mediated space of Twitter.

Drawing from "ritualization," tweets seem a-gestural and the term "expression" seems perfectly able to capture what the tweeting individual is trying to "express." However, it is easy to forget that any computer-mediated communication has acquired gestural conventions which also "never seem to remain innocent." Though the gestural conventions may be mediated through graphical avatars, emoticons, or even unintended typed characters, these can be considered "gestures" and they are laden with meaning. For example, on Twitter, one can decipher a sigh or pause through subtle and not-so-subtle textual cues (e.g., a ". . ." for an explicit pause). This is a critical point and one supported by the literature that users "compensate textually" in computer-mediated communication (Herring 2008).

In terms of participation framework, computer-mediated communication which is public has a "perceptual range" which cannot actually be fully perceived by the speaker of the word. That being said, there is a "perceptual range" which is at least partially perceived by the sender of the tweet and those who receive the tweet in their Twitter timelines have a "participation status relative" to the tweets. What I mean by this is that the person sending the tweet knows that there is a potential audience for it and that the readers of the tweet have different participation statuses relative to the tweet. Specifically, a tweet by an individual or group may have triggered the tweet. Or it could be a more subtle relationship. Regardless, this participation status is important to understanding social communication on Twitter.

Lastly, and most importantly, is Goffman's idea of embedding. For him, embedding signifies the distinction between the situational circumscription of speaker and the fluidity of who "owns" those utterances. Specifically, he argues that utterances have subjects, but the original utterer need not be preserved in the utterance itself. Additionally, he observes that this "embedding capacity" (1981: 3) is part of our general linguistic ability to embed utterances in "any remove in time," rather than just in "the situated present." Goffman's theoretical perspective is particularly suited to understanding Twitter because of his development of embedding. Specifically, tweets when they have been broadcasted to the Twitter universe ("Twitterverse") become removed from the situational cir-

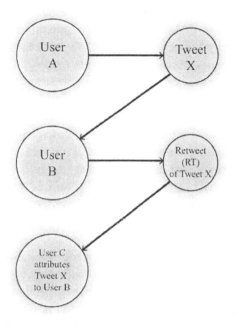

Figure 3.1   Twitter attribution

cumscription which face-to-face communication provides. Tweet utterances, as the utterances Goffman is referring to, also have subjects. However, the circulation of tweets is largely dependent on whose name the utterance is being attributed to, rather than who is the original utterer. So, if an unknown person sends a profound tweet, it is most likely destined to never be read. Of course, this is true of any medium in that reception depends on audience. But the ability of Twitter to re-embed tweets into the situational space of another Twitter user (through retweets) generates wholly new audiences which feel the utterance to be originating from the retweeter. This is particularly interesting because the retweet most often bears reference to the original Twitterer (through an at-mention (e.g., @whitehouse)). However, this part of the tweet is usually unconsciously or consciously ignored (see figure 3.1).

Furthermore, embedding is also particularly useful in theorizing Twitter as it also refers to our linguistic ability to fluidly temporalize utterances. Though Twitter, as a medium, can be synchronous in communicative interactions (if Twitterer and tweet recipient are both online at the same time), it most often has some element of asynchronicity. That being said, when tweets are retweeted, they become re-embedded into the situated present of the recipient. And if that recipient retweets, the new recipients also view the tweet utterance in their situated present. Because in virtual spaces "the interacting parties meet in time rather than in a place" (Knorr Cetina 2009: 79), it is useful to think of what I term "synthetic embedding," which places primacy on "response presence" (Goffman 1983) rather than physical place. That being said, synthetic embedding, like physical embedding, reformulates the space it is embedded in, which happens to be a virtual space.

The difference with Twitter is that the audience range of tweets is not always in congruence with the perceptual range (or indeed intended range) of the original Twitterer. The original tweeter intends the tweet to circulate to their immediate followers. They are not always consciously aware that their tweets have the potential to travel much farther. This is a key distinction between synthetic embedding and embedding. Kwak et al. (2010: 6) note that once a tweet is retweeted (regardless of the number of followers the original Twitterer has), it reaches an audience (mean) size of 1,000. This is quite significant as an "everyday" tweet posted by an ordinary individual has a potentially large readership if it is retweeted. Therefore, like any utterances with intended audiences, tweets are not only synthetically embedded in some time frame, but also audience contexts. And if tweets do become retweeted, they experience synthetic re-embedding in both a different temporal frame and potentially different social context.

The above does not take into account replies to tweets and the responses to these replies. Rather, it has been restricted to a single tweet utterance and the ways in which we can theorize its production, perception, and reproduction. However, a critical function of Twitter and a reason for its popularity is the ability for users to reply to one another. When replying to a tweet or directing a tweet to a specific user, the site prefixes the reply with an "@" and the intended recipient sees this in their Twitter page when they log on. Like face-to-face communication, utterances on Twitter generate responses. Similarly, these responses are, following Goffman (1981: 5), "realized at different points in 'sequence time'." Conversations on Twitter become marked by the exchange of responses which can be aggregated into a sequence (by time) and this forms a "coherent" conversation.[5] However, having a conversation on Twitter can be more like sitting in a room with a door, not knowing who is going to pop their head round and respond or who is listening behind the door. Additionally, it could be several people coming through that door within seconds of each other. On top of that, there could be any number of other rooms out there with someone retweeting your tweet, and they have respondents. If the user identification of the originating Twitterer is retained (through an at-sign), the originating Twitterer has the ability to see who is retweeting and responding. They can choose to become a respondent to a retweeter, thereby opening the door to one or many of these other rooms. For example, Barack Obama retweeted (RT) a tweet from @ whitehouse, welcoming Russian President Medvedev to Twitter. Anyone can retweet this tweet, reply to it, or retweet it with modified text. Each of these configurations entails differences in audience and perceived authorship.

Ultimately, there is a sense of boundedness of the retweet to the new utterer. However, anyone, not just the originating Twitterer, can open any of these doors or they can form a new room and "own" the tweet. This type of computer-mediated communication does have a history in forms of copy-and-paste communication (e.g., if someone copied a discussion idea from one email to another, they become considered the original utterer). However, within the etiquette of emailing lists, the original utterer is preserved and it is customary for an original poster (OP) – even if on another site or mailing list – to be referred to or thanked (Hansen et al. 2010).

Conclusion

> I immediately asked the obvious question: why would some-one want to Twitter? Evan Williams put it this way: "The question 'Why are we interested in this stuff?' – 'Why is this entertainment?' could be flipped on its head when we ask, 'Why is fictionalized, non-real entertainment, normal enter-tainment, interesting?' People are in the world and that's real." (Niedzviecki 2009: 129)

Twitter co-founder Evan Williams believes that the lives of ordinary people are "real," and fictional entertainment which has become the norm is "non-real." The posting of perceived "banal" tweets such as what one had for breakfast or what one is wearing have led some to dismiss Twitter. However, from Williams's point of view, this is what is "real" and the real is interesting. Another aspect that has fueled critics of Twitter is the medium's terseness. Trying to communicate in the restricted format of 140 characters seems unduly limited to some. For some of Twitter's critics (e.g., Keen 2010), it may even be considered a threat to our current modes of commu-nication. They argue that new media more generally is leading to the impoverishment of grammar, vocabulary, spelling, and so on (Tucker 2009). This is not a "new" argument. Rather, as Baym (2010: 1) argues, every new communications medium sees a cohort of critics who consider the medium as "shal-low." Additionally, she highlights that the critics of electronic messages have seen them as "vacuous" (p. 10) and that "new media often stir[s] up fears of moral decline" (p. 41).

It is also important to note that many of the things which are concisely tweeted are also expressed tersely not only in other mediated forms, but in face-to-face communication as well. Not all communication needs to be verbose. Goffman refers to these as "truncated verbal forms" (1981: 7). If we are asking someone which direction a subway station is, or how much a newspaper costs, a couple of words will satisfy the questioner. Those such as Keen (2010) who argue that Twitter heralds the death of meaningful communication may be failing to appreciate this. The key to understanding "talk" on Twitter is not to get drawn into a privileging of verbosity in speech acts. This is a slippery slope, ending, more often than not, in stratified communication. Rather, the assumption needs to be made that the actors in Twitter are satisfied by the sub-140-character responses they receive.

Following Goffman (1981: 10), another important conclusion of this chapter is that a "basic normative assumption about talk is that, whatever else, it should be correctly interpretable in the special sense of conveying to the intended recipients what the sender more or less wanted to get across." They need not "agree" with the message, they just need to be in agreement "as to what they have heard" (ibid.). Or, put into linguistic theory, "illocutionary force" (the conventional intention of a statement) is what needs to be in agreement, rather than "perlocutionary effect" (the effect of the statement on the hearer, or in achieving a particular goal). I would add, though, that the recipients of tweets may not be intended and that illocutionary force can be diminished as tweets become increasingly removed from the original tweeting speaker. However, the medium ultimately tends toward the privileging of verbatim tweets rather than insuring the preservation of intended meaning (i.e., what the original speaker "wanted to get across").[6]

Ultimately, this chapter has sought to further our understanding of Twitter by extending interactionist and other social theory. By exploring literature on media democratization, self-production, technological determinism, and interactionism, some basic theoretical frameworks have been introduced by which to understand Twitter's roles in social communication. It has been emphasized that our uses of social media are products of larger social, political, and economic forces and the theoretical frames introduced in this chapter are critical to meaningfully understanding Twitter. The next chapters build from this theoretical base in order to explore questions of how Twitter has potentially changed self-production, how we communicate, interaction orders, the synchronicity of social interaction, the way people use language (including shifts in verbosity), and power relations between interactants. Later chapters will explore specific topical areas and empirical case studies to investigate these questions.

CHAPTER FOUR

Twitter and Journalism

Twitter is real time flow of worldwide consciousness.

@deevaeva

If Twitter is a conduit for a global stream of consciousness, it logically follows that the medium is a barometer for revealing everything, from the occurrence of natural disasters to the public perception of political candidates. This chapter explores this potential awareness of "worldwide consciousness" through the examination of Twitter and journalism. Twitter can be understood as a news environment in which news is always present. That includes both professional journalists and "citizen journalists," who cover "news" in their cities, towns, and countries. Likewise, news is highly present through the retweeting of links to news stories. Also considered in this chapter is the question of Twitter as a more democratic space for news production and consumption. Through new forms of Twitter-mediated journalism, the medium may be changing journalistic norms, including the transparency of journalistic practice and a greater role of citizen journalists in overseeing news production.

Twitter has been prominently associated with journalism, both in terms of shifts in journalistic practice as well as its facilitating of citizen journalism. An interesting aspect of Twitter is its function as an "ambient" news environment (Hermida 2010b), a media space where news is always present. In Twitter's case, both banal and profound news is present in this ambient environment. This news is produced and consumed by a wide range of individuals, ranging from

professional journalists to non-professional citizen journalists. In this way, Twitter presents an opportunity for many
types of journalisms rather than strictly traditional modes of
journalistic production and consumption. Moreover, the roles
of news producer and consumer are often blurred on Twitter.
The medium has also influenced some of the ways in which
journalists conduct news work. Specifically, as an ambient
news space where news is in the air, Twitter-savvy journalists with their finger on the social media pulse are often on
the lookout for newsworthy scoops. They can contact Twitter
users who they think are breaking interesting news. As discussed later in this chapter, the reporting journalists need not
even be in the physical location of breaking-news events when
citizen journalists are on the ground giving them updates via
Twitter (which can include embedded photographs).

Two key themes are explored in this chapter: Twitter as an
ambient news environment and as a space for multiple journalisms. In terms of the latter, detailed attention is given to
the specific case of citizen journalists and Twitter. The site's
role in being the first to report on the Mumbai bomb blasts
in 2008 and the downed U.S. Airways flight in 2009 are
used as case studies to help illustrate citizen journalism and
Twitter. Also explored here is the question of whether Twitter
has transformed ordinary individuals into citizen journalists
whom the newsreading public follows, or whether their voices
are merely subsumed by traditional media. In other words, has
Twitter really produced a new space in which ordinary people
meaningfully interact with other ordinary people around the
world who have rich insider accounts pertaining to diverse
forms of socioeconomic life? An argument is made that ordinary people on Twitter are producing news and consuming
news (especially "breaking news") produced by other ordinary
people. However, counter-arguments are presented which
make the case that perhaps the individual tweets and Twitter
users breaking news stories experience a short-lived fame
as the public follows stories of interest through professional

news media outlets. Ultimately, the rise of citizen journalism on Twitter highlights the complex roles of ordinary people in update cultures and how what one may tweet merely as a simple update can become transformed into "news," whether traditional media picks up the tweet or it is retweeted at a large scale (i.e., a Twitter community itself determines "news").

Twitter as a News Environment

There has been some discussion and scholarship on Twitter and journalism around the idea of "ambient news" (Burns 2010; Hermida 2010b). This idea conceptualizes Twitter as a space whose ambient environment always contains news (the analogy here is to oxygen in our physical ambient environment). Hermida (2010b: 301) argues that "lightweight" and "always on" communication services can create ontologies where news is part of the "mental model" of these technologies' users. He adds that Twitter can be thought of as "an awareness system" (ibid.), which facilitates awareness between users even when they are not physically proximate. The awareness is always there, but central attention is activated at moments "when a user feels the need to communicate." The difference between Twitter and visiting the website of a newspaper is that in the former, news is always present, but potentially at the periphery for a user. Other information or particular individuals may be taking center stage. Hermida offers an interesting model for considering Twitter as an "ambient media system" in that news information is received "in the periphery of their awareness [. . . and] does not require the cognitive attention of, for example, an e-mail" (ibid.). In other words, individual tweets do not inherently represent valuable pieces of information ipso facto. In chapter 3, I conceive of Twitter as consisting of nested "digital objects," which can be composed of anything from a couple of tweets to the combination of tweets, retweets, and hashtags. Hermida's notion of Twitter as an ambient news space is particularly useful in seeing how digital objects may emerge which catch a user's attention and are drawn from periphery to center (whereas an individual tweet may not have the gravity to do this). Collective approvals of, for example, a news story through retweets from certain users can engage tweet consumers in different ways. An important aspect of understanding Twitter as an ambient news space is recognizing that "completeness of awareness is not the goal" (Hermida 2010b: 303). It is useful to think back to the analogy of Twitter as a radio (made in chapters 2–3). If one had complete awareness of the radio's total band of frequencies, one would be deluged (think of 25 radios all blaring different stations in a room). If all frequencies of one's Twitter feed took center stage simultaneously, this type of incomprehensible cacophony would occur. Rather, for most users, their Twitter feed works more like a single radio station, albeit disjointed, which is always on, though someone can be checking email or working and Twitter can be in the periphery. But if something comes to our attention, the Twitter feed, like the radio station, can come to the center of our cognitive field. The key is that Twitter, unlike a singularly focused radio station, always has news in the ambient environment (excepting news radio, of course). Though not referring to Twitter, Hargreaves and Thomas put it well: "News is, in a word, ambient, like the air we breathe" (cited in Hermida 2010a). This has implications both to news consumption and production. Journalists can "sense" news just as it is unfolding. They could see a digital object constituted of important tweets emerge and decide to contact Twitterers, or research the story on the ground.

New Journalisms

Besides adding to journalists' source mix, Twitter has changed some journalistic practices and norms. For example, Lasorsa et al. (2011: 19) found that Twitter led to journalists "more freely express[ing] opinions," a behavior which directly challenges "the journalistic norm of objectivity (impartiality and nonpartisanship)." They also found a contingent of journalists on Twitter who use the medium for "providing accountability and transparency regarding how they conduct their work" (Lasorsa et al. 2011: 19). This is an important aspect of how Twitter is shaping some aspects of journalistic practice. Some of the shifts have come about through processes on Twitter that involve users "patrolling" the emergence of news and its authenticity or journalistic rigor. Bruns (2005) describes the process of "gatewatching," wherein users are engaged in "highlighting, sharing, and evaluating the relevant material released by other sources" (Bruns and Burgess 2011: 2). Through sometimes critical evaluations of news, journalists can be held accountable very quickly after an article has been published. In other words, Twitter's ambient news environment has gained an increasingly evaluative role on traditional media, where journalists have "to maintain the trust of audiences" on Twitter (Lasorsa et al. 2011: 23). Journalistic norms have been particularly affected in these ways over the last century (ibid.: 19) as more "democratizing" technologies from the telephone to blogs have emerged.

The medium can also facilitate more collaborative journalistic practices wherein journalists invite Twitter users to "participate in the news production process" (Lasorsa et al. 2011: 26) by eliciting feedback on an article or retweeting unedited messages they think are relevant to a breaking-news event. Another key way in which new media more generally has been shaping journalistic practice is crowdsourcing, where the "wisdom of the crowds" (Surowiecki 2004) is leveraged to analyze large amounts of data or check materials. Bruns (2011) gives the example of how the *Guardian* newspaper in the UK created a web portal which enabled the public to review British government ministers' expenses during the 2009 "MPs expenses scandal." He claims that the project was a "success" because it leveraged this form of crowdsourcing (2011: 117) to scour the details of scores of receipts and expense forms. Twitter also presents interesting forms of crowdsourcing for journalists and, as the medium matures further, crowdsourcing initiatives by journalists may become more common.

Citizen Journalists Breaking News Through Twitter

Twitter has received significant media attention in its uses of disseminating information during breaking-news events, including the 2008 Mumbai bomb blasts (Dolnick 2008), the 2011 News International phone-hacking scandal (Geere 2011), political movements in the 2011 "Arab Spring" (Warf 2011), and the January 2009 crash of US Airways Flight 1549 (Beaumont 2009).[1] In the latter event, Janis Krums, a passenger on the Midtown Ferry, took a picture of the downed US Airways jet floating in the Hudson[2] and uploaded it to Twitter before news crews even arrived on the scene (see figure 4.1). Krums not only uploaded his tweet and photograph with ease, but also continued tweeting as he helped with aid efforts. In an instant, he was transformed from Florida-based businessman to both citizen journalist and emergency aid worker. During the Mumbai bomb blasts in 2008, Twitter was used to circulate news about the attacks (Beaumont 2008). Seconds after the first blasts, Twitter users were providing eyewitness accounts from Mumbai. For example, on November 26, 2008, the day of the attacks, @ShriNagesh tweeted "a gunman appeared infront of us, carrying machine gun-type weapons & started firing. I just turned & ran in opp direction," and @Dupree tweeted "Mumbai terrorists are asking hotel reception for rooms of American citizens and holding them hostage on one floor." On November 27, @Ashokjjr tweeted "Oberoi fire under control now," and @sengupta tweeted, "Trident fire seems under control" (all tweets cited in BBC News 2008). Though limited to 140 characters, the information contained in these tweets was invaluable to individuals in Mumbai as well as news media outlets throughout

Figure 4.1 Miracle on the Hudson; photograph by Janis Krums
(www.janiskrums.com; Twitter:@jkrums)

the world. Traffic on Twitter with the #mumbai hashtag grew to such a volume on November 27 that the Indian government asked Twitter users to halt their updates: "ALL LIVE UPDATES – PLEASE STOP TWEETING about #Mumbai police and military operations" (BBC News 2008). Some reports indicated that the Indian government was worried that the terrorists were garnering inside information about the situation from Internet media sites including Twitter (*Courier Mail* 2008).

Not only was news in the case of both Flight 1549 and the Mumbai bomb blasts disseminated nearly instantaneously through Twitter, but tweets also included linked photographic documentation. Krums' emotive image was used by traditional news organizations around the world. In the face of deep budget cuts, media outlets are hard-pressed to have people on the ground picking up stories this quickly. Twitter, on the other hand, has at its disposal a virtual army of citizen journalists ready to tweet at a moment's notice from their mobile phones or mobile devices. As "smartphones" (e.g., iPhones and Android phones) penetrate markets further, a higher percentage of this army can seamlessly embed pictures into their tweets. At the time of writing, almost half of American adults own smartphones (Smith 2012). Additionally, almost a third of American adults use mobile location-based services (Zickuhr and Smith 2011) and half of American adult mobile users have apps installed (Purcell 2011). In the American context, a very large segment of the population is capable of sending tweets with linked photographs. A significant number of these users have location-based services enabled, which would associate location with their tweets. Furthermore, as mentioned previously, it is relatively easy for a user to tweet from their phone. Most smartphone users with a Twitter-based app could take a picture and send a tweet in under 45 seconds and newer iPhones have the ability to tweet as a standard built-in feature. This seamless convergence of photographic and textual information from everyday "citizen journalists" made Twitter a news source during the post-election protests in Iran (Morozov 2009),[3] the 2011 earthquake in Japan (Doan et al. 2011), the elections in Moldova (Barry et al. 2009; Mungiu-Pippidi and Munteanu 2009), and the 2011 "Arab Spring" movements in the Middle East and North Africa (Benn 2011).

The Rise of Twitter-based Citizen Journalists?

Rebillard and Toubol (2010) concluded that the egalitarian promises of the Internet as a tool for citizen journalists have not panned out. Rather, professional news media websites are mostly built around content from professional journalistic sources and most "citizen journalism" online relies and links back to professional news media websites. Nonetheless, Twitter has made possible some interesting cases of citizen journalism, as discussed in the previous section. Indeed, in the case of US Airways Flight 1549, it was a citizen journalist, Janis Krums, who took a picture of the downed aircraft and circulated it to the Twitterverse from his iPhone (see figure 4.1) before the traditional media even had any idea of the disaster. Similarly, in the case of the Mumbai bomb blasts, those "reporting" on the destruction were ordinary Indians. A question of interest in this chapter is whether this signals the rise of citizen journalism or whether it is merely a new means for traditional media to crowdsource stories (and even crowdsource free photographic documentation). Either way, this is a question with significant implications. Jen Leo, a blogger for the *Los Angeles Times*, wrote about Krums' iconic photograph, asking whether it is "becoming more interesting to turn to citizen journalism than traditional broadcast media for coverage?" (Leo 2009). Part of this question, of course, is contingent on the legitimacy of Twitter as a news source itself. Ross McCulloch (2009) of the Third Sector Lab blog emphasizes how Flight 1549 marked a turning point for Twitter's legitimacy:

> With the press of a few buttons on his iPhone, Janis Krums changed the way the world looks at twitter. While the traditional news networks were still searching for the plane in the Hudson, [his] photo was already spreading like wildfire across the twittersphere.

From McCulloch's perspective, the tipping point whereby Twitter became considered a potentially legitimate source of breaking news was Flight 1549. Not only could interested individuals see Krums' photograph online, but they could also send tweets directly to him, posing questions and requesting clarification. Indeed, Krums' @jkrums Twitter following rocketed from 150 to nearly 6,000. Krums participated in Twitter-led discussions, including one on the Third Sector Lab site. What is particularly unique in this type of citizen journalism is that consumers of Krums' account were able to build (or at least perceive) a rapport with Krums himself. Though this case highlights the use of citizen journalism in breaking news stories, it does not displace the usefulness of traditional news media (or length-unrestricted blogs in the realm of new media) to cover in-depth or longer-running issues and matters. Bianco (2009: 305), for example, argues that Twitter has "notably proved to the world its capacity to transmit real-time information," but is not a medium best designed for reporting "issues and campaigns across a protracted period of time."

Though Twitter is not displacing traditional media from Bianco's (2009) perspective, news organizations have found the medium useful in their coverage of breaking news. Minutes after Krums posted the "The Miracle on the Hudson" photograph on Twitter, media outlets were calling his mobile phone asking for up-to-the-minute information and requesting interviews. As Bianco (2009: 305) notes, within half an hour of taking the picture, Krums was interviewed live by MSNBC. McCulloch (2009) points out that though this event may have been a means by which Twitter was legitimatized, this newfound victory was not at the expense of "old media" in that the "newspapers and TV news stations didn't pay a penny to the likes of Reuters and AP when US 1549 hit the Hudson [. . . as they] all got their big photo for free that day" through the Internet. In a similar vein, there have been cases where governments have banned journalists from reporting from their countries. The 2009 election in Iran is the most well-known example. As Palser (2009) notes, major international news organizations such as CNN relied on information from social networking and social media websites, including Twitter. During Twitter's infancy, the use of social media by journalists remained exceptional rather than the norm. Lariscy et al. (2009) found that only 7.5 percent of journalists they interviewed indicated social media is "very important to their work" while 56.5 percent were neutral or considered social media to be "of little or no importance." More recent work argues that "the news industry embraces various forms of social media to help them remain competitive in their news-gathering" (Dickinson 2011: 1). Additionally, sportswriters are increasingly using social media as part of their source mix (Reed 2011), an unsurprising move given the use of Twitter by prominent athletes (Thomas 2011).

However, live news dissemination from citizen journalists is not without its detractors. For example, in May 2009, Daniel MacArthur, a researcher at the Wellcome Trust Institute in Cambridge, UK, tweeted live reports from the Cold Spring Harbor Laboratory (CSHL) "Biology of Genomes" conference. His tweets (and blog entries) came to the attention of CSHL via an online news source and the conference organizers amended their conference rules and regulations to prohibit tweeting, blogging, and other Internet-based reporting during conferences unless express permission was obtained from the presenter being talked about (Bonetta 2009). MacArthur's case highlights the fact that the organizers of scholarly conferences, and indeed presenters, are not only worried about privacy and intellectual property, but they are also worried about tweets which cast a presentation as boring, unpleasant, or a waste of time (such as one bioengineer who tweeted:

"sitting in a boring conference presentation"). The question to which attention is drawn by cases such as MacArthur's is what constitutes citizen journalism itself and where the boundaries should be drawn between professional journalism and citizen journalism online (Miller 2008; Rebillard and Touboul 2010; Thorsen 2008). Though the literature on this is divergent, it generally converges on the idea that Internet technologies, as Thorsen (2008: 936) in his work on Wikinews argues, present a "challenge to traditional journalistic norms."

Twitter as Communal News Space

Part of these changes in journalistic norms involve more communal journalistic practices. Computer-mediated communication has, as Castells (2000) argues, created a new "social morphology," which is dominated by networks. "Virtual communities" have been noted for their ability to transcend geographical constraints (Rheingold 1993). However, they also represent interesting dialogic spaces where a seemingly individualistic interlocutor is actually being listened to by the larger virtual community. Not only does communication in such spaces become simultaneously individualistic and communal, but so does the negotiation of the culture of news production and consumption. The (re)construction of communication and culture on Twitter represents a particularly interesting case in comparison to social network sites such as Facebook. Specifically, Twitter is a "public space" with anyone able to see, respond, or forward ("retweet") messages. This is in distinction to Facebook's friend-focused environment where individuals have more limited access to the Facebook profiles of others. On Twitter, users can break news, comment on larger political issues, local concerns, and fads – all publicly.

Hashtag categories illustrate the ability of Twitter to be both an individual and communal news space simultaneously. For example, #breakingnews, a hashtag used to tweet breaking news, has been a regular hashtag topic. Any tweets with #breakingnews are aggregated into a communal meta-thread which represents what Twitter users consider breaking news at the moment. During the blizzards in the UK in January 2010, this was also the case with individuals tweeting about local snow experiences through the hashtag #uksnow, forming a communal thread on the topic which was simultaneously individualistic. Furthermore, a claim (albeit easily refutable) can be made that Twitter has made opinion the result of a "democratic" confluence of voices, rather than the privileging of elite individual or institutional voices. Regardless, we can also see the act of tweeting breaking news or experiences in the blizzards as a means to affirm individuals' identities rather than as an intended form of journalism. DiMicco and Millen (2007), in their work researching the use of Facebook at a large software development company, found that employees used status updates to, for example, affirm their identity as business professionals[4] or, on the other hand, as fresh out of college.[5] In other words, #breakingnews or #uksnow tweets are being used by some as a means to assert their individual and group identities (see chapter 3 for a fuller discussion). And even if these individuals tweet without journalism in mind, it may be that a "journalistic community" surrounding a hashtag topic nonetheless emerges. Cox (2008) has argued that similar unintended communities have emerged on the photo-sharing website Flickr.

Digital Divides and Twitterized Journalism

As this chapter has discussed, Twitter has fostered an active ambient news environment with many forms of journalism emerging (from professional to citizen journalism). However, it should be noted that news production and consumption on Twitter remain a socially stratified practice. Marginalized populations often lack or have limited net access in their households (Witte and Mannon 2010), and even amongst

children – a demographic which is painted as a homogene-
ously net-savvy generation – digital divides based upon lines
of class and other socioeconomic factors continue to exist
(Livingstone and Helsper 2007).[6] Hobson (2008) has per-
suasively argued that the Internet continues to be "raced"
and racial digital divides remain pervasive (Kolko et al. 2000;
Nakamura 2002, 2008); Twitter is no exception to this.
Another important distinction that needs to be made in terms
of digital divides is that between access to the Internet and
being "Internet savvy" – an understanding that sees Internet
use as different for different kinds of users (DiMaggio et al.
2001). For instance, Cox (2008) found that most users of
Flickr, a popular photo-sharing website, are males working
in new media or computer fields, students, and youth. In
terms of access, studies have shown that broadband Internet
access continues to grow in the EU and America (Polykalas
and Vlachos 2006; Shampine 2003). However, access does
not inherently translate into equal usage. Specifically, people
with disabilities (Ellcessor 2010) and populations which are
socioeconomically marginalized are more likely to use the
Internet for the most simple of tasks (often email) and remain
ignorant of or ill versed in the use of Web 2.0 tools (Witte and
Mannon 2010). At a more basic level, Hargittai (2006) found
that respondents with lower educational levels had a higher
frequency of spelling and typographical errors when using
Internet search engines, resulting in an Internet experience
which is limited from the start.

Digital divides also continue to be age-related (Witte and
Mannon 2010). Though "silver surfers" as a category continues to rise in numbers, they represent only a small percentage
of users online and, more importantly, are not representative
of Internet-usage patterns amongst older individuals in general. A case in point is the ongoing protest by pensioners in the
UK against the elimination of paper cheques. Many argue that
their physical disabilities and lack of IT skills (and PCs) make
online banking difficult or impossible. The thought of losing

paper cheques is downright frightening to them, whereas the Internet-enabled middle classes were already using online bill payment systems at the start of the millennium (Hayashi and Klee 2003).

The amplification of digital divides in the face of more advanced Internet applications should not be read as fodder for a Luddite argument. Rather, technology can be harnessed to more equitably disseminate news. For example, the reach of text messages is less socially stratified than tweets given the levels of mobile penetration in many countries. Text message-based information services have successfully been deployed in lesser-developed countries. For example, FrontlineSMS[7] was used during the 2004 Indian Ocean tsunami to keep disaster-affected individuals informed.[8] Additionally, text messages are frequently used to disseminate health messages in lesser-developed countries (Kaplan 2006). The point here is to be aware of how digital divides affect news production and consumption on Twitter.

Another limitation of Twitter is the issue of information integrity. Tweets regarding breaking news, disasters, and public health epidemics can be misleading, incorrect, or even fraudulent (Goolsby 2009). In the case of the 2009 swine flu pandemic, tweets tagged with #swineflu often contained false or misleading information. Similarly, during the 2011 UK riots, misinformation on Twitter potentially created further tension and unrest (Geere 2011). For instance, Geere (2011) observes that a widely circulated tweet which linked to an image of tanks and soldiers was claiming to be proof of the British army assembling in central London. Rather, the image turned out to be of an army presence in Egypt. Geere (2011) also gives the example of how a set of tweets "even claimed that rioters had attacked the London Zoo and set free a selection of animals, including a tiger."[9] Again, this was a hoax. Marginalized and vulnerable populations are disproportionately affected by such information. It is impossible to monitor the integrity of information flowing on Twitter. Though individuals can follow trusted news outlets on Twitter, some users can and do pose as traditional news organizations by employing a username which sounds or looks like a newspaper or television station. Indeed, someone who posed as the Dalai Lama on Twitter attracted 20,000 followers in 48 hours (Moore 2009). Though Twitter eventually shut down this impersonating account, the openness of the medium enables significant fraudulence and the implications of this should not be underestimated.

Conclusion

This chapter has sought to explore how journalism has been influenced by Twitter and, if so, how? Because of Twitter's ubiquity in developed countries (and increasingly in developing countries), it has become an important "ambient" news environment (Hermida 2010b). Specifically, news is always present: it is in the environment of Twitter. This chapter has discussed how news need not always be at the center of a Twitter user's cognitive field. Rather, like a radio, a user's Twitter timeline could be playing in the background and if the user becomes interested in a particular story, Twitter moves from the ambient periphery to the active center. Some of this is facilitated by digital objects on Twitter, the confluence of tweets, hashtags, retweets, pictures, and hyperlinks. The update culture on Twitter lends itself particularly well to new forms of journalism. In this chapter, shifts towards collaborative journalistic practices (e.g., crowdsourcing) and citizen journalism have been explored.

Research has shown that print media readership is declining (Gulati and Just 2006; Wahl 2006) and that, as Vivian Schiller (cited in Emmett 2008) of NYTimes.com observes, "social media [. . .] is one of several essential strategies for disseminating news online – and for surviving [as a news organization]." As Zeichick (2009) notes, news organizations are increasingly sending tweets with the headlines of their breaking-news stories. In the field of journalism, it is easy to see how social media is redefining centuries-old journalistic practices. "Citizen journalists," non-professional journalists, are taking pictures from their smartphones and embedding them in tweets, and this material has now become part of some journalists' source mix. As newspapers cut back on staff, citizen journalists fill the void, always ready to "report" via Twitter what they consider to be an important scoop.

Another issue which is pertinent to journalism and Twitter is the persistence of digital divides. As this chapter has argued, there remain persisting digital divides in many Western countries, which keep marginalized and vulnerable populations away from Twitter. Though new social networks and communities of knowledge are supported by Twitter, they are strongly socioeconomically stratified. This keeps Twitter inaccessible to much of the newsreading public, relegating the medium to the more technologically literate "Twittering classes" (this is especially true in developing countries). Furthermore, the issue of information integrity on Twitter (e.g., misleading swine flu updates and news hoaxes about the 2011 UK riots) also disproportionately affects marginalized populations. Hoaxes and patent misinformation can potentially have disastrous ramifications on vulnerable populations if issues of health, for example, are concerned. Ultimately, news production and consumption on Twitter are highly stratified.

Though we must be cognizant of digital divides and differing levels of information literacy, this is not to say that Twitter has not altered news production and consumption. Indeed, journalistic norms surrounding transparency and accountability have been affected by Twitter's ambient news environment (Hermida 2010b). Just as journalists use crowdsourcing to help with stories, the crowds are watching journalists on Twitter. Journalists on Twitter have had to open the gates to their craft, bringing news production more into the public eye, at least in terms of higher levels of accountability (Hayes et al. 2007). This chapter has also illustrated how professional

news media have become more open to using tweets for picking up breaking news such as the downing of Flight 1549 and
the Mumbai bomb blasts. When tweets have been picked up
by major media outlets in cases such as these, this coverage
has brought attention to Twitter itself. However, the public
ultimately takes interest in the stories themselves and not so
much in the original source tweets or the individual Twitterer
responsible for breaking the story. If this is the case (and chapter 3 has discussed this further), Twittering citizen journalists
are ephemeral, vanishing after their 15 minutes in the lime-
light. In most instances, they are left unpaid and unknown.
Those citizen journalists who do become "known" represent
elites in the medium. This is an interesting tension in that
Twitter is viewed as an alternative news media. Yet, as Poell
and Borra (2011: 14) found in the case of the 2010 Toronto
G20 protests, the "resulting account was based on the obser-
vations and experiences of a small group of insiders." In other
words, Twitter's citizen journalism is not exempt from the
hierarchies endemic in traditional media industries. Rather,
new forms of elitism are emerging.

Ultimately, Twitter has gained prominence as a powerful
media outlet. Shirky (cited in Last 2009) argues that the 2009
anti-government Iranian protests were "transformed by social
media" and, through Twitter, "people throughout the world
are not only listening but responding." In 2011, many in the
media asserted a similar conclusion in reference to the "Arab
Spring" social movements (see chapter 6 for a fuller discussion). Though Shirky's conclusion is itself debatable,[10] it is
important to respond to his assertion that global citizens are
not only consuming breaking news but producing news in a
globalized Twitter-mediated public sphere, which emphasizes
an instantaneous "stream of news [which] combines news,
opinion, and emotion" (Papacharissi and de Fatima Oliveira
2012: 1). Even Mark Pfeifle of the usually cautious *Christian
Science Monitor* argued that Twitter should be given the Nobel
Peace Prize (Last 2009). Such a conclusion, however, perhaps

ignores the fact that much of the talk on Twitter is monological, or just never listened to or responded to (a phenomenon Cox (2008) argues is characteristic of Web 2.0 in general). That being said, the power of the medium lies in the fact that profound tweets appear side by side with banal ones – second by second, minute by minute, and hour by hour. It is from this perspective that Twitter affords citizen journalists the possibility to break profound news stories to a global public and to interact with journalists in new ways. Even if professional news media dominates coverage of the story and the original Twitterer is left with only 15 minutes of fame, the power of Twitter to citizen journalism should not be underestimated. Additionally, Twitter has facilitated new journalistic practices and is shaping journalistic norms such as transparency.

CHAPTER FIVE

Twitter and Disasters

> I woke in the earthquake now.
>
> @aracatxoxo, a Japanese Twitter user

As the tweet above illustrates, some users tweet during a natural disaster. That tweet was sent by a user in Japan on November 23, 2011, almost immediately after an earthquake registering 6.1 on the Richter scale was reported in Honshu, Japan. Another user, @W7VOA, a reporter for *Voice of America*, tweeted around the same time: "Quake in Tokyo; That one woke me out of a deep sleep at 0425." As these tweets suggest, the information conveyed by the messages may not be rich in each individual instance. However, collectively, as seen in the 2011 Tōhoku earthquake in Japan, the information disseminated and gleaned can be of great value to disaster victims and relief workers alike. This chapter explores the significance of Twitter during and in the aftermath of natural disasters.

Throughout this book, Twitter has been explained as a communications technology which is best understood as part of a larger trend towards "update cultures." As discussed in previous chapters, there is a pervasive culture in quite a few countries where individuals take a picture and want to share it online, or have had an exceptional meal and want to update their friends about the amazing restaurant they found. However, there are gradients of the type of updating that occurs on Twitter (i.e., updating ranges on the spectrum between banal and profound). Previous chapters have paid close attention to updating about the banal (chapters 2 and 3).

However, the previous chapter began the discussion of more extraordinary forms of updates through citizen journalism. In this chapter, the update culture is discussed in the context of diverse people being in extreme situations that they feel the world needs to be updated about: disasters. On Twitter, citizen journalists have updated the world during earthquakes, plane crashes, tsunamis, wildfires, and other disasters. In all of these situations, people felt the need to update via tweets.

The focus of the previous chapter was to discuss Twitter's role in terms of changes to journalistic practice. This chapter seeks to understand the nuances of update cultures by examining one extreme end of the continuum from banal to profound tweets (extreme disasters). Disasters are specifically useful for understanding Twitter in that those who are affected are completely broken from normal routines, potentially at risk of injury or death, anxious about the short term, and usually in some form of shock or other trauma. Additionally, Internet access can be severely limited or potentially dangerous if traveling is needed for access. Yet individuals in disaster epicenters tweet. And they use Twitter in new and innovative ways in these situations. Here, the unique case of Twitter and disasters is explored, to understand both Twitter's specific role and some of the complexities surrounding update cultures.

Gathering news information about disasters is an act of following a fast-moving target. In the minutes between news broadcasts, things on the ground can change so rapidly in particularly acute disasters. Traditional news media often cannot catch up in a timely manner. Before the Internet became pervasive, television (and, before that, radio) served as the first line for individuals to access fast-breaking news regarding disasters. Now social media has become an important source of disaster information. In particular, Twitter is commonly used by individuals to follow breaking news regarding disasters, and to keep abreast of the updates that may be coming in frequently throughout the day. Twitter and similar social media sites are inherently built for individual users to subscribe to flows of information, a structure that works efficiently for information dissemination during disasters. In the case of Twitter, users who are interested in breaking news often "follow" the Twitter feeds of traditional news media. What is also particularly unique to Twitter is that users can then elect to follow the updates of users who they feel are close to a disaster. Twitter users can choose to follow the tweets of those "reporting" on the disaster (e.g., traditional and citizen journalists as discussed in the previous chapter) or they can simply read the feeds of these users. In other words, disasters offer a particularly unique case to see the ways in which journalistic practice has been changed by Twitter, a key theme discussed in the previous chapter. This chapter begins by introducing the study of disasters. It discusses the social embeddedness of disasters and then provides a historical context through an exploration of relevant information technology and disasters literature. The use of Twitter in recent disasters, including the 2011 Tōhoku Japan earthquake and the 2010 Pakistan floods, is explored last. These cases serve to present an examination of Twitter's differential usage in developed and developing countries, and to highlight extreme forms of update culture (e.g., a user tweeting as they feel the earth shake under them).

Disaster as Socially Mediated

Disasters, as Clarke (2004: 137) observes, may be destructive, but are ultimately "prosaic" and, as such, help us glean "important things about how and why society works as it does." (The same holds true for understanding how Twitter "works" during disasters.) Sorokin (1943: 244), in his seminal *Man and Society in Calamity*, noted that disasters "offer an opportunity to examine many aspects of social life which in normal times are hidden." Forms of kindness between members of a community or existent social hierarchies are made highly visible in disaster situations, despite less altruistic behavior at other times. For example, in the aftermath of the 2004 Indian Ocean tsunami, the Sri Lankan government tried to appropriate land from devastated coastal villages for hotel development.[1] During the 1971 San Fernando earthquake in California, Steinberg (2000: 178) notes that middle-class individuals were quickly approved for federally funded loans, while the poor, elderly, and ethnic minorities were largely ignored.[2] Despite these inequalities, disaster situations have the ability to activate "disaster communities," usually ad hoc communities of people affected by or involved with a disaster. Using the case of a munitions ship explosion in Halifax, Canada, in 1917, Samuel Prince (1920: 19) argued that the violence of disaster situations creates a state of "flux" from "which it [life] must reset upon a principle, a creed, or purpose" and, from this, "a new sense of unity in dealing with common problems" (Prince 1920: 139) can emerge.

Like in Halifax, contemporary natural disasters cause a flux and various virtual communities can emerge in a common creed of reconstruction. The cyber-presences of disaster communities have blurred a disaster's physical spatial borders as individuals and aid agencies in disaster-struck areas form online coalitions (Murthy 2011a). Fischer's (1998: 18) observation that "[g]roups of survivors tend to emerge to begin automatically responding to the needs of one another" is affirmed virtually in some disaster cases (though not in others). Whether these were activist oriented or scientific (e.g., sedimentary change and water supply issues), individuals and groups in some twenty-first-century disasters have worked together virtually. Online communities can be important to the social fabric of certain segments of disaster victims. For example, from the day the 2004 Indian Ocean tsunami hit subcontinental shores, the web forum and chat sections of India's and Sri Lanka's most popular websites filled with posts. On the popular Indian site rediff.com, a bevy of sympathetic posts appeared on December 26, 2004, the day the tsunami hit the Indian subcontinent. One year after the tsunami, the forum section of the popular Sri Lankan website spot.lk hosted several discussion threads in which users posted images and text (including in the Tamil language) in remembrance of victims of the disaster.

Scholarship on disasters illustrates that new media spaces such as these functioned as collective spaces which brought together disparate people and communities who experienced similar traumas (Palen 2008; Yan 2009). Though they are relatively recent phenomena, these digital communities of disaster victims are reminiscent of what Barton (1969: 226–7) termed communities with "segmental integration." What he meant by this was that the community had "close ties" within particular social "segments," but had "few ties" between the segments (ibid.). Applied to virtual communities, groups could have "close ties" online, but not necessarily to other groups of online posters. However, Barton (p. 227) argues that despite this diversity between segmental groups, "intense discussion and awareness within all groups" can occur as "each has some of its members affected" by the disaster.

Loft (2005) suggests that blogs (the longer-length cousin of Twitter) can encourage community-building.[3] Specialized roles emerge on media including blogs, and solidarity can develop from the specialized roles that people have in this virtual community. In my research on new media and disasters (Murthy 2011a), I found that tsunami-related blogs can be understood as communities through the complex mesh of online interactions between those with missing relatives, individuals affected locally by the aftermath, aid workers, volunteers (specialist and non-specialist), and the general public (some encouraging donations and others to express support online). Just the fact of empathetic expressions of support by anonymous virtual participants in a community is powerful. In the 2007 Virginia Tech shooting, anonymous individuals contributed their condolences to an online virtual Memorial in Second Life, and this was found to be meaningful by those affected by the disaster (Hughes et al. 2008).

Information Technology and Disasters

The diffusion of innovative technologies within a state of extreme disaster seems at some level counterintuitive. Rather than conjuring up ad hoc networks of Twitter users, which update others of road closures and fatalities, one would think a disaster would sweep away any proclivity for technological invention. However, as Pitirim Sorokin (1943: 243) prophetically noted in the 1940s, disaster can "stimulate and foster" society's "scientific and technological work." Twitter becomes, in some disasters, one of the tools for this innovative work Sorokin is alluding to. That being said, the introduction of new technologies in disaster situations, as Bates and Peacock (1987: 305) note, is not a zero-sum game. They give the example of a society where water was traditionally obtained from public fountains or watering places. Besides serving the purpose of obtaining water, they also functioned as key community spaces where women met and socialized. In reconstruction efforts, these villages could be given piped water to their houses or village centers (perhaps due to well contamination), an action which Bates and Peacock (1987: 305–6) argue constitutes a change in social life (e.g., for women who regularly socialize at fountains). Additionally, if victims turn to Twitter because of a disaster, tweeting may persist as part of their life after the disaster. However, in this situation, Twitter most likely "augments" (Jurgenson 2012) their social communication rather than eliminating or severely reducing face-to-face interactions.

Cutting-edge communications networks have historically been associated with developed countries. Recent scholarship shows that this trend is changing (Hughes et al. 2008; Liu et al. 2008; Shklovski et al. 2008; Sutton et al. 2008). The ability to tweet and post YouTube videos of your "disaster experience" has the potential for normally marginalized individuals and groups to update the world about their situation. This is hardly unproblematic. Although it fosters a perceived sense of empowerment amongst disaster victims,[4] there is also a globally induced pressure to update the world by "representing"[5] one's village/town/city/country, as international media scramble to arrive in remote disaster-stricken areas.

Whether the people have become more empowered or not, online dispatches from developing countries (despite usually coming from social and economic elites) not only shape international views of disaster victims, but can also affect aid campaigns.[6] For example, Flickr photographs and blog posts regarding the 2008 Cyclone Nargis disaster in Myanmar flowed out of the country while traditional forms of news dissemination were severely limited. One blogger who had multiple fractures managed to find an operational hospital and posted comments and a picture, commenting on the ordeal.[7] Similarly, a Malaysian businessman, *azmil77*, who happened to be visiting Myanmar during the cyclone, took a series of moving eyewitness photographs and posted them almost immediately onto Flickr.[8] An intense discussion of comments ensued on his album. Another Flickr album contains photographs taken in Yangon by Jyotish Nordstrom, the founder and director of a voluntary preschool for impoverished local children.[9] In the album's description, details are given on how to send donations to the school. Though on a small scale and usually dependent on local digital knowledge, these representations of disaster experiences via social media can provide a counterbalance to sometimes exploitative and ethnocentric accounts,[10] and tweets coming out of disaster areas can have similar effects.

Before specifically exploring Twitter and disasters, it is useful to further examine the history of information-sharing technology in disasters. As in other chapters, this historical context is critically important to viewing Twitter alongside other sociotechnical innovations in disaster communication. Stephenson and Anderson's (1997) forward-looking essay "Disasters and the Information Technology Revolution," though well over a decade old now, remains a useful review of the subject. Beginning with "time-sharing" mainframes (where clusters of users shared room-sized computers) in the 1970s, to the advent of personal computers in the 1980s, they argue that disaster relief operations have been heavily shaped by technological change. They observe that online modem-networked bulletin boards (very early precursors to Twitter), such as ADMIN in Australia and the Emergency Preparedness Information Exchange (EPIX) in Canada, had been adopted by a small minority of emergency professionals by the late 1980s (Stephenson and Anderson 1997: 311). They single out the 1990s as having perhaps the most profound effect to disaster relief operations, with innovations in digital radio, Geographic Information Systems (GIS), email (and email list servers), Gopher (software used to create information portals), remote sensing, and the Internet.[11] Fischer (1998) also notes that disaster victims in the United States during the 1990s could complete online applications for disaster relief from the Federal Emergency Management Agency (FEMA) website directly, and that the information on various websites (governmental and otherwise) announced disaster mitigation and response. It is important to reflect on the evolution of information technology and disasters not only to contextualize the importance of these changes, but also to remember that these technologies have not always been ubiquitous. The same goes for tweets during disasters – something that has become ubiquitous in developed countries.

During contemporary disasters, the world not only expects and assumes a barrage of tweets, but also digital videos and photographs that chronicle the events surrounding a disaster. But, in 1995, the use of the Internet as "a self-help network" for relaying information about the Kobe earthquake in Japan (through digital maps, digital photographs, and online forums) was noteworthy (Stephenson and Anderson 1997: 315). Similarly, the use of web pages during flooding in North Dakota and Manitoba in April and May 1997 "played a crucial role [. . .] in maintaining a sense of community among evacuated people dispersed throughout the region" (Stephenson and Anderson 1997: 317). This latter point that the Internet can (and has over a decade) influenced social cohesion during natural disasters is one compellingly made by Shklovski et al. (2008). That said, there are downsides to increasing Internet and telephony usage during disasters. Specifically, a greater reliance on the Internet also translates to a greater demand on electricity. Additionally, using mobile devices to upload videos and photos can easily overload cellular phone systems and cause outages. (Twitter is an interesting exception in that tweets are low bandwidth consumers; individuals can tweet more regularly and from more locations in the disaster area, whereas video uploading is often a much more difficult action to accomplish.) In the case of the 2004 Indian Ocean tsunami, the disaster created large-scale interruptions to the electricity and telephone grids. In developed countries, this is much less of a problem. For example, in the U.S., in the run-up to Tropical Storm Bonnie in 2010, AT&T (which, at the time, was the exclusive carrier for iPhones in the U.S.) publicly announced it was increasing network capacity to cope with potential outages from mobile Internet use.

Twitter and Disasters

As already noted, Twitter has been prominently associated with contemporary disasters (especially in the case of the 2011 Tōhoku Japan earthquake). Research on the usage of social media and disaster events has been growing, covering a range of sites, including social networking, photo repository, and microblogging sites (Kireyev et al. 2009). The discussion of natural disasters on Twitter has been part of a general trend that has brought Twitter significant mainstream attention. As McCulloch (2009) argues, the downing of US Airways Flight 1549 in the Hudson River in New York in 2009 and Twitter's use in covering the story legitimized the site as a journalistic space (a case discussed in detail in the previous chapter). Specifically, the media used by Janis Krums to circulate a picture taken on his iPhone of the downed aircraft was Twitter's photo-sharing portal, TwitPic. This happened well before any news crews arrived and many major news media used his iPhone picture in print media, with the Associated Press eventually purchasing distribution rights. And MSNBC had him on the phone within 30 minutes of him tweeting.

The October 2007 wildfires in Southern California were perhaps the first natural disaster that put Twitter on the map. As Hughes and Palen (2009: 1) note, Twitter was used "to inform citizens of the time-critical information about road closures, community evacuations, shifts in fire lines, and shelter information." A man-made disaster in which Twitter became important and, indeed, controversial was that of the Mumbai bomb blasts of 2008, where everyday Indians were tweeting about which hotels had been taken over by armed gunmen, where fires were still burning, and where shots had been fired (see chapter 4). Because tweets are so short, researchers have found them to be a medium especially well suited to communicating real-time information during disasters (Hughes and Palen 2009). As Palen et al. note (2010), "the implications of social media are significant for mass emergency events." In their case study of the 2009 Red River Valley flood, they found significant cases of individuals tweeting about their disaster experience as well as about aid organizations involved (Palen et al. 2010). Additionally, social media are being used by government officials to assist in organizing volunteer efforts during disasters (Tucker 2011).

Twitter and the 2011 Tōhoku Japan earthquake
On March 14, 2011, an earthquake with a 9.0 magnitude hit northeast Japan (with the earthquake's epicenter off of the Oshika Peninsula of Tōhoku). Many coastal cities were affected and aftershocks were felt until late April. This

earthquake was the most powerful to have ever hit Japan and is considered to be the fifth largest global earthquake since 1900 in magnitude (Kelley 2011). In the earthquake's aftermath, telephone networks were unreliable, but the Internet was relatively stable, enabling affected individuals to communicate by Twitter, email, and Skype (Tamura and Fukuda 2011). As Horiuchi (2011) observes, "Twitter proved robust and functional" when mobile phone networks were overloaded. The bulk of Tōhoku-related hashtags were #prayforjapan, #japanquake, #tsunami, and #japan (Tucker 2011). Twitter was also used by medical professionals to disseminate time-sensitive medical information/advice. For example, doctors in Japan used Twitter to notify patients where to locate medicine (Tamura and Fukuda 2011). These tweets were retweeted and circulated within relevant networks. The combination of Twitter with on-the-ground assistance was found to be beneficial to the health of victims (Tamura and Fukuda 2011). As for US Airways Flight 1549, tweets were timely in this case.

Twitter was even carrying reliable earthquake reports of Tōhoku before CNN began reporting on the disaster (Tucker 2011). The first tweet regarding the earthquake ("Earthquake!") happened one minute and 25 seconds after the earthquake hit and was in Japanese (Doan et al. 2011). The first English tweet came 46 seconds later. The tweets during the earthquake and in the aftermath were found to be related to the earthquake/tsunami, radiation (from the Fukushima nuclear power plant), and post-traumatic anxiety (ibid.). The first tsunami-related tweet came six minutes after the earthquake ("I can see tsunami is coming!!!!") from a citizen journalist tweeting in Japanese (ibid.). Tweets covered a wide range of topics, ranging from shortages of food and supplies to expressions of high levels of anxiety. What this pattern reveals is that tweets were flowing rapidly from the moment the Tōhoku earthquake was felt and useful information was succinctly conveyed in a timely fashion.

Japan is reported as having the eleventh largest number of Twitter users in the world and has had a Japanese-language version of the site since 2008 (Okazaki et al. 2011: 64). Because of its large user-base and high frequency of earthquakes, researchers had already begun investigating Twitter and earthquake notification in Japan before the Tōhoku earthquake, and found that the first tweet after an earthquake in Japan generally occurs within a minute (Okazaki et al. 2011). However, Twitter's ability to filter important information from experts during disasters is questionable. Rather, Twitter's infrastructure is based around prioritizing the circulation of tweets from more "popular" Twitter users, rather than making a distinction of whether they have expertise in an area. For example, in the aftermath of the Tōhoku earthquake, scientists unsuccessfully tried to assuage the public via Twitter that the health impacts from the leaking Fukushima nuclear reactor were minimal beyond a 20–30 km radius of the reactors (McCartney 2011). Though the next case we will be exploring, the 2010 Pakistan floods, is different both in the type of disaster and locale, tweets from popular Twitter users – especially celebrities – were disproportionately influential. The engagement of "development celebrities" (Goodman and Barnes 2011), celebrities who see themselves as ambassadors of development politics, will also be explored in the next section.

The 2010 Pakistan floods
The 2010 Pakistan floods were the third most popular trending topic in 2010 in Twitter's News Events category (Twitter.com 2010).[12] The floods caused enormous loss of life, significant environmental destruction, and a large-scale humanitarian crisis. The United Nations quickly labeled the situation in Pakistan as a "catastrophe." There were 1,802 people reported dead and 2,994 injured (Associated Press of Pakistan 2010). The United Nations World Food Programme estimated that 1.8 million people "were in dire need of

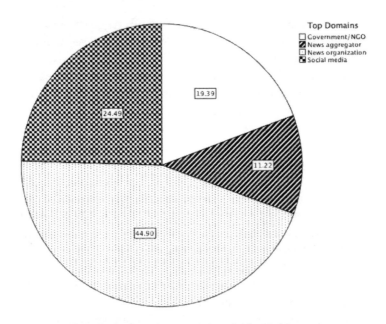

Figure 5.1   Top 100 domain categories which #Pakistan tweets linked to

water, food and shelter" (*The Irish Times* 2010). In the case of the floods, the vast majority of the affected population consisted of digital have-nots prior to the flooding. National broadband penetration was a mere 0.31 percent (International Telecommunication Union 2010). Additionally, the areas affected are predominantly home to Urdu-language speakers, rather than English-language speakers.

I investigated the 2010 Pakistan floods on Twitter by studying 113,862 tweets with the trending hashtag "Pakistan" (collected during August 2010).[13] Which websites people were linking to in their tweets were also examined. What is immediately noteworthy is that traditional media was the most frequently linked media form during the 2010 Pakistan floods (see figure 5.1). This finding highlights several aspects of Twitter's use in this case. Twitter users place primacy on circulating information from traditional news media rather than information/news from social media (which includes blogs). In many ways, this affirms an argument that Twitter as a whole does not give much voice to alternative news sources (including alternative disaster accounts from citizen journalists). Rather, CNN, the BBC, and other traditional media dominate the list of sites that individuals tweeting during the floods were linking to. Although this indicates the continuing strength of traditional media, it does not high-light the eclipse of social media. Rather, it affirms the place of traditional news media alongside social media in disasters (Li and Rao 2010).

In terms of content, most Pakistan-related tweets refer to the floods in passing and often recommend a news article. Many users retweet headline stories tweeted by traditional news organizations. One of the questions this book has explored is how transformative Twitter – as a medium – is in terms of forming communities, whether around health (see chapter 7) or social movements (see chapter 6). In the case of disasters, the scholarship has argued that Twitter can facilitate the formation of effective disaster communities (Hughes and Palen 2009; Vieweg et al. 2010). However, if most are tweeting in passing, does a disaster "community" emerge?

Although these communities can and do exist – for instance, individuals in a disaster zone tweet the location of victims or report road closures (Palen et al. 2010) – the majority are tweeting news stories from traditional media. Additionally the vast majority of users are only tweeting once about the floods (see figure 5.2). Such infrequent involvement points to the fact that these users are not part of a cohesive disaster community. Rather, Twitter users passively retweet about humanitarian crises, political movements, and other "causes" from the comfort of their chair (akin to the "slacktivism" discussed in chapter 6). This low-stakes involvement in the disaster creates

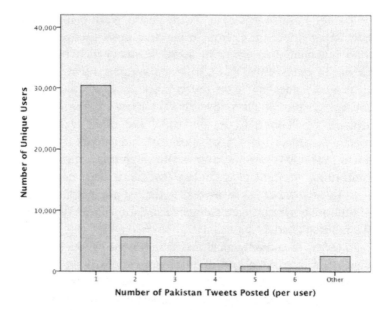

Figure 5.2   Frequency of tweets per user with Pakistan trending topic tag

a public identity for themselves as global individuals who are immersed in humanitarian causes. It takes just a second to tweet about a disaster and one's followers potentially see a user as an empathetic cosmopolitan. Rather than deep engagement, these masses of users are only superficially engaged with a disaster or other humanitarian event.

This behavior should not be viewed as normatively inferior to tweets contributed from on-the-ground aid workers and citizen journalists. Rather, these types of users themselves are qualitatively different and not comparable. What the involvement of these casual tweets reveals is a relatively high level of focused interest toward the floods. Interestingly, many Twitter users (with the majority in Western countries) at least had the floods on their mind, even if it was in passing (see figure 5.2). This is further substantiated by the fact that

Pakistan was one of the top trending topics of 2010 (Twitter. com 2010).[14]

The Pakistan floods also shed light on whose tweets are being picked up and being circulated. Besides traditional news media, are tweets from users in Pakistan experiencing the disaster first hand among the tweets that are most retweeted? No. Out of the top 20 at-mentions, a celebrity (Jemima Khan) outranks UNICEF. Four of the top 10 are celebrities (Jemima Khan, Lance Armstrong, Stephen Fry, and Justin Bieber). Two are news media (the *New York Times* and the *Huffington Post*) and two are governmental/non-governmental organizations (the U.S. State Department and UNICEF). Either Twitter users believe celebrities could impact the lot of disaster-affected victims or the data reflects Twitter's propensity to involve celebrities in all topics, regardless of their expertise or relevance. The scholarship on Twitter supports the latter (Cha et al. 2010). In other words, users with a significant number of at-mentions were the exception rather than the rule. Specifically, the directedness of the conversations regarding the Pakistan floods had a significant weight toward mentioning celebrities rather than individuals or organizations on the ground in Pakistan. Additionally, only 10 of the top 100 users who were at-mentioned and one of the top 20 at-mentioned users were located in Pakistan, which supports the theory that Twitter functioned more as a clearing house of "news" passing through the hands of mainstream media or celebrities during the disaster, rather than Pakistani individuals and institutions. Research in celebrity studies highlights the emergence of "development celebrities," celebrities who have cultivated influence in development politics through a variety of modes, including Twitter (Goodman and Barnes 2011). Prominent celebrities have had their "development celebrity" status emphasized via Twitter by tweeting about disasters such as the Haitian earthquake:

> celebrities like Paris Hilton, Dannii Minogue, Chris Martin and Ben Stiller took to their Twitter accounts to, in the words

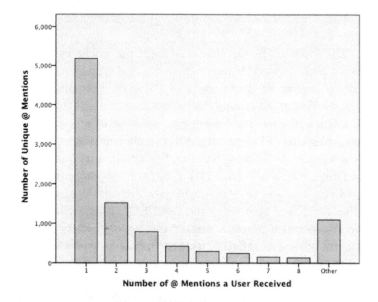

Figure 5.3 Frequency of at-mentions per user with Pakistan
trending topic hashtag

of Stiller, alert their followers after the Haitian earthquake
that "People in Haiti need our help and attention right
now" (Thompson 2010); Wyclef Jean Tweeted that he was
". . . on my way to the DR to get to Haiti. Please urge your
councilmen, governors, etc; we need a state of emergency
for Haiti" and that "Haiti today faces a natural disaster
of unprecedented proportion, an earthquake unlike anything the country has ever experienced" (Thompson 2010).
(Goodman and Barnes 2011)

Twitter provides a highly efficient medium for "development
celebrities" to make known their development credentials. In
the case of Stiller, only a vague tweet about Haiti is tweeted,
but it makes clear Stiller's interest in the Haitian disaster.

The authority and influence of celebrities within the case
of the Pakistan floods (as well as in Twitter in general) are
also important points that should not be underestimated.

Tweets by celebrities are also retweeted the most (see table 5.1). Out of the 15 tweets most retweeted, nine were by celebrities. Only two non-celebrity individuals appear in this list. Celebrities are most interested in raising awareness about the floods and money for assistance through their tweets (see table 5.1). The U.S. State Department is the only governmental institution in the list. Much of the significance of this retweet list is derived from what is absent from it. Specifically, there are no citizen journalists reporting on the floods from the ground. Indeed, there are no individuals from Pakistan who appear in the list. From the vantage point of retweets, Twitter seems to be disproportionately focused as a medium for celebrities to promote fundraising efforts rather than disseminating first-hand information about the floods. That said, tweets by social-media savvy Pakistanis did help raise money during the disaster (Toosi 2011). However, the majority of retweeted messages are linked to celebrities or other influential Twitter users. Celebrities ultimately had a powerful voice within the context of the Pakistan floods, a voice that is seemingly louder than individual journalists and individuals in Pakistan.

This highlights the larger power of celebrities within Twitter and within update cultures. Many individuals follow celebrities because they are interested in their updates on celebrity culture (Hargittai and Litt 2011), whether these are banal or profound. Individuals are tuning into celebrity Twitter feeds whether to read their breakfast selection, romantic interest, or about development causes. Another way to think about celebrities tweeting on disasters is as "brokers," who introduce large sections of the public to a disaster the celebrity thinks matters (e.g., Ben Stiller's tweet about the Haitian earthquake). The retweeting of a celebrity tweet can potentially have real impacts on the prominence of disasters from the eyes of Twitter users in developed countries. The knock-on effect could be increased media attention. Ultimately – if one sees Twitter as a powerful political force

Table 5.1 Top 15 retweets with identifiable users

(numbers 5 and 13 had no identifiable users and were categorized as spam)

Ranking	Retweet text
1	RT @Yunaaaa: Flood-affected children in north-western Pakistan urgently need aid – Help @UNICEF help these children – Please visit http: ...
2	RT @JemKhan: My article re Pakistan floods. Please read, RT, donate if poss. Thanks http://www.thesundaytimes.co.uk/sto/public/article37 ...
3	RT @DalaiLama: His Holiness the Dalai Lama prays for the loss of life caused by floods in Pakistan, India, and landslides in Drugchu htt ...
4	RT @rainnwilson: We give a billion a year to Pakistan which aids the Taliban. Why not give it to the poor or to the debt?
6	RT @Sascha1976: Wat #carglasszuigt kan, kan ook voor een goed doel... Hashtag #giro555open om Pakistan te helpen. 14 miljoen mensen hebb ...
7	RT @oncefelin: Moscow mortuaries full. Floods in India. Floods in China. Floods in Pakistan. Millions affected. Climate change is real. ...
8	RT @stephenfry: Amazing article by @JemKhan on Pakistan, its floods, its future and what we can do. http://bit.ly/95Knjq
9	RT @UncleRUSH: 20 million left homeless by Pakistan flooding...plz raise awareness
10	RT @StateDept: Text \SWAT\" to 50555 from your phone to contribute $10 to help flood victims in #Pakistan. http://go.usa.gov/cxS #UNHCR #UN"
11	RT @TheEconomist: How the heatwave in Russia is connected to floods in Pakistan http://econ.st/cvZWWX #economist #heatwave #russia #pakistan
12	RT @stephenfry: To donate to Red Cross http://bit.ly/aW9DAs or to give £5 text DONATE to 70700. Those stricken by the Pakistan floods ne ..
14	RT @TheVijayMallya: My website-mallyainparliament.in hacked by d Pakistan Cyber Army Shocked when I opened site to update it Saw the Pak ...
15	RT @QueenRania: Dire needs in Pakistan for flood-affected children – Help @UNICEF Please help these children by visiting http://www.unic ...

– these public elevations of a disaster to prominence could potentially influence governmental humanitarian aid decisions (that is, if politicians see Twitter as a barometer of constituent sentiment).

Conclusion

This chapter has explored the unique situation of Twitter and disasters, extreme events which render visible many aspects of social life which are otherwise obscured or invisible. When a disaster strikes, otherwise disparate groups become joined together across the common experience of being disaster victims. In this way, Twitter may be helping form far-reaching communities that transcend traditional socioeconomic barriers. Or it may be reinforcing these hierarchies. A key reason this chapter explored disasters rather than another area is that disasters are highly unique in their extreme nature and their ability to instantaneously affect everyone regardless of social position. Most disaster victims feel anxious and, at a minimum, disoriented. Some may have even witnessed death (and tweeted about it). This extreme situation can lead to an update culture whose content can be highly profound. Additionally, the stakes of getting tweets out from a disaster zone can be much higher. Lives could potentially be saved through tweets warning people of flash-flood areas or other dangerous situations. Therefore, even if Internet access is difficult to come by, some individuals may feel a direct need to update the world of what they know about a disaster situation.

Even if their tweets do not save a life, one thing is certain. The world turns to Twitter to learn of minute-to-minute detail during disasters. This chapter has discussed how Twitter has shaped journalistic practice, using disaster reporting as a case study. Disaster victims who are tweeting to help other victims also simultaneously become citizen journalists. This practice has not infringed upon the role of traditional media and disaster reporting. Rather, it has augmented the information available to journalists in their reporting (i.e., being much more timely and far-reaching in their reports). Examining Twitter's use during natural disasters reveals both the forest and the trees. We see individual citizen journalists, aid workers, and victims going to great lengths to interact with each other on Twitter. However, the macro view suggests that those who have a powerful voice regarding any topic on Twitter (i.e., celebrities and other "popular" Twitter users) have the most powerful voice during natural disasters. For example, Kate Gosselin, Kim Kardashian, and Jersey Shore's Snooki were tweeting in anticipation of Hurricane Irene in 2011 (Fox News Philadelphia 2011). This is a trend not restricted to disasters, but includes many topics on Twitter (Cha et al. 2010). The fact that celebrities including Stephen Fry, Jemima Khan, Rainn Wilson, Yuna Kim, and Russell Simmons commanded the most retweets during the 2010 Pakistan floods (see table 5.1) reveals how much of a celebrity-oriented culture many of Twitter's trending topics have developed. Indeed, celebrities appear to be at the forefront of Twitter-based fundraising efforts for flood victims.

In this chapter, the twofold significance of this has been explored. First, celebrity cultures are powerful and involve the ability to set the agenda regarding important events far beyond celebrity gossip. Second, as "development celebrities," their voice within disaster discourses is indicative of update cultures themselves. Specifically, Twitter users see celebrities as a key source of "important" updates, whether about Hollywood gossip, fashion trends, or important world events. Celebrities command our attention on a range of topics regardless of their superficial engagement and they can steer discourse on Twitter in terms of raising disasters to prominence, which potentially has real impacts on fundraising efforts.

This chapter also highlights the varying locales and types of disasters that are tweeted. Twitter's more extensive use in the 2011 Tōhoku Japan earthquake reveals that, in a country with exceptionally high rates of Twitter use per capita, the medium was perceived as having significant effects on aid efforts, public health, and rescue operations. Though the two disasters are different (floods versus an earthquake/tsunami), they were similar in becoming trending topics on Twitter. However, in Pakistan's case, Western Twitter users (especially celebrities) were most responsible for the propagation of tweets and the catapulting of #pakistan to one of the most popular trending topics of 2010. In the case of Tōhoku, many tweets were in Japanese and originating from users in Japan. This is significant because it highlights the differing uses of Twitter by users in developed versus developing countries. Japan and other developed (or emergent affluent economies, such as Brazil) have large Twitter user-bases and are able to have agency, control, and voice regarding disasters which occur on their home soil. In developing countries, updates usually have to travel through celebrities or other highly followed Twitter users. As discussed in chapter 6, it was mostly Twitter users outside of Egypt who were tweeting about Egypt during the Arab Spring, and it is these users who received attention in traditional media coverage rather than Egyptians. In other words, Twitter may not be changing the power of both Western individuals and traditional news media; rather, Twitter seemingly echoes this power relationship.

Overall, Twitter presents a valuable mode of dissemination when disasters hit countries that are well connected (e.g., Japan), but less-connected countries are more dependent on Western users and an extremely small Twittering elite (e.g., as was the case in Pakistan). Nevertheless, the effect of one tweet during a disaster can be profound or, as Serino puts it, "In 140 characters, [. . . a] person on a cell phone on a beach can tell hundreds of people around them that a tsunami is coming" (cited in Tucker 2011). Disasters present us with unique glimpses of the complexity of update cultures. On the one hand, updating the world can seem banal and evidence of a moral decay (if one agrees with the arguments of Twitter pessimists). On the other hand, a tweet from that person on the beach is still a terse update, but one that is extremely profound.

CHAPTER SIX

Twitter and Activism

> Looks like there is some action in the air http://t.co/
> mpɪulhFQ 2 pm March from Washington Square to
> Liberty Plaza. #OWS #Occupy #TheOther99.
>
> @TimCast

The tweet above is part of the stream of tweets from the Occupy Wall Street-related hashtags of #OWS and #Occupy. Occupy Wall Street was a series of activist movements started in New York City in 2011 to protest against perceived financial inequalities symbolized by Wall Street. The movement spread to many global cities. #TheOther99 refers to the hashtag used by the Occupy and related movements which seek to redress the wealth disparity gap in the U.S. (in which wealth is ultra concentrated amongst the richest 1 percent of the American population at the expense of the remaining 99 percent of the American population). The tweet is attempting to solicit participants for an Occupy Wall Street-related march at 2 p.m. in New York City on the day the tweet was posted. The march is part of a campaign within Occupy Wall Street for environmental justice. This chapter explores the role of Twitter in activism and whether tweets like the one above can bring feet to the street during social movements. It takes as its focus the 2011 "Arab Spring" movements in the Middle East and North Africa, and evaluates what role Twitter may have played in the movements.

Facebook and Twitter turned out to be far more effective agents of change than any "martyrdom" attacks on apostates, crusaders and Zionists – the most familiar objects of hatred in the jihadi lexicon. (Black 2011)

Twitter has been prominently associated with wide-ranging forms of sociopolitical activism. One of the prominent associations is with the so-called "Arab Spring," a rough grouping of diverse anti-government movements in the Middle East and North Africa (MENA) in late 2010 and early 2011. The movements, which included Tunisia, Egypt, Libya, Bahrain, Syria, and Yemen (with substantial protests occurring in many other countries in the region), received particular media attention for the ways in which Twitter was used in them. Whether or not Twitter "turned out to be [a] far more effective [agent] of change," as Black (2011) argues above, Twitter became recurrently associated with MENA movements since 2009 and #iranelection was the top Twitter news story in 2009. Like the case of the downing of US Airways Flight 1549, discussed in chapter 4, the unrest in Tunisia in 2011 hit Twitter before mainstream international media (Moore et al. 2011), making it a valuable news source for international journalists and news-consuming individuals around the world. Though it is tempting to label many of the movements as Twitter revolutions, this does not accurately capture the medium's role. Marcell Shewaro, a prominent Syrian blogger, observes that "[t]he street led the bloggers" in the case of the Syrian unrest (cited in Moore et al. 2011). Or, paraphrasing Shewaro, the street led the tweeters. This is in distinction to some scholarship which has found that the "efficacy of the streets has changed" and that new media has become a critical center of progressive political resistance and protest (Raley 2009). This chapter explores activist movements and Twitter by critically examining the case of the Egyptian unrest in January 2011 ("25 January Revolution"), though it refers to other countries grouped into the collective Arab Spring uprisings. This chapter will make the argument that it is important to critically approach Twitter's use in these movements. Specifically, the idea of technological determinism will be explored and the case will be made that Twitter has great potential in organizing activists' movements (as seen in Egypt), but we should be careful about concluding Twitter's value ipso facto or Twitter as "causing" these very diverse movements. Additionally, Twitter's impact on complex, large-scale sociopolitical activism will be examined through Mark Granovetter's sociological work which argues that there is "strength" in having a multitude of "weak" connections (the type of connections Twitter most often facilitates). Though the chapter does not present original empirical data, it synthesizes empirical data from an array of sources in order to present comprehensive conclusions on Twitter's role in the Arab Spring. The chapter provides a more nuanced conclusion to Twitter's role in recent social movements without falling victim to a strict binary distinction of whether Twitter caused/didn't cause the 25 January and other revolutions associated with the Arab Spring.

Cairo Tweeting

Egypt has experienced varying levels of control of media content in contemporary times (Amin 2002). During the 25 January Revolution, the Egyptian government began by targeting online social platforms, including Facebook and Twitter, and then moved to the communication infrastructure itself (Dunn 2011: 16). In Egypt, at the time of the unrest, there were approximately 3.5 million registered Facebook users (which amounts to roughly 4.21 percent of the population), 12,000 registered Twitter users (which amounts to roughly .00014 percent of the population), and 13.5 million Internet users (which amounts to roughly 16.27 percent of the population) (Dunn 2011: 18; United Nations Department of Economic and Social Affairs 2010: 63). Figure 6.1 provides a visual representation (with Twitter users almost invisible to the visual field).

Given this data, it is clear that the percentage of the Egyptian population who was tweeting or consuming tweets

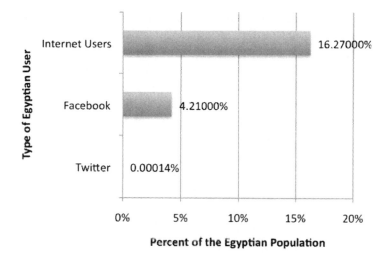

Figure 6.1   Internet, Facebook, and Twitter users in Egypt

was miniscule. That is not to say that .00014 percent of the
Egyptian population could not start the movement. Rather,
the actual direct reach of Twitter within Egypt was extremely
minimal. That said, the perception of the Egyptian government concerning online social networking and social media
was that they were a threat. This can be partially explained by
media representation of Twitter's and Facebook's influence,
but also Twitter's reach outside of Egypt. International mainstream news media were regularly using scoops garnered
from Twitter as an integral part of their source mix (Lotan et
al. 2011). Whether it was over-egging the pudding by Western
journalists, or for other reasons, the Egyptian authorities shut
down the Internet for five days in January of 2011. Because this
Internet shutdown had major impacts on what Dunn (2011:
20) terms "apolitical" groups of Egyptian society, including
the business community, these previously apathetic groups
began to exhibit anti-government sentiment. Ultimately,
what we can conclude is that the tiny base of Twitter users in
Egypt did not matter in terms of the real effects Twitter had

on Egypt. If anything, global news media hype potentially had more of a causal effect on Egypt. Specifically, Twitter's perception as a threat by the authorities mattered more than any concerted statistical quantification of the pervasiveness of the medium in the country. We can extrapolate this to mean that user uptake of Twitter is not the sole variable in activism.

The Egyptian authorities ultimately stoked massive interest by everyday Egyptians in Twitter through the Internet shutdown. The notoriety of/interest in Twitter reached the level where Google worked with Twitter to quickly develop a "speak2tweet" system enabling Egyptians to dial an international number and leave a message which would be recorded and tweeted with a #Egypt hashtag. Tweets could also be listened to by dialing the number. The situation had reached a point where P. J. Crowley, the U.S. Assistant Secretary of State at the time, felt compelled to tweet:

> We are concerned that communication services, including the Internet, social media and even this #tweet, are being blocked in #Egypt. (Farber 2011)

Though his view is the opposite of the Egyptian government's, Crowley's normative position on the utility of Twitter and other social media to Egypt is quite similar to that of the Egyptian government in that both ultimately legitimize Twitter and its role in the social movements in Egypt in 2011. The fact that Crowley emphasized that his tweet might even be blocked additionally legitimates the power of individual tweets (i.e., his). What is particularly interesting is that it is not individual tweets per se which most fueled activism, but, as Hassanpour (2011: 2) argues, Egypt's Internet shutdown (which involved blocking Twitter a day before Facebook), which he describes as acting more as a "catalyst of the revolutionary process and hastens the disintegration of the status quo." In other words, his conclusion is highly counterintuitive in that we would expect the disruption of tweets and Facebook updates to have fragmented revolutionary unrest, rather than strengthen it. Additionally, because government loyalists were using Twitter to launch "smear campaigns against opposition forces" (Tomlinson 2011), the blocking of Twitter – simultaneously and serendipitously – diminished the medium's use as a tool of repression.

Hassanpour (2011: 4) observes that "[i]n the absence of the mass media, information is communicated locally" and local face-to-face communication with friends, family, colleagues, and one's local community is a powerful contributor to on-the-ground revolutionary movements. Specifically, "it forced more face-to-face communication, i.e. more physical presence in streets" (ibid.: 28). Looking at the "schedule" of when the Egyptian government shut down different services also reveals an interesting pattern. Twitter was blocked on January 25, 2011, Facebook on January 26, 2011, and – a whole six days after Twitter was blocked – Cairo's Al-Jazeera bureau was shut down on January 30, 2011 (ibid.: 32). Should we take this to mean that tweets were perceived as more threatening than traditional satellite news reporting done by Al-Jazeera? Ultimately, by March 2011, the number of active Twitter users in Egypt is estimated at over 131,000 (Salem and Mourtada 2011: 16), more than a tenfold increase from January 2011.

Twitter Revolution?

On a more macro level, over 122,000 tweets with keywords pertaining to the Egyptian movements were circulated during January 16–23, 2011, jumping to over 1.3 million during January 24–30, 2011 (O'Dell 2011). Though tweets containing Egypt-related keywords and hashtags jumped over tenfold in January 2011, this should not be conflated with the medium's influence in the movements or even whether it "started" the movements. Indeed, various contemporary movements in the Middle East and North Africa have been labeled as "Twitter revolutions" (Christensen 2011; Warf 2011). As discussed earlier in chapter 3, it is critical that we evaluate the actual uses of

Twitter rather than falling into the trap of being technologically deterministic in terms of the medium. Claiming that the movements in Iran, Egypt, Tunisia, Bahrain, and other MENA states were the result of social networking sites and social media is, according to Warf (2011), an untenable point. Warf (2011: 166) not only observes that a mere 0.3 percent of Iranians are on Twitter, but also adds that it is highly unrealistic to think that it was the case that "dictatorships staffed with passive bumbling incompetents [were] patiently wait[ing] to be toppled by savvy young Arab bloggers and cyber-dissidents." Or, as Moore et al. (2011) put it, "Could a simple text message, sent by enough people, depose dictators everywhere?" A key observation by Warf is that Twitter, Facebook, and mobile phones may have "enabled" mass movements in the Arab Spring, but they did not "cause" them. Rather, he argues that it was high unemployment, persistent poverty, and frequent police brutality that were key factors in civil unrest in the region (Warf 2011: 167). El-Din Haseeb (2011: 118) argues that an over-emphasis on the role of social media in the Arab Spring uprisings is at the expense of understanding these events as the result of over 40 years of accumulated political consciousness. This slip in logic in terms of causality and new media is one which Morozov (2009; 2011) frequently highlights in his work.

Ultimately, in the case of Iran, when only 0.3 percent of the Iranian population has a Twitter account, it seems premature to label it a "Twitter Revolution." In Libya, 5.5 percent of the population uses the Internet, and in Yemen, it drops to 1.8 percent (The World Bank 2010). Nonetheless, the "Arab Spring" uprisings, collectively including anti-government movements in Egypt, Tunisia, Yemen, Syria, Libya, and Bahrain in 2011, have been treated by some media commentators as "Twitter Revolutions" (Beaumont 2011). Though social media and social networking technologies played a part in organizing activist movements and, especially, disseminating information out of MENA countries to the West, Twitter ultimately is a communications medium. Like any communications medium, it is merely a tool, and imbuing it with more meaning diverts attention from the fact that Twitter's use and its perception of utility is socially constructed. Rosen (2011) captures this well:

> Internet schminternet. Revolutions happen when they happen. Whatever means are lying around will get used.

The logic here is that modes of communication have historically been integral to revolutions (whether it be the telegraph, rotary phone, cell phone, email, or Twitter). McLuhan (1952: 192) remarks that "[there] have been so many domestic and social revolutions associated with the consequences of the mechanization of writing." Historicizing Twitter's role within social movements in the broader context of technology and political change becomes crucial because, as Motadel (2011) argues, that "communication has played a role in spreading revolutionary ideas throughout history." Mowlana (1979: 111) observes that in the Iranian revolution of 1978–9, "new" media technology was important to the movement:

> the Iranian revolution was also aided by *these modern mass media.* "Small media" – cassette tapes, Xerox, tape recorders, and telephone – could be used to communicate and still escape the control of the regime. From Paris, Ayatollah Khomeini sent his messages through telephone and tapes to Iran, where they were copied by the thousands and made their way through the informal and traditional communication networks to the nation. This method of communication provided both the credibility and excitement of oral messages and the permanence and accessibility of written messages. (Mowlana 1979: 111, my emphasis)

During the late 1970s, these "small media" were the Twitter of the time. Many countries leveraged these "democratic" technologies to record and disseminate written and oral revolutionary messages (Fandy 1999), or to create impromptu "radio stations" with a cassette deck attached to a speaker (Sheldon 1991).

One of the differences emblematic of Twitter (and similar social media) in comparison to previous modes of communication – stretching back to a letter carried by ship and more recently email – is that it is near instantaneous, multiplex, globalized, socially networked, and public. This, as opposed to earlier forms of communication, has not just speeded up information dissemination, but the ways in which activists can organize. In this way, Twitter as a medium is "revolutionary," but so was the telegraph, as Motadel (2011) argues (though the telegraph's messages were slightly longer than tweets[1] as senders had to include words containing the sender's information (Green 1889: 37)). Motadel (2011) observes that even trains and steamers speeded up communication delivery significantly. In other words, time has incrementally become less and less of a barrier. Along with space, time has become "compressed" (Robertson 1992). As a medium, Twitter extends this type of time/space compression that the telegraph revolutionized.

"Twitter Can't Topple Dictators"

Rosen (2011) wrote "The "Twitter Can't Topple Dictators" article, a now notorious online piece, in which he argues that a genre of journalism has emerged which took the title of Rosen's article as their premise. Perhaps the most controversial piece of journalism in the genre is Malcolm Gladwell's (2010) article in *The New Yorker*. Contra Lotan et al. (2011), Gladwell makes the argument that revolutions are not tweeted. Rather, he agrees with Morozov (2009) that recent social activism (e.g., Iran and Moldova) is being inappropriately associated with Twitter. His argument is particularly compelling in that it draws from the empirical facts that very few Twitter accounts existed in Iran during the movement (Morozov 2009) and almost all #iranelection tweets were in English (Gladwell 2010). Indeed, he cites Esfandiari (2010) who comments that "no one seemed to wonder why people trying to coordinate protests in Iran would be writing in any language other than Farsi." This is a fundamental question. Prima facie, it appears that the association of these movements with Twitter and Facebook was more of a journalistic and diplomatic invention, rather than a reality on the ground. However, though it may not have been a frontline tool on the ground, it was highly effective in quickly getting messages out of the MENA region and into the hands of Western journalists, as Lotan et al. (2011) argue.

Gladwell broadens his argument beyond revolutions in the MENA region and argues that Twitter is, generally speaking, not ideal for carrying out revolutions, movements that inherently need a tightly organized hierarchy. He makes the argument that Twitter is about loose networks of "followers" rather than a structured organization with leadership. Gladwell gives the example of events during the American civil rights movement, which he terms "high-risk": actions which involved the real possibility of injury or even death, but which had an immense potential for social change. He labels their organization "militaristic." This leads him to the succinct conclusion that "Activism [. . .] is not for the faint of heart." This also leads Gladwell to conclude that these types of activism need "strong ties" rather than "weak ties." Following the sociologist Granovetter's (1973) seminal work on the subject, Nelson (1989: 380) sums up the former as ties which are "frequent contacts that almost invariably have affective, often friendly, overtones and may include reciprocal favors," while the latter are "infrequent contacts that because they are episodic, do not necessarily have affective content." In terms of the strength of ties, Granovetter (1973: 1361) conceptualizes tie strength as based around "combination of the amount of time, the emotional intensity, the intimacy (mutual confiding), and the reciprocal services which characterize the tie." While Granovetter makes a case for the strength of weak ties, Nelson (1989: 381) highlights that the strength of strong ties is that they are likely to foster a less conflictual situation.

Indeed, in Gladwell's example of the civil rights movement, participants became involved through strong ties (a friend, roommate, or family member who was part of the movement) and, as such, developed a stronger commitment to the cause, which helped breed a cohesive network. Ultimately, Gladwell decides Twitter is of minimal use to high-risk activism which requires substantial commitment and dedication to a cause, and concludes that it is best used for "buffing the edges" of existing social orders. In other words, Twitter, from Gladwell's perspective, is better for boycotting a company over a specific product, or lobbying for the release of a particular political prisoner, than for bringing down a government.

In a way, the elephant in the room is not whether strong ties can foster successful activist movements, but whether the strength of weak ties Granovetter hypothesizes can be sufficiently coalesced on Twitter and similar social media to foster successful activist movements. In an age of Twitter and Facebook status updates, where some think talk online is mere "web chatter," could social media spur the sort of action that strong ties can engender? Put another way: can a tweet convince people to take to high-risk streets? Of course, this is a straw man. Even Martin Luther King generally needed more than 140 characters to capture people's hearts. But he ultimately persuaded followers to make significant personal sacrifices for the movement, including participating in high-risk marches and sit-ins.

The key question that needs to be asked is whether a tweet or a group of tweets can bring feet to the street. In some cases, this is possible and in others it is not. Always, this is something that needs to be evaluated on a case-by-case basis. In cases of low risk, there seems a greater likelihood of people being mobilized by tweets. However, even in low-risk cases, often there seems to be an online/offline disconnect. For example, Moore et al. (2011) give the example of the #walk2work hashtag used in Uganda in February 2011 to coordinate street-level protests against rising fuel and food costs. They conclude that though "the movement seemed strong on Twitter, it failed to catch on in the streets" (Moore et al. 2011). Or, put in terms of leadership, "[the] online arena proves ideal at coordinating protests but not so much at forging leaders" (Tomlinson 2011). However, in high-risk situations, it is even harder to discern whether activism brewed on Twitter can alone muster the strong ties needed for people to hit the streets. This is an important distinction.

Ultimately, Gladwell's argument, though compelling on many levels, creates a strict binary between weak and strong ties. This position forces a choice between the two, when such a choice need not be made. Bennett and Toft (2009: 258) argue that a combination of weak and strong ties (which they refer to as thin and thick network ties) is a desirable configuration for many modern activist movements. Their work on the 2003 anti-Iraq War protests, and the ongoing Fair Trade movements in the U.K. and U.S., highlights not only the efficiency of combining online weak-tie networks with more centralized strong-tie networks, but also emphasizes that not all movements need strong ties. They observe that political mobilization to drive an election campaign may work best with centrally organized authority, but the Fair Trade movement they studied thrived with "bottom-up," "decentralized" actors participating when an issue they were interested in came up, such as lobbying McDonald's or Monsanto (Bennett and Toft 2009: 250). Additionally, another issue with Gladwell's argument is that it seems to imply that large-scale online networks on Twitter effortlessly appear without involving strong tie-based coalition-building. However, these networks regularly involve a confluence of complex, often transnational networks, which include both offline and online interactions and weak/strong ties. As the global 2011 Occupy Wall Street campaigns highlight, modern social movements can use Twitter's efficiently distributed weak-tie networks to disseminate real-time information about an activist movement, or to recruit participants. Additionally, movements that actively involve Twitter may be reaching out to new audiences who historically have not been involved in social or political organizations. This is a critical point. Put another way, as formal memberships in collective organizations have declined (Putnam 2000), loose-tie networks are left to fill in the void. So, ultimately, pitting strong-tie against weak-tie networks is at the expense of including these latent informal networks of potentially interested activists. It should also be noted that the privileging of strong-tie networks in some cases may be elitist. Many mobilization efforts are cash-strapped and if movements are organized via digital technologies the cost is greatly reduced (Bennett and Toft 2009: 247). So, even if the effective strength of weak ties is not equal to that of strong ties (and this is not inherently the case), there are issues of access and reach that Gladwell does not fully take into account.

Tweeting Information from #Syria and #Egypt to the World?

In the case of the Arab Spring, weak ties played an important role both because of cost and a need to disseminate information from the MENA region to the West. Many of these movements were not looking for Twitter to bring feet to, for example, Tahrir Square, but rather to transmit up-to-the-minute updates to Western media in the face of telephone and other communication outages. Many MENA governments have banned or severely restricted social media in recent years. Interestingly, in February 2011, Syria decided to remove a ban on social media sites, including Facebook and YouTube, which had been instituted in 2007 (Mroue 2011). However, as Tomlinson (2011) notes, shortly afterwards the government was reported to have kidnapped and tortured civilian activists to obtain their Facebook passwords, in order to target other suspected activists or scupper their planned actions. Twitter was used in MENA revolutions both by anti-government activists to transmit updates and by governments to find and detain activists. Also, several MENA states created "phantom" Twitter accounts (i.e., automated spam-generating accounts), using these to post banal information with a trending hashtag to dilute activist messages (e.g., this was done in Syria, with tweets about falafels and the weather, to dilute the #syria hashtag). Twitter and Facebook, Comninos (2011) believes, lend themselves to being used by authorities to "spy" on activists and to uncover their identities to make arrests. Christensen (2011: 156) observes that the Iranian government uses new media to monitor Internet users and argues that "it [new media] served to simplify surveillance, disinformation, and repression." Another issue with Twitter is that of information integrity. Global dissemination of breaking news can also spread rumors and misinformation (see chapter 4 for a fuller discussion). Fearn-Banks (2010: 58) argues that "Citizen journalists have nothing and no one preventing them from disseminating misinformation to a global audience in seconds." Esfandiari (2010) gives the example of rumors being spread on Twitter during the Iran unrest of "police helicopters pouring acid and boiling water on protesters [, but . . . a] year later it remains just that: a rumor." As a medium, Twitter's skill in propagating information can just as easily be turned to campaigns of misinformation. Additionally, as Lotan et al. (2011: 1380) argue, rumors on Twitter are often difficult to detect as misinformation. As was the case in Iran in 2009, social media can be highly effective as a mode of facilitating "impromptu social networks" (Morán et al. 2010) for activism, but the corporeal violence deployed by some dictators is being used to counter digital dissent.

But, even if the efficacy of digital dissent is being curbed by repression, the fact of the matter is that tweets got out of MENA countries even when mobile networks were shut down (Idle and Nunns 2011: 65). These tweets provided a constantly updating stream of information to the world from Egypt (Idle and Nunns 2011). Interestingly, social media also served as a powerful tool of news dissemination to other

MENA countries with restricted national news media. Idle and Nunns (2011) observe that Egyptians "were avid recipients of [Twitter] reports coming out of Tunisia," and they argue that Egyptian tweets had a knock-on effect, that "inspire[d] uprisings across the region." Egyptians saw Tunisian tweets not only as a "first-hand" source of information during the events, but also as a vital source of information, given incomplete media coverage by the Egyptian press. Importantly, the tweets served as a catalyst to already fomented revolutionary feelings. With a revolution brewing in their backyard, the tweets flowing from Tunisia – even if they did not directly contribute to the movements – helped draw international attention to the region. Though many Tahrir activists were not involved online, the tiny minority of English-speaking activists tweeting from Tahrir did have tweets picked up by the international news media and those on Twitter in Egypt felt that they "were not only talking to their fellow Egyptians but to the international media and the world" (Idle and Nunns 2011: 20).

Twitter Didn't Topple Dictators, But it Rattled Them

Even in Tahrir, there was no single leadership. Shehata et al. (cited in Hassanpour 2011) state that "Nobody was in charge of Tahrir," and "a lot of those who joined the protests on January 25 in Tahrir were not aware of the Facebook campaign, they had heard about it from the protesters in the square and surrounding streets." Morozov (2011: 16), speaking about the "Green Movement" in Iran, agrees, observing that people in Tehran "didn't need to go online to notice that there was a big public protest going on in the middle of Tehran [as the . . .] raging horns of cars stuck in traffic were a pretty good indicator."

In looking at the number of active Twitter users in the MENA region between January 1 and March 30, 2011, coun-

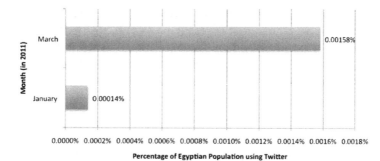

Figure 6.2   Egyptian population using Twitter (January and March 2011)

tries with the highest Twitter user-bases (over 100,000) are Israel, Kuwait, Saudi Arabia, Egypt, Qatar, the UAE, and Turkey (Salem and Mourtada 2011). Only Egypt is an "Arab Spring" country.[2] However, Egypt has a large population and its Twitter user-base, estimated at just over 131,000 by March 30, 2011, translates to a mere 0.00158 percent of the population (see figure 6.2), which puts it as having extremely low Twitter user penetration comparative to other MENA countries (Salem and Mourtada 2011: 16–17, 24). That said, the number of Twitter users in Egypt from January to the end of March, 2011, is estimated to have increased over tenfold from about 12,000 (Dunn 2011) users to 131,000 (Salem and Mourtada 2011). This is indeed significant in and of itself, as it provides empirical data that suggests a rapid growth in Twitter usage during the 25 January Revolution.

Interestingly, tweet volume in MENA states roughly doubled during a day of protests or particular civil unrest. For instance, Tunisia's tweet volume on January 14, the day of protests there, doubled from roughly 4,000 to 8,000 (Salem and Mourtada 2011: 21) and, interestingly, tweet volume in Egypt more than doubled on January 14 as Egyptians tweeted about the events in Tunisia (Salem and Mourtada 2011: 20). As discussed previously, some have dismissed these data given the extremely low penetration of Twitter in many MENA states. Others have argued that coverage of Twitter has been micro-focused around individual Twitter users, making it difficult to discern Twitter's impact. For example, Esfandiari (2010) discusses the case of @oxfordgirl – an Iranian-born writer, former journalist in Tehran, and Twitter user from Oxford, England – who was profiled by the mainstream British press as a "prominent and much-followed source during the [Iranian] protests" and as "Ahmadinejad's nemesis" (Weaver 2010a, 2010b). And @oxfordgirl states that she coordinated individual movements on the street and warned people to stay away from particular streets where the Iranian militia was waiting (Weaver 2010b). In the case of Iran, @oxfordgirl believes that "Twitter has saved lots of lives by warning people not to go down certain roads" (Weaver 2010b). Esfandiari (2010) sees @oxfordgirl as emblematic of the "myopic" focus of Twitter and its role in Iran. Specifically, she argues that the focus on individual "prominent" Western-based Twitter users brings increased exposure to individual Twitter users, but did little for activists on the ground in Tehran. Esfandiari (2010) also disputes the legitimacy of @oxfordgirl's claim of being a quasi air traffic controller of street-level movements.

An example of a prominent Twitter user during the Egyptian movements is Wael Ghonim, the Head of Marketing for Google Middle East and North Africa. Ghonim started a Facebook page in June 2010, titled "We are all Khaled Said" (Kirkpatrick and Preston 2011). The page was initially launched to raise awareness of a young Egyptian business-man who was tortured to death by Alexandria police. Ghonim ultimately used this Facebook page and his highly followed Twitter profile (@ghonim) to help recruit online followers to the 25 January protests. *Time Magazine* listed him in its 2011 TIME100 list of most influential people of the year for his contribution to the 25 January Revolution (*Time Magazine* 2011). Ghonim himself was jailed and tortured for 11 days in early 2011 for his role in the "We are all Khaled Said" Facebook page. Ghonim was prolific on Twitter, and he has become known for labeling the 25 January Revolution as "Revolution 2.0" and comparing it to Wikipedia, in that 25 January, like Wikipedia, was a grassroots user-contributed revolution without individual contributors receiving credit (CBS 2011). Papacharissi and Oliveira (2011) label him as one of the digitally prominent "opinion leaders" of 25 January.

Take these two cases together (and many more cases abound of prominent "game-changing" tweeters during the Arab Spring and precursing movements) and what emerges – what Esfandiari (2010) terms "the real role that Twitter played" – is that Twitter helped focus the international spotlight on these events and disseminate timely, personal, and relevant breaking news to international news media and the global public. As a medium, what is impressive is the dissemination power of Twitter to circulate this information from Tahrir and other activist hotspots to networks and subnetworks of Twitter users around the world. Tweets from activists in Tahrir ended up being covered by international news media and were picked up quickly. This dissemination was not only important in terms of circulation of information, but also critical to building "unprecedented moral solidarity" (Esfandiari 2010). It was also an important tool for maintaining links between activist movements in various MENA countries and even farther afield. That said, empirical research reveals that perhaps Twitter was of more value to the revolution outside of Egypt than within. As previously discussed, Twitter had even caught the attention of high-ranking State Department officials. However, only 1 percent of (relatively well-off) Egyptians reported using Twitter for 25 January-related information, with the bulk using television and word-of-mouth (see figure 6.3).

The data illustrated in figure 6.3 is unsurprising in that, as Hounshell (2011a: 22) observes, "many Egyptian Twitterati

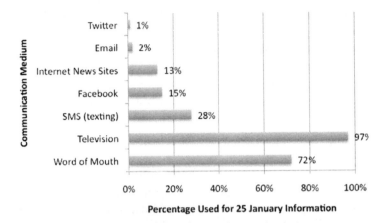

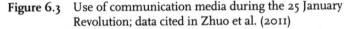

Figure 6.3   Use of communication media during the 25 January Revolution; data cited in Zhuo et al. (2011)

are upper-crust graduates of the American University in Cairo," and Gitlin (2011) observes that they are "tech-savvy, cosmopolitan, often from elite origins, well educated and tend to speak excellent English." In other words, the Twitterati was not representative of the general Egyptian population. But that is not inherently relevant to the medium's impact within social movements. Zhuo et al. (2011) argue that social media sites brought together young, urban Egyptian men (and I would add "elite") into a "networked individualism" (Rainie and Wellman 2012), where disparate individuals became formed into loosely structured networks. This argument provides a more nuanced conclusion to Twitter's role in social movements without falling victim to a strict binary distinction of whether Twitter caused/didn't cause the revolution.

Conclusion

[W]e believe we're going to put our experience on a CD-Rom and give an iPad to these would be democrats in Tunisia and Egypt, and they're going to replicate what's taken us eight centuries to produce. I think that's probably not going to happen and it speaks to the kind of ahistorical viewpoint that we bring to the world. (Scheuer in Moore 2011).

This chapter has sought to understand Twitter's role in activist movements by exploring the specific case of the 2011 "Arab Spring" uprisings. Diverse positions (favorable and unfavorable to Twitter) were presented in order to critically evaluate the effect of social media on a set of highly prominent activist movements. The factors that contributed to these movements in various Middle East and North African (MENA) countries were also diverse. The economic situation played a central role in demonstrations in Egypt and Tunisia, religious tensions were important to unrest in Syria and Bahrain, and tribal differences played a part in movements in Libya and Yemen (Hadar 2011b). The use of Twitter reveals the fact that information about the revolutions from ordinary people had a potentially global reach. However, though the message may have gotten across, was the medium (Twitter), paraphrasing McLuhan, the "message," which ultimately "massaged" us into a feeling of cybertopia? There are scores of voices in the camps of the cybertopians and cyberdystopians who, in the case of the former, argue for Twitter to be given a Nobel Peace Prize (Pfeifle 2009) and, in the case of the latter, argue that Twitter is emblematic of ineffectual "pseudo-laptop/iPad revolutionaries" (Hadar 2011a), where Twitter's role in the movements is a canard. An important point to understand from this tension is to pay heed to McLuhan's distinction between medium and message, and to understand that the medium itself can easily become the message. In other words, did Twitter itself become the message heard or did the medium actually play a crucial role in helping form, articulate, and ultimately disseminate the message? Specifically, what was the causal relationship – if any – between the multitude of tweets sent and activist movements? Or, as Morozov (2011: 16) puts it, "If a tree falls in the forest and everyone tweets about it, it may not be the tweets that moved it." Mehdi Yahyanejad, who runs one of the most popular Farsi-language websites, Balatarin, believes that Twitter's impact inside Iran was non-existent, and adds that the Iranian "Twitter Revolution" consisted of "Americans tweeting among themselves" (cited in Esfandiari 2010). Hounshell (2011b: 20) concludes that Twitter's role in the Arab Spring has been as a "real-time information stream for international-news junkies." Hounshell's conclusion, despite holding water, ends up being excessively reductive. Specifically, during the Arab Spring, Twitter was a more multifunctional medium across not only the MENA region, but globally. Twitter served three purposes for Egyptian activists: (1) a real-time information stream maintained by Egyptian citizen journalists (for Egyptian consumption); (2) a means for local information and updates to reach an international audience (including international journalists); and (3) a means to organize disparate activist groups on the ground. Perhaps its greatest impact was in the second purpose and its least in the third purpose.

Another important conclusion we can draw is that though we think Twitter's mode of internationalizing otherwise "national" revolutions is unique, revolutions, along with other types of rises and falls of state power, have historically been "germane international events" whose domestic and international causal forces cannot be neatly untangled into a "hermetic" separation (Philpott 2001). However, what is different is that citizen journalists in Egypt, Tunisia, Libya, and other countries were part of that international revolutionary process in an almost real-time interactive experience.

In fact, much of Twitter's prominence in relation to the "Arab Spring" arose from individuals in the West tweeting and retweeting. Lotan et al. (2011) studied tweets during the 25 January Revolution and found that @exiledsurfer, a Vienna-based "activist," was an integral part of information flow to journalists during the 25 January Revolution. Cases like this raise the important question of what actually constitutes activism in social media (as @exiledsurfer is based in Austria and not Egypt). Gladwell's (2010) answer is that becoming an "activist" on Twitter is a low-risk proposition in most cases;[3] @exiledsurfer, for example, was not putting himself at personal risk.[4] Terms to describe the perceived low-stakes effort of online activism have emerged, labeling these activists as "latte activists," "armchair warriors," and "slacktivists" (Siegle 2005; Vitak et al. 2011). Needless to say, it is "low effort" to sip one's half-carb, skinny soy latte in a Starbucks and retweet an #egypt tweet to your followers. However, it is, in many ways, a wholly different qualitative proposition to be tweeting from inside MENA countries, where government officials were recruited to carefully monitor Twitter to track down and detain these activists. The argument that emerges is not new, but remains just as important. The social, political, and economic context of any mediated social communication needs to be carefully interpreted to pass normative judgments on that social communication itself.

In other words, judging an #egypt tweet requires a lot of context. Though retweeting an #egypt tweet can be reductively judged as "slacktivism," would the same verdict be applied if those retweets from Western Twitter users not only led to greater global awareness about #egypt, but also led to increased fundraising for humanitarian relief? Therefore, even if the tweets from Egypt did not "help" the movements in Egypt themselves, they did raise global awareness, which directly led to increased diplomatic pressure and humanitarian aid. This may not have been revolutionary per se, but it had some discernible impact. Gladwell's answer, as discussed in this chapter, concerns the privileging of strong-tie networks. However, weak ties have a lot to offer modern transnational mobilizations. Bennett and Toft's (2009: 252) work on transnational activism and social networks highlights that weak ties can "empower individuals to mobilize their own diverse political networks." Twitter may have also democratized participation in the movement. Ultimately, even if tweets did not bring feet to the Egyptian streets, they helped facilitate a diverse global network of individuals who participated in a wide-ranging set of mobilization efforts (from the retweeters in Starbucks to those sending letters to their Congresspeople/ Ministers, or participating in activist movements both online and offline).

CHAPTER SEVEN

Twitter and Health

got told at clinic today my cancer has come back.
Need urgent surgery and then chemo before
Christmas x.

@SupernurseJane

As the tweet above illustrates, individuals are tweeting about their health. In this particular case, the user tweeting has been told her cancer has relapsed and she needs surgery and chemo. The posting of such intimate health information has become a familiar sight on Twitter. This chapter explores some of the ways Twitter is being used by patients, medical researchers, and doctors. The medium is critically examined to highlight both the pros and cons of Twitter's health-related uses. It also illustrates ways in which our bodies have become a subject of Twitter's update culture. The medium's update cultures have been discussed in previous chapters as being highly pervasive in our lives. However, tweeting about one's body marks an even greater shift in this direction. The following chapter investigates some of the ways in which Twitter and its role of updating may become particularly routinized in the lives of some users.

In chapter 5, the profundity of disasters was used to highlight some of the complexities of update cultures and how everything from the banal to the profound is tweeted. Another spectrum that tweets cover is that of the public and the private. Previous chapters have discussed the historical trend towards more disclosure of "private" information in the public sphere (especially chapter 3). Twitter's ease, location independence, and its ubiquitous role in the routines of many users have led to very intimate tweets. An important example of this is Twitter's use in health. An individual's body has traditionally been a very private domain. Tweeting about the state of our bodies in detail sheds light on several important areas of the medium. Not only does it reveal many interesting aspects of Twitter's pervasiveness in traditionally private spheres, but the posting of tweets about health also potentially affects the relationships between doctors and patients as well as giving authority and expertise to non-medical professionals (especially fellow patients and their families).

Traditionally, patients have received health-related information by meeting personally with health professionals, and would normally only share details of their condition in this environment or with someone close to them. As the popularity of online social networking and social media sites has increased, individual patients, their families, and their caregivers have bypassed the traditional controls of the healthcare and life-science industries by volunteering private information about themselves on publicly accessible Internet sites. Additionally, they have become more trusting of health messages on these sites. According to data from the American Health Information National Trend Survey, 23 percent of respondents reported using a social networking site (Chou et al. 2009: 3). One reason for this is that these individuals form support networks with strangers who have the same chronic illness.

This is not a phenomenon restricted to Twitter, but rather, as Orsini (2010: 3) observes, that people are able to use new media to create support communities on virtual social networks such as patientslikeme.com. Rajani et al. (2011) see this trend as potential evidence that online social networks, including Twitter, may be "good for your health." They make the argument that because of online health networks, illness has "virtually been removed as [a factor] contributing to social isolation and it is now not uncommon for individuals to have networks that number in the hundreds" (Rajani et al. 2011: 819). They add that these virtual networks can function as support groups that motivate others to follow weight loss and other treatment regimes. Put in the context of Twitter, some have observed that tweets can help encourage, for example, diabetics to follow exercise regimes (Hawn 2009). The rise of these health-related communities on Twitter is a particularly unique case in that tweets about one's health may be very regular and involve both a stable and shifting audience. Not only are these fellow Twitter users a trusted audience (despite the public nature of Twitter), but the Twitterverse is imbued as a space which has some level of authority and expertise in health-related matters. This is not to say that Twitter is replacing doctors. However, health professionals have also started tweeting, as some of them have seen the importance of Twitter to patients.

This chapter also introduces how Twitter is used by individuals who have/had a significant health event (as well as by their families). Twitter is used by them to find out about new treatment options, referrals to specialists, and as a support network (to monitor and support each other in terms of medications, treatments, and clinical trials). These networks also serve a role in political activism and patient advocacy. This chapter presents two brief case studies – Lou Gehrig's disease and cancer – to illustrate how Twitter has become involved in our health. Besides tweets updating others about one's health, the posting of treatment or health status as a tweet can also generate immediate responses from known individuals and strangers. The immediacy of tweet responses can also foster a feeling of "telepresence," the notion that one's communicators are an unmediated "present" rather than relating through mediated communication (see chapter 3 for a fuller discussion). In other words, we can feel a "physical" community within Twitter, which has an *audience* who shares our highs and lows and can potentially "be there" for us when we receive a shocking diagnosis. One can even make the argument that society has become more and more atomistic and individu-alistic, with certain community structures becoming weak or inaccessible (Putnam 2000), and, in this context, Twitter becomes an important venue for people to share with others their concerns, joys, and downright fears about their health. For example, instead of going to a local community center to participate in a weekly cancer support group, these individuals may opt to turn to their keyboards and smartphones, gaining strength and support one tweet at a time.

Twitter-mediated Healthcare

Public and private boundaries regarding health have shifted. For some, telling the world about one's health has become part of the larger trend of an "update culture" (see chapters 1–3). For them, updating others about their health via Twitter is on a continuum that includes anything from updating others about what they had for breakfast to the break-up of a relationship. Though the boundaries of public and private have been shifting historically regarding health (e.g., call-in radio shows with doctors), Twitter represents an acceleration of this trend. Not only does Twitter provide a medium for indi-viduals to write about their health at the time (e.g., "I just got diagnosed with cancer" or "Coming down with the flu"), but it connects these messages to other health messages on Twitter through hashtags. Additionally, this act of sharing one's health situation (sometimes even from a doctor's office) fur-ther highlights shifts toward a powerful update culture which includes the "status" of our bodies. For example, individuals tweeting about diagnoses may be updating the world about having cancer, but, usually, their intended target audience is their family and friends. However, as discussed previously, there is a dissonance between perceived and actual audiences on Twitter.

Nonetheless, Twitter has become more ubiquitous in health contexts.[1] Take the example of a hysterectomy and uterine prolapse surgery of a 70-year-old woman in Iowa which was tweeted real time through 300 tweets posted by a hospital official from a computer immediately outside of the operating room's sterile area (cited in Krowchuk 2010: 6). The woman gave consent for the surgery to be tweeted so that her family could track the operation from the waiting room (and one family member tracked the procedure from her workplace) (Crumb 2009). A 2011 episode of *Grey's Anatomy* fictionalizes such occurrences through a portrayal of doctors tweeting during a surgery. However, a more representative example of Twitter's use by healthcare institutions is the Boston Public Health Commission (@healthyBoston), which tweets every couple of days regarding public health. During the H1N1 pandemic, they used Twitter to inform the local community of vaccine clinics and to correct common public misconceptions that there was a wait for the vaccines (Tucker 2011).

As the Iowa case highlights, a key difference with Twitter is that responses are often almost synchronous and can occur regularly throughout the day as individuals check their timelines at work, home, and on their smartphones. One does not even have to be waiting in the hospital to keep tabs on a family member's surgery. Indeed, the Twitter stream in this example contained detailed information that those in the waiting room were not synchronously receiving. Additionally, as Licoppe (2004) has shown, repeated mediated interactions foster "telepresence," the perception of mediated communication as face-to-face communication. For example, a video call using Skype is perceived by the conversation participants as being face-to-face rather than being mediated by Skype (see chapter 3 for a fuller discussion of this). In the Iowa case, family members could – via Twitter – feel as if they were "there" in the hospital. As McNab (2009: 566) puts it: "Instant and borderless, it [Twitter] elevates electronic communication to near face-to-face." Grandparents can follow births and far-flung relatives can relieve their anxieties during a loved one's operation via tweets. Twitter also potentially provides a unique historical opportunity for more accurate health information to be disseminated to broader audiences. McNab (2009: 566) observes that, "one fact sheet or an emergency message about an outbreak can be spread through Twitter faster than any influenza virus." Lastly, Twitter changes the relationship between health institutions (including individual doctors) and the public in that previously monologic health dicta and warnings can now be interrogated, individually situated, or affirmed through an interaction with the institution or person tweeting that information.

Similarly, Twitter presents new opportunities for patient support networks. Hawn (2009: 364) describes the case of Rachel Baumgartel, 33, a diabetic who lives in Boulder, Colorado, and sends tweets almost daily on "what she had for breakfast, what her hemoglobin A1c level is, or how much exercise she got on the elliptical equipment at the gym." As Hawn notes, Baumgartel often receives reply tweets from followers, which encourage her to stick to her "arduous health regimen." Hawn finds that those who are chronically ill are successfully using social media, including Twitter, in this way. Baumgartel herself observes:

> Because I have people who follow me on Twitter ... it means I have some kind of audience that is caring for me in the background. It's helpful if I'm having a rough day, if things are not going so well with my blood sugar. I find support there, and it keeps me in line, too. (cited in Hawn 2009: 365)

The example of Baumgartel reveals the complex interplay in which tweets can reveal private health information (like hemoglobin A1c levels), while the regular disclosure of this information via tweets to an amorphous audience led to the formation of a more coherent audience – a support community – which had real impacts on Baumgartel's life.

Vance et al. (2009: 135) argue that Twitter lends itself to a "medical support group format" and offers the example of a

Twitter user who uses her timeline as a network for mothers of children who have attention deficit disorder. The importance of such uses is that they repurpose Twitter in innovative ways to create new health communities. In this case, the focus is not on individual tweets, but a single Twitter profile is used much like a Facebook group, and tweets that need to be pushed out can be. Heaivilin et al.'s (2011: 1047) work on tweets referring to dental pain found that users' tweets describe levels of pain, treatments taken, and the effect of this pain on their lives. They believe that Twitter may be a useful medium for dental professionals to disseminate relevant health information, including recommendations to visit the dentist if they experience certain symptoms. As a support group, Heaivilin et al. (2011: 1050) argue that individuals "may find comfort in the fact others are simultaneously facing the challenge" of the same medical condition. This illustrates one way in which individuals are using Twitter to ask fellow users for medical advice (e.g., dental pain management). The last example highlights some of the ways in which not only doctor/patient relationships may be changing due to the medium, but also that the authority and legitimacy of fellow Twitter users as sources of medical advice is reasonably high. The importance of this should not be underestimated.

Within the healthcare community, Twitter is being used by medical researchers and doctors to interact with each other to enhance drug discovery. Interestingly, it is also being used by medical researchers to directly interact with patients. One example is the Amyotrophic Lateral Sclerosis Untangled (ALSU) Twitter research project.[2] Begun in 2009, ALSU uses Twitter to connect with people with ALS (commonly known as Lou Gehrig's Disease) by asking people with ALS to tweet about alternative and off-label treatments with the hashtag "ALSUntangled" (Bedlack and Hardiman 2009). This information is then used by researchers at the ALSU project, which includes 66 members (The Alsuntangled Group 2010). The ALSU Project has over 600 followers and responds to

Has **ALSUntangled** heard of Dr. Wu's Stem Cell Treatment Center in Beijing?
Twitter - Aug 6, 2010

RT @ALSUntangled: Some individuals report decreased pain. No evidence of benefit beyond this. Why is Marinol withheld from #ALS patients?
Twitter - Jul 26, 2010

ALSUntangled: Some individuals report decreased pain. No evidence of benefit beyond this.
Twitter - Jul 25, 2010

New blog post: Stowe/Morales treatments investigated by @ALSUntangled
Stowe/ Morales treatments are investigated by ALSUntangled ≤ MND ... -
wordpress.com
Twitter - Jul 22, 2010

@alsuntangled What can you tell me about the benefits of acupuncture for ALS patients?
Twitter - Jul 21, 2010

Stowe/Morales unproven MND treatment has been investigated by @ALSUntangled: ... - definately worth a blog post! KJ
Informa Healthcare - Amyotrophic Lateral Sclerosis - 11(4):414 ... -
informahealthcare.com
Twitter - Jul 21, 2010

Figure 7.1   @ALSUntangled Twitter Stream (usernames redacted)

individual questions from Twitter users publicly. For example, one Twitter user asked whether pulsed electromagnetic field therapy has been found effective in ALS. The ALSU team tweeted back that they would be investigating this specific question. This type of interaction potentially represents a turn in scientific research, where patients can have direct feedback into the formulation of research questions and interact directly with prominent researchers. Individuals with ALS and their caregivers are able to interact directly with ALSU via Twitter (see figure 7.1). Additionally, their tweets can be seen by members of the public, thereby creating a publicly accessible record of these discussions. When designing the ALSU project, Bedlack and Hardiman (2009) chose Twitter as they believe that the medium is "simple" to join and to use. However, the ALS network on Twitter is far from simple. Specifically, in addition to discussing AOTs, individuals with ALS and their caregivers become part of a broader ALS support and knowledge network. The ease of communication likely fosters more regular interactions. And the time and effort it takes to tweet @ALSUntangled is minimal for Twitter users with ALS. This potentially breaks down traditional barriers and signals fundamental shifts in doctor/researcher/patient boundaries. Additionally, users of Twitter such as ALSU legitimize the medium's role in health. Lastly, it illustrates how tweets, considered by some as banal updates, can be of direct use in profound medical research.

ALSUntangled is an interesting case as it is attached to a prominent ALS-research center. This trust and reputation of ALSUntangled has facilitated high levels of sharing about a patient's or a family member's ALS situation and treatment experiences via tweets. Similarly, the individual doctors who are regularly tweeting command a high level of trust both within the ALS patient community and the medical community itself (e.g., one ALSUntangled tweet asks a doctor who has been tweeting within the ALSUntangled hashtag to send his CV to the ALSU research team). Not only does this trust lead to cases of people asking them about potential tests, treatment options, and referrals, but also reveals the presence of a far-reaching network of followers (who receive this doctor's tweets). As Twitter offers dialogic interaction, any of these followers at any time can choose to respond to one of these doctors' tweets or ask an unrelated question regarding their personal ALS or other medical situation. In the case of ALS, Twitter may be breaking down boundaries between doctors, researchers, and patients, which could ultimately have real impact on the psychological and physical well-being of ALS patients. However, this example also highlights that the divulging of private health information most likely needs a trusted mediator (in this case, Johns Hopkins University's ALS center).

The shift of health information from monologic to dialogic

Traditionally, health organizations, non-profit organizations, and other health-related institutions have followed a monologic dissemination model, where the consumers of this information do not interact with its creator. For example, a health organization issues a swine flu warning, but receivers of this warning do not have the opportunity to ask questions or interact with the health organization. McNab (2009: 566) argues that social media has shifted this relationship in the context of health information in that it "has changed the monologue to a dialogue, where anyone with Internet access can be a content creator and communicator." This is part of a larger trend in media more generally which has seen a shift from unidirectional mass media to interactivity. Chapter 4, for example, highlighted shifts toward interactive journalistic practices. Media has become more interactive, with readers able to comment on content and have discussions with other readers or even the author (Chung 2008). Electronic books have also marked significant shifts in interactivity (Larson 2010). In other words, media is becoming generally more dialogical. In the case of health, medical information itself becomes a product of a dialogic community mediated by information technology. Joshua Schwimmer, a nephrologist at Lenox Hill Hospital, believes that part of Twitter's popularity amongst doctors is that it creates "instant online communities of people with similar interests" (cited in Victorian 2010: 16). The instantaneity helps build the community. Individuals tweeting perceive an active audience rather than tweeting into a black hole. This expanded audience also potentially translates to an extended reach of tweets and relevant health information being usefully propagated.

In the case of ALSUntangled, Twitter was found to extend the reach of ALS clinical trials. Similarly, TrialX is a company that has turned to Twitter to try to match patients with targeted clinical trials. As the TrialX blog[3] notes, their application searches Twitter for any tweet with "@trialx CT." Patients interested in finding a suitable clinical trial send tweets such as "@trialx CT find studies for my father 62 with pancreatic cancer in Raleigh area." The TrialX application searches its database for a suitable clinical trial and then tweets back a link to a website with matching trials. A co-founder of TrialX believes that the system will increase participation in clinical trials as it will increase people's awareness of trials and provide "a simple way" to gain information about participating in trials (Terry 2009: 509).

Examples such as ALSUntangled and TrialX highlight how the interactivity of the medium has provided new ways for the healthcare community to interact with patients. Rather than clinical trials posters on hospital walls or even posts on Internet forums, Twitter-mediated platforms such as ALSUntangled allow a highly interactive experience with researchers. This represents a potential shift in the norms of medical research itself. However, regardless of the promise of these Twitter-mediated research spaces, it is most likely that many patients will feel uncomfortable publicly tweeting their age, health information, and location. The boundaries between public and private have shifted significantly, but just how much are patients willing to reveal? Indeed, this cuts to a larger issue of Twitter and health: privacy.

Potential downsides: from privacy issues to medical misinformation

As Vance et al. (2009: 133) note, social media is underused by public health professionals. Only 16 percent of U.S. hospitals surveyed use Twitter officially (Thaker et al. 2011: 707). Privacy is a major issue which keeps hospital uptake low and Orsini (2010: 3) rightly highlights that the leaking of patients' personal information onto Twitter would create a Health Insurance Portability and Accountability Act (HIPAA) violation in the case of American patients. Patients may inadvertently offer "too much information" in their tweets. Or they may tweet to a doctor and expect a response (which the doctor most likely cannot provide due to privacy legislation in most countries). Hawn (2009: 363) echoes this and warns that "the possibility of spreading . . . problematic information" is more likely with the increased adoption of new media. Chou et al. (2009: 3) add that though "the participatory nature of social media entails an open forum for information exchange," this also leads to a greater possibility of disseminating "noncredible, and potentially erroneous, health information." This is part of a larger issue of information integrity on Twitter (Murthy 2011b). Rajani et al. (2011) state that if virtual support groups replace support that would have been provided by healthcare professionals, they may receive medical misinformation as opposed to validated information from the healthcare community. This is an important point. Indeed, some believe that medical professionals need to be present online to ensure the integrity of health information that the public receives given that patients increasingly consume health information online, as a lack of participation by physicians may ultimately lead to their declining influence in individuals' medical decision-making (Kubetin 2011).

Twitter can also be used to correct prevalent medical misinformation. For example, H. Michael Dreher, a professor and registered nurse of 25 years, tweets under @RNmakingsense to provide "quick, concise health information" to his followers and, given his experience, feels comfortable "being a filter for health information" through Twitter (Dreher 2009: 220). In another example, the American Cancer Society (ACS) credits Twitter with rectifying "a long-standing communication problem" in which blogs and other Internet sites were stating that the ACS was recommending routine screening for prostate cancer (Butcher 2009: 36–8). After tweeting that the ACS recommends men consult with their doctor on the necessity of screening, they have found that blogs and the mainstream media have picked this up.

However, others argue that health professionals using social media run the risk of sharing personal information if they respond to the questions of patients on a site like Twitter (Twaddell, cited in Krowchuk 2010: 7). Additionally, Otto (2011) observes that doctors believe that "offhand remarks" on social media "could show up later in legal proceedings." In highly litigious countries such as the U.S., this is particularly relevant. Privacy is also an issue in terms of clinical interactions. For example, Michael Lara, a board-certified psychiatrist and neurologist, had a patient track him down on Twitter and ask him questions specific to his treatment options (Terry 2009: 508). Lara had his staff contact the patient by telephone to resolve the issue and to also make clear that Twitter was not an appropriate medium to contact Lara (Terry 2009: 508). Certainly, the prospect of patients publicly tweeting at any time about sensitive medical questions and remaining in an expectant state is not "just what the doctor ordered." The relationship between doctors and patients can be very personal. However, its intimacy does have various formal constraints and Lara's case highlights this.

Other potential downsides have to do with medical professionals and institutions "following" people on Twitter. Specifically, some in the healthcare industry are worried that the act of following may be conflated with an endorsement of that particular Twitter user. Terry (2009: 508) gives the example of the Anne Arundel Medical Center, an American hospital which maintains a Twitter profile, but has decided to have a disclaimer on their page which makes this clear. That being said, the act of following may be perceived by other Twitter users as an endorsement regardless of any disclaimer. The act of following users on Twitter usually indicates (though not always) some level of – even miniscule – interest in that user. Equating this to the validation of that user is a slippery slope, but a slope that continues to be well greased.

Another issue is differential access to Twitter given persisting digital divides (Lenhart et al. 2010; Madden 2010; Witte and Mannon 2010). As discussed in previous chapters,[4] Twitter is socially stratified along class, racial, gender, age, and other lines. Patients from lower socioeconomic backgrounds may be unable to use social media due to the cost of a computer or Internet-enabled phone (Krowchuk 2010: 7), the lack of English-language literacy (Warschauer et al. 2004), or poorer writing skills (Warschauer 2003: 117). Liang and Mackey (2011: 824) observe that pharmaceutical companies use Twitter accounts for direct-to-consumer advertising where tweets advertising specific treatment options are sent to users. Some marginalized groups may lack the social capital[5] to responsibly consume this hyper-targeted advertising. Chou et al. (2009: 3) also note the presence of a "double divide" where those without Internet access are doubly impacted in that they are unable to obtain health information freely available on the Internet. That said, McNab (2009: 566) reports that approximately one in four people globally use the Internet and that the World Summit of the Information Society has made a commitment "to connect villages . . . health centres and hospitals with ICTs" by 2015 (cited in McNab 2009: 566). Additionally, developing countries have increased mobile phone usage (which includes the introduction of ultra-low-cost cellular (ULC) phones (Blau 2006)). Though many of the phones being purchased in developing countries have only basic Internet services, Kahn et al. (2010) argue there are opportunities for mobile health (m-health), which involve basic mobile phones. Twitter may be an ideal medium for pushing vital health information to these individuals with basic mobile phones via text messages.

Cancer Networks and Twitter

The illnesses which tend to have the most active Twitter networks are either chronic or life-changing. Cancer patients, their friends/family, and a diverse set of oncology-related professionals are prominent examples of active health networks on Twitter. Cancer survivors are very active on Twitter.[6] Some users insert the phrase "cancer survivor" into their Twitter biographies, affirming this part of their Twitter persona. The case of cancer networks on Twitter presents a glimpse not only of how doctors and health institutions are dialogically interacting with individuals, but also how these networks have an international reach and, most of the time, involve strangers, rather than strengthening existing offline relationships. Though some patients do follow their doctor's Twitter timeline (if they are Twitter users), most often doctors and health institutions are interacting with "far-flung" colleagues or members of the public (Victorian 2010). In the case of cancer, Butcher believes that Twitter is "transforming the cancer care community" by engaging individuals in one-to-one conversations, connecting with oncology professionals who would not necessarily cross paths, as well as assisting oncology researchers in finding clinical trial participants (Butcher 2009). She gives the example of the Vanderbilt-Ingram Cancer Center and their planned use of Twitter to locate clusters of people who are interested in lung cancer as well as lung cancer survivors and use these networks to inform these targeted individuals about the clinical trials they are scheduled to conduct (Butcher 2009). The clinical trial literature frequently discusses under-representation of certain groups (Rochon et al. 2004), and Twitter may be an ideal medium to make these trials more inclusive given the high rate of use of Twitter by, for example, African Americans (Hargittai and Litt 2011).

As discussed earlier in this chapter, these recruitment efforts are premised on the far reach of cancer networks on Twitter. For example, the Know Cancer group (@know_cancer) has over 21,000 followers. Indeed, some individual oncologists have large followings as well. For example, Butcher (2010b) gives the example of Naoto T. Ueno (@TeamOncology), a doctor at the M.D. Anderson Cancer Center in the U.S. and a cancer survivor, who tweets in English and Japanese and has about 5,500 followers. In the past, he has tweeted about emergent oncology research such as proceedings from the Asian

Clinical Oncology Society conference in Japan. This aspect of the public being able to follow medical conferences through Twitter is something McNab (2009) highlights. Ueno also uses Twitter to correct misinformation regarding cancer. For example, one of his tweets which criticized a breast cancer screening program in Japan led to the program undergoing a "rethink" (Butcher 2010b: 38). Ueno is an interesting case in that he tweets in the evening in Japanese and during the day in English, so that Twitter users in Japan are online when he is tweeting in Japanese. His Twitter timeline straddles two distinct sociolinguistic spaces within Twitter itself. Second, he makes a point of tweeting about aspects of his daily life, especially food and music, alongside tweets about cancer. At the time of writing, his timeline included tweets about Japanese pop music he listens to and a link to an article in *Oncology Times*, which discusses his work on inflammatory breast cancer. He believes that by tweeting about non-cancer topics, he draws an audience "that has nothing to do with cancer," but when he tweets about cancer (which he does about 40 percent of the time), these followers still pay attention to his cancer-related tweets (Butcher 2010b: 38). From his perspective, Twitter "is fantastic in the way that you can disseminate information to people who don't care about cancer." This aspect of drawing in individuals who may be interested in one part of your life into another part of your life is a unique aspect of the medium, and one in which social networks are intentionally or unintentionally bridged. Of course, this characteristic of Twitter is not limited to health. As discussed in chapter 5, some celebrities regularly tweet about humanitarian crises in addition to other topics (e.g., Hollywood gossip). Though not a bait and switch, this ability of Twitter to expose followers to "unexpected" topical information is important. Indeed, it shapes the ways in which Twitter is able to disseminate information to non-homophilous groups (see chapter 3 for a discussion of homophily).

Another active oncologist using Twitter is Dr. Anas Younes,

also of the M.D. Anderson Cancer Center. Butcher (2010a) interviewed Younes and describes how he has configured his computer to search for every mention of "lymphoma" posted on Twitter. He uses these incoming tweets as a basis to reach a large number of people, whether he knows them personally or not. For instance, a stranger directed the following tweet to him:

> @DrAnasYounes Hi i need your advice pls, both parents had non hodgkins lymphoma, my dad died, do my genes increase my chance of getting it?

Dr. Younes quickly responded that there is currently no genetic test to predict familial lymphoma. This sort of inter-action between a member of the public (of an unknown location) and a prominent oncologist is a product of Twitter's ability to connect health practitioners with new audiences. It also highlights how Twitter is changing some doctor/patient relationships by not only breaking down traditional barriers between doctors and patients, but also connecting patients with doctors who are experts in the field (regardless of where they live). These interactions can also potentially eclipse racial (Manfredi et al. 2010), gender (Celik et al. 2009), and other barriers between doctors and patients. Older patients are also keen to use electronic communication with their doctors (Singh et al. 2009). Teens report that they find it difficult to discuss drug use and sexual health topics and feel less anxi-ety using computer-mediated communication (Lenhart et al. 2010: 4). Twitter may be shaping medical practice by pro-viding an avenue for these groups to interact with interested medical professionals.

Twitter also enables doctors to keep a finger on the pulse of what patients are interested in or worried about. As for the case of journalism discussed in chapter 4, doctors can use Twitter as an awareness system in which health is in the ambient environment of the medium. Steven Tucker, an American oncologist based in Singapore, notes that Twitter is an excellent platform for you to listen to patients as well as

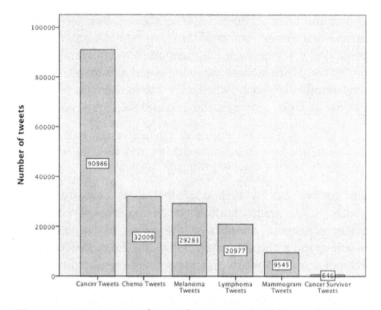

Figure 7.2 Frequency of tweets by cancer-related keywords

interested members of the public (Butcher 2010a: 8). Ueno, a cancer survivor himself, stresses the importance of Twitter to patient empowerment. Indeed, he feels this is the "most important thing" regarding his use of Twitter (Butcher 2010b: 38). Specifically, individuals diagnosed with cancer, carers, and family members can use Twitter to gather information on particular cancer treatment options and clinical trials, but can also put questions about their specific cases to leading oncologists in the field. Patients, carers, and family perceive this level of agency as a critically important utility of Twitter. Chou et al. (2009: 3) argue that online social networks "may increase perceived social support." Importantly, they add that social media has facilitated an increase in patient-generated content, which is "seen as more democratic and patient controlled, enabling users to exchange health-related information that they need and therefore making information more patient/consumer-centered" (Chou et al. 2009: 3). As Turner (2010) argues, this is part of a perceived "turn" in which new media breaks down traditional power relations between content creators and public consumers. In other words, patients become both authors and content consumers, giving them more of a locus of control.

I explored some of these questions empirically through a six-month study of cancer-related tweets.[7] The study will be briefly introduced as it gives another example of how Twitter is used in update cultures focused on health. A total of 90,986 cancer-related tweets was collected during the six-month period of 2010–11 (with the breakdown listed in figure 7.2). Most individuals tweeting were from the U.S. and, out of the top 15 cities being tweeted from, only three were non-U.S. (London, Toronto, and Sydney). The majority of tweets referred to chemotherapy or melanoma (see figure 7.2). Throughout this book, it has been argued that Twitter is part of a larger societal trend toward "update cultures." In the case of cancer, the succinctness of the medium, combined with users' desire to update their friends, family, and the larger Twitterverse of their everyday and exceptional health circumstances, contributes to an update culture. For example, some tweets collected in this study aim to inform their audience of the commencement of chemotherapy treatment and to update about ongoing treatment. Individuals were found tweeting that they have a chemotherapy appointment today, that they are anxiously waiting at their appointment, or they have just had treatment and feel physically and emotionally exhausted.

A significant pattern which emerges is that individuals see Twitter as a means to share aspects about their (or a loved one's) chemotherapy regime, which includes tweets proclaiming final chemotherapy sessions as well as some in which chemotherapy is attributed to their cancer's remission. In other words, users often tweet about chemotherapy multiple times and in diverse contexts. For some, updating about their chemotherapy is similar to diary writing. Others who, for example, are having difficulty with side effects may be actively soliciting responses of support from fellow Twitter users.[8]

In the case of melanoma, an interesting trend emerges which often includes users tweeting about their own experiences of melanoma, the loss of a family member, and organizations fundraising or providing melanoma-related information. For instance, at the time of writing, tweets ranged from a user who discussed losing her father to melanoma a decade earlier, to another user tweeting about how she had melanoma two years ago and has to be vigilant about moles. Another user tweeted about wanting to get a tan, but refusing to use a tanning bed for fear of melanoma. Clearly, there is a diversity of melanoma-related tweets across the spectrum, from current patients to skeptical tanners. In the case of chemotherapy-related tweets, individuals either had or were having chemotherapy, or knew of people in that situation. The melanoma tweets varied more widely. However, what they share in common with chemotherapy tweets is that the succinctness of the tweet, combined with its efficient and wide-ranging distribution, encourages users to tweet as a form of diary writing and as a means to solicit support.

These insights into Twitter intuitively make sense. In the collected data, there regularly appear tweets from individuals who have just received their diagnosis and are about to start chemotherapy. In these cases, why would someone post such a personal tweet to a public audience that is potentially very large? Like many of the other situations presented in this book, Twitter, as a medium, is able to solicit timely personal information. An individual who has just received a diagnosis of a life-changing disease is most likely not going to sit down in the doctor's waiting room and write a blog post or fire off emails to everyone they know. However, tweeting only takes a minute and has become so routine for some people that their tweet about a cancer diagnosis may be tweeted almost quasi-unconsciously. In other words, it has become second nature – or perhaps routinized – for some individuals to tweet things that are both banal and profound in their lives. Additionally, the shock of the event may not have fully percolated so that person's habitual routine continues (tweeting and all). Other individuals may have a desire to tell the world of this life-changing situation. Update cultures inherently encourage us to share. Alongside the erosion of public/private boundaries surrounding one's health, and the need for many individuals to affirm their identities (and that they, as individual beings, are important), it is not surprising to see update cultures emerge in regards to health. Ultimately, for individuals to tweet that they have just received a cancer diagnosis and are fearful about chemotherapy only takes a minute, but the act "publishes" an intimate aspect of our lives. It concretizes our thoughts and includes our friends, family, and anyone who is interested into a potential dialogue with this part of our lives. This is part of Twitter's function as a micro-blog in that, like blogs, it is giving voice to its author. Additionally, this publishing of our innermost thoughts can be perceived by posters as self-affirming. In a world where communities are not tightly integrated and our voice may feel weak, tweets might be perceived by their authors as empowering. This is particularly felt if other Twitter users reply to these tweets.

Cancer Retweeted

Retweets play a powerful role in determining the impact of a tweet in terms of visibility within Twitter and beyond.[9] In the data collected for the study mentioned in the previous section, retweets behaved in a similar way. Tweets that were retweeted significantly snowballed into more retweets. This is interesting for several reasons. In the previous section, individual tweets soliciting support during chemotherapy were mentioned. However, these tweets usually have a small audience and are not retweeted (unless tweeted by celebrities or other users with large followings). The question this raises is just how far the voice of ordinary Twitter users can reach. In other

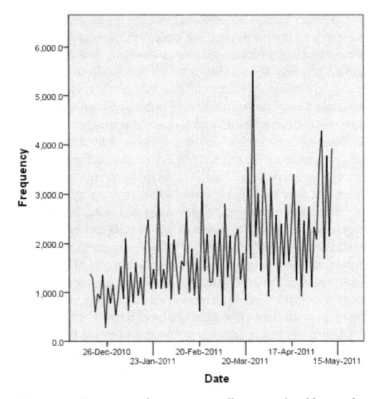

Figure 7.3   Frequency of tweets across all cancer-related keywords

words, what is the reach of tweets that inform of a cancer diagnosis or update on chemotherapy progress? It seems that these tweets succeed as not only part of a diary process, but also fulfill our need to update one's own "domain" on Twitter. Individuals who are tweeting about their health are not seeking to have their tweets become "viral." Rather, their audience is usually themselves and their followers (what can be thought of as a "domain" within the larger Twitterverse). These domains are not islands, strictly speaking, but the propagation of these health-related tweets are the exception rather than the rule.

However, some tweets do become viral. In the study mentioned in the previous section, five noticeable retweet events occurred (see figure 7.3) that were thought to be important by the larger Twitter community. In late October 2010, Aidan Reed, a five-year-old boy from Clearwater, Kansas, who was diagnosed with acute lymphoblastic leukemia (James 2010) was the subject of the spike. Aidan enjoys drawing monsters and his aunt, Mandi Ostein, came up with the idea for Aidan to sell his pictures online through etsy.com, an online marketplace for handmade and vintage goods, to help fund his medical treatment and the family's unforeseen expenses (James 2010). A tweet with a link to Aidan's etsy store was significantly retweeted. Ostein had expected to sell 60 prints by Thanksgiving of 2010, but ultimately sold 7,000 at $12 apiece (Cohen 2010). One of the most common iterations of the tweet was:

> Here's Aidan's blog (he's 5, has leukemia, is selling his monster drawings on Etsy to pay for his chemo). (<http://aidforaidan.wordpress.com/about/>)

On October 27, 2010, @abolishcancer, an established cancer charity group retweeted this tweet to their tens of thousands of followers, which resulted in the tweet traversing many subnetworks within Twitter and leading to a jump both in the "chemo" data set as well as the aggregate cancer data set. The case of Aidan Reed reveals how a particular cancer story became picked up by influential Twitter users and ultimately caught the eye of @abolishcancer, which resulted in large-scale retweeting. This retweet surge led to ABC, CNN, and other traditional news media picking up the story, which in turn snowballed into more retweeting. This example highlights how Twitter's dissemination model facilitates the construction of "events" on the medium that Twitter users have taken notice of (a parallel to the emergence of viral videos on YouTube).

In 2011, a surge of lymphoma-related tweets was spurred by a Leukemia & Lymphoma Society charity triathlon event.

In February 2011, tweets peaked when Hologic became the first company to obtain U.S. Food and Drug Administration (FDA) approval for 3D breast tomosynthesis, a type of three-dimensional mammogram which could potentially detect certain breast cancers at an earlier stage than traditional mammography techniques. Similarly, in March 2011, tweets spiked regarding Bristol-Myers Squibb's experimental melanoma drug, Yervoy, whose clinical trials reported significant results in the treatment of patients with metastatic melanoma (Hobson 2011). A follow-on rise occurred in June 2011 when Yervoy's second-phase clinical trials were announced, reporting prolongation of life of patients with metastatic melanoma.

Interestingly, this reveals that the most prominent cancer-related events on Twitter are either charity-oriented or caused by perceived important drug discoveries. These findings reveal some of the ways in which cancer discourse exists on Twitter and what is considered important. The case of Aidan Reed also highlights that Twitter has been important to individual cancer patients rather than exclusively to established cancer charities and drug companies (though the latter dominates major jumps and Aidan Reed is the exception rather than the rule). Examining these changes in tweet volume gives us insights not only into larger patterns of health and Twitter, but also what events are considered most important to users. Specifically, only the event of Aidan Reed is "grass-roots." The tweets regarding Reed started in a small domain and spread across Twitter as a whole, ultimately crossing over and catching the eye of mainstream media. Reed became a micro-celebrity on Twitter. Indeed, there are various other cases of patients who have gained mainstream media attention (albeit, often just 15 minutes of fame) due to an unusual, attention-grabbing circumstance popularized on Twitter. A similar process occurs when tweets from citizen journalists are picked up by the mainstream media.[10]

The other spikes are attributable to events that had already caught the eye of the media (i.e., major charity events and drug discoveries). In these cases, activity on Twitter mirrors coverage by traditional media sources. In Reed's case, Twitter had real impact on his cancer experience. The interesting tension of Twitter is that there is a sea of tweets with cancer patients seeking support. Reed's case moved from semi-private domains to the radar of @abolishcancer and then its reach exponentially increased. What this highlights is one of Twitter's unique abilities as a medium to make one a "star" within the community (i.e., a micro-celebrity). Are the legions of others whose tweets are not noticed left in the lurch? Not exactly. For if the posters get satisfaction and validation of their health situation by being noticed within their own domain, that is not only sufficient, but keeps them eager and willing to update their small circle of followers. In other words, people are not necessarily tweeting about their health to be noticed at the level of Reed, but desire to be noticed within their domain or to publish their own thoughts (e.g., as a diary).

Conclusion

Because health can often be a very intimate topic, an individual's decision to tweet such information is illustrative of several of the larger themes this book has been exploring. Namely, the case of health helps explain the shifting of public/private boundaries, tweets as part of an update culture, and Twitter as a means to publicize information to a wide audience. In the past, discussing one's insulin levels or being diagnosed with cancer was usually relegated to the private domain. Tweeting about such personal medical situations may prima facie seem downright shocking. However, it is emblematic of larger trends in which private health information is being volunteered publicly. A very unique aspect of Twitter is the ease with which the medium allows individuals to tweet about their health. The time it takes to tweet about having just been diagnosed with brain cancer compared with writing a blog entry or other publication on the Internet is exponentially quicker. This cost efficiency of Twitter should not be underestimated. It is a key reason why the medium is able to draw out such intimate, extemporaneous tweets from its users. Many of those tweeting would not write a blog entry from their doctor's waiting room about being anxious prior to a chemotherapy appointment, but do not hesitate to pick up their smartphone for 45 seconds and tweet about it. This perceived seamlessness is an important aspect of social communication in the Twitter age.

Another area this chapter has examined through health is Twitter's role in update cultures. Like Facebook, Twitter is built upon eliciting updates of everything from the minutiae of users' lives to the profound. These tweets appear side by side, fostering a unique tension between the banal and profound. As society continues to become more individualized, our ability to socially update others in our community continues to become increasingly challenging. With fewer tight-knit communities (Putnam 2000), our desire to update people about our health has not decreased. However, this need has found an outlet in computer-mediated communication, including Twitter. The tweeting of health information develops into part of some individuals' socialization and becomes further cemented when others "update" via Twitter regarding their health. And when friends, family, colleagues, and others reciprocally update on Twitter about their health, the culture of updating becomes further legitimized. This is crucial to users' continued perception of the social need to not only update, but to update at such a personal level. Furthermore, update cultures also offer participants an opportunity to monologue. Twitter provides them with a one-person audience, themselves, in which they can write about their health – almost in a diary fashion – and the act of tweeting itself can be cathartic. Though the larger audience may not be felt (boyd and Marwick 2010) in these autobiographical exercises, the uniqueness of Twitter is the seamless permeability of the individual's intimate domain and the larger Twitterverse. For instance, strangers may find a tweet announcing a lymphoma diagnosis and send a tweet of support to that Twitter user. It is due to its ability to reduce social exclusion that Rajani et al. (2011) claim that Twitter may potentially be "good for one's health."

This chapter has also examined how retweets can demarcate health events on Twitter that are considered important. Research mentioned in the chapter highlights some of the events that resulted in surges of Twitter traffic around a particular cancer-related tweet. Though a tweet from a single user who does not have many followers (i.e., a normal Twitter user) can become noticed by the larger Twitterverse, this is of course the exception rather than the rule. In fact, in the research presented, only one case out of the five mentioned can be considered grassroots (i.e., gaining attention via organic growth in Twitter itself rather than from prior media coverage). The most heavily retweeted cancer-related tweets concern major drug discoveries such as new treatments that have experienced promising results in clinical trials. What is interesting is that these are "events" which had already garnered the attention of traditional broadcast media and Twitter ends up re-emphasizing and rebroadcasting these stories. What is unique about the medium is what happens if someone's tweet is picked from the crowd and, for example, Lance Armstrong directs a tweet with encouragement to fight hard in the cancer battle, or CNN contacts the person for an interview. Clearly, these are exceptional circumstances. Albeit rare, the sheer fact that a small number of users become microcelebrities on Twitter and gain mainstream media attention can be considered one reason why people tweet. In the same way, though the vast majority of musicians posting videos on YouTube do not get scouted by major record labels, Justin Bieber did. The Internet in general has ameliorated some of the barriers of entry to the celebrity world by enabling individuals to first attain a celebrity status online before crossing over to mainstream success (Gamson 2011). For this reason, some musicians keep uploading videos, hoping that the next one will make them a YouTube celebrity (Strangelove 2010). The same holds true for some who tweet about their health. Some hope the crippling health bills their treatment has brought will catch the attention of someone like Oprah and a check will be sent in the mail. This is based on a hope that ordinary people can become extraordinary via Twitter. Again, as long as the dream of such celebrity intervention is kept alive, the sheer rarity of such events remains insignificant for some who tweet about their health.

This chapter has also explored the ways in which Twitter may be affecting the relationship between and amongst doctors and patients. Individuals are using the medium to create support communities and to interact with doctors more directly. Doctors and medical researchers are using the medium to interact with each other and to specifically target patients to involve them in targeted clinical trials or in other research. Though the use of Twitter within cancer communities mentioned in this chapter signals important shifts in social communication regarding health, the use of social media by health institutions and individual doctors remains, by most measures, minimal. Only a relatively small number of hospitals are officially using social media (Victorian 2010: 16). However, the public adoption of social media in terms of health-related topics has become much more common (Heaivilin et al. 2011; Prier et al. 2011). This signals shifts in who has authority and expertise in health. In these Twitter-based health communities, other patients and their family members are viewed as authority figures whose medical advice is considered valuable. Like the shifts in journalistic practice highlighted in chapter 4, these changes mark potential shifts in health practices.

Though some populations (especially marginalized ones) remain on the wrong side of the digital divide, other vulnerable populations such as youth are increasing their use of social media (Chou et al. 2009; Lenhart et al. 2010). Twitter has an enormous potential to target this population on issues such as sun safety awareness, tobacco cessation, and human papillomavirus vaccination education (Vance et al. 2009: 133). In the U.S., Twitter is used by African Americans at a higher rate than by non-Hispanic whites (Hargittai and Litt 2011), and this demographic area continues to experience differential health access (Blendon et al. 1995). Vance et al. (2009: 135) add that individual physicians have the potential to make significant impacts on large groups through Twitter by simple action recommendations, such as reminding people to wear their daily sunscreen. It is this ability of Twitter to have a larger reach that is attractive to some medical professionals. Joel Toph, a nephrologist in Detroit, believes that "out of any other way that I could get to talk to people about nephrology, this [Twitter] is the widest audience" (cited in Victorian 2010: 17). However, this reach also extends the dissemination of negative health messages. For instance, Prier et al. (2011) find that Twitter is routinely used by bars, clubs, and restaurants to promote tobacco use at their establishments. As a communications medium, it is a value-independent messenger.

CHAPTER EIGHT

Conclusion

SOCIETY IS CRAZY!!! PEOPLE ASK TO BE
STALKED THESE DAYS . . . follow me on twitter . . .
follow me on twitter . . . FOLLOW.
@VERBALARTISAN

The tweet above is commenting on the idea that people use
Twitter as a means for self-promotion (or, in the words of this
tweeter, they "ask to be stalked"). As this book has explored,
critics of Twitter have emphasized this egocentric side of
the medium. However, placing primacy on more egocentric
tweets is at the expense of the fact that many tweets on Twitter
are also highly communal. It is this irony of individual/
communal (and banal/profound) side by side that makes
Twitter a particularly interesting object of analysis. This
chapter brings together the diverse range of theory and case
studies raised throughout the book to draw broad conclusions
about social communication in the Twitter age.

Though a young communications medium, Twitter has
shaped many aspects of our social, political, and economic
lives. This book has sought to begin a critical conversation
not just about Twitter, but also about social media and the
"update cultures" they support. Specifically, it has been
argued that a nuanced approach to understanding Twitter
reveals that the medium is part of a larger historical trend
toward update cultures, social norms that encourage us to
share more in the public sphere (from intimately private
aspects of one's life such as a cancer diagnosis to very public
events such as an earthquake tremor). The Twitterverse as a

whole contains vast arrays of complex, highly intermeshed networks, which reveal a highly efficient awareness system which powers Twitter's update culture. As Twitter has been studied here ultimately as a network, it is fitting to present many of the ideas discussed as a network. Figure 8.1 illustrates how this book has connected a wide array of themes that span a variety of disciplines in order to understand the nuances of Twitter. Many of the key themes discussed, such as update cultures, "ambient" news, Twitter as an awareness system, and the medium's ability to foster engaged communities, are illustrated as central in figure 8.1. My hope is that this diagram can help readers connect the dots between theory and practice, public and private, and historical and modern that the book has navigated. To bring together some of these diverse themes, this chapter re-examines Twitter through three frames: (1) history and theory; (2) voice and influence; and (3) aware communities. The aim is to not only provide some discernible conclusions about Twitter, but to also help spur further discussion of Twitter.

History and Theory

[N]o matter how much technology reduces the intellectual and social isolation of people, their metaphysical isolation is little affected. (McLuhan 1952: 189)

Marshall McLuhan's work has shaped the study of emergent communication technologies profoundly. His analysis of radio and television continues to be valuable to modern understandings of Internet technologies. To provide broader conclusions on social communication in the Twitter age, I will refer to a couple of McLuhan's ideas that comment on technology and community, technology and communicative reach, and technology and celebrities. It is easy to lose sight of the political, social, and economic nuances of social media. In the context of Twitter, McLuhan is helpful in framing an argument that the

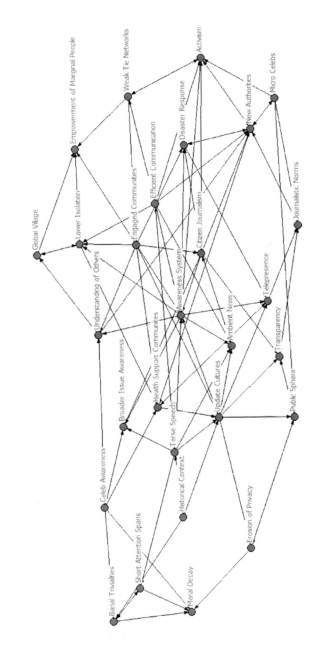

Figure 8.1 Interactions of themes discussed in this book

medium may be increasing our intellectual and social integration globally but, at a micro-social level, it does not inherently integrate us with our local social climate (neighbors, local community, etc.). In other words, Twitter aids us in more tightly integrated globalized communication, McLuhan's (1967) "global village," but may not be helping local community structures. But does tweeting integrate us more with our local community? For instance, can we tweet "thinking about going to dinner tonight . . . anyone want to join?" and, in the process, reduce our social isolation? Theoretically, yes. However, answering in the affirmative to these questions supposes that people will tweet in these ways rather than about celebrity gossip or news headlines, for example.

Questions like these are important and have been covered throughout this book via both theory and practice. However, the medium of Twitter is still relatively in its infancy and further empirical work needs to be conducted to more solidly answer the impact of the medium on social, political, and economic cultures. What is clear is that social communication is highly shaped by changes in technology and Twitter is no exception. McLuhan (1952: 189) observes that in the age of communication by "unassisted human voice," reach was highly localized, but with the advent of the written word, "its range in time and space was [. . .] given enormous expansion." I have argued that social communication in the Twitter age continues this expansion along the spectrum that originated with early writing. If email moved us exponentially up the spectrum, communicating via Twitter and similar social media represents another enormous expansion of the spectrum in terms of instantaneous, global, and multiplexed communication. Rather than being locked in a binary analysis of Twitter (e.g., it has strengthened communities/weakened communities), a more productive approach is to view the Twitter age as part of a historical continuum.

This book has explored this continuum by focusing on the telegraph and its reception in the eighteenth and nineteenth centuries. Like Twitter, the telegraph had scores of critics who feared its terseness and believed the medium would kill off letter writing. The telegraph's supporters saw its global reach and immediacy of communicating messages as an epochal shift in global connectedness. Its opponents saw the telegraph as the bringer of moral decay. This book has argued that Twitter has faced both similar praise and criticism. However, the two technologies are different in many ways. Twitter, unlike the telegraph, is multicast and incorporates a social network (followers and following). Twitter also draws from the structure of social networking technologies like Facebook. Unlike the telegraph, Twitter is public (in terms of tweets), audiovisual, and free to use. In the eighteenth century, messages were not sent "down the wire" by ordinary people several times a day. Rather, telegraph messages were used more sparingly. Tweets, however, do not require a trip to the telegraph operator and can be sent at any time and from any place. Unlike the infrequent telegraph message, tweets can produce a quasi "stream of consciousness." And when tweets rapidly fire between people, there is a feeling by users that their communication is no longer mediated. The immediacy of tweets generates a sense of "being there" with one's interlocutors (this idea of "telepresence" is discussed in chapter 3).

Voice and Influence

Another question this book has explored concerns whose voices rise above the flood of tweets. I have discussed how "celebrities" form the bulk of the Twitterati and exert disproportionate influence on the shape of discourse in Twitter (see chapter 5). McLuhan (1952: 195) explored the construction of celebrity status and concludes that "the intimacy and immediacy of the flexible television camera and screen are much less favorable to the star system than the movie camera and its giant screen onto which are poured such dreams as money can buy." The question McLuhan raises is between media rather than within a single medium. So, is the "intimacy and immediacy" of Twitter "less favorable to the star system" of television and film? If anything, this is a straw man. Bar the occasional exception, the most followed users on Twitter are celebrities because of their fame outside of Twitter (rather than their fame being "homegrown" on Twitter). At the time of writing, the top 10 most followed users in ascending order are Lady Gaga, Justin Bieber, Katy Perry, Rihanna, Shakira, Britney Spears, Kim Kardashian, Barack Obama, Taylor Swift, and Selena Gomez (@twitaholic 2012). The top 100 list reads much the same. A dystopic reading would see this as affirmation of Kierkegaard's claim that modernity is an age of indolence (see chapter 3). However, I have argued here that one's "banal" activity on Twitter (like following celebrity gossip) is as much a part of many people's identity as discussing current events. Indeed, it may be even more important to them. By ignoring this, we risk applying an elite bias to understanding Twitter.

Twitter is, of course, a corporate business. In its initial stages, it was focused on user growth. Currently, it has begun the process of increasing revenues. Its advertising models have raised controversy amongst Twitter users. One question which periodically crops up on Twitter is whether promoted tweets and trending topics (which are paid advertising services) reshape discourse on Twitter. Empirically, the effect is not highly discernible yet (though Twitter and other social media are in early days in terms of advertising strategies). The top Twitter news story in 2009 was #iranelection and, in 2010, the Gulf Oil Spill (Twitter 2010). The top five hashtags in 2010 were #rememberwhen, #slapyourself, #confession-time, #thingsimiss, and #ohjustlikeme (Twitter 2010). None of these were "promoted." However, promoted trending topics can have discernible influence on content generation/dissemination on Twitter. For example, in November 2010, the *Washington Post* sponsored #Election to promote their election day coverage. The Conan O'Brien show, in 2010, sponsored #ConanShowZero. (In a promoted trending topic, the sponsor's tweets appear at the top of the stream.) An interesting case is Europcar's promotion of #myextrahour, which they used to pipe to billboards in the UK.[1] And, if drug companies were to sponsor trending topics, the implications – legally, politically, socially, and economically – would be imminently discernible.

Of course, if those promoted tweets are significantly retweeted, that will have more direct effects on Twitter's modes of originating popular discourse. The terminology used by marketing professionals is between "organic" and "promoted" trending topics. The label of "organic" implies more of a grassroots development of a topic, whereas the "promoted" version aims to skip the grassroots building of a topic. As you can imagine, skipping the construction of a support base can have consequences on the popularity of a topic. Promoted topics have changed Twitter in that they have brought monetization into tweet audience reception. However, as the statistics from Twitter show (Twitter 2010), "organic" topics are the most popular. Given the continuing power and reach of organic topics, this book has considered to what extent ordinary people have voice and influence on Twitter. This question has been explored through the role of citizen journalists (see chapters 4–6), patients as health authorities (see chapter 7), and everyday people as activists (see chapter 6). In many cases, celebrities and traditional media have overwhelming voice and influence. However, in other cases such as health communities, individual patients can be viewed as authorities whose voice Twitter has helped make legitimate.

"Aware" Communities

In this book, the aim has been to explore the larger implications of Twitter on modern social, political, and economic life. Part of this exploration has involved examining the ways in which Twitter is individualistic and communal. Barry Wellman, whose work has extensively covered the social implications of the Internet and the rise of a more networked society (Wellman 1999; Wellman and Haythornthwaite 2002), remarked (in reference to the role of GPS navigation systems) that the technology is framed as "me-centric" as opposed to the society-centric focus that reading a physical map gives us (i.e., a greater context of our surroundings).[2] In a me-centric world, the focus is on you/your life/things from your vantage point, and is myopically oriented to "the moment." It, from Wellman's point of view,[3] can also illustrate where your life is going (in terms of your momentum), whereas a society-centric view places primacy on your role in society as part of a collection of people. Though it appears that Twitter is me-centric, this binary does not seem to describe Twitter as well as it does the GPS, the reason being that Twitter, as discussed, can help maintain communities (especially ad hoc ones) that resemble more society-centric formations, such as the cancer support groups (discussed in chapter 7) and communities in the aftermath of a disaster (discussed in chapter 5). The binary is useful in highlighting how Twitter can be viewed from two oppositional perspectives. But our social lives are not constructed from a mutually exclusive relationship between me-centric and society-centric. Rather, many of our daily activities straddle both. Twitter follows suit and is simultaneously individualistic and communal (as well as banal and profound). Furthermore, Twitter's (real/perceived) role in major news events (ranging from the downing of US Airways Flight 1549 to the 2011 Arab Spring movements and Tōhoku earthquake in Japan) is framed as society-centric. The fact that Twitter has become mainstream through these events continues to change its demography and the ways in which the medium is used. Though social communication in the Twitter age may seem me-centric, there is more happening than meets the eye. One glance at the stream of tweets after a disaster provides evidence of society-centric awareness systems such as the "ambient" news environment discussed in chapter 4. Though I have argued that Twitter should not be viewed as a toppler of governments, perhaps, at another level, tweeting together can introduce us to new people and new ideas locally and globally. It may be making us aware of broader issues and engaging us with non-homophilic communities. At 140 characters at a time, tweeters support a complex update culture which, in many ways, represents a thriving – albeit disjointed – group capable of both the banal and profound.

The Future

Twitter is a very active medium and presents a wide range of possible areas to study. This book has started the conversation rather than concluding it. For example, one area not explored here is censorship, a subject that has been invoked in reference to newsgroups, websites, blogs, and many other Internet spaces. In terms of Twitter, an example from August 2011 comes to mind. I was on Twitter and saw a retweet of Peter Daou's (@peterdau) tweet: "Unbelievable: Is Twitter REALLY allowing #reasonstobeatyourgirlfriend to be a trending topic??!" Twitter activists responded to the #reasonstobeatyourgirlfriend with the hashtags #violenceisnotfunny and #140reasonsdvisnotajoke (led by @feministing). The latter hashtag was picked up by prominent Twitter users, including @nationalnow (the U.S.-based National Organization of Women) and @Fem2pto who used this hashtag to counter tweets encouraging domestic violence. Despite this response, a significant number of users asked for the hashtag to be censored. Cases like this abound on Twitter. Clearly, Twitter has political, social, and economic effects, and the multitude of specific cases could never be fully captured in a book like this. Ultimately, it is a communications medium and its perception and use are socially constructed. Issues ranging from bullying to excessive intrusions of privacy are important to understanding Twitter and, indeed, its future. However, the medium has also fostered innovative social formations built on extensive weak-tie networks, which have updated the world during disasters or helped solve problems through crowdsourced collective intelligence. Like every "new" communications medium, Twitter will be eclipsed at some point in the future. The American Library of Congress is archiving tweets and one day historians will study selections of the enormous corpus of text generated by the Twitterverse. For better or for worse, one thing is clear: Twitter has shaped modern social communication.

"Til da end" – @SazzyIsDaBest_9

Notes

CHAPTER 1 WHAT IS TWITTER?

1 Other sites include Blellow, Jaiku, Plurk, and Foursquare.
2 In practice, the question is not indicative of the responses, as they can and do encompass anything of interest to the user from what one is doing to commenting on an issue (Michaud, cited in Honeycutt and Herring 2009: 1).
3 As long as the user has not restricted access to their tweets. A minority of users make their tweets "protected," a status by which only approved "followers" of their tweets have access to them. In this case, a Twitter-based "conversation" could only occur with permitted followers.
4 Biz Stone is also a Twitter co-founder.
5 Clapperton (2009: xxvi) offers a simple definition of social media as "an Internet-based tool that allows the reader to engage with the writer or with a community online and in public."
6 A now defunct microblogging service that was acquired by Facebook.
7 Except for the small minority of users who make their Twitter profiles private.
8 Twitter has been labeled a microblog technology due to the medium's combination of "text messaging with the instant messaging cultures of the PC and Internet, as well as blogging and social networking" (Goggin 2011: 125). Microblogging services, like Twitter, are one type of social media.
9 For example, a 14-year-old girl from London, Serena Beakhurst, went missing in January 2011 and tweets about her case were retweeted by celebrities, which raised the profile of the case. Ultimately, the London Metropolitan police found Serena.
10 Personal interview.

CHAPTER 2 CONTEXTUALIZING TWITTER

1 The advent of Internet-based technologies has often been understood through the "global village" (Hanson 2007; Jefferis 2002; Levinson 2001; Wellman 1999).

CHAPTER 3 THEORIZING TWITTER

1 Tying this back to Goffman, these changes in social communication are part of "ego" and "personal feelings," and are critical to understanding Twitter and, especially, its role in self-production.
2 Bakhtin and Holquist (1981) refer to this as a "dialogic community."
3 Furthermore, we should not underestimate the startling ability of states to pull the plug, as occurred in Egypt in 2011.
4 Of course, the ability to fly off here and there is not possible for everyone. For example, marginalized asylum-seekers and other underprivileged migrants reading those billboards in London have no other choice than mediated communication. Therefore, privileging face-to-face communication over mediated communication in cases such as these is itself stratified by class.
5 However, this assumes that the response exchanges can be paired into "dialogic units," as Goffman (1981: 6) refers to them.
6 Additionally, the diminishing of the illocutionary force of tweets may be accelerated when non-native English speakers enter the predominantly English Twitterverse. But, paradoxically, Twitter may be increasing illocutionary force for non-native speakers of the global lingua franca who enter into this English-dominated media space because it may require less English-language competency.

CHAPTER 4 TWITTER AND JOURNALISM

1 See chapter 6.
2 See: <http://twitpic.com/135xa>.
3 Though this is not without its downsides (Morozov 2009).
4 A group they term "Living in the Business World."
5 A group they term "Reliving the College Days."
6 Furthermore, far from being concerned about tweeting, these

households are more focused on getting food on the table. This situation has been amplified by the current economic recession.

7 See: <http://www.frontlinesms.com/>.

8 Of course, Twitter and text messaging are not mutually exclusive. Indeed, far from it.

9 See: <http://yfrog.com/kh807bmj>; accessed 08/26/2011.

10 For example, Morozov (2009) argues that the "Iranian Twitter revolution" was itself a construction of the American media.

CHAPTER 5   TWITTER AND DISASTERS

1 The Sri Lankan government's land grab of prime coastal property for hotel development, rather than returning the land to the villagers who had lived on it for generations, makes this painfully clear in the aftermath of the 2004 Indian Ocean tsunami (Cohen 2011).

2 He adds that 90 percent of loan applications from inner-city South Central Los Angeles were refused (Steinberg 2000: 178).

3 These would be the online equivalent of what the sociologist Émile Durkheim (1964) refers to as communities with "organic" forms of solidarity.

4 When they are given a podium in cyberspace, it becomes even more tempting to equate this with a high level of agency amongst disaster victims. Lastly, access to these technologies is highly stratified in "developing" nation-states (Hoffman 2004).

5 These "representations" are, following de Certeau, understood not as absolute representations. Rather, a key significance of them is the way in which they are consumed.

6 Online donations to tsunami relief agencies were unprecedented. The American wing of the NGO Action Against Hunger raised over $400,000 online in the first 10 days after the tsunami, an amount just short of the organization's total 2004 donations (Aitchison, cited in Glasius et al. 2005: 7).

7 See: <http://myamarnews.blogspot.com>.

8 See this Flickr album at: <http://www.flickr.com/photos/azmil77/>.

9 See this Flickr album at: <http://www.flickr.com/photos/laurieloul/sets/72157604973621519/>.

10 See Leach's (2005) critique of the reporting of the 2004 Indian Ocean tsunami.

11 See Stephenson and Anderson (1997: 311–15).
12 Trending topics appear in a box within the profile pages of all Twitter users. Additionally, given this placement within Twitter as well as search engine results, users are known to be guided to trending topics (Abrol and Khan 2010). See chapter 1 for a further discussion on the importance of trending topics.
13 There were 300 Twitter users selected from this sample for further study (the 100 users with the most tweets, the 100 most at-mentioned users, and 100 randomly selected users).
14 But it also reveals that Western users were the ones who enabled Pakistan to become a trending topic, rather than users based in Pakistan (the U.S. had the highest frequency of tweets; almost double that of Pakistani Twitter users).

CHAPTER 6 TWITTER AND ACTIVISM

1 At an average of 200 characters and the 95th percentile at 250 characters (Davies and Barber 1973).
2 Of course, this depends on what criteria is applied to defining "Arab Spring" countries.
3 Excepting the fact that governments detained and arrested some individuals based on Twitter activity.
4 Though other expatriate Twitter activists, including @oxfordgirl, feared reprisals on family in MENA countries.

CHAPTER 7 TWITTER AND HEALTH

1 This is part of a larger trend: 61 percent of adult Americans look online for health information (Fox and Jones 2009: 2). Of these "e-patients," 41 percent "have read someone else's commentary or experience about health or medical issues on an online news group, website, or blog" (ibid.: 3). Additionally, 15 percent of e-patients "have posted comments, queries, or information about health or medical matters" ibid.: 17). Though the last percentage may seem small, it is statistically significant, and this sharing of personal health information on social networking sites represents a starting rather than ending point. From 2009 to 2010, social networking use among Internet users aged 50–64 grew from 25 percent to 47 percent (Madden 2010: 2).
2 See: <http://twitter.com/ALSUntangled>.

3 See: <http://blog.trialx.com/2009/03/now-you-can-talk-to-twitter-and-find.html>.

4 See chapters 4–5.

5 See chapter 3 for a discussion of social capital.

6 Cancer survivors are a group considered "lost in transition" in terms of healthcare support (Hewitt et al. 2006). Twitter may be providing them with a solution to this situation.

7 All tweets containing five cancer-related keywords – "chemo," "lymphoma," "mammogram," "melanoma," and "cancer survivor" – were collected from December 15, 2010, to May 12, 2011.

8 The data confirms this.

9 See chapters 1–3.

10 See chapter 4 for a fuller discussion.

CHAPTER 8 CONCLUSION

1 See: <http://en.ooh-tv.com/images/Europcar-Launches-First-Dynamic-Twitter-_E809/JCDecaux_Europcar_i_on_Cromwell-Road_de.jpg>.

2 Email sent to the email list of the Communication and Information Technology section of the American Sociological Association (CITASA) by Barry Wellman on July 9, 2011.

3 Email sent to the email list of the Communication and Information Technology section of the American Sociological Association (CITASA) by Barry Wellman on July 9, 2011.

Glossary

@	see "at mention"
at-mention	an at-mention (abbreviated as @ or referred to as a "mention") is used within Twitter as a means for users to direct tweets to specific user(s); discussions on Twitter often leverage at-mentions in order for speaker and recipient to be easily identifiable (e.g., "@BarackObama Hello!")
direct message	this refers to a private tweet between two individuals; direct messages (often abbreviated as DM) are like an email or instant message which is not published publicly to one's followers
DM	see "direct message"
fail whale	when Twitter has been over capacity (especially during major world events), a picture of a whale is displayed and this image has become known as the "fail whale"
FF	see "Follow Friday"
follow	this indicates that one has elected to "subscribe" to the tweets of another user to be displayed in their timeline (see "timeline")
Follow Friday	on Fridays, Twitter users use the hashtag (#FF) to suggest Twitter users to follow
follower	a user who has elected to follow you (see "follow"); a list of followers including a total number of followers is listed on a user's profile page

following	this refers to users one follows (see "follow")
hashtag	this refers to subject classifiers within tweets; by using # before any text, a user can identify their tweet with a larger conversation topic (e.g., #ukriots)
lists	groups of Twitter users can be associated with a list which any Twitter user can curate; lists are public and span everything from professional groups to lists of musical groups
profile	the equivalent of a "homepage" on Twitter; a user's biographical information, profile picture, published tweets, followers, and following are displayed
promoted	trending topics (see "trending topics") are placed at the top of the trending topic list or tweets are placed at the top of search results for a fee paid to Twitter
reply tweet	a tweet which replies to another Twitter user(s) directly via an at-mention (see "at-mention")
retweet	this is the term given to the act of forwarding tweets written by others; a retweet (often abbreviated as RT) is viewable by one's followers
RT	see "retweet"
timeline	a list of all tweets which are displayed real-time; one's own timeline displays one's tweets as well as tweets by others
trending topics	Twitter maintains lists of hashtags which are the most popular hashtags at the time; these are prominently visible on the site
twaddict	a colloquial expression referring to an individual who is perceived as addicted to Twitter
tweeps	this term is derived from the colloquial word "peeps," which refers to one's friends or "peoples." On Twitter, this has been

	extended to refer to one's Twitter friends (i.e., one's followers on Twitter)
tweet	messages on Twitter; tweets are restricted to 140 characters and are usually publicly visible to anyone regardless of whether they have a Twitter account
tweeter	a Twitter user
twilliterate	a colloquial term referring to those who are unfamiliar with Twitter; it was made particularly popular through a viral YouTube video called "The Twitter Song"
twitiquette	Twitter etiquette
Twitterati	an elite set of Twitter users; this more often refers to celebrity Twitter users who are highly active in the medium (e.g., Justin Bieber, Paris Hilton, and Stephen Fry)
twitter-crastination	a colloquial expression referring to the use of Twitter as a procrastination tool
Twitterer	see "tweeter"
twitterpated	a colloquial expression referring to being overwhelmed by tweets
Twitterverse	the entire user community of Twitter; generalizations about the Twitter population often invoked this term
twug	a Twitter hug which can be used in many contexts ranging from between friends to within support communities on Twitter

References

@twitaholic 2012 "The Twitaholic.com Top 100 Twitterholics based on followers," at: <http://twitaholic.com/>.

Abrol, S. and Khan, L. 2010 "TWinner: understanding news queries with geo-content using Twitter," *Proceedings of the 6th Workshop on Geographic Information Retrieval*, Zurich, Switzerland: ACM.

Adkins, B. A. and Nasarczyk, J. 2009 "Asynchronicity and the 'time envelope' of online annotation: the case of the photosharing website, Flickr," *Australian Journal of Communication* 35(3): 115–40.

Adorno, T. W. and Bernstein, J. M. 1991 *The Culture Industry: Selected Essays on Mass Culture*, London: Routledge.

Allen, R. C. 1992 *Channels of Discourse, Reassembled: Television and Contemporary Criticism*, 2nd edn., Chapel Hill, NC: University of North Carolina Press.

Alsuntangled Group, The 2010 "ALSUntangled No. 5: Investigating the Stowe/Morales ALS Protocol," *Amyotrophic Lateral Sclerosis* 11(4): 414–16.

Amin, H. 2002 "Freedom as a value in Arab media: perceptions and attitudes among journalists," *Political Communication* 19(2): 125–35.

Associated Press of Pakistan 2010 "1,802 confirmed dead in floods: Kaira." *Associated Press of Pakistan*, Islamabad: Associated Press of Pakistan.

Austin, M. 2011 *Useful Fictions: Evolution, Anxiety, and the Origins of Literature*, Lincoln, NB: University of Nebraska Press.

Ayoo, P. O. 2009 "Reflections on the digital divide and its implications for the internationalization of higher education in a developing region: The Case of East Africa," *Higher Education Policy* 22(3): 30–18.

Bakhtin, M. M. and Holquist, M. 1981 *The Dialogic Imagination: Four Essays*, Austin, TX: University of Texas Press.

Barabási, A.-L. 2003 *Linked: How Everything is Connected to Everything Else and What it Means for Business, Science, and Everyday Life*, New York: Plume.

Barry, E., Khalip, N., Schwirtz, M., and Cohen, N. 2009 "Protests in Moldova explode, with a call to arms on Twitter," *The New York Times*, New York: The New York Times; available at: <http://www.nytimes.com/2009/04/08/world/europe/08moldova.html?_r=2&ref=todayspaper>.

Barton, A. 1969 *Communities in Disaster: A Sociological Analysis of Collective Stress Situations*, Garden City, NY: Doubleday & Company, Inc.

Bates, F. L. and Peacock, W. G. 1987 "Disasters and social change," in R. R. Dynes, B. D. Marchi and C. Pelanda (eds.), *Sociology of Disasters: Contribution of Sociology to Disaster Research*, Milan: Franco Angeli Libri.

Baudelaire, C. 1965 "The modern public and photography," part 2 of "The salon of 1859," in J. Mayne (ed.), *Art in Paris, 1845–1862*, London: Phaidon Publishers; distributed by New York Graphic Society Publishers, Greenwich.

Bauman, Z. 2000 *Liquid Modernity*, Cambridge, UK: Polity.

Baym, N. K. 2010 *Personal Connections in the Digital Age*, Cambridge, UK, and Malden, MA: Polity.

BBC News 2008 "As it happened: Mumbai attacks 27 November," BBC News.

Beaumont, C. 2008 "Mumbai attacks: Twitter and Flickr used to break news," *The Telegraph*, London: Telegraph Media Group Ltd; available at: <http://www.telegraph.co.uk/news/worldnews/asia/india/3530640/Mumbai-attacks-Twitter-and-Flickr-used-to-break-news-Bombay-India.html>.

Beaumont, C. 2009 "New York plane crash: Twitter breaks the news, again," *The Telegraph*, London: Telegraph Media Group Ltd; available at: <http://www.telegraph.co.uk/technology/twitter/4269765/New-York-plane-crash-Twitter-breaks-the-news-again.html>.

Beaumont, P. 2011 "Friends, followers and countrymen: The uprisings in Libya, Tunisia and Egypt have been called 'Twitter revolutions' – but can social networking overthrow a government? Peter Beaumont reports from the Middle East on how activists are really using the web," *Guardian*, February 25, 2011, p. 4, London: Guardian Newspapers Limited.

Bedlack, R. and Hardiman, O. 2009 "ALSUntangled (ALSU): a scientific approach to Off-Label Treatment Options for People with ALS Using Tweets and Twitters," *Amyotrophic Lateral Sclerosis* 10(3): 129–30.

Benedictus, L. 2010 "Twitter's old hat if you've used The Notificator," *Guardian*, June 15, 2010, London: Guardian News and Media Limited;

available at: <http://www.guardian.co.uk/technology/2010/jun/15/ the-notificator-precursor-of-twiitter>.

Benn, T. 2011 "The flowers of the Arab spring grow from buds of free information," *New Statesman* 140(5048): 12.

Bennett, W. L. and Toft, A. 2008 "Identity, technology, and narratives: transnational activism and social networks," in A. Chadwick and P. N. Howard (eds.), *Routledge Handbook of Internet Politics*, London and New York: Routledge, pp. 246–60.

Berman, M. 1982 *All That is Solid Melts into Air: The Experience of Modernity*, New York: Simon and Schuster.

Bianco, J. S. 2009 "Social networking and cloud computing: precarious affordances for the 'prosumer'," *Women's Studies Quarterly* 37(1&2): 303–12.

Bianculli, D. 1992 *Teleliteracy: Taking Television Seriously*, New York: Continuum.

Black, I. 2011 "Death of Bin Laden: analysis: al-Qaida's influence slips from marginal to almost irrelevant in light of Arab Spring: uprisings bypassed forces of militant Islamism Twitter and Facebook had more effect than 'martyrs'," *Guardian*, May 3, 2011, p. 16, London: Guardian Newspapers Limited.

Blair, W. 1915 *I Hear a Little Twitter and a Song. Words by G. Plass*, Cincinnati: J. Church Co.

Blau, J. 2006 "Talk Is cheap," *IEEE Spectrum* 43(10): 14–16.

Blendon, R. J., Scheck, A. C., Donelan, K., Hill, C. A., Smith, M., Beatrice, D., and Altman, D. 1995 "How white and African Americans view their health and social problems," *JAMA: The Journal of the American Medical Association* 273(4): 341–6.

Bliven, B. 1924 "How radio is remaking our world," *20th Century Magazine* 108: 149.

Boaz, J. 1802 *A Few Particulars Respecting Mr. Boaz's Patent Telegraph*, London: Unknown.

Bolger, N., Davis, A., and Rafaeli, E. 2003 "Diary methods: capturing life as it is lived," *Annual Review of Psychology* 54(1): 579–616.

Bonetta, L. 2009 "Should you be tweeting?," *Cell* 139(3): 452–3.

Boon, S. and Sinclair, C. 2009 "A world I don't inhabit: disquiet and identity in Second Life and Facebook," *Educational Media International* 46(2): 99–110.

Bourdieu, P. 1984 *Distinctio : A Social Critique of the Judgement of Taste*, Cambridge, MA: Harvard University Press.

boyd, d. 2007 "Why youth ♥ social network sites: the role of networked publics in teenage social life," *The John D. and Catherine T. MacArthur Foundation Series on Digital Media and Learning*: 119–42.

boyd, d. m. and Ellison, N. B. 2008 "Social network sites: definition, history, and scholarship," *Journal of Computer-Mediated Communication* 13(1): 210–30.

boyd, d. and Marwick, A. E. 2011 "I tweet honestly, I tweet passionately: Twitter users, context collapse, and the imagined audience," *New Media & Society* 13(1): 114–33.

boyd, d. m., Golder, S., and Lotan, G. 2010 "Tweet, tweet, retweet: conversational aspects of retweeting on Twitter," *2010 43rd Hawaii International Conference on System Sciences*, Koloa, Kauai, Hawaii.

Bracken, C. C. and Skalski, P. D. 2009 *Immersed in Media: Telepresence in Everyday Life*, New York: Routledge.

Bruns, A. 2005 *Gatewatching: Collaborative Online News Production*, New York: P. Lang.

Bruns, A. 2011 "Gatekeeping, gatewatching, real-time feedback: new challenges for Journalism," *Brazilian Journalism Research* 7(2): 117–36.

Bruns, A. and Burgess, J. E. 2011 "New methodologies for researching news discussion on Twitter," in *The Future of Journalism*, 8–9 September 2011, Cardiff: Cardiff University (unpublished); available at: <http://eprints.qut.edu.au/46330/>.

Bryant, J. and Miron, D. 2004 "Theory and research in mass communication," *Journal of Communication* 54(4): 662–704.

Bull, M. 2005 "No dead air! The iPod and the culture of mobile listening," *Leisure Studies* 24(4): 343–55.

Burgess, J. and Green, J. 2009 *YouTube: Online Video and Participatory Culture*, Cambridge, U.K., and Malden, MA: Polity.

Burns, A. 2010 "Oblique strategies for ambient journalism," *M/C Journal* 13(2).

Butcher, L. 2009 "How Twitter is transforming the cancer care community," *Oncology Times* 31(21): 36–9.

Butcher, L. 2010a "Oncologists using Twitter to advance cancer knowledge," *Oncology Times:* 32(1): 8–10.

Butcher, L. 2010b "Profiles in oncology social media: Naoto T. Ueno, MD, PhD – @teamoncology," *Oncology Times* 32(13): 38–9.

Butler, J. G. 2010 *Television Style*, New York: Routledge.

Callcott, J. G. 1863 *The First Twitter of Spring. Part Song, Written by W. S. Passmore*, London: Foster & King.

Castells, M. 1996 *The Rise of the Network Society*, Cambridge, MA, and Oxford: Blackwell.

Castells, M. 2000 "Materials for an exploratory theory of the network society," *British Journal of Sociology* 51(1): 5–24.

CBS 2011 "Wael Ghonim and Egypt's new age revolution" *60 Minutes*, USA.

Celik, H., Lagro-Janssen, T., Klinge, I., van der Weijden, T., and Widdershoven, G. 2009 "Maintaining gender sensitivity in the family practice: facilitators and barriers," *Journal of Evaluation in Clinical Practice* 15(6): 1220–25.

Cha, M., Haddadi, H., Benevenuto, F., and Gummadi, K. 2010 "Measuring user influence in Twitter: the million follower fallacy" *Fourth International AAAI Conference on Weblogs and Social Media*, George Washington University.

Chou, W.-y. S., Hunt, Y., Beckjord, E. B., Moser, R., and Hesse, B. 2009 "Social media use in the United States: implications for health communication," *Journal of Medical Internet Research* 11(4): 48.

Christensen, C. 2011 "Twitter revolutions? Addressing social media and dissent," *The Communication Review* 14(3): 155–7.

Christian Science Monitor, The 2011 "What Chávez and Obama have in common: Twitterplomacy," *Christian Science Monitor*, available at: <http://www.csmonitor.com/Innovation/Tech/2011/0322/What-Chavez-and-Obama-have-in-common-Twitterplomacy>.

Chung, D. S. 2008 "Interactive features of online newspapers: identifying patterns and predicting use of engaged readers," *Journal of Computer-Mediated Communication* 13(3): 658–79.

Clapperton, G. 2009 *This is Social Media: How to Tweet, Post, Link and Blog Your Way to Business Success*, Chichester, U.K.: Capstone.

Clark, A. 2003 *Natural-born Cyborgs: Why Minds and Technologies are Made to Merge*, New York: Oxford University Press.

Clarke, L. 2004 "Using disaster to see society," *Contemporary Sociology* 33(2): 137–9.

Cohen, E. 2010 "Aidan's art helps pay for his own cancer care," *CNN Health*, December 3, 2010, edn., Atlanta, GA: CNN.

Cohen, E. 2011 "Tourism and land grab in the aftermath of the Indian Ocean tsunami," *Scandinavian Journal of Hospitality and Tourism* 11(3): 224–36.

Coleman, J. S. 1988 "Social capital in the creation of human capital," *American Journal of Sociology* 94(S1): S95–S120.

Comninos, A. 2011 "Twitter revolutions and cyber crackdowns: user-generated content and social networking in the Arab Spring and beyond," Association for Progressive Communications (APC); available at: <http://www.apc.org/en/system/files/AlexComninos_MobileInternet.pdf>.

Connor-Linton, J. 1999 "Competing communicative styles and crosstalk: a multi-feature analysis," *Language in Society* 28(01): 25–56.

Courier Mail 2008 "Terrorists turn technology into weapon of war in Mumbai" *Courier Mail*, Queensland: Queensland Newspapers;

available at: <http://www.couriermail.com.au/news/world/terrorists-and-technology/story-e6freop6-1111118178210>.

Cox, A. M. 2008 *Flickr: A Case Study of Web2.0*, vol. 60, Bradford, UK: Emerald.

Crawford, K. 2009 "Following you: disciplines of listening in social media" *Continuum: Journal of Media & Cultural Studies* 23(4): 525–35.

Crumb, M. J. 2009 "Twitter opens a door to Iowa operating room" *The Associated Press*; available at: <http://www.omaha.com/article/20090901/AP09/309019855>.

Davies, D. W. and Barber, D. L. A. 1973 *Communication Networks for Computers*, London and New York: John Wiley.

Dayan, D. 1998 "Particularistic media and diasporic communications," in T. Liebes, J. Curran, and E. Katz (eds.), *Media, Ritual, and Identity*, London and New York: Routledge.

De Choudhury, M., Sundaram, H., John, A., Seligmann, D. D., and Kelliher, A. 2010 "'Birds of a feather': does user homophily impact information diffusion in social media?"; available at: <http://arxiv.org/abs/1006.1702>.

Delanty, G. 2006 "The cosmopolitan imagination: critical cosmopolitanism and social theory," *The British Journal of Sociology* 57(1): 25–47.

Dent, J. D. 1795 *The Telegraph, or, a New Way of Knowing Things: A Comic Piece, as Performed at the Theatre Royal, Covent Garden, with Universal Applause*, London: J. Downes & Co.

Derks, D., Bos, A. E. R., and von Grumbkow, J. 2008 "Emoticons in computer-mediated communication: social motives and social context," *CyberPsychology & Behavior* 11(1): 99–101.

DeVoe, K. M. 2009 "Bursts of information: microblogging," *Reference Librarian* 50(2): 212–14.

Dickinson, R. 2011 "The use of social media in the work of local newspaper journalists," *The Future of Journalism Conference*, Cardiff, UK: Cardiff University.

DiMaggio, P., Hargittai, E., Neuman, W. R., and Robinson, J. P. 2001 "Social implications of the Internet," *Annual Review of Sociology* 27(1): 307–36.

DiMicco, J. M. and Millen, D. R. 2007 "Identity management: multiple presentations of self in Facebook," *Proceedings of the 2007 International ACM Conference on Supporting Group Work*, Sanibel Island, Florida, USA: ACM.

Doan, S., Vo, B.-K., and Collier, N. 2011 "An analysis of Twitter messages in the 2011 Tōhoku Earthquake," in *Lecture Notes of the Institute for Computer Science, Social Informatics and Telecommunications*

Engineering, vol. 91, New York: Springer, pp. 58–66; available at: <http://rd.springer.com/chapter/10.1007/978-3-642-29262-0_8>.

Dolnick, S. 2008 "Bloggers provide raw view of Mumbai attacks: dramatic siege threw user-generated corner of the Internet into high gear," Redmond, WA: msnbc.com.

Dreher, H. M. 2009 "Twittering about anything, everything, and even health," *Holistic Nursing Practice* 23(4): 217–21.

Dreyfus, H. L. 2009 *On the Internet*, 2nd edn. London: Routledge.

Dunn, A. 2011 "The Arab Spring: revolution and shifting geopolitics – unplugging a nation: state media strategy during Egypt's January 25 uprising," *The Fletcher Forum of World Affairs Journal* 35(2): 15–24.

Durant, A. 2010 *Meaning in the Media: Discourse, Controversy and Debate*, Cambridge, U.K.: Cambridge University Press.

Durkheim, É. 1964 *The Division of Labor in Society*, New York: Free Press of Glencoe.

Ebner, M. and Schiefner, M. 2008 "Microblogging – more than fun?," *Proceedings of IADIS Mobile Learning Conference 2008*: 155–9.

Ellcessor, E. 2010 "Bridging disability divides," *Information, Communication & Society* 13(3): 289–308.

Ellerman, E. 2007 "The Internet in context," in J. Gackenbach (ed.), *Psychology and the Internet: Intrapersonal, Interpersonal, and Transpersonal Implications*, 2nd edn. Amsterdam and Boston, MA: Elsevier/Academic Press.

Ellison, N. B., Steinfield, C., and Lampe, C. 2007 "The benefits of Facebook 'friends': social capital and college students' use of online social network sites," *Journal of Computer-Mediated Communication* 12(4): 1143–68.

Emmett, A. 2008 "Networking news," *American Journalism Review* 30(6): 40–43.

Enteen, J. B. 2010 *Virtual English: Queer Internets and Digital Creolization*, New York and London: Routledge.

Esfandiari, G. 2010 "The Twitter devolution," *Foreign Policy*, June 7; available at: <http://www.foreignpolicy.com/articles/2010/06/07/the_twitter_revolution_that_wasnt>.

Ewalt, D. M. 2003 "All eyes on cell phones," *InformationWeek* (961): 51–8.

Fandy, M. 1999 "CyberResistance: Saudi opposition between globalization and localization," *Comparative Studies in Society and History* 41(1): 124–47.

Farber, D. 2011 "P. J. Crowley's Twitter diplomacy" *CNN.com WorldWatch*, Atlanta, GA: CNN.

Fearn-Banks, K. 2010 *Crisis Communications: A Casebook Approach*, 4th edn., New York: Routledge.

Fischer, C. S. 1992 *America Calling: A Social History of the Telephone to 1940*, Berkeley, CA: University of California Press.

Fischer, H. W. 1998 *Response to Disaster: Fact Versus Fiction & Its Perpetuation: the Sociology of Disaster*, 2nd edn., Lanham, MD: University Press of America.

Forster, E. M. [1909] 1997 *The Machine Stops and Other Stories*, London: André Deutsch.

Fox News Philadelphia 2011 "Kate Gosselin, Snooki Tweet About Irene," *myfoxphilly.com*, August 27, 2011 edn., Philadelphia, PA: Fox News.

Fox, S. and Jones, S. 2009 "The social life of health information," *Pew Internet & American Life Project*, Washington, DC: Pew Research Center.

Gadamer, H.-G., Weinsheimer, J. and Marshall, D. G. 2004 *Truth and Method*, 2nd edn. London and New York: Continuum.

Gamson, J. 2011 "The unwatched life is not worth living: the elevation of the ordinary in celebrity culture," *PMLA* 126(4): 1061–9.

Geere, D. 2011 "Twitter spread misinformation faster than truth in UK riots," *Wired Magazine*; available at: <http://www.wired.co.uk/news/archive/2011-08/09/twitter-misinformation-riots>.

Gigliotti, C. 1999 "The ethical life of the digital aesthetic," in P. Lunenfeld (ed.), *The Digital Dialectic: New Essays on New Media*, Cambridge, MA: MIT Press, pp. 46–63.

Gilder, G. 1994 "Life after television, updated," *Forbes ASAP*; available at: <http://www.seas.upenn.edu/~gaj1/tvgg.html>.

Gitlin, T. 2011 "Sandmonkey: 'too stupid to govern us'," *Dissent* 58(3): 5–7.

Gladwell, M. 2010 "Small change," *New Yorker* 86(30): 42–9.

Glasius, M., Kaldor, M., and Anheier, H. 2005 "Introduction," in M. Glasius, M. Kaldor, and H. Anheier (eds.), *Global Civil Society 2005/06*, London: Sage.

Goffman, E. 1959 *The Presentation of Self in Everyday Life*, Garden City, NY: Doubleday.

Goffman, E. 1981 *Forms of Talk*, Oxford: Blackwell.

Goffman, E. 1983 "The interaction order: American Sociological Association, 1982 presidential address," *American Sociological Review* 48(1): 1–17.

Goggin, G. 2011 *Global Mobile Media*, Abingdon, Oxon, and New York: Routledge.

Goodman, M. K., and Barnes, C. 2011 "Star/poverty space: the making of the 'development celebrity'," *Celebrity Studies* 2(1): 69–85.

Goolsby, R. 2009 "Lifting elephants: Twitter and blogging in global perspective," in *Social Computing and Behavioral Modeling*, New York: Springer; available at: <http://dx.doi.org/10.1007/978-1-4419-0056-2_2>.

Granovetter, M. S. 1973 "The strength of weak ties," *American Journal of Sociology* 78(6): 1360–80.

Green, N. 1889 "Are telegraph rates too high?," *The North American Review* 149(396): 569–79.

Guattari, F. 1995 *Chaosmosis*, Bloomington, IN: Indiana University Press.

Gulati, G. J. J. and Just, M. R. 2006 "The establishment strikes back: newspapers and online news," *Conference Papers – Southern Political Science Association*: 1–10.

Hadar, L. T. 2011a "Start the Twitter revolution without me," *Cato Institute Blog*, vol. 2011; available at: <http://www.cato.org/publications/commentary/start-twitter-revolution-without-me>.

Hadar, L. T. 2011b "This is a struggle for power, not Arab Spring," *The Business Times*, Singapore: Singapore Press Holdings.

Hansen, D. L., Shneiderman, B. and Smith, M. 2010 "Visualizing threaded conversation networks: mining message boards and email lists for actionable insights," in A. An, P. Lingras, S. Petty, and R. Huang (eds.), *Active Media Technology*, vol. 6335, Berlin/Heidelberg: Springer.

Hanson, J. 2007 *24/7: How Cell Phones and the Internet Change the Way We Live, Work, and Play*, Westport, CT: Praeger.

Hargittai, E. 2006 "Hurdles to information seeking: spelling and typographical mistakes during users online behavior," *Journal of the Association for Information Systems* 7(1): 52–67.

Hargittai, E. and Litt, E. 2011 "The tweet smell of celebrity success: explaining variation in Twitter adoption among a diverse group of young adults," *New Media & Society* 13(5): 824–42.

Hartley, J. 1999 *Uses of Television*, London and New York: Routledge.

Harvey, D. 1989 *The Condition of Postmodernity: An Enquiry into the Origins of Cultural Change*, Oxford: Blackwell.

Haseeb, K. E.-D. 2011 "On the Arab 'Democratic Spring': lessons derived," *Contemporary Arab Affairs* 4(2): 113–22.

Hassanpour, N. 2011 "Media disruption exacerbates revolutionary unrest: evidence from Mubarak's natural experiment," *APSA 2011 Annual Meeting Paper*.

Hawn, C. 2009 "Take two aspirin and tweet me in the morning: how Twitter, Facebook, and other social media are reshaping health care," *Health Affairs* 28(2): 361–8.

Hayashi, F. and Klee, E. 2003 "Technology adoption and consumer payments: evidence from survey data," *Review of Network Economics* 2(2): Article 8.

Hayes, A. S., Singer, J. B., and Ceppos, J. 2007 "Shifting roles, enduring values: the credible journalist in a digital age," *Journal of Mass Media Ethics* 22(4): 262–79.

Heaivilin, N., Gerbert, B., Page, J. E., and Gibbs, J. L. 2011 "Public health surveillance of dental pain via Twitter," *Journal of Dental Research* 90(9): 1047–51.

Heidegger, M. 1977 *The Question Concerning Technology, and Other Essays*, New York: Garland Pub.

Hermida, A. 2010a "From TV to Twitter: how ambient news became ambient journalism," *Media/Culture Journal* 13(2); available at: <http://papers.ssrn.com/sol3/papers.cfm?abstract_id=1732603>.

Hermida, A. 2010b "Twittering the news," *Journalism Practice* 4(3): 297–308.

Herring, S. C. 2001 "Computer-mediated discourse," in D. Schiffrin, D. Tannen, and H. E. Hamilton (eds.), *The Handbook of Discourse Analysis*, Oxford: Blackwell, pp. 612–34.

Hewitt, M. E., Ganz, P. A., Institute of Medicine (U.S.), and American Society of Clinical Oncology (U.S.), 2006 *From Cancer Patient to Cancer Survivor: Lost in Transition: An American Society of Clinical Oncology and Institute of Medicine Symposium*, Washington, DC: National Academies Press.

Hobson, J. 2008 "Digital whiteness, primitive blackness," *Feminist Media Studies* 8(2): 111–26, London: Routledge.

Hobson, K. 2011 "A.M. Vitals: Bristol-Myers Squibb's melanoma drug improves survival," *Wall Street Journal Blogs*, New York: Dow Jones & Co; available at: <http://blogs.wsj.com/health/2011/03/22/a-m-vitals-bristol-myers-squibbs-melanoma-drug-improves-survival/>.

Hoffman, B. 2004 *The Politics of the Internet in Third World Development: Challenges in Contrasting Regimes with Case Studies of Costa Rica and Cuba*, New York: Routledge.

Honeycutt, C. and Herring, S. 2009 "Beyond microblogging: conversation and collaboration via Twitter," *HICSS '09. 42nd Hawaii International Conference on System Sciences.*

Horiuchi, N. 2011 "Japan post-earthquake," *Nature Photonics* 5(9): 508.

Hounshell, B. 2011a "A guide to the foreign policy Twitterati," *Foreign Policy* 187: 22.

Hounshell, B. 2011b "The revolution will be tweeted," *Foreign Policy* 187: 20–21.

Hughes, A. L. and Palen, L. 2009 "Twitter adoption and use in mass convergence and emergency events," *6th International ISCRAM Conference*, Gothenburg, Sweden.

Hughes, A. L., Palen, L., Sutton, J., Liu, S. B., and Vieweg, S. 2008 "'Site-seeing' in disaster: an examination of on-line social convergence," *5th International ISCRAM Conference*, Washington, DC.

Huyssen, A. 2000 "Present pasts: media, politics, amnesia," *Public Culture* 12(1): 21–38.

Idle, N. and Nunns, A. 2011 *Tweets from Tahrir: Egypt's Revolution as it Unfolded, in the Words of the People Who Made it*, New York: OR Books.

International Telecommunication Union 2010 *Fixed Broadband Subscriptions*, available at: <http://www.itu.int/ITU-D/ict/statistics/>.

International Telecommunications Union 2011 *Key Global Telecom Indicators for the World Telecommunication Service Sector*, Geneva, Switzerland: International Telecommunications Union.

Irish Times, The 2010 "Anger builds as disaster affects three million," August 4, 2010, p. 8, Dublin: *The Irish Times*.

James, Susan Donaldson 2010 "Little boy battles cancer with monsters," ABC World News with Diane Sawyer (November 11), available at: <http://abcnews.go.com/Health/CancerPreventionAndTreatment/aid-aidan-sells-4000-monster-drawings-boy-leukemia/story?id=121 13304>.

Java, A., Xiaodan, S., Finin, T., and Tseng, B. 2007 "Why we twitter: understanding microblogging usage and communities," *Proceedings of the 9th WebKDD and 1st SNA-KDD 2007 Workshop on Web Mining and Social Network Analysis*, San Jose, California: ACM.

Jefferis, D. 2002 *Internet: Electronic Global Village*, New York: Crabtree.

Jue, A. L., Marr, J. A., and Kassotakis, M. E. 2010 *Social Media at Work: How Networking Tools Propel Organizational Performance*, 1st edn., San Francisco, CA: Jossey-Bass.

Jurgenson, N. 2012 "Augmented collectives: revolution, occupation, protest, riots, flash mobs at the intersection of atoms and bits" *Eastern Sociological Society Annual Meeting*, New York.

Kahn, J. G., Yang, J. S., and Kahn, J. S. 2010 "'Mobile' health needs and opportunities in developing countries," *Health Affairs* 29(2): 254–61.

Kaplan, W. 2006 "Can the ubiquitous power of mobile phones be used to improve health outcomes in developing countries?," *Globalization and Health* 2(1): 1–14.

Katz, E. and Lazarsfeld, P. F. 1955 *Personal Influence: The Part Played by People in the Flow of Mass Communications*, Glencoe, IL: Free Press.

Keen, A. 2010 "Reinventing the Luddite: an interview with Andrew Keen," *Futurist*, 44(2): 35–6, Bethesda, MD: World Future Society.

Kelley, T. 2011 "Environmental health insights into the 2011 Tōhoku Japan earthquake disaster," *Environmental Health Insights* 2011: 21.

Kierkegaard, S. and Dru, A. 1962 *The Present Age and Of the Difference between a Genius and an Apostle. Translated and with an introduction by Alexander Dru*, London and Glasgow: Collins.

Kireyev, K., Palen, L., and Anderson, K. 2009 "Applications of topics models to analysis of disaster-related Twitter data," *NIPS Workshop on Applications for Topic Models: Text and Beyond*, La Jolla, CA: Neural Information Processing Systems Foundation.

Kirkpatrick, D. and Preston, J. 2011 "Google executive who was jailed said he was part of Facebook campaign in Egypt," *New York Times*, February 7, 2011, New York: New York Times.

Knorr Cetina, K. 2009 "The synthetic situation: interactionism for a global world," *Symbolic Interaction* 32(1): 61–87.

Kolko, B. E., Nakamura, L., and Rodman, G. B. 2000 *Race in Cyberspace*, New York: Routledge.

Krowchuk, H. V. 2010 "Should social media be used to communicate with patients?," *MCN The American Journal of Maternal/Child Nursing* 35(1): 6–7.

Kubetin, S. K. 2011 "A lesson in taking social media to the medical level," *Internal Medicine News* 44(7): 75.

Kwak, H., Lee, C., Park, H. and Moon, S. 2010 "What is Twitter, a social network or a news media?," *Proceedings of the 19th International Conference on World Wide Web*, Raleigh, North Carolina: ACM.

Lariscy, R. W., Avery, E. J., Sweetser, K. D., and Howes, P. 2009 "An examination of the role of online social media in journalists' source mix," *Public Relations Review* 35(3): 314–16.

Larson, L. C. 2010 "Digital readers: the next chapter in e-book reading and response," *The Reading Teacher* 64(1): 15–22.

Lasorsa, D. L., Lewis, S. C., and Holton, A. E. 2011 "Normalizing Twitter," *Journalism Studies* 13(1): 19–36.

Last, J. V. 2009 "Tweeting while Tehran burns," *Current* 515: 9–10.

Leach, S. L. 2005 "How to tell story of the dead without offending the living," *Christian Science Monitor* 97(38): 11.

Lenhart, A., Purcell, K., Smith, A., and Zickuhr, K. 2010 "Social media & mobile internet use among teens and young adults," *Pew Internet & American Life Project*, Washington, DC: Pew Research Center.

Leo, J. 2009 "Citizen journo Janis Krums twitters amazing Hudson plane crash photo from ferry," *Los Angeles Times*, Los Angeles: Los

Angeles timesgroup: available at: <http://qa.travel.latimes.com/daily-deal-blog/index.php/citizen-journo-janis-3851/>.

Levinson, P. 2001 *Digital McLuhan: A Guide to the Information Millenium*, London and New York: Routledge.

Li, J. and Rao, H. R. 2010 "Twitter as a rapid response news service: an exploration in the context of the 2008 China Earthquake," *Electronic Journal of Information Systems in Developing Countries* 42(4): 1–22.

Li, Q. 2006 "Cyberbullying in Schools," *School Psychology International* 27(2): 157–70.

Liang, B. A. and Mackey, T. 2011 "Direct-to-consumer advertising with interactive Internet media," *JAMA: The Journal of the American Medical Association* 305(8): 824–5.

Licoppe, C. 2004 "'Connected' presence: the emergence of a new repertoire for managing social relationships in a changing communication technoscape," *Environment and Planning D: Society and Space* 22(1): 135–56.

Liebmann, M. 1996 *Arts Approaches to Conflict*, London: Jessica Kingsley Publishers.

Liu, S. B., Palen, L., Sutton, J., Hughes, A. L., and Vieweg, S. 2008 "In search of the bigger picture: the emergent role of on-line photo sharing in times of disaster," *5th International ISCRAM Conference*, Washington, DC.

Livingstone, S. 2008 "Taking risky opportunities in youthful content creation: teenagers' use of social networking sites for intimacy, privacy and self-expression," *New Media Society* 10(3): 393–411.

Livingstone, S. and Helsper, E. 2007 "Gradations in digital inclusion: children, young people and the digital divide," *New Media Society* 9(4): 671–96.

Loft, J. B. 2005 "Understanding community weblogs" unpublished Ph.D. thesis, South Dakota State University.

Lotan, G., Graeff, E., Ananny, M., Gaffney, D., Pearce, I., and boyd, d. 2011 "The revolutions were tweeted: information flows during the 2011 Tunisian and Egyptian revolutions," *International Journal of Communication* 5: 1375–1405.

McAulay, L. 2007 "Unintended consequences of computer-mediated communications," *Behaviour & Information Technology* 26(5): 385–98.

McCartney, M. 2011 "Panic about nuclear apocalypse overshadows Japan's real plight," *BMJ* 342: 1845; available at: <http://www.bmj.com/content/342/bmj.d1845.full>.

McCulloch, R. 2009 "The man who changed twitter," *Third Sector Lab*: Third Sector Lab; available at: <http://thirdsectorlab.co.uk/?p=27>.

McLuhan, H. M. 1952 "Technology and Political Change," *International Journal* 7(3): 189–95.

McLuhan, M. 1962 *The Gutenberg Galaxy: The Making of Typographic Man*, Toronto: University of Toronto Press.

McLuhan, M. and Fiore, Q. 1967 *The Medium is the Massage*, New York: Random House.

McLuhan, M. and Fiore, Q. 1968 *War and Peace in the Global Village: An Inventory of Some of the Current Spastic Situations that Could be Eliminated by More Feedforward*, 1st edn., New York: McGraw-Hill.

McNab, C. 2009 "What social media offers to health professionals and citizens," *Bulletin of the World Health Organization* 87: 566.

McPherson, M., Smith-Lovin, L., and Cook, J. M. 2001 "Birds of a feather: homophily in social networks," *Annual Review of Sociology* 27(1): 415–44.

Madden, M. 2010 "Older adults and social media," *Pew Internet & American Life Project*, Washington, DC: Pew Research Center.

Manfredi, C., Kaiser, K., Matthews, A. K., and Johnson, T. P. 2010 "Are racial differences in patient–physician cancer communication and information explained by background, predisposing, and enabling factors?," *Journal of Health Communication* 15(3): 272–92.

Manovich, L. 2001 *The Language of New Media*, Cambridge, MA, London: MIT Press.

Menchik, D. A. and Tian, X. 2008 "Putting social context into text: the semiotics of e-mail interaction," *American Journal of Sociology* 114(2): 332–70.

Miller, R. 2008 "The new journalism: its audience participation time," *EContent* 31(6): 30–34.

Minsky, M. 1980 "Telepresence," *OMNI Magazine*: 45–51.

Modern Mechanix and Inventions magazine 1935 "Robot messenger displays person-to-person notes in public," *Modern Mechanix and Inventions Magazine*: 80.

Moore, A. 2011 "Imperial hubris of the war on terror," *Lateline*, Australian: Australian Broadcasting Corporation.

Moore, J., Ford, P., Lynch, S., Delaney, M., and Montlake, S. 2011 "Social media day: did Twitter and Facebook really build a global revolution?," *Christian Science Monitor*, available at: <http://www.csmonitor.com/World/Global-Issues/2011/0630/Social-media-Did-Twitter-and-Facebook-really-build-a-global-revolution>.

Moore, M. 2009 "'Dalai Lama' Twitter account suspended after exposed as fake," *The Telegraph*, London: Telegraph Media Group Ltd; available at: <http://www.telegraph.co.uk/news/newstopics/

howaboutthat/4577342/Dalai-Lama-Twitter-account-suspended-aft er-exposed-as-fake.html>.

Morán, A. L., Rodríguez-Covili, J., Mejia, D., Favela, J., Ochoa, S., Kolfschoten, G., Herrmann, T., and Lukosch, S. 2010 "Supporting informal interaction in a hospital through impromptu social networking," *Collaboration and Technology*, Vol. 6257, Berlin: Springer, pp. 305–20.

Morozov, E. 2009 "Iran: Downside to the 'Twitter Revolution'," *Dissent* 56(4): 10–14.

Morozov, E. 2011 *The Net Delusion: The Dark Side of Internet Freedom*, 1st edn., New York: Public Affairs.

Morris, T. 2009 *All a Twitter: A Personal and Professional Guide to Social Networking with Twitter*, Indianapolis, IN: Que.

Motadel, D. 2011 "Waves of revolution," *History Today* 61(4): 3–4.

Mowlana, H. 1979 "Technology versus tradition: communication in the Iranian Revolution," *Journal of Communication* 29(3): 107–12.

Mroue, B. 2011 "Syria Facebook, YouTube ban lifted: reports," *The Huffington Post*; available at: <http://www.huffingtonpost. com/2011/02/08/syria-facebook-youtube-ba_n_820273.html>.

Mungiu-Pippidi, A. and Munteanu, I. 2009 "Moldova's 'Twitter revolution'," *Journal of Democracy* 20(3): 136–42.

Murdock, G. 1993 "Communications and the constitution of modernity," *Media Culture and Society* 15(4): 521–39.

Murthy, D. 2010 "Muslim punks online: a diasporic Pakistani music subculture on the Internet," *South Asian Popular Culture* 8(2): 181–94.

Murthy, D. 2011a "New media and natural disasters," *Information, Communication & Society*: 1–17; see: <http://www.tandfonline.com/ doi/abs/10.1080/1369118X.2011.611815#preview>.

Murthy, D. 2011b "Twitter: microphone for the masses?," *Media, Culture & Society* 33(5): 779–89.

Murthy, D. Forthcoming "Towards a sociological understanding of social media: theorizing Twitter," *Sociology*.

Nakamura, L. 2002 *Cybertypes: Race, Ethnicity, and Identity on the Internet*, New York: Routledge.

Nakamura, L. 2008 *Digitizing Race: Visual Cultures of the Internet*, Minneapolis, MN: University of Minnesota Press.

Nelson, R. E. 1989 "The strength of strong ties: social networks and intergroup conflict in organizations," *The Academy of Management Journal* 32(2): 377–401.

Niedzviecki, H. 2009 *The Peep Diaries: How We're Learning to Love Watching Ourselves and Our Neighbors*, San Francisco, CA: City Lights Books.

Nosko, A., Wood, E., and Molema, S. 2010 "All about me: disclosure in online social networking profiles: The case of FACEBOOK," *Computers in Human Behavior* 26(3): 406–18.

O'Dell, J. 2011 "How Egyptians used Twitter during the January crisis," New York City: Mashable.com; at: <http://mashable.com/2011/02/01/egypt-twitter-infographic/>.

Oh, J. 2009 "Korean tacos open new avenue " *The Korea Herald*, Seoul: Financial Times Group; available at: <http://view.koreaherald.com/kh/view.php?ud=20090417000026&cpv=0>.

Okazaki, Makoto, and Yutaka Matsuo 2008 "Semantic twitter: analyzing tweets for real-time event notification," in John G. Breslin, Thomas N. Burg, Hong-Gee Kim, Tom Raftery, and Jan-Hinrik Schmidt (eds.), *Proceedings of the 2008/2009 International Conference on Social Software: Recent Trends and Developments in Social Software* (BlogTalk 08/09), Berlin: Springer-Verlag, pp. 63–74.

Orsini, M. 2010 "Social media: how home health care agencies can join the chorus of empowered voices," *Home Health Care Management & Practice* 22(3): 213–17.

Otto, M. A. 2011 "Social media facilitate medical communication: experts debate risks and benefits of engaging in Twitter, Facebook, texting, and blogs," *Internal Medicine News* 44(2): 55.

Palen, L. 2008 "Online social media in crisis events," *EDUCAUSE Quarterly* 31(3): 76–8.

Palen, L., Starbird, K., Vieweg, S. and Hughes, A. 2010 "Twitter-based information distribution during the 2009 Red River Valley flood threat," *Bulletin of the American Society for Information Science and Technology* 36(5): 13–17.

Palser, B. 2009 "Amateur content's star turn," *American Journalism Review* 31(4): 42.

Papacharissi, Z. and Oliveira, M. d. F. 2011 "The rhythms of news storytelling on Twitter: coverage of the January 25th Egyptian uprising on Twitter," *World Association for Public Opinion Research Conference*, Amsterdam.

Papacharissi, Z. and Oliveira, M. d. F. 2012 "Affective news and networked publics: the rhythms of news storytelling on #Egypt," *Journal of Communication* 62(2): 266–82.

Pfeifle, M. 2009 "A Nobel Peace Prize for Twitter?," *Christian Science Monitor* (July 6): 9. Available at: <http://www.csmonitor.com/commentary/opinion/2009/0706/p09s02-coop.html>.

Philpott, D. 2001 *Revolutions in Sovereignty: How Ideas Shaped Modern International Relations*, Princeton, NJ: Princeton University Press.

Poell, T. and Borra, E. 2011 "Twitter, YouTube, and Flickr as platforms of alternative journalism: the social media account of the 2010 Toronto G20 protests," *Journalism*; available at: available at <http://jou.sagepub.com/content/early/2011/12/14/146488491143 1533.abstract>.

Polykalas, S. E. and Vlachos, K. G. 2006 "Broadband penetration and broadband competition: evidence and analysis in the EU market," *Info – The Journal of Policy, Regulation and Strategy for Telecommunications* 8: 15–30.

Prier, K. W., Smith, M. S., Giraud-Carrier, C., and Hanson, C. L. 2011 "Identifying health-related topics on twitter: an exploration of tobacco-related tweets as a test topic" *Proceedings of the 4th International Conference on Social Computing, Behavioral-Cultural Modeling and Prediction*, College Park, MD: Springer-Verlag.

Prince, S. H. 1920 "Catastrophe and social change: based upon a sociological study of the Halifax disaster," unpublished Ph.D. thesis, New York: Columbia University.

Purcell, K. 2011 "Half of adult cell phone owners have apps on their phones," in The Pew Internet and American Life Project, Washington, DC: Pew Research Center.

Putnam, R. D. 2000 *Bowling Alone: The Collapse and Revival of American Community*, New York: Simon & Schuster.

Rainie, L. and Wellman, B. 2012 *Networked: The New Social Operating System*, Cambridge, MA: MIT Press.

Rajani, R., Berman, D. S. and Rozanski, A. 2011 "Social networks – are they good for your health? The era of Facebook and Twitter," *QJM* 104(9): 819–20.

Raley, R. 2009 *Tactical Media*, Minneapolis, MN, and London: University of Minnesota Press.

Rebillard, F. and Touboul, A. 2010 "Promises unfulfilled? 'Journalism 2.0' user participation and editorial policy on newspaper websites," *Media Culture Society* 32(2): 323–34.

Reed, S. 2011 "Sports journalists use of social media and its effects on professionalism," *Journal of Sports Media* 6(2): 43–64.

Rettie, R. 2009 "Mobile phone communication: extending Goffman to mediated interaction," *Sociology* 43(3): 421–38.

Rheingold, H. 1993 *The Virtual Community: Homesteading on the Electronic Frontier*, Reading, MA: Addison-Wesley.

Riva, G. and Galimberti, C. 1998 "Computer-mediated communication: identity and social interaction in an electronic environment," *Genetic, Social and General Psychology Monographs* 124(4): 434–64.

Robertson, R. 1992 *Globalization: Social Theory and Global Culture*, London: Sage.

Rochon, P. A., Mashari, A., Cohen, A., Misra, A., Laxer, D., Streiner, D. L., Clark, J. P., Dergal, J. M., and Gold, J. 2004 "The inclusion of minority groups in clinical trials: problems of under representation and under reporting of data," *Accountability in Research* 11(3–4): 215–23.

Rosen, J. 2011 "The 'Twitter can't topple dictators' article," in J. Rosen (ed.), *PressThink*, vol. 2011, New York: Jay Rosen; available at: <http://pressthink.org/2011/02/the-twitter-cant-topple-dictators-article/>.

Rosenthal, A. 2008 "Gerald M. Phillips as electronic tribal chief: socio-forming cyberspace," in T. Adams and S. A. Smith (eds.), *Electronic Tribes: The Virtual Worlds of Geeks, Gamers, Shamans, and Scammers*, 1st edn., Austin, TX: University of Texas Press.

Salem, F. and Mourtada, R. 2011 "Civil movements: the impact of Facebook and Twitter," *Arab Social Media Report* 1(2): 1–29.

Saussure, F. d., Bally, C., Riedlinger, A., and Sechehaye, A. 1916 *Cours de linguistique generale*, Paris: Payot.

Schonfeld, E. 2011 "Twitter reaches 200 million tweets a day, but how many come from bots?," *Techcrunch*, at: <http://techcrunch.com/2011/06/30/twitter-3200-million-tweets/>.

Shah, N. 2008 "From global village to global marketplace: metaphorical descriptions of the global Internet," *International Journal of Media and Cultural Politics* 4(1): 9–26.

Shampine, A. L. 2003 *Down to the Wire: Studies in the Diffusion and Regulation of Telecommunications Technologies*, New York: Nova Science Publishers.

Shehata, D., El-Hamalawy, H., and Lynch, M. 2011 "Youth movements and social media: their role and impact," *From Tahrir: Revolution or Democratic Transition Conference*, Cairo, Egypt.

Sheldon, A. 1991 "Giving voice to the poor," *Foreign Policy* (84): 93–106.

Shirky, C. 2010 *Cognitive Surplus: Creativity and Generosity in a Connected Age*, New York: Penguin Press.

Shklovski, I., Palen, L., and Sutton, J. 2008 "Finding community through information and communication technology in disaster response," *Proceedings of the 2008 ACM Conference on Computer Supported Cooperative Work*, San Diego, CA, USA: ACM.

Siegle, L. 2005 "Armchair warrior," *The Observer* magazine, March 6, 2005, p. 55.

Singh, H., Fox, S. A., Petersen, N. J., Shethia, A., and Street, R. L. 2009 "Older patients' enthusiasm to use electronic mail to communicate with their physicians: cross-sectional survey," *Journal of Medical Internet Research* 11(2): 13.

Smith, A. 2012 "Nearly half of American adults are smartphone owners," in The Pew Internet and American Life Project, Washington, DC: Pew Research Center.

Snow, J. 2009 "So, can I like, twitter you some time?," *FREEwilliamsburg*, New York: FREEWilliamsburg; available at: <http://www.free williamsburg.com/so-can-i-like-twitter-you-some-time/>.

Sorokin, P. A. 1943 *Man and Society in Calamity: The Effects of War, Revolution, Famine, Pestilence upon Human Mind, Behavior, Social Organization and Cultural Life*, New York: E.P. Dutton & Company, Inc.

Spitzberg, B. H. 2006 "Preliminary development of a model and measure of computer-mediated communication (CMC) competence," *Journal of Computer-Mediated Communication* 11(2): 629–66.

Standage, T. 1998 *The Victorian Internet: The Remarkable Story of the Telegraph and the Nineteenth Century's On-line Pioneers*, New York: Walker and Co.

Steinberg, T. 2000 *Acts of God: The Unnatural History of Disasters in America*, New York: Oxford University Press.

Stephenson, R. and Anderson, P. S. 1997 "Disasters and the information technology revolution," *Disasters* 21(4): 305–34.

Strangelove, M. 2010 *Watching YouTube: Extraordinary Videos by Ordinary People*, Toronto and Buffalo, NY: University of Toronto Press.

Surowiecki, J. 2004 *The Wisdom of Crowds: Why the Many are Smarter than the Few and How Collective Wisdom Shapes Business, Economies, Societies, and Nations*, 1st edn., New York: Doubleday.

Sutton, J., Palen, L., and Shklovski, I. 2008 "Backchannels on the front lines: emergent uses of social media in the 2007 Southern California wildfires," *5th International ISCRAM Conference*, Washington, DC.

Tamura, Y. and Fukuda, K. 2011 "Earthquake in Japan," *The Lancet* 377(9778): 1652.

Terry, M. 2009 "Twittering healthcare: social media and medicine," *Telemedicine and e-Health* 15(6): 507–10.

Thaker, S. I., Nowacki, A. S., Mehta, N. B., and Edwards, A. R. 2011 "How U.S. hospitals use social media," *Annals of Internal Medicine* 154(10): 707–8.

Therborn, G. 2000 "At the birth of second century sociology: times of reflexivity, spaces of identity, and nodes of knowledge," *British Journal of Sociology* 51(1): 37–57.

Thomas, J. A. 2011 "Twitter: the sports media rookie," *Journal of Sports Media* 6(1): 115–20.

Thorsen, E. 2008 "Journalistic objectivity redefined? Wikinews and the neutral point of view," *New Media Society* 10(6): 935–54.

Time Magazine 2011 "The 2011 TIME 100," *Time Magazine* (May 2); available at: <http://www.time.com/time/specials/packages/arti cle/0,28804,2066367_2066369,00.html>.

Times, The 1796 "Yesterday a TELEGRAPH was erected over the Admiralty," vol. issue 3504, London: The Times.

Times, The 1900 "The Post Office (Letters to the Editor)," *The Times*, vol. issue 36250, London: The Times.

Tomlinson, H. 2011 "Online dissent has mobilised millions but found no leaders," *The Times*, 1st edn., London: Times Newspapers Ltd.

Toosi, N. 2011 "Young Pakistanis blog, tweet to push for change," *MSNBC.com* (June 16); available at: <http://www.msnbc.msn. com/id/43424657/ns/technology_and_science-tech_and_gadgets/t/ young-pakistanis-blog-tweet-push-change/>.

Tucker, C. 2011 "Social media, texting play new role in response to disasters: Preparedness, communication targeted," *The Nation's Health* 41(4): 1, 18.

Tucker, P. 2009 "The dawn of the postliterate age," *Futurist* 43(6): 41–5.

Turner, G. 2010 *Ordinary People and the Media: The Demotic Turn*, London: SAGE.

Twitter 2010 "2010 Year in review," at: <http://yearinreview.twitter. com/trends/>.

Twitter.com 2010 "2010 trends on Twitter," *Twitter.com*, San Francisco, CA: Twitter Inc.

United Nations Department of Economic and Social Affairs 2010 *World Statistics Pocketbook*, New York: United Nations.

Vance, K., Howe, W., and Dellavalle, R. P. 2009 "Social Internet sites as a source of public health information," *Dermatologic Clinics* 27(2): 133–6.

Victorian, B. 2010 "Nephrologists using social media connect with far-flung colleagues, health care consumers," *Nephrology Times* 3(1): 1, 16–18.

Vieweg, S., Hughes, A. L., Starbird, K., and Palen, L. 2010 "Microblogging during two natural hazards events: what twitter may contribute to situational awareness," *Proceedings of the 28th International Conference on Human Factors in Computing Systems*, Atlanta, GA: ACM.

Vitak, J., Zube, P., Smock, A., Carr, C. T., Ellison, N., and Lampe, C. 2011 "It's complicated: Facebook users' political participation in the 2008 election," *CyberPsychology, Behavior & Social Networking* 14(3): 107–14.

Wahl, A. 2006 "Red all over," *Canadian Business* 79(4): 53–4.

Wajcman, J. 2008 "Life in the fast lane? Towards a sociology of technology and time," *British Journal of Sociology* 59(1): 59–77.

Waldman, D. 1977 "Critical theory and film: Adorno and 'the culture industry' revisited," *New German Critique* (12): 39–60.

Walther, J. B. 1996 "Computer-mediated communication," *Communication Research* 23(1): 3–43.

Warf, B. 2011 "Myths, realities, and lessons of the Arab Spring," *The Arab World Geographer* 14(2): 166–8.

Warschauer, M. 2003 *Technology and Social Inclusion: Rethinking the Digital Divide*, Cambridge, MA: MIT Press.

Warschauer, M., Knobel, M., and Stone, L. 2004 "Technology and equity in schooling: deconstructing the digital divide," *Educational Policy* 18(4): 562–88.

Wasserman, T. 2012 "Twitter says it has 140 million users," Mashable.com.

Watts, D. J. 2003 *Six Degrees: The Science of a Connected Age*, 1st edn., New York: Norton.

Weaver, M. 2010a "Special report: Iran: social media: the 'Twitter revolution' that never materialised," *Guardian*, June 10, 2010, p. 19, London: Guardian Newspapers Limited.

Weaver, M. 2010b "Twitter: Ahmadinejad's nemesis, online from Oxfordshire," *Guardian*, February 11, 2010, p. 17, London: Guardian Newspapers Limited.

Wellman, B. 1999 *Networks in the Global Village: Life in Contemporary Communities*, Boulder, CO: Westview Press.

Wellman, B. and Haythornthwaite, C. (eds.) 2002 *The Internet in Everyday Life*, Oxford: Blackwell.

Williams, R. and Williams, E. 1990 *Television: Technology and Cultural Form*, 2nd edn., ed. Ederyn Williams. London: Routledge.

Witte, J. C. and Mannon, S. E. 2010 *The Internet and Social inequalities*, 1st edn., New York: Routledge.

World Bank, The 2010 "World development indicators," Washington, DC: The World Bank.

Yan, Qu, Philip Fei Wu, and Xiaoqing Wang 2009 "Online community response to major disaster: a study of Tianya Forum in the 2008 Sichuan earthquake," *Hawaii International Conference on System Sciences*, pp. 1–11, 42nd Hawaii International Conference on System Sciences, January 2009, Waikoloa, Big Island, Hawaii.

Yuan, Y. C. and Gay, G. 2006 "Homophily of network ties and bonding and bridging social capital in computer-mediated distributed teams," *Journal of Computer-Mediated Communication* 11(4): 1062–84.

Zeichick, A. 2009 "A-twitter over Twitter," *netWorker* 13(1): 5–7.

Zhuo, X., Wellman, B., and Yu, J. 2011 "Egypt: the first Internet revolt?," *Peace Magazine* 27(3): 6.

Zickuhr, K. and Smith, A. 2011 "28% of American adults use mobile and social location-based services," in The Pew Internet and American Life Project, Washington, DC: Pew Research Center.

Index

Page numbers for illustrations are shown in italics.

The Future of
Global Oil Production

*Facts, Figures, Trends and
Projections, by Region*

ROGER D. BLANCHARD

I.C.C. LIBRARY

McFarland & Company, Inc., Publishers
Jefferson, North Carolina, and London

HD
9560
.B49
2005

LIBRARY OF CONGRESS CATALOGUING-IN-PUBLICATION DATA

Blanchard, Roger D., 1953–
    The future of global oil production : facts, figures, trends and
projections, by region / Roger D. Blanchard.
        p.   cm.
    Includes bibliographical references and index.

    ISBN 0-7864-2357-9 (softcover : 50# alkaline paper) ∞

    1. Petroleum industry and trade.   2. Petroleum industry and
trade — Forecasting.   I. Title.
    HD9560.B49   2006
    333.8'2320112 — dc22   2005029543

British Library cataloguing data are available

©2005 Roger D. Blanchard. All rights reserved

No part of this book may be reproduced or transmitted in any form
or by any means, electronic or mechanical, including photocopying
or recording, or by any information storage and retrieval system,
without permission in writing from the publisher.

Cover photograph © 2005 Digital Vision

Manufactured in the United States of America

McFarland & Company, Inc., Publishers
    Box 611, Jefferson, North Carolina 28640
    www.mcfarlandpub.com

Contents

1/06 B&T 29.95

Abbreviations in Figures and Tables

ANWR	Arctic National Wildlife Refuge
b	barrels
btu	British thermal unit
/d	per day
DEA	Danish Energy Authority
EUR	estimated ultimate recovery
FSU	former Soviet Union
Gb	billion barrels
GOM	Gulf of Mexico
J	joules
kJ	kilojoules
mb	million barrels
MMS	Minerals Management Service
NGLs	natural gas liquids
NPD	Norwegian Petroleum Directorate
NPR-A	National Petroleum Reserve-Alaska
OPEC	Organization of Petroleum Exporting Countries
prod.	production
psi	pounds per square inch
Qbtu	Quadrillion British thermal units
TLHs	total liquid hydrocarbons
UAE	United Arab Emirates (Abu Dhabi and Dubai)
UK	United Kingdom
US	United States
US DOE/EIA	United States Department of Energy/Energy Information Administration
USGS	United States Geological Survey
WEC	World Energy Council
WTI	West Texas Intermediate
/y	per year

Introduction

Writing a book that thoroughly and accurately assesses future global oil production is quite a challenge, for several reasons. First, most countries provide only sparse field level oil production data, making it difficult to assess the status of their oil fields. Second, they provide oil reserves data that are essentially worthless. Third, the United States Geological Survey (USGS), which assesses global oil resources, appears to provide overly optimistic estimates of undiscovered resources and reserves growth. Drawing on these USGS assessments, the United States Department of Energy/ Energy Information Administration (US DOE/EIA) provides overly optimistic projections of future global oil production.

Oil reserves data are published in *Oil & Gas Journal* and *World Oil*, but the data come from the governments of the associated countries. Many national governments are motivated to inflate data for various reasons. To make matters worse, many countries do not update their oil reserves data, so the same data are published year after year even though production should reduce reserves if replacement oil is not discovered. A further problem is that there is no universally agreed upon definition for oil reserves, and different countries use different definitions.

In the U.S., reported reserves have to conform to the requirements of the Securities and Exchange Commission (SEC). In accordance with SEC rules, only proven reserves are reported. Proven reserves correspond to the volume of oil that oil companies are sure can be extracted at the time of reporting. Proven reserves represent less than what will ultimately be extracted because they don't include probable reserves. Probable reserves are reserves beyond proven reserves that can probably be extracted before production is terminated. The underreporting of reserves, due to the lack of inclusion of probable reserves, leads to "reserves growth" as oil that has not been previously reported as proven reserves gets added to that category. Some governments report proven + probable reserves, but that is rare.

1

Besides global oil resource assessments, the USGS also provides technically recoverable oil resource assessments for the U.S., excluding federal offshore waters. The Minerals Management Service (MMS) provides oil resource assessments for federal offshore waters. The estimates that the USGS and MMS provide for U.S. oil resources are very impressive, although evidence indicates that they are highly inflated relative to expected ultimate recovery. Chapter 1, "Oil Production in the United States," explores the latest assessment by the USGS and compares it to what recent oil production history suggests will ultimately be extracted.

Members of the Organization of Petroleum Exporting Countries (OPEC) reported huge increases in oil reserves during the second half of the 1980s (see Table 1).

Little new oil was discovered by members of OPEC during that period, so why did they report large increases in reserves? In the middle 1980s, the price of oil dropped dramatically, and that led to a decline in OPEC oil revenues. Within OPEC, oil production quotas are tied to oil reserves. To bring in more money after the oil price collapse, members of OPEC increased their reported reserves, which increased their production quotas. The term "political reserves" has been coined to represent the inflated reserves by members of OPEC. In the pages of *Oil & Gas Journal* and *World Oil*, oil reserves for members of OPEC carry the same weight as those from the U.S.

During the recent U.S.–Iraq war (2003) and its aftermath, the media frequently reported that Iraq had oil reserves of 112 Gb (Gb represents

Table 1— Reported Reserves for OPEC Countries
(data from Campbell, "The Imminent Peak of World Oil Production")

Year	Iran	Iraq	Kuwait	Saudi Arabia	Venezuela	U.A.E.
1980	58.0	31.0	65.4	163.3	17.9	29.4
1981	57.5	30.0	65.9	165.0	18.0	30.4
1982	57.0	29.7	64.5	164.6	20.3	31.9
1983	55.3	41.0	64.2	162.4	21.5	31.9
1984	51.0	43.0	63.9	166.0	24.9	31.8
1985	48.5	44.5	90.0	169.0	25.9	31.9
1986	47.9	44.1	89.9	166.8	25.6	32.4
1987	48.8	47.1	91.9	166.6	25.0	32.4
1988	93.0	100.0	91.9	167.0	56.3	96.2
1989	92.9	100.0	91.9	167.0	58.0	96.2
1990	92.9	100.0	94.5	257.5	59.0	96.2
1995	88.2	100.0	94.0	258.7	64.5	96.5

Estimates of Most Probable Reserves by PetroConsultants Inc. (1996)

Year	Iran	Iraq	Kuwait	Saudi Arabia	Venezuela	U.A.E.
1996	64.7	77.4	52.0	222.6	27.4	58.7

"gigabarrel," one billion barrels). In 1987, Iraq reported reserves of 47.1 Gb, but the value was increased to 100 Gb in 1988. Reported reserves remained at 100 Gb until 1996, when the value was increased to 112 Gb. Since 1996, Iraq's reported reserves have remained around 112 Gb. During the period 1980–2002, Iraq's reserves figures came from the Saddam Hussein government, not necessarily the most trustworthy source of data and information. In 1996, Petroconsultants Inc. was reporting Iraq's oil reserves as 77.4 Gb. Petroconsultants and its recently restructured entity, the IHS Group, have maintained oil field data for countries throughout the world over many years. The Petroconsultants estimate of Iraq's reserves seems to have missed the media's attention even though it's probably a more reasonable estimate. The 112 Gb figure is more impressive and maybe that's why it attracted so much media attention.

For oil reserves data to be valid, a universally recognized definition and independent assessments would be required. Reserves figures would have to be updated by subtracting annual production. Many countries would never submit to those requirements, because governments benefit from the opaqueness of the present method of reporting reserves.

In recent years, global oil reserves have been reported in *Oil & Gas Journal* and *World Oil* as being greater than 1000 Gb.[1] The U.S. media occasionally report the global oil reserves figure as a means of assuring the public that all is well with oil supplies. The validity of national oil reserves figures should call into question the validity of the global total.

Oil Definitions

Oil, as defined in this book, consists of crude oil + condensate. It is composed of a mixture of hydrocarbons, compounds containing carbon and hydrogen, with carbon chain lengths in the range of ~ 5 to ~15 carbons. **Condensate** consists of gaseous hydrocarbons in the ground which condense when brought to the surface.

Production data for crude oil typically include condensate, but not always. Sometimes data sources don't state explicitly what is included in their production figures. Adding to the confusion, different sources of production data can have significantly different production values. As an example, the US DOE/EIA publishes oil production data for U.S. states, as does *Oil & Gas Journal*. In the case of coastal states, the values can be dramatically different. The most extreme example is that of Louisiana, for which the US DOE/EIA reported production as 256,000 b/d in 2002 while *Oil & Gas Journal* reported 1,501,110 b/d.[2,3] The difference between the two values is the amount of production from federal offshore waters, which *Oil & Gas Journal* includes but the US DOE/EIA doesn't. Neither source specifies whether they included production from federal waters.

When media sources report data concerning oil production, they typically aren't clear about what is included in the production figures they report. Figures can include crude oil, condensate, natural gas liquids, refinery gain and other hydrocarbon liquids or any combination of those components. Typically what they report is the production for all of the components mentioned above.

Natural gas liquids (NGLs) consist of the heavier hydrocarbon components of natural gas that are condensed out at natural gas processing plants. Natural gas consists mainly of methane, a one-carbon hydrocarbon, but there can be hydrocarbon components with chain-lengths up to ~5.

A **refinery** is a facility that separates oil into fractions such as gasoline, kerosene, fuel oil, etc. The refining process is accomplished by heating the oil and condensing out different fractions at different temperatures. **Refinery gain** arises from the refinery products being less dense than the input crude oil. This leads to a gain in volume.

Other hydrocarbon liquids consist mainly of alcohol components that are used for fuel purposes. Methanol, a one-carbon alcohol, and ethanol, a two-carbon alcohol, are used in pure form as fuel or as a fuel additive to make mixtures such as gasohol.

Total liquid hydrocarbons (TLHs), as defined in this book, consist of crude oil, condensate, natural gas liquids, refinery gain and other hydrocarbon liquids. In 2003, global oil production was ~69 mb/d, while TLHs production was ~79 mb/d.[4] Oil makes up about 86% of global TLHs production. In the U.S., domestic oil production only makes up ~65% of TLHs production because NGLs and refinery gain production values are so high.

Conventional oil, as defined in this book, is oil that either flows out of the ground as a result of reservoir pressure or can be pumped out of the ground. It does not include oil production that requires steam stimulation for extraction, such as extra heavy oil and "in situ" oil sands production. In conventional oil production, reservoir pressure is often enhanced with the injection of water or gas.

Unconventional oil, as defined in this book, includes extra heavy oil and oil obtained from tar sands, oil shale and coal. Getting oil from unconventional sources may require steam injection for extraction, extensive processing or chemical conversion. Unconventional oil production is generally expensive, energy intensive and not conducive to high production rates. Conventional oil production, by contrast, is generally cheap, not energy intensive and conducive to high production rates. Most oil obtained to date is from conventional oil sources. The most extensively developed unconventional oil source is the Athabasca Oil Sands in Alberta, Canada (see Chapter 3).

An important term relative to oil production is **estimated ultimate recovery (EUR)**. EUR is the ultimate amount of oil that is expected to have been extracted from an oil field, oil basin, state, country, or other area when oil production is terminated.

Oftentimes, governments and oil companies report volumes of oil for discoveries in terms of **oil-in-place**, although they don't clearly specify the reported volume as such. Oil-in-place represents the total volume, every drop, of oil in a reservoir. Oil-in-place values can be very impressive, but the volumes of recoverable oil will be considerably less than the oil-in-place values. It appears that the purpose of reporting oil-in-place values is to deceive investors or the public about how much oil will ultimately be extracted from fields.

A barrel of oil contains 42 U.S. gallons. Prefixes are used to express large numbers of barrels. A gigabarrel represents a billion barrels and is abbreviated **Gb**. A megabarrel represents a million barrels and is abbreviated mb. In this book, volumes of oil will be expressed as barrels, **mb** or Gb. Production rates will be expressed as barrels/day (b/d), thousand barrels/day (tb/d) or million barrels/day (mb/d).

Oil fields are classified by size corresponding to their EUR values. Table 2 provides an oil field size identification list.

According to L.F. Ivanhoe et al., approximately 94% of all conventional oil that had been discovered as of January 1, 1990, was originally contained in 1331 fields larger than 100 mb.[5] It's the larger oil fields that really matter in terms of global oil production. A mere 120 of the world's largest oil fields produced ~32 mb/d of oil in 2000, almost half of the world's daily production that year. The world's 15 largest oil fields produced approximately 22% of the world's daily oil production in 2000.[6]

Table 3 contains oil production data for fields that produced at least 300,000 b/d as of 2000. Only 5 of the 26 fields in Table 3 were discovered after 1970 and only 1 after 1980. For the pre–1970 fields in Table 3, summed production was over 14,000,000 b/d, ~21% of the world's daily production in 2000. The top 4 fields in Table 3 produced ~12% of the world's daily supply in 2000 while the post-1970 fields produced ~5%.

Most of the world's supergiant and megagiant fields were discovered long ago, and with few exceptions, fields found in the last 15 years have been much smaller. There are several projects under development or in the planning stages that will ultimately produce at least 300,000 b/d (see

Table 2 — Oil Field Size Identification

Field Size Identification	EUR Range (Gb)
Megagiant	> 50
Supergiant	5 — 50
Giant	0.5 — 5
Major	0.1 — 0.5
Large	0.05 — 0.1
Medium	0.025 — 0.05
Small	0.01 — 0.025
Very Small	0.001 — 0.01
Tiny	0.0001 — 0.001
Insignificant	0 — 0.0001

Table 4), but they will not be able to maintain production at a high level for the extended periods that the old supergiant and megagiant fields were able to.

Even very large oil fields ultimately decline, and several of the fields in Table 3 have experienced significantly production declines. For example, the Prudhoe Bay field has declined 73.2% and the Samotlor field about 91% since their highest production rates in the late 1980s. As Prudhoe Bay and Samotlor fields illustrate, when large fields decline, they can decline rapidly. In the case of the Prudhoe Bay field, gas is now injected into the field and the number of wells has almost tripled since the 1980s, yet production continues to decline (see Chapter 1).

Numerous other fields listed in Table 3 are already declining, possibly declining, or should soon start declining. In China, the Daqing field (#4) has been declining for several years and will drop below 1 mb/d in 2003. The Venezuelan fields in Table 3 are producing significantly less than they were in the 1970s. Production from the Cantarell (#2) and Marlim (#10) fields has increased rapidly in recent years but will soon start declining. It appears that the Troll (#20) and Ekofisk (#23) fields reached peak production in 2002. Unfortunately, there is little publicly available data of oil production rates for Middle East fields listed in Table 3 to determine their production status.

Megagiant and supergiant fields contain immense volumes of oil. The Ghawar field, Saudi Arabia, is the largest field ever discovered, with an EUR of possibly 110–120 Gb.[7] The second largest field, the Burgan field in Kuwait, has an EUR of ~70 Gb.[8] To place those volumes in perspective, the world presently consumes ~78 mb of TLHs each day, or about 28 Gb a year.

Table 4 contains a list of projects that should reach a production rate of at least 300,000 b/d. Most of the fields involved are in the Middle East.

Table 3 — The World's Top Producing Oil Fields
(most data in Table 3 are from Simmons, "The World's Giant Oilfields." Prudhoe Bay data are from the Alaska Department of Revenue, Troll and Ekofisk data are from the Norwegian Petroleum Directorate, Daqing and Shengli data are from *Oil & Gas Journal*, and Marlim field data are from Jean Laherrere. Some of the estimated maximum production values are from *Oil & Gas Journal*.)

Field, Country	Discovery Date	Daily Production (b/d)	Estimated Maximum Production (b/d)
1. Ghawar, Saudi Arabia	1948	4,500,000 (2000)	6,300,000
2. Cantarell, Mexico	1976	1,879,000 (2002)	1,879,000
3. Burgan, Kuwait	1938	1,500,000 (2000)	1,800,000
4. Daqing, China	1959	1,006,000 (2002)	1,108,000
5. Kirkuk, Iraq	1927	900,000 (2000)	1,500,000
6. Rumailia North, Iraq	1958	700,000 (2000)	1,200,000
7. Abqaig, Saudi Arabia	1940	600,000 (2000)	800,000
8. Shayba, Saudi Arabia	1975	600,000 (2000)	600,000
9. Shengli, China	1962	534,000 (2000)	673,000
10. Marlim, Brazil	1985	521,000 (2001)	521,000
11. Safaniyah, Saudi Arabia	1951	500,000 (2000)	1,250,000
12. Zuluf, Saudi Arabia	1965	500,000 (2000)	600,000
13. Rumailia South, Iraq	1953	500,000 (2000)	≥800,000
14. Bu Hasa, Abu Dhabi	1962	450,000 (2000)	≥680,000
15. Prudhoe Bay, U.S.A.	1968	415,000 (2002)	1,550,000
16. Berri, Saudi Arabia	1964	400,000 (2000)	800,000
17. Zakum-Lower, Abu Dhabi	1963	400,000 (2000)	unknown
18. Zakum-Upper, Abu Dhabi	1963	400,000 (2000)	unknown
19. Lagunillas, Venezuela	1925	396,000 (1996)	≥940,000
20. Troll, Norway	1979	365,000 (2002)	365,000
21. Samotlor, Russia	1961	320,000 (2000)	3,500,000
22. Bachaquero, Venezuela	1930	310,000 (1996)	≥739,000
23. Ekofisk, Norway	1971	300,000 (2002)	300,000
24. Gachsaran, Iran	1937	300,000 (2000)	≥911,000
25. Ahwaz Bangestan, Iran	1958	300,000 (2000)	≥1,090,000
26. Khafji, Neutral Zone	1961	300,000 (2000)	unknown

Table 4 — Major Planned Oil Projects
(from Simmons "The World's Giant Oilfields")

Field	Country	Estimated Peak Production (b/d)
1. Azadegan	Iran	300,000–400,000
2. Desht-e-Abadan	Iran	unknown
3. West Qurna	Iraq	possibly 400,000
4. Rataw	Iraq	possibly 600,000
5. Nahr Umar	Iraq	400,000–500,000
6. Qatif Expansion	Saudi Arabia	possibly 500,000
7. Khurais Rehabilitation	Saudi Arabia	possibly 800,000
8. Priobskoye	Russia	550,000
9. Ghadames	Algeria	300,000
10. Kashagan	Kazakhstan	1,200,000
11. ACG Megastructure	Azerbaijan	1,000,000

Energy Profit Ratio

Possibly the most important aspect of any energy source used by humans is energy profit ratio, EPR. It is the ratio of the energy content of a fuel relative to the energy needed to obtain the fuel.

$$EPR = \frac{\text{energy content of fuel}}{\text{energy needed to obtain fuel}}$$

The higher the EPR value for a fuel, the higher the net energy yield for the fuel and the more valuable the fuel is. Conventional oil, coal and natural gas have high EPR values relative to other fuels. The EPR value for 1970s U.S. oil production was 23.0 according to Gever et al.[9] The fact that so many U.S. oil wells are now marginal stripper wells (wells that produce less than 10 barrels/day) means that the EPR value for U.S. oil production would be much lower today. By comparison, the EPR for oil obtained from Athabasca Oil Sands is only 1.5 according to Walter Youngquist.[10] The 1.5 value means that for every three barrels of oil produced from Athabasca Oil Sands, it requires the energy equivalent of 2 barrels of oil to produce it. There is a lot of hype concerning future use of hydrogen as a fuel source. One problem with hydrogen is that the EPR is much less than 1, meaning much more energy is needed to produce the hydrogen than the energy content of the hydrogen produced. Table 5 lists some published EPR values.

It's the relative values in Table 5 that should be considered important rather than their accuracy. According to the US DOE, ethanol obtained from corn has an EPR value of 1.35. David Pimental estimates the EPR value for ethanol obtained from corn at <1. Whatever the actual EPR value for ethanol obtained from corn, at best it provides a low net energy yield relative to conventional fossil fuels.

U.S. Energy Supply

Table 6 contains U.S. energy supply data for 1990, 1995 and 2000 based upon energy source. The values in Table 6 are in quadrillion (1 x 10^{15}) Btu (British Thermal Units), which probably doesn't mean much to most people. In terms of TLHs, U.S. consumption in 2000 was 19.7 mb/d, or about 7.2 Gb/y. That was nearly 30% of global TLHs consumption in 2000. In 2003, the U.S. is expected to consume ~20.3 mb/d, or ~7.4 Gb/y. For natural gas, U.S. consumption was 23.45 trillion cubic feet (tcf) in 2000, 26.4% of the world's total. For coal, U.S. consumption was 1.084 billion tons in 2000, 21.3% of the world's total.[11]

Table 5 — Energy Profit Ratio Values for Various Fuels
(Gever et al., *Beyond Oil: The Threat of Food and Fuel in the Coming Decades*; Shapouri et al., "Estimating the Net Energy Balance of Corn Ethanol"; Pimentel, "Energy and Dollar Costs of Ethanol Production with Corn" Youngquist, Geodestinies.)

Fuel Source	*Energy Profit Ratio*
Oil and Gas (Domestic Wellhead)	
1940s	Discoveries >100.0 (Gever et al.)
1970s	Production 23.0, Discoveries 8.0 (Gever et al.)
Coal	
1950s	80.0 (Gever et al.)
1970s	30.0 (Gever et al.)
Ethanol (from sugarcane)	0.8–1.7 (Gever et al.)
Ethanol (from corn)	1.35 (Shapouri et al.), <1 (Pimentel)
Oil Shale (western Colorado, U.S.)	~1 (Youngquist)
Oil Sands (Athabasca Region, Canada)	1.5 (Youngquist)
Hydrogen from Water	<<1*

* Based upon basic principles of thermodynamics, more energy must be consumed to make H_2 than the energy obtained by oxidizing the H_2.

Table 6 — U.S. Energy Supply (Qbtu)
(data from the US DOE/EIA, http://www.eia.doe.gov/)

Energy Source	*1990*	*1995*	*2000*
Solar Energy*	0.063	0.073	0.075
Wind	0.032	0.033	0.051
TLHs	33.55	34.55	37.96
Natural Gas	19.30	22.16	23.11
Coal	19.25	20.02	22.41
Hydroelectric	3.11	3.45	3.05
Wood	2.19	2.42	2.60
Nuclear	6.16	7.18	8.01
Total	83.66	89.89	97.26

*Includes solar thermal and solar photovoltaic.

Growth of total energy consumption was 16.3% from 1990 to 2000 for the U.S., while growth of TLHs consumption was 13.1% for the same period. Table 7 distinguishes U.S. energy supply in terms of source percentage composition values for 1990, 1995 and 2000.

What Table 7 illustrates is that TLHs, coal and natural gas make up the bulk of U.S. energy supply and that there was no significant change in percent composition of energy sources from 1990 to 2000. TLHs, coal and natural gas provided 89.03% of total U.S. energy supply in 2000, up from 86.18% in 1990. Environmentalists talk extensively about solar and wind energy becoming significant energy sources in the future, but the data in Table 7 show that they make up a minute amount of U.S. energy supply

Table 7 — U.S. Energy Supply (% Composition)
(data from the US DOE/EIA, http://www.eia.doe.gov/)

Energy Source	1990	1995	2000
Solar Energy*	0.075	0.081	0.071
Wind	0.038	0.037	0.052
TLHs	40.10	38.44	42.23
Natural Gas	23.07	24.65	23.76
Coal	23.01	22.27	23.04
Hydroelectric	3.72	3.84	3.14
Wood	2.62	2.69	2.67
Nuclear	7.36	7.99	8.24

*Includes solar thermal and solar photovoltaic.

and that their contribution is growing at a snail's pace. In 1990, solar and wind energy provided 0.11% of total U.S. energy supply. In 2000, solar and wind energy provided 0.12% of total U.S. energy supply. The US DOE/EIA projects that in 2025 solar and wind energy will provide 1% of total U.S. energy supply.[12]

Table 8 contains data of changes in U.S. energy supply by source from 1990 to 2000. TLHs, coal and natural gas provided the dominant increases. The use of solar energy increased 0.16% while wind energy increased 0.43% relative to TLHs. Solar and wind energy will not contribute significantly to U.S. energy supply anytime soon.

Total U.S. energy consumption increased from 9.58 QBtu in 1900 to 97.05 QBtu in 2001, a factor of ~10.[13] The US DOE/EIA is projecting that total U.S. energy consumption will increase to 139.07 QBtu in 2025, a 43.3% increase over 2001.[14] Figure 1 is a graph of historical and projected total U.S. energy consumption from 1900 through 2025. Historical data are from 1900 through 2001. The oil crisis of 1973 led to a decrease in U.S. energy consumption for a few years, and the oil crisis of the late 1970s and early 1980s led to a decrease in consumption from 1979 to 1983. The oil crises led to the creation of Corporate Average Fuel Economy (CAFE) standards for motor vehicles, a shift in electrical power generation from oil to coal, and a large decrease in oil use for space heating. Those measures helped reduce U.S. total liquid hydrocarbons demand by several million barrels/day.

Figure 2 is a graph containing historical and projected U.S. total liquid hydrocarbons consumption, as well as U.S. field production of oil + natural gas liquids. Historical consumption data are from 1900 through 2001 and production data are for the period 1949–2001. Figure 2 illustrates the growing gap between TLHs consumption and field production of liquid hydrocarbons in the U.S. The forecast of TLHs consumption indicates that the gap will expand in the future.

Table 8 — Changes in U.S. Energy Supply by Source (1990 to 2000)
(data from the US DOE/EIA, http://www.eia.doe.gov/)

Energy Source	% Increase Relative Energy Increase (Qbtu)	to TLHs Increase
Solar Energy**	0.007	0.16
Wind	0.019	0.43
TLHs	4.41	-
Natural Gas	3.81	86.39
Coal	3.16	71.66
Hydroelectric	-0.06	-1.36
Wood	0.42	9.52
Nuclear	1.85	41.95

*Includes solar thermal and solar photovoltaic.

World Energy Supply

Table 9 contains data for world energy supply by source for 1990, 1995 and 2000. Total global energy supply increased by 12.3% from 1990 to 2000, while TLHs supply increased by 13.9%. The largest increases in energy supply occurred in the category Other (36.0%), hydroelectric (21.8%) and natural gas (19.7%). Coal use decreased by 1.9% from 1990 to 2000.

Table 10 contains percentage composition values of world energy supply by source for 1990, 1995 and 2000.

Total liquid hydrocarbons, natural gas and coal made up 85.3% of total global energy consumption in 2000, down from 86.8% in 1990.

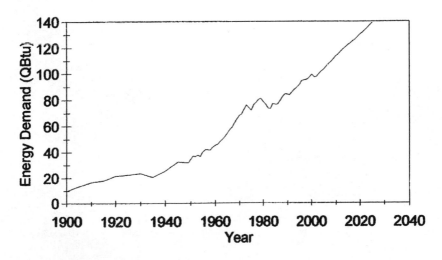

Figure 1— Historical and projected U.S. total energy consumption (data from the US DOE/EIA).

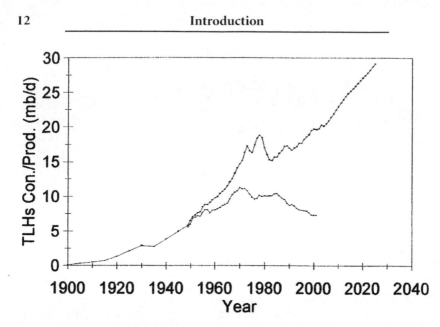

Figure 2 — U.S. total liquid hydrocarbons consumption (upper line) and field production of oil + natural gas liquids (lower line) (data from the US DOE/EIA).

Figure 3 is a graph of historical and projected total global energy consumption. Total global energy consumption increased from ~35 QBtu in 1900 to 404.0 QBtu in 2001, a factor of ~10 increase. The US DOE/EIA

Table 9 — World Energy Supply by Source (QBtu)
(data from the US DOE/EIA, http://www.eia.doe.gov/)

Energy Source	1990	1995	2000
TLHs	136.35	141.48	155.25
Natural Gas	75.91	80.26	90.83
Coal	94.29	91.84	92.51
Hydroelectric	22.55	25.70	27.46
Nuclear	20.31	23.21	25.52
Other			
(Geothermal, Solar, Wind, Wood and Waste Electric)	3.94	4.78	5.36
Total	353.35	367.27	396.93

Table 10 — World Energy Supply by Source (%)
(data from the US DOE/EIA, http://www.eia.doe.gov/)

Energy Source	1990	1995	2000
TLHs	38.59	38.52	39.11
Natural Gas	21.48	21.85	22.88
Coal	26.68	25.01	23.31
Hydroelectric	6.38	7.00	6.92
Nuclear	5.75	6.32	6.43
Other			
(Geothermal, Solar, Wind, Wood and Waste Electric)	1.12	1.30	1.35

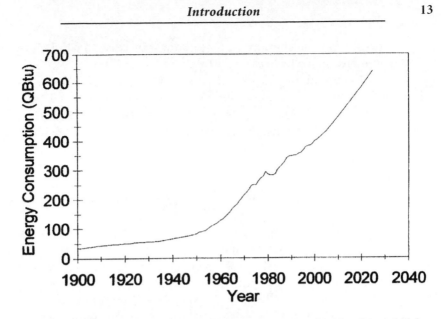

Figure 3 — Historical and projected total global energy consumption (historical data from Jean Laherrere [1900–1969] and US DOE/EIA [1970–2025]).

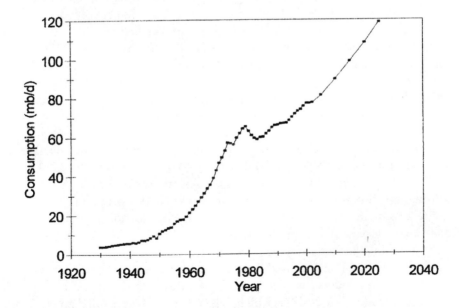

Figure 4 — Historical and projected global TLHs consumption. (historical data from Colin Campbell [1930–1969] and the US DOE/EIA [1970–2001]).

projects that total global energy consumption will increase to 640.1 QBtu in 2025, an increase of 58.5% over 2001.[15]

Figure 4 is a graph of historical and projected global TLHs consumption from 1930 to 2025. Global TLHs consumption increased from 3.72 mb/d in 1930 to 77.12 mb/d in 2001, a factor of ~21. The US DOE/EIA projects that global TLHs consumption will increase to 118.8 mb/d in 2025, an increase of 54.0% over 2001.[16]

The Importance of Oil

Environmentalists like to claim that oil can be easily replaced by other forms of energy, particularly solar and wind, that don't have the environmental consequences of oil. After the oil crises of the 1970s, there was an unprecedented level of energy research in the U.S., which can be appreciated by looking at issues of *Chemical & Engineering News* during the late 1970s and early 1980s. When the price of oil declined in the middle 1980s, the level of energy research dropped with it. In spite of all the energy research that was conducted during the late 1970s and early 1980s, there was no significant change in the percent composition of our energy sources. Through the 1980s and 1990s, environmentalists rallied around electric vehicles as a replacement for petroleum-fueled vehicles. General Motors introduced the EV1 electric vehicle in 1996 to offer Americans an electric vehicle option. Production of the EV1 was terminated in 2000 after few vehicles were sold or leased. Now environmentalists have rallied around hybrid and fuel cell vehicles. The possible impacts of those vehicles, as well as other alternatives to conventional oil use, are evaluated in Chapter 10. Why haven't alternative forms of energy or alternative transportation systems replaced oil use up to this point? What makes oil so valuable?

First, because oil is a liquid, it is easily transported at high rates through pipelines or in large volumes on ships. The Alaskan oil pipeline, ~4 feet in diameter, carried ~2 mb/d when oil production peaked from the North Slope of Alaska in the late 1980s. An Ultra Large Crude Carrier (ULCC) oil tanker can carry ~1 mb of oil across seas.

Second, in the early to middle stages of a large conventional oil fields life, oil can be produced at high production rates with the application of very little work; the EPR is very high. The Ghawar field, Saudi Arabia, is producing ~4.5 mb/d, while the Burgan field, Kuwait, is producing ~1.5 mb/d. Very little effort or energy is expended in producing oil from those fields relative to the amount of energy obtained. Even for smaller fields, the EPR is high relative to the EPR of other fuels.

Table 11— Enthalpy of Combustion Values for Various Fuels
(enthalpy data were obtained from Petrucci et al., *General Chemistry: Principles and Modern Applications*, 2001)

Fuel	Enthalpy of Combustion (Kilojoules/mole*)
Octane	-5103
Ethanol	-1278
Methanol	-638
Hydrogen	-286

A joule is a unit of energy and a mole of molecules consists of 6.02 × 10²³ molecules

Table 12 — Energy Densities for Common Fuels
(enthalpy data were obtained from Petucci et al.)

Fuel Source	Energy Density (kJ/gallon)	% Relative to Octane
Octane	118,690	–
Ethanol	82,958	69.9
Methanol	59,579	50.2
H_2 (at 5000 psi and 25.0°C)	6,020	12.8
CH_4 (at 5000 psi and 25.0°C)	16,888	35.5

Third, the hydrocarbon components of oil have very high enthalpy of combustion values. Enthalpy of combustion is the amount of energy released when a specific amount of substance is burned. Table 11 compares the enthalpy of combustion for octane, a component of oil, with enthalpy of combustion values for other fuels.

Based upon the data in Table 11, it would take about 18 times more hydrogen molecules, 8 times more methanol molecules and 4 times more ethanol molecules to obtain the same amount of energy obtained from octane.

Fourth, the energy density, energy/unit volume, of oil components is much higher than that for other fuels. The high energy density of oil components makes them particularly valuable as transportation fuels due to the small volume required for containing a high energy content. Table 12 has energy density values for various fuels.

The energy densities of H_2 and CH_4 are much lower than octane because they are gases. In gases, the molecules are much farther apart than in a liquid, even when gases are compressed to very high pressure. The low energy densities of gaseous fuels make them poor choices for transportation applications even if they are compressed. For vehicles powered by gaseous fuels, the fuel tanks must be much larger, the vehicle must get much better mileage per unit of fuel, the vehicle must be refilled more frequently, or some combination of the three must be used.

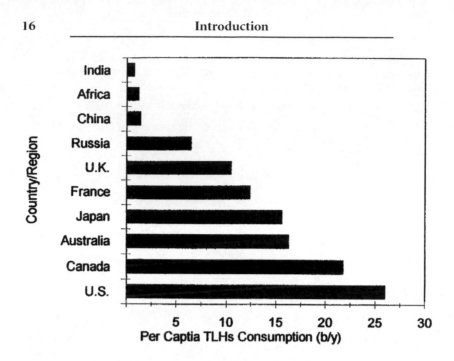

Figure 5 — Per capita TLHs consumption for selected countries and Africa (energy data from the US DOE/EIA, population data from GeoHive: Global Statistics).

Uses of Oil

The main use of oil in the U.S. is for transportation, where about 66% of the oil supply is used. Over 95% of all transportation in the U.S. is fueled with oil, the remainder being mainly electric powered trains and subways. About 26% of the U.S. oil supply is used by industry as a feedstock in the petrochemical industry, to power industrial equipment or for heating purposes. Industrial equipment includes bulldozers, road graters, cranes, tractors, etc. Logging, construction, trucking, air transportation and agriculture rely heavily on oil to power the equipment used in those industries. Residential and commercial use of oil accounts for about 7% of total U.S. demand. Natural gas is more popular than oil for space heating purposes, but oil is still widely used in New England and the Middle Atlantic states. At one time substantial amounts of oil were used for electrical generation in the U.S., but since the oil crises of the 1970s, oil use for that purpose has been dramatically curtailed. Today only about 1% of the U.S. electrical supply is generated from oil.[17]

The U.S. uses the highest per capita level of TLHs of any industrialized country in the world. Per capita TLHs consumption for developing countries is considerably less than for developed countries, as Figure 5 illustrates.

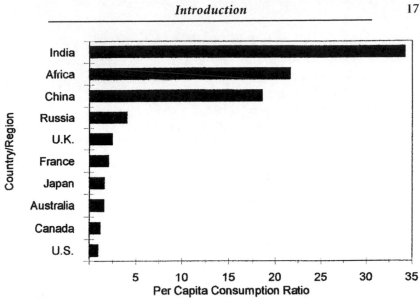

Figure 6 — Per capita consumption ratio of the U.S. relative to selected countries and Africa (energy data from the US DOE/EIA, population data from GeoHive: Global Statistics).

People in developing countries certainly have a desire to live the American lifestyle; they want motor vehicles and other modern conveniences. Because of their desires, TLHs consumption in developing countries is rising rapidly. In China, TLHs consumption increased 86% for the period 1992–2001, an average increase of 6.65%/year. In India, TLHs consumption grew by 67% for the period 1992–2001, an average increase of 4.90%/year. Oil consumption in Africa has not grown nearly as rapidly as in China and India, but it still grew about 20% for the period 1992–2001.[18] Most of the projected global growth in TLHs consumption over the next 20 years is expected to come from developing countries.

Figure 6 is a graph of the ratio of U.S. per capita consumption relative to the per capita consumption for selected countries and Africa. U.S. per capita TLHs consumption is over 34 times that of India, over 21 times that of Africa, over 18 times that of China, about 2.5 times that of the U.K. and about 2 times that of France. When comparing the U.S. to other industrialized nations, the data suggest that the U.S. could reduce its TLHs consumption significantly and still maintain a relatively high standard of living. Japan and Western Europe, in particular, have more extensive mass transit systems than the U.S., which reduces their per capita demand for TLHs. It would be possible for the U.S. to develop a much better mass transit system than it has, but it would be expensive and take time. Present U.S. attitudes towards mass transit do not suggest that extensive expansion is possible in the near future. Americans have a love affair with their personal motor vehicles, and it appears that most Americans are unwilling to give them up.

Developing countries have a great capacity for further increasing their per capita TLHs consumption. If only China and India increased their per capita consumption to the level of Russia, a country that has a low per capita TLHs consumption compared to the U.S., consumption for those two countries would have to increase by 33.7 mb/d over the present consumption level.

Creation and Trapping of Oil

Many people think that oil can be found nearly everywhere. All that is necessary is to drill a well deep enough to find the oil. The idea deludes people into thinking that oil will always be available in whatever quantities necessary.

The harsh reality is that oil is not found nearly everywhere. In fact, it is found in quite limited locations. There are geological reasons why places such as Texas, the North Sea and Saudi Arabia contain large quantities of oil and why much of the world contains little or no oil.

The origins of oil spring from the death of aquatic microorganisms, particularly algae. When conditions for microorganisms are optimal — abundant nutrients and warm water — microorganisms can grow in profusion and die in profusion. Most dead microorganisms get oxidized — that is, react with oxygen — before they settle to the bottom of a water body. Some portion of the microorganisms that settle out get eaten by bottom-feeding organisms. If the microorganisms settle out in a non-oxidizing environment, they can build up over time. That occurs in marine troughs and deep lakes. In certain locations, the dead microorganisms can make up 10% or more of the deposited sediment. Conditions that create a high concentration of deposited microorganisms occur only rarely.

Over time the microorganisms get buried with other sediment. Bacteria within the sediment feed on the organic matter that make up the microorganisms, creating CO_2 and CH_4, leaving behind an organic material called kerogen. The kerogen sinks further into the earth as it is buried by ever more sediment. As the Kerogen sinks, the temperature rises. The rising temperature breaks down the kerogen, resulting in the creation of oil. Oil is generally formed at depths of 2000 to 4500 meters (6,000 to 14,000 feet), a region called the oil window. The sediment that sinks into the earth gets compressed over time to form rock. This rock, containing a high concentration of organic matter, is called source rock. It is the source of oil. Source rock is a prerequisite for the existence of oil within a geographic region. Many regions around the world have no source rock, and hence no oil.

After oil is formed, it has to collect in a reservoir for it to be of any value to humans. The high pressure within the source rock forces the oil out. The oil migrates upward, toward lower pressure. If an impermeable layer of rock prohibits further migration, the oil will be trapped below the layer. If an impermeable layer doesn't exist, the oil will migrate to the surface where it can evaporate or be oxidized. Oil typically gets trapped in locations where rocks have been folded or faulted. In order for a trap to be effective, the overlying rock has to act as an efficient seal.

The requirements of source rock plus effective traps limit the geographic locations of economically viable oil fields. At the global level, geologists have mapped where oil can be expected and where it will not be expected. For the most part, the regions of the world with geology amenable to oil generation and trapping have been explored. The oil industry is now in the process of exploring the remaining geologically worthwhile locations: the deep-water Gulf of Mexico (offshore U.S. and Mexico), Campos Basin (offshore Brazil), the deep-water Atlantic Ocean off West Africa, and the Caspian Sea. Extensive exploration has already taken place in these locations. Exploration results in the Caspian Sea have been relatively discouraging, although the US DOE/EIA was still claiming that there was 217 Gb of oil in the Caspian Sea region not that long ago.[19] One supergiant field, the Kashagan field, containing a high-sulfur, low-grade crude, was discovered in the Caspian Sea in 2000. Several major oil companies involved in the discovery of the field have sold their interest in it, suggesting the oil is not sufficiently valuable. Beyond the Kashagan field, there have been no major discoveries in the region in the last 5 years.

Oil Exploration and Production Technology

Considerable technological progress has been made over the years to aid in the exploration and production of oil. As a result, the process is now extremely efficient. In the early days, oil seeps were used to identify locations to drill for oil. Later, geologists used surface geology, fossils from surface rocks and micro-fossils from auger holes to assess the oil geology of a region. Instrumental techniques were developed over time, including refraction seismology (1925), electric well logs (1930), analog reflection seismology (1935), digital reflection seismology (1965) and 3-D digital reflection seismology (1978). Reflection seismology involves setting off explosive charges and monitoring the energy waves reflected back from the underground rock interfaces. The echoes provide a picture of the underground rock structure and are used to determine drilling locations. Today with 3-D seismology, petroleum geologists can get a 3-dimensional picture of the earth's subsurface.

Rotary drilling rigs (1920), offshore drilling barges (1950), deep-water drillships (1956), semi-submersible rigs (1964) and horizontal drilling (1985) have made production more efficient and expanded the area from which oil can be extracted. Semi-submersible rigs have made offshore oil exploration relatively simple, even in the worst of conditions. A semi-submersible rig has a drilling platform mounted on two submerged pontoons that are unaffected by wave action. Horizontal drilling and multilateral wells are in common use today. Horizontal drilling involves a well that is initially drilled downward, but is made to deviate in a horizontal direction up to ~6 miles. Multilateral wells involve multiple branches drilled from a single borehole.

To accelerate the extraction of oil from a field, water or gas is injected into the reservoir to force the oil out. For fields containing heavy oil, steam injection is commonly used to reduce the viscosity of the oil so it can be extracted.

Exploration is technically possible virtually everywhere on earth, though (as previously mentioned) the number of sites where oil can actually be found is limited by geological circumstance. In locations that do contain oil, production is technically possible even in the most challenging environments.

Divergent Views of the Global Oil Resource

Presently there is a vigorous debate concerning the magnitude of the global oil resource and when global production will peak. On one side of the debate are the disciples of the petroleum geophysicist M.K. Hubbert. The Hubbert Model of oil discovery and production predicts that, over a large producing region, the discovery rate will rise from zero up to a peak and then decline from the peak back to zero.[20,21] The production curve will have a similar profile but lag behind the discovery curve (see Figure 7). The model assumes that there will be unrestrained exploration and devel-

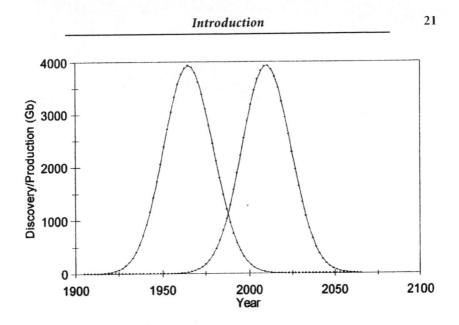

Figure 7 — The Hubbert Model showing discovery (first curve) and production (second curve) rates for oil.

opment over the large area and that there will be a large number of oil fields within the producing region. If those assumptions aren't met, the discovery and production profiles will deviate from the profiles shown in Figure 7.

Economists often promote the opposing view, frequently termed the cornucopian view, although the view is not limited to economists. For cornucopians, the world has infinite resources. In terms of oil, if an oil shortage develops, the price will go up, stimulating more exploration, which will lead to new discoveries and a higher level of production. Cornucopians argue that there is still plenty of the earth's surface that has never been explored for oil. When it is explored, the earth will provide ample quantities of oil.

Cornucopians may also argue that production will increase within producing countries where production has been declining when the price of oil increases. Table 13 illustrates that higher prices, at least in the short run, have had little impact upon stemming the decline of production in mature producing countries.

The summed decline for the 10 countries in Table 13 for 2002–2003 was 4.78% while for 2003–2004 it was 5.63%. It can be argued that the 2003–2004 decline was made larger by the impact of Hurricane Ivan (in September) on U.S. oil production. If only the first 8-months data is used for the U.S., the summed decline for the 10 countries was still 5.32%.

Table 13 — The Impact of Price on Oil Production for Mature Producing Countries

(The countries in this table are the top ten producing countries that appear to be in long-term decline. Oil prices are for West Texas Intermediate (WTI). The data in this table are from the U.S. DOE/EIA except for Norway, whose data are from the Norwegian Petroleum Directorate.)

Year	2002	2003	2004	% Decline 2002–2003	%Decline 2003–2004
Oil Price	$26.07	$31.04	$41.38		
Country/ Production (mb/d)					
U.S.	5.746	5.681	5.430	-1.13	-4.42
Norway	3.150	3.068	2.964	-2.60	-3.39
U.K.	2.292	2.093	1.845	-8.68	-11.85
Indonesia	1.267	1.171	1.113	-7.58	-4.95
Oman	0.897	0.781	0.751	-12.93	-3.84
Argentina	0.757	0.741	0.691	-2.11	-6.75
Egypt	0.631	0.618	0.594	-2.06	-3.88
Australia	0.626	0.512	0.455	-18.21	-11.13
Colombia	0.577	0.538	0.529	-6.76	-1.67
Syria	0.511	0.464	0.410	-9.20	-11.63
Summed Production (mb/d)	16.454	15.667	14.782	-4.78	-5.63

A third argument cornucopians make is that oil companies are continually improving the efficiency of oil extraction. As the argument goes, years ago oil companies expected to extract only 30% of the oil in a field. Today they expect to extract 50% of the oil in a field. Someday essentially all of the oil in a field will be extractable. Increasing the percentage of extractable oil will dramatically increase the conventional oil resource.

Cornucopians like to state that numerous predictions of an imminent global oil production decline never materialized in the past and thus won't anytime soon. In the cornucopian view, if there were a limit to the conventional oil resource, ample quantities of oil could be obtained from nonconventional oil resources. Alternatively, the world has abundant quantities of hydrogen, which can substitute for oil.

Cornucopians like to criticize M.K. Hubbert because in his original 1956 presentation introducing the Hubbert Model, he predicted that the EUR for the U.S. would be 150–200 Gb. It now appears that the ultimate recovery for the U.S. will be ~250 Gb. At the time of Hubbert's 1956 presentation, there was no oil production from Alaska and the deep-water GOM. In his 1981 paper, he frequently referred to the 1956 presentation and made it explicitly clear that his prediction applied only to the contiguous 48 states and continental shelf. The ultimate recovery from that region will be ~197 Gb, within the 150–200 Gb range he predicted.

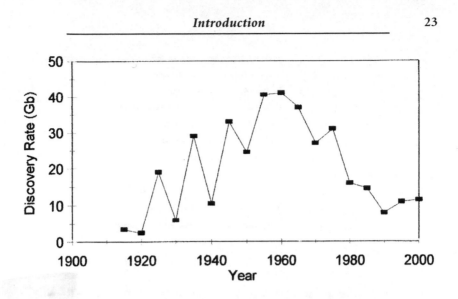

Figure 8 — Oil discovery rate (5 year average) (the 1990–2003 data are from Jean Laherrere; data prior to 1990 are from Ivanhoe, "Get Ready for Another Oil Shock").

Global Oil Discovery Rate

Figure 8 is a graph of global oil discovery rate versus time. The global oil discovery rate peaked during the 1960–1965 period at ~41 Gb/y and has generally declined since then. Since 1980, the global oil production rate has exceeded the global oil discovery rate. For 2000–2003, the average global oil discovery rate was ~11.25 Gb/year while global oil production was 24.9 Gb/year.[22]

Global Estimated Ultimate Recovery

Figure 9 is a chart of published estimates for ultimate global conventional oil recovery. Estimates have generally fluctuated around 2000 Gb. Cumulative global oil production at the end of 2003 was ~955 Gb. At the present oil consumption rate of ~25 Gb/year, the midway point for an EUR of 2000 Gb would occur in 2005.

In their recent World Petroleum Assessment 2000 (WPA2000), the USGS estimated an ultimate recovery of over 3000 Gb.[23] There has been harsh criticism of the USGS concerning the WPA2000. The basic points of criticism are:

1. With the U.S. estimate of undiscovered oil included in the world total, the mean undiscovered volume of oil in the WPA2000 is 724 Gb. The WPA2000 states that the undiscovered oil will potentially be added

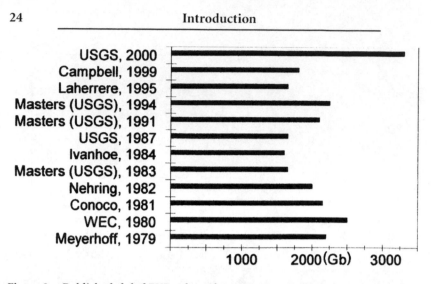

Figure 9 — Published global EUR values (from MacKenzie, "Oil as a Finite Resource: When Is Global Production Likely to Peak?).

to reserves during the period of 1995–2025. That corresponds to a discovery rate of ~24 Gb/y. In no year since 1995 have discoveries come close to 24 Gb, suggesting that the estimate of undiscovered oil is inflated.

2. With the U.S. estimate of reserve growth included in the world total, the mean reserves growth figure is 674 Gb. That figure is based upon the U.S. experience where much of the oil was discovered before technical assessment techniques were available and where SEC rules lead to an underreporting of reserves.

3. Based upon the WPA2000, the International Energy Outlook 2001 (IEO2001) by the US DOE/EIA projected that North Sea oil production would peak at 6.7 mb/d in ~2006 and decline slowly after the peak.[24] North Sea oil production actually peaked in 1999 at 5.95 mb/d and is now declining rapidly, averaging 5.31 mb/d in 2003. The US DOE/EIA had to significantly lower their North Sea oil production projection in their IEO2003 (see Chapter 3).[25]

Also in their IEO2001, the US DOE/EIA projected that Colombia's oil production would exceed 1 mb/d by 2010.[26] Colombia's oil production peaked in 1999 at 816,000 b/d and is declining rapidly, averaging 538,000 b/d in 2003.[27] In their IEO2003, the US DOE/EIA downgraded Colombia's future oil production rate but still expects production to rise to ~650,000 b/d by 2010, which appears unlikely.[28]

Table 14 — The World's Top 16 Oil Producing Countries in 2003
(data from the US DOE/EIA, http://www.eia.doe.gov/)

Rank	Country	Production (mb/d)	Rank	Country	Production (mb/d)
1	Saudi Arabia	8.85	9	Venezuela	2.34
2	Russia	8.18	10	Canada	2.31
3	United States	5.74	11	Nigeria	2.24
4	Iran	3.78	12	Kuwait	2.18
5	China	3.41	13	United Kingdom	2.07
6	Mexico	3.37	14	Brazil	1.55
7	Norway	2.85	15	Libya	1.42
8	United Arab Emirates	2.35	16	Iraq	1.31

The World's Top Oil Producing Countries

Table 14 contains a list of the world's top 16 oil producing countries in 2003. The world's top 16 oil producing countries produced 53.95 mb/d in 2003, 77.70% of the world's total of 69.43 mb/d.

Sources of Data

The main sources of data for this book include the US DOE/EIA, *Oil & Gas Journal*, the Minerals Management Service (MMS), the Norwegian Petroleum Directorate (NPD), the Danish Energy Authority (DEA), Alaska Department of Revenue, Simmons and Company International and the Railroad Commission of Texas. Also, international petroleum geologists Jean Laherrere and Colin Campbell provided invaluable data. Some graphs only show production data through 2001 or 2002 because those are the most recent available data.

Production Forecasts

Many chapters of the book compare production forecasts by the US DOE/EIA to those of Colin Campbell and Richard Duncan. Duncan is a frequent author of articles in various oil industry journals. Campbell and Duncan made their forecasts in the late 1990s, while the IEO2003 was used for the US DOE/EIA forecasts. Forecasts are also compared to recent production data.

Cumulative Production Values

Cumulative production values at the end of 2002 or 2003 are provided for fields and countries in this book. Values were generally determined by adding published production values since 1992 to the 1992 cumulative production data in *Oil & Gas Journal*, the last year they published cumulative production values. For some fields— Prudhoe Bay, Marlim, Statfjord, Oseberg, Gullfaks and others—cumulative production values were calculated directly based upon production data from sources other than *Oil & Gas Journal*.

1

Oil Production in the United States

The United States has been among the world's top oil producing countries since "Colonel" Edwin Drake successfully drilled for oil near the town of Titusville, Pennsylvania, in 1859. Presently the U.S. is the world's 3rd highest oil producing nation behind Saudi Arabia and Russia. Drake's success led to a wild drilling boom in western Pennsylvania that was later repeated in numerous other states. In the late 1800s, oil was used mainly to make kerosene for lighting purposes. During that period, gasoline was considered worthless and was typically discarded. With the advent of the automobile and the decline in kerosene use for lighting purposes due to electrical lighting, gasoline became a principal product of refined petroleum.

Pennsylvania's peak years for oil production came early with maximum production occurring in 1891 at over 86,000 b/d (see Figure 1.1).[1] The oil production graph for Pennsylvania shows that production can continue for a long time after maximum production occurs, but at a much lower production level. Pennsylvania now produces ~6,000 b/d, enough to supply the liquid hydrocarbon needs of the U.S. for about 37 seconds/day. Through 2002, Pennsylvania's cumulative oil production was 1.37 Gb.[2]

Along with Pennsylvania, Ohio and West Virginia became major oil producing states in the late 1800s. Ohio achieved a production rate of over 65,000 b/d in 1896 while West Virginia reached a peak of over 44,000 b/d in 1900 (see Appendix A for production profiles of U.S. states).[3] By today's standards, the production rates for Pennsylvania, Ohio and West Virginia prior to 1900 were insignificant.

Between 1900 and 1920, four states that would become major oil producers started their ascendancy up the production charts: Texas, California, Kansas and Oklahoma. Louisiana, now America's top oil producing

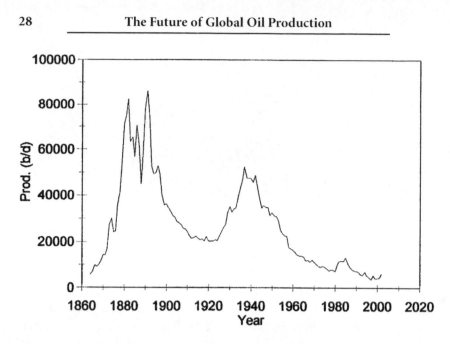

Figure 1.1— Pennsylvania's oil production (data from the American Petroleum Institute [1864–1997] and *Oil & Gas Journal* [1998–2002]).

state, had a relatively low production rate in the early 1900s from salt domes along the Gulf Coast. Production didn't take off until after 1930. Interestingly, for most of the period from 1900 to 1930, Oklahoma had a higher production rate than either Texas or Louisiana. Through 2001, the states of Texas, California, Kansas, Oklahoma and Louisiana produced 74.1% of the cumulative U.S. production.[4,5]

Oil Production in Texas

Texas became an important oil producing state after the discovery of the Spindletop field, near Beaumont, in 1901. Spindletop's oil was contained in a salt dome structure in which the reservoir pressure was exceedingly high, high enough that early wells blew out at 75,000 b/d. Spindletop led to the first oil boom in Texas, although it only lasted for a few years before the reservoir pressure collapsed due to a wanton disregard for reservoir management. As Anthony Lucas, involved in the discovery of Spindletop, said concerning Spindletop, "The cow was milked too hard; moreover, she was not milked too intelligently."[6]

After Spindletop further discoveries led to growth in the Texas oil industry, but it was the discovery of the "Black Giant" in 1930 that really made Texas the oil producing capital of the nation and world. The Black

Giant, or East Texas field, was discovered by Dad Joiner through the application of luck, since no geologic knowledge was applied to the discovery process. By 1931, production from the Black Giant had climbed to over 1 mb/d. The rate of oil production was so high that it caused the price of oil to fall to pennies a barrel while production costs were around 80 cent a barrel. Low oil prices led The Railroad Commission of Texas to proration oil, limit production, to maintain the price at a set level. State prorationing proved to be ineffective at stopping what was termed "hot oil" production, oil produced illegally, so the federal government interceded to control production nationally. The Oil Code of the National Industrial Recovery Act (1933) set monthly quotas for each state and this was sufficient to maintain the price of oil between $1.00 and $1.18/barrel during the period 1934–1940.[7] After World War II, oil consumption in the U.S. increased rapidly and eliminated the need to limit production. From the early days of the U.S. oil industry through 1947, the U.S. had been a net oil exporter. In 1948, U.S. oil imports exceeded exports for the first time, even with flat-out U.S. production.

Getting back to the Black Giant, the reservoir is about 45 miles long and 5–10 miles wide. It is the largest field ever discovered in the lower 48 states with an EUR of ~5.5 Gb. From 1993 to 2002, the Black Giant's production declined steadily from 82,568 b/d to 15,680 b/d.[8] Today's production rate is a long way from the ~1 mb/d of 1931. Approximately 98% of the Black Giant's initial oil endownment has been produced.

Figure 1.2 is a graph of Texas' oil production. Texas' oil production reached its peak in 1972 at 3.57 mb/d.[9] In 2003, production was 0.984 mb/d, a decline of 2.59 mb/d (72.4%) from the peak.[10]

A common belief among Americans is that oil companies hold back oil production for the day when the price will be much higher. Thus, companies stand to make "windfall" profits when the price rises. The production profile of Texas calls that belief into question. Prior to 1973, the price of oil had been fairly constant at ~$3.00/barrel for many years. Due to the oil crisis of 1973, the price of oil increased to ~$13/barrel. During the oil crisis of the late 1970s/early 1980s, the price of oil increased to ~$35/barrel (or ~$50 in 1990 dollars). In spite of the two crisis-induced price increases, oil production in Texas declined steadily.

Once oil production starts declining in a mature oil producing region such as Texas, the easily extractable oil has been extracted and it requires an increasing amount of work to extract the remaining oil. Wells that once required no pumping because high reservoir pressure forced the oil out ultimately require pumping as the reservoir pressure declines. Over time, the wells pump less and less oil. A substantial increase in the price of oil

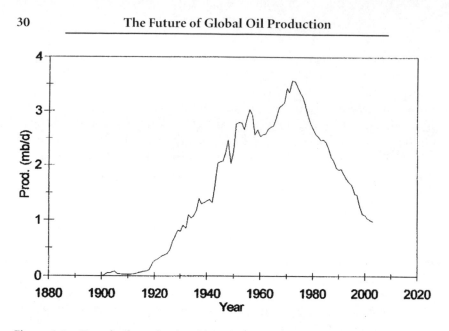

Figure 1.2 — Texas' oil production (data from the American Petroleum Institute [1890–1997] and the Railroad Commission of Texas [1998–2003]).

will have little effect on the declining production trend unless there are previously undeveloped oil fields to exploit. The U.S. now has approximately 500,000 low production stripper wells (wells that produce less than 10 barrels/day) with an average production rate of ~2 b/d. Wells that get capped typically produce considerably less than 1 b/d. Table 1.1 contains the average production rate/well for 7 selected states.

Of the 31 U.S. states for which oil production data is provided in Appendix A, 13 have an average production rate/well of less than 3 b/d. Once a well has been capped, it's expensive to restart the well and there is no assurance that oil flow can be regained, thus there is little incentive for oil companies to restart capped wells. The moral of this story is not to expect a surge in Texas' oil production even if the price of oil skyrockets. Texas may no longer be the top oil producing state in the U.S., but the ultimate recovery for Texas, ~ 75 Gb, will far exceed the ultimate recovery from any other state.

Table 1.1 — Average Oil Production Rate per Well
(Barrels/Day/Well) for Selected States*

Year	Ohio	Pennsylvania	New York	Michigan	Oklahoma	Texas	Alaska
1991	0.83	0.31	0.29	10.57	3.23	10.14	1191.66
2001	0.57	0.28	0.12	5.75	2.23	8.68	492.20

*(Based upon data from Oil & Gas Journal, 2nd December issues, 1971–2003.)

Oil Production from Other Major Oil Producing States in the US/48

California's oil production rose rapidly in the early 1900s with production centered around Los Angeles. Oil discoveries were initially made in the Los Angeles Basin in the 1890s. Major fields were also discovered in the San Joquin Valley from 1890 to 1910. California led the nation in oil production from 1903 through 1914 before Oklahoma took the lead. One of the large early discoveries was Signal Hill, just south of LA, discovered in 1921. Oil production from Signal Hill helped propel California to the top oil producing state again from 1923 through 1926. After 1950, significant production occurred offshore in the Santa Maria-Partington, Santa Barbara-Ventura and LA Basins. California's oil production reached its maximum rate in 1985 at 1.16 mb/d.[11] By 2002, production had declined to 0.788 mb/d (see Figure 1.3).[12]

Initially, Louisiana's oil production came from salt domes along the Gulf of Mexico (GOM) coast during the early 1900s. In 1947, Kerr-McGee struck oil 10 miles off the Louisiana coast which heralded the development of an offshore oil industry. Louisana's oil production peaked in 1971 at 2.56 mb/d (see Figure 1.4).[13] After the 1971 peak, production declined rapidly until a second minor price induced peak occurred in the middle 1980s. Since the middle 1990s, Louisiana's oil production has risen rapidly due

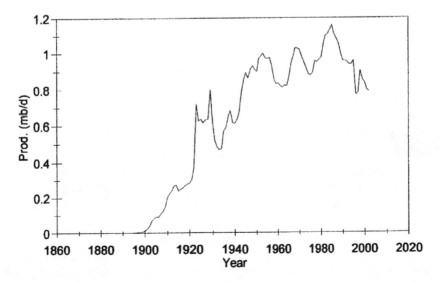

Figure 1.3 — California's oil production (Data from the American Petroleum Institute [1870–1997] and Oil & Gas Journal [1998–2002]).

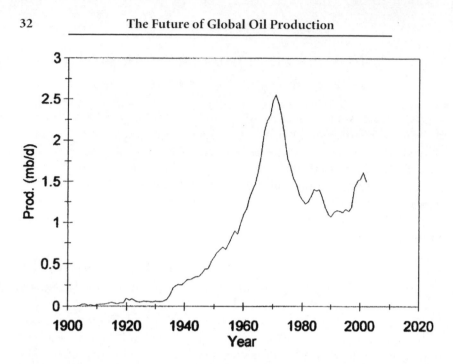

Figure 1.4 — Louisiana's oil production (Data from the American Petroleum Institute [1900–1997] and *Oil & Gas Journal* [1998–2002]).

to oil development in the deep-water GOM. Most of the oil that comes from federal waters in the GOM originates in the central region of the GOM. The oil goes to terminals in Louisiana and is included as part of Louisiana's oil production. Louisiana's onshore oil production (~280,000 b/d) only made up a small portion (~17.5%) of its total oil production (1.50 mb/d) in 2002.[14,15]

Oklahoma's oil production began with a series of discoveries in the early 1900s, the largest of which was the Glenn Pool. The early discoveries provided Oklahoma with the oil necessary to compete with California as the top oil producing state during the period 1900–1928, before Texas took over the top spot. The 1926 discovery of the Greater Seminole field lead to a spike in Oklahoma's oil production in 1927 at 761,027 b/d.[16] That was the high point for Oklahoma's oil production. Production is now in steady decline with the 2002 production rate at 182,581 b/d, 24.0% of the 1927 maximum.[17]

The first oil discovery in the plains states was made in Kansas during the 1890s, but significant sustained production in Kansas didn't occur until after 1915. Through the 1930s and 1940s production rose steadily, ultimately reaching a maximum of 340,285 b/d in 1956.[18] By 2002, the production rate had declined to 89,647 b/d, 26.3% of the 1956 maximum.[19]

Oil Production in the US/48
Excluding the Gulf of Mexico

The oil production profile for the lower US/48 states, excluding the Gulf of Mexico, is similar to that of Texas due to the strong influence Texas' production has had on U.S. production (see Figure 1.5).

For this region, production peaked in 1971 at 8.40 mb/d. By 2001, production had declined to 3.10 mb/d, a decline of 63.1%.[20,21] During the 1992–2001 period, oil production from this region declined at an average rate of 4.46%/year. The production curve after 2001, in Figure 1.5, is based upon the average decline rate for the 1992–2001 period. Figure 1.5 includes a minor amount of production from Pacific federal offshore waters, 0.92 Gb, as of 1999. The ultimate recovery for this region will be ~180 Gb of oil, based upon Figure 1.5.

The purpose for showing the graph in Figure 1.5 is to compare future production from this region, based upon the graph, with the most recent national oil and gas assessment by the USGS, completed in 1995. In their U.S. assessments, the USGS assesses only the onshore portion of the U.S. and states waters. The Minerals Management Service, MMS, assesses federal offshore oil and gas resources. Table 1.2 shows the national assess-

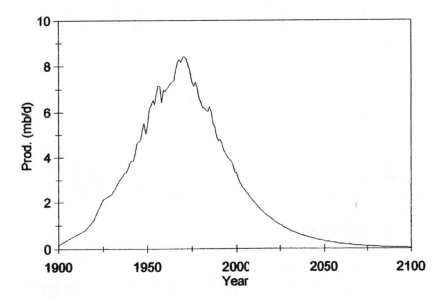

Figure 1.5 — Historical [1900–2001] and projected [2002–2100] oil production for the lower US/48 states, excluding the Gulf of Mexico (Data from the US DOE/EIA and MMS).

Table 1.2 — 1995 USGS Oil Assessment for the U.S.
(1995 National Assessment of United States Oil and Gas Resources, United States Geological Survey)

Source of oil	Volume (Gb)
Undiscovered Conventional Oil Resources	30.3
Reserve Growth in Conventional Fields	60.0
Measured Proven Reserves	20.2
Total	110.5

ment results by the USGS for technically recoverable conventional oil resources, as of January 1, 1994.

The total reserves figure given in Table 1.2 includes 27.7 Gb of Alaskan reserves which must be subtracted from the total for comparison to Figure 1.5. The difference gives 82.8 Gb, the amount of oil that the USGS expects to be technically recoverable from the onshore US/48 and state waters after Jan. 1, 1994.

Cumulative production from the region was 145.4 Gb, as of January 1, 1994. Based upon the graph in Figure 1.5, the ultimate recovery from this region will be 180.2 Gb and the amount of oil recoverable after January 1, 1994 will be 34.8 Gb. The USGS assessment concludes that 2.38 times that amount of oil is technically recoverable after January 1, 1994 from this region.

There appears to be a consistent pattern of over-estimations for recoverable oil resources in the U.S. by the USGS and MMS. Using assessment results from the USGS and MMS, the US DOE/EIA then makes overly optimistic forecasts of future production for the U.S. and world. In a debate concerning U.S. oil resources dating back to the 1950s, M.King Hubbert, petroleum geophysicist for Shell Oil Company, predicted that U.S. oil production from the contiguous U.S. and offshore continental shelf would be 150–200 Gb with peak production occurring between 1966 and 1971.[22] His 1956 presentation to the American Petroleum Institute did not explicitly state that his estimate was for the contiguous U.S. and offshore continental shelf but his 1981 paper, which extensively refers to his 1956 presentation, makes it clear that his estimate was for this region.[23] It appears that the ultimate recovery for the contiguous U.S. and continental shelf will be approximately 197 Gb (see Figure 1.7).

In the USGS oil resource assessment of 1961, the USGS was estimating that the ultimate recovery for the U.S. would be 590 Gb,[24] but the contiguous U.S. and continental shelf make up most of the U.S. so the bulk of the 590 Gb should be expected to come from that region. Through the 1960s after 1961, the Assistant Chief Geologist for the USGS, Vincent E. McKelvey, who was responsible for official Survey estimates, issued successive reports estimating that the ultimate recovery for the U.S. would be about 600 Gb with peak production occurring around 2000.[25] With peak production for the U.S. occurring in 1971, Hubbert proved to be on the mark. The USGS estimated ultimate recovery for the U.S. during the 1960s is ~2.4 times what will ultimately be recovered for the total U.S. (see Table 1.7).

To address inflated assessment values by the USGS, subsequent display of USGS estimates for technically recoverable oil resources will be accompanied by a value identified as the Expected Recovery Volume (ERV). The ERV is the USGS technically recoverable volume of oil divided by a factor of 2.38. The ERV is a more plausible estimate of the amount of oil that will actually be recovered. The USGS now provides economically recoverable volumes in their assessments, typically at $18/barrel and $30/barrel, but their economically recoverable volumes are still considerably higher than corresponding ERV values.

Oil Production in the Shallow-Water Gulf of Mexico

Oil production from the Gulf of Mexico's (GOM's) continental shelf started in the late 1940s and reached its highest level, over 1 mb/d, in the early 1970s (see Figure 1.6).[26] This region is also called the shallow-water GOM with production occurring in water depths up to 1000 feet. There

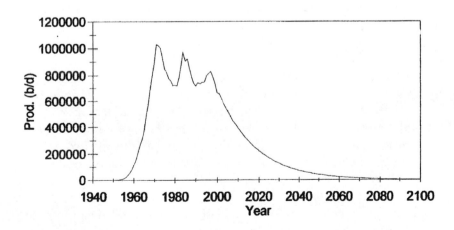

Figure 1.6 — Historical [1950–2001] and projected [2002–2100] oil production from the shallow-water GOM (Historical data from the MMS).

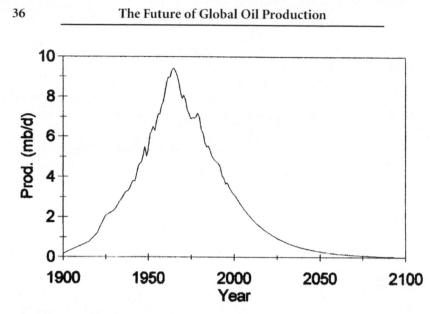

Figure 1.7 — Historical [1900–2001] and projected [2002–2100] oil production from the US/48, excluding the deepwater GOM (Historical data from the US DOE/EIA and MMS).

was a second peak in the 1980s, associated with elevated oil prices during the oil crisis of the late 1970s/early 1980s, and a third peak in the late 1990s. The third peak can be attributed to the use of advanced exploration and production technology and extension of production onto the slope of the continental shelf. The production profile of the shallow-water GOM deviates from the Hubbert Model for several reasons. First, government leasing of offshore territory in the GOM expanded with time. Second, offshore exploration and production technology improved tremendously over the time period of shallow-water development.

Oil fields in the shallow-water GOM are now typically declining at 10–15%/year and the region has been extensively explored. The average size for new field discoveries is 6 Mb, which is tiny.[27] Because of the high decline rates of mature fields and the small size of new discoveries, future production is projected to decline at the rate it has during 1997–2001, 5.54%/year. The production curve after 2001 in Figure 1.6 is based upon the 5.54%/year decline rate. In that case, the ultimate recovery from the shallow-water GOM would be 15.1 Gb.

Adding the production from the shallow-water GOM (Figure 1.6) to the US/48 graph (Figure 1.5) gives Figure 1.7.

In Figure 1.7, oil production peaked in 1971 at 9.42 mb/d.[28,29] In 2001, oil production from this region had declined to 3.94 mb/d, a decline of

5.48 mb/d (58.2%) since 1971.[30,31] The ultimate recovery from this region, based upon Figure 1.7, is 196.9 Gb.

Oil Production in the Deep-Water GOM

Oil exploration in the deep-water GOM, water depths greater than 1000 feet, started in the 1970s and expanded in the 1980s. Production from this region was paltry prior to the 1995 Deep-Water Royalty Relief Act. The act, along with advances in technology, stimulated rapid development. Deep-water development is very expensive, as Table 1.3 illustrates, and the high cost of development will be a limiting factor in terms of small field development.

The MMS estimates that the undiscovered technically recoverable amount of oil in the GOM is 37.1 Gb, as of January 1, 1999.[32] That figure appears to be unrealistic as it pertains to what will ultimately be recoverable. The 37.1 Gb figure is for discoveries in all of the GOM but presumably most of the oil would come from the deep-water GOM since the shallow-water GOM in the western and central gulf has been extensively explored and the eastern GOM is not oil prone. As an approximation, it's assumed that the ultimate recovery from the deep-water GOM will be the same as for the shallow-water GOM, 15.1 Gb. Colin Campbell estimates the EUR for the U.S. deep-water GOM will be as high as 10.5 Gb.[33] Using the 15.1 Gb ultimate recovery figure, a plausible oil production curve is shown in Figure 1.8.

Peak production in Figure 1.8 occurs in 2013/2014 at 1.59 mb/d. By the end of 2002, there were 147 oil field discoveries in the deep-water GOM.[34] Table 1.4 lists the 10 largest discoveries in the deep-water GOM.

The Thunderhorse field is expected to come on-line during 2005–2007 and is projected to produce 250,000 b/d at maximum production. Because of the expense associated with deep-water field development and production, fields generally achieve a high maximum production rate early in production and decline rapidly within a few years after start-up. The Thunderhorse field is sufficiently large that it should be able to maintain a high plateau production rate for 4–8 years.

Table 1.3 — Deep-Water GOM Oil Developments
(Data from the Minerals Management Service)

Project	Development Cost
Diana/Hoover Fields	$1.1 Billion
Atlantis Field	$2.6 Billion
British Petroleum Deepwater Oil Pipeline	$1 Billion

Table 1.4 — Top 10 Largest Deep-Water GOM Oil Fields
(data are from the Minerals Management Service and from Skrebowski, "Oil Field Mega Projects 2004")

Field	Discovery Date	EUR (Mb)
Thunderhorse	1999	1500*
Holstein	1999	Up to 1000*
Atlantis	?	Up to 875*
Mad Dog	1998	Up to 800
Tahiti	2002	Up to 700*
Great White	2002	500*
Mars	1989	456.3
Ursa	1990	239.1
Auger	1987	224.4
Ram-Powell	1985	185.7

* Includes gas converted to barrels of oil equivalent

Using the MMS assessment, the U.S. DOE/EIA projects a production profile for the deep-water GOM that does not even peak before 2025 (see Figure 1.9).[35] Based upon Figure 1.9, cumulative production through 2025 would be 15.3 Gb, with production still rising.

In their July 2003 Oil Market Report, the International Energy Agency projected that GOM oil production would increase by 135,000 b/d in 2003, aided by the start-up of the Na Kika, Medussa, Matterhorn, Habanero and

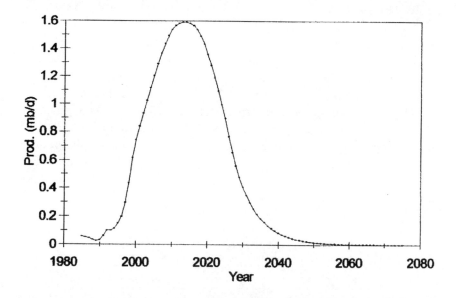

Figure 1.8 — Historical [1985–2001] and projected [2002–2075] oil production from the deep-water GOM (Historical data from the MMS).

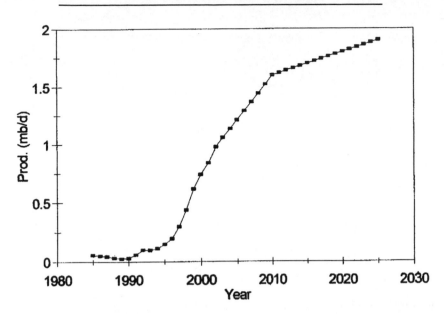

Figure 1.9 — US DOE/EIA production projection for the deep-water GOM Historical [1985–2001] and projected [2002–2025] oil production (Historical data from the MMS).

Horn Mountain deep-water fields. For 2004, they project that GOM oil production will increase 180,000 b/d, aided by the start-up of the Front Runner, Devil's Tower and Gunnison deep-water fields.[36]

Oil Production in Alaska

Alaska's oil production commenced with developments in the Cook Inlet region of southern Alaska in the late 1950s. Production from the region reached a maximum production rate of about 220,000 b/d in 1971 (see Figure 1.10).

Cumulative production from the Cook Inlet region was 1.28 Gb at the end of 2002.[37] The Alaska Department of Natural Resources is projecting that oil production will be terminated in 2021 at which time cumulative production will be ~1.4 Gb.[38]

It was the discovery of the supergiant Prudhoe Bay field in December 1967 that ultimately lead to Alaska becoming the top oil producing state in the U.S., at least for a while. After the Prudhoe Bay discovery, development was slowed by engineering problems due to the harsh conditions

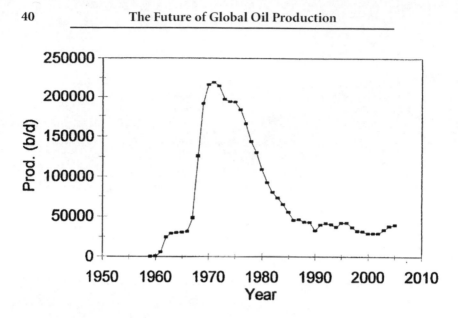

Figure 1.10 — Oil production from the Cook Inlet region of Alaska (Data from the Alaska Department of Revenue).

of the north, claims by Alaskan natives and opposition by environmental groups. Environmental opposition gained overwhelming momentum after the Santa Barbara oil blowout in 1969 which hindered further development until 1973. Because of the 1973 OPEC oil embargo, which fostered deep concerns within the U.S. government over dependence upon OPEC oil, an oil pipeline was approved from the North Slope of Alaska down to Valdez, through which North Slope oil would flow. In 1977 production started from the Prudhoe Bay field and Alaska's oil production rose rapidly.

The Prudhoe Bay field is the largest field ever discovered in the U.S. and Canada, and one of the largest ever found globally. By 1980, the Prudhoe Bay field was producing over 1.5 mb/d. In 1981, production started from the giant Kuparak field, which reached a production rate of 300,000 b/d in 1988. Those two fields alone produced over 90% of Alaska's oil production during the late 1980s. Even supergiant fields ultimately decline and the Prudhoe Bay field started declining in 1989 (see Figure 1.11). Since 1987, when production reached its highest rate, the Prudhoe Bay field has declined at an average rate of 9.6%/year, with an overall decline of 74.2%. In 2002, the field produced 415,000 b/d.[39]

Figure 1.12 is a graph of annual production versus cumulative production for the Prudhoe Bay field. The benefit of this graphical presentation is that extrapolating a line through the declining data points to the x-axis provides a good estimate of the field's ultimate recovery. In the case

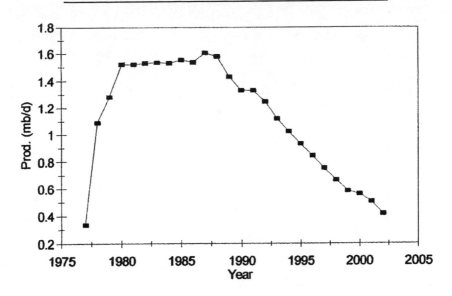

Figure 1.11— Prudhoe Bay field oil production (Data from the Alaska Department of Revenue).

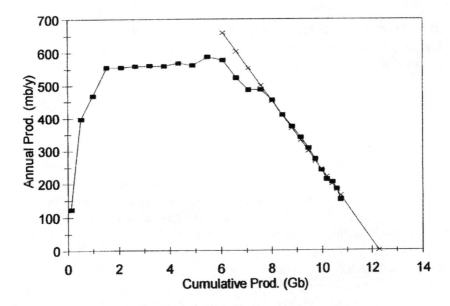

Figure 1.12 — Plot of annual production versus cumulative production for Prudhoe Bay field oil production [rectangles] and best-fit line to x-axis [X] (Data from the Alaska Department of Revenue).

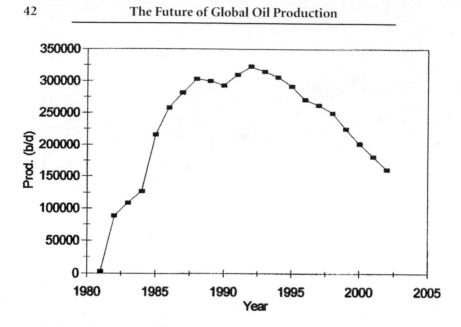

Figure 1.13 — Kuparak field oil production (Data from the Alaska Department of Revenue).

of the Prudhoe Bay field, the ultimate oil recovery will be approximately 12.3 Gb. At the end of 2002, 10.7 Gb of oil had been produced from the Prudhoe Bay field, 87.0% of the EUR.[40]

The Kuparak field reached its highest production rate in 1994 at 323,000 b/d.[41] It has declined at an average rate of 7.3%/year since then with an overall decline of 50.2% (see Figure 1.13). The Kuparak field will ultimately produce ~2.4 Gb of oil. In recent years, minor fields (satellites) around the Prudhoe Bay and Kuparak fields have been brought on-line to slow the rate at which oil production declines from the region.

A third North Slope field, Point McIntyre, also achieved a high production rate but is now in steep decline (see Figure 1.14). It has been declining at an average rate of 22.6%/year since 1997 with an overall decline of 72.9%. It will ultimately produce ~0.4 Gb of crude oil.

Because the Prudhoe Bay field dwarfs all other North Slope fields, Alaska's oil production has declined in parallel with the Prudhoe Bay field (see Figure 1.15). Through 2000, 78% of the cumulative production from the North Slope had come from the Prudhoe Bay field.[42]

Alaska's oil production peaked in 1988 at 2.02 mb/d. By 2000, production had declined to just over 1 mb/d for an average decline rate of 5.77%/year from 1988 through 2000.[43] There was a slight increase in production from 2000 through 2002 due to the introduction of the Alpine

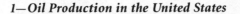

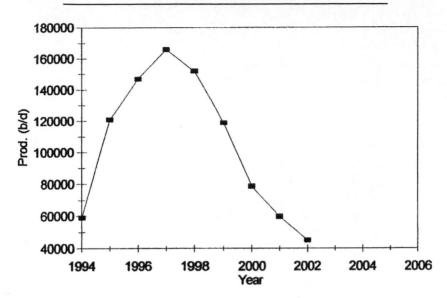

Figure 1.14 — Point McIntyre field oil production (Data from the Alaska Department of Revenue).

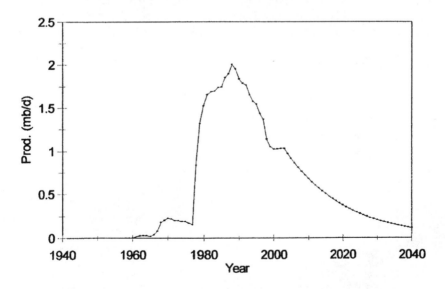

Figure 1.15 — Alaska's historical [1958–2002] and projected [2003–2040] oil production from presently active oil fields (Data from the Alaska Department of Revenue).

and Northstar fields, as well as numerous satellites of the Prudhoe Bay and Kuparak fields.

The Alpine field is one of the largest fields found in the U.S. over the last two decades. It will ultimately produce about 0.43 Gb. Production from the field has risen to over 100,000 b/d (2003). The Northstar field is located in the Beaufort Sea and is producing ~70,000 b/d (2003).[44] Because the Northstar field's EUR is so low, 0.13 Gb, production will start to decline in the next few years, whereas the Alpine field's production can probably be maintained at the 100,000 b/d level for another 2–5 years.

The production projection after 2002 in Figure 1.15 is for presently active fields only. It is based upon the assumptions that 2003 production will be the same as 2002, which appears valid as of December 2003, and that there will be a return to an average decline rate of 5.77%/year after 2003. The Figure 1.15 projection is similar to projections by the US DOE/EIA and Alaska Department of Natural Resources for presently active fields.[45,46]

Back in the early 1980s there was considerable excitement concerning a huge underground structure in the Beaufort Sea about 65 miles northwest of the Prudhoe Bay field. Oil companies had visions of another Prudhoe Bay field, if not something larger. In December 1983 the structure was breached only to discover it was filled with salt water, a $2 billion salt water hole.[47]

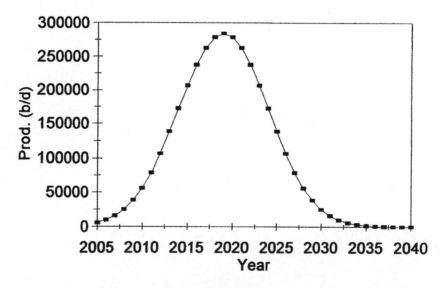

Figure 1.16 — A plausible oil production curve for further development on the North Slope, excluding the Arctic National Wildlife Refuge.

There is still latitude for further oil development in the central r of the North Slope and National Petroleum Reserve-Alaska, NPR-A, just west of the central region. The Clinton administration opened 4.6 million acres of the NPR-A to oil and gas development and the Bush administration opened 9 million acres in late 2003. Exploration of the 4.6 million acres started in 1999. Through late Nov. 2003, there had been no significant oil discoveries reported. The oil industry argues that they don't want to report discoveries when further acreage will be leased because other companies would bid up acreage prices. If there had been a significant discovery, it would be difficult to suppress that information for long.

Figure 1.16 is a plausible production profile for production from NPR-A and currently undeveloped resources of the central region based upon the ERV for the region.[48] Figure 1.16 assumes that production starts in 2005 and peaks in 2019 at ~284,000 b/d.

Oil Production in the
Arctic National Wildlife Refuge

There has been considerable debate for at least 20 years over opening the Arctic National Wildlife Refuge (ANWR) to oil and gas development. The debate will probably continue until ANWR is opened due to a

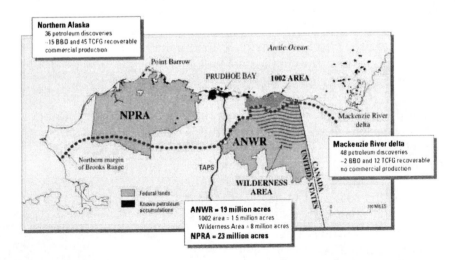

Figure 1.17 — Diagram showing the Arctic National Wildlife Refuge (U.S. Geological Survey).

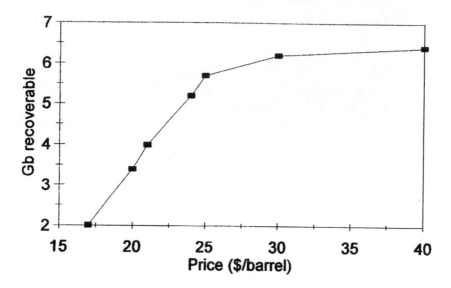

Figure 1.18 — Economically recoverable reserves in the 1002 area based upon the USGS analysis, prices are in 1996 dollars.

future oil crisis. ANWR is located in the northeastern corner of Alaska (see Figure 1.17).

In a 1998 assessment of ANWR's oil and gas potential, by the USGS, it was estimated that approximately 83% of the recoverable oil would be in the northwest half of the refuge. The study region of the USGS assessment included the 1002 area of ANWR (north of the Brooks Range), native lands within the refuge area and state waters out to the three mile limit of jurisdiction. The USGS estimated that the mean technically recoverable amount of oil was 7.7 Gb in the 1002 area and 2.7 Gb from native lands and state waters for a total of 10.4 Gb.[49]

The USGS report includes an economic assessment of the 1002 area. Figure 1.18 is a graph showing their estimate of recoverable oil in the 1002 area versus price. If the price of oil is assumed to be $40/barrel, the total study area, including state waters and native lands, would contain 8.6 Gb of economically recoverable oil, based upon the USGS assessment.

The ERV value for ANWR is 4.4 Gb, including state waters and native lands. Based upon the 4.4 Gb value, Figure 1.19 is a plausible graph of ANWR oil production versus time assuming production starts in 2010. Peak production occurs in 2024 at 940,000 b/d.

Colin Campbell makes the case that a unique set of geologic circumstances occurred in the Prudhoe Bay area that was not duplicated west and east of Prudhoe Bay. He does not expect ANWR to produce significant quantities of oil.

Based upon the USGS's technically recoverable estimate, the US DOE/EIA has estimated that maximum ANWR production would be 1.00–1.35 mb/d and that it would occur 20–30 years after production begins.[50] Since it took 11 years for initial North Slope production to reach its peak, it's unclear why it would take 20–30 years to reach peak produc-

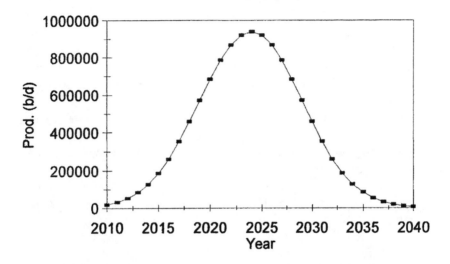

Figure 1.19 — A plausible production profile for ANWR oil production based upon an EUR of 4.4 Gb.

Table 1.5 — Impact of ANWR Oil Production
on Future U.S. Production

	2000	*2015*	*2020*	*2025*
US/48, excluding deep-water				
GOM production (mb/d)	3.95	2.03	1.60	1.26
Deepwater GOM production (mb/d)	0.74	1.58	1.36	0.90
Production from presently active				
Alaskan oil fields (mb/d)	1.02	0.50	0.38	0.28
ANWR production (mb/d)	0.00	0.19	0.68	0.92
Other Alaskan Production* (mb/d)	0.00	0.21	0.28	0.14
Total U.S. production (mb/d)	5.71	4.51	4.30	3.50
Oil demand (mb/d)**	15.12	17.61	18.12	18.39
Oil imports (mb/d)**	9.41	13.10	13.82	14.89
% imports	62.2	74.4	76.3	81.0
Increase in oil imports from 2000 (mb/d)		3.69	4.41	5.48

*Other Alaskan production includes production from NPR-A and further development in the cen-tral region of the North Slope. Production is assumed to start in 2005
**Only includes crude oil and condensate

tion in ANWR. Due to the cost of oil development on the North Slope, there is an incentive for oil companies to produce oil as quickly as possible.

What impact would ANWR production have on future U.S. oil production and imports? Table 1.5 shows the impact of ANWR oil production in 2015, 2020 and 2025 relative to 2000. Production numbers in Table 1.5 are based upon Figures 7, 8, 15, 16 and 19. Projected U.S. oil demand is from the Annual Energy Outlook 2003 by the US DOE/EIA.[51]

The projected production for Other Alaskan Production does not include future production, if any, from the Arctic Ocean. Only the Northstar field, just offshore, is producing oil and there appears to be no rush for further development in the Arctic Ocean. Table 1.5 also doesn't include oil production from federal offshore waters that are currently under a leasing moratorium.

Obviously all of the numbers in Table 1.5 will be off to some degree, but the point of the exercise is to show that a decline in U.S. oil production and an increase in imports will occur even if ANWR is opened to oil development. Oil production from ANWR will not solve the problem of high U.S. dependence on oil imports. If the U.S. government actually had a goal of reducing U.S. oil imports, a far more important component of the effort would be decreasing oil demand. There appears little likelihood of a serious effort to reduce U.S. oil demand in the foreseeable future.

It has been estimated that the minimum operational flow through the Trans-Alaska Oil Pipeline (TAPS) would be approximately 300,000 b/d.[52] The minimal operational flow limit of the pipeline insures that the ultimate recovery from the North Slope will be less than what could be pumped from North Slope fields before they dry up.

Total U.S. Oil Production

Figure 1.20 is a graph of historical and projected total U.S. oil production. Maximum production occurred in 1971 at 9.64 mb/d. The production increase that occurred in the late 1970s and early 1980s was due to the combined effects of Alaskan North Slope oil production coming on-line and the high price of oil during that period, which led to an oil drilling boom in the U.S. In 2003, production was 5.74 mb/d, a decline of 3.90 mb/d since 1971 (40.5%).[53]

Figure 1.20 consists of historical data through 2001 and projected data beyond 2001. Projected data comes from Figures 7, 8, 15, 16 and 19. Rapid

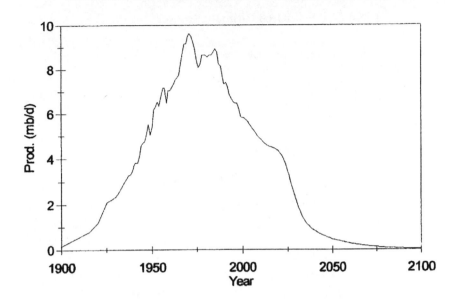

Figure 1.20 — Historical [1900–2001] and projected [2002–2100] total U.S. oil production (Historical data from Colin Campbell [1900–1959] and the US DOE/EIA [1960–2001]).

Table 1.6 — Assessed Oil Resources
for Specific Regions of the U.S.

(Data are from or based upon data from the Outer Continental Shelf Petroleum Assessment, 2000, by the Minerals Management Service and data from the Alaska Department of Natural Resources)

Assessment Year	Region	USGS/MMS oil Assessment Volume (Gb)	Expected Recovery Volume (Gb)
2000	Pacific Federal Waters	10.7	4.5
2000	Alaska Federal Waters	24.9	10.5
2000	Atlantic Federal Waters	2.3	1.0
1998	ANWR	10.4	4.4
1995	Undiscovered Resources in the Central Region and NPR-A of Alaska North Slope	3.0	1.3
Totals		53.7	21.7

development of ANWR, the deep-water GOM and the remainder of the Alaskan North Slope would slow the U.S. production decline between 2000 and 2020. After 2020, U.S. production will decline rapidly. The graph does not include further oil development in the Arctic Ocean and federal offshore waters that are under an oil-leasing moratorium.

Table 1.7 — Estimated Ultimate Recovery for the U.S.

Region	Ultimate Production (Gb)
U.S./48 Excluding Deepwater GOM	196.9
Presently Active North Slope Fields	20.9
Table 1.6 Total	21.7
Deep-Water GOM	15.1
Southern Alaska	1.4
Total	256.0

The Estimated Ultimate Recovery for the U.S.

As previously stated, the USGS and MMS have made recent oil and gas assessments of onshore and offshore regions in the U.S. Table 1.6 lists the values reported by the USGS and MMS, along with the ERV values.

Using the values of Table 1.6, as well as previously stated values, Table 1.7 provides the estimated ultimate recovery for the U.S. The value for the U.S./48, excluding the deepwater GOM, is the ultimate production based upon Figure 1.7. The value for presently active North Slope fields is based upon Figure 1.15. The value for the deep-water GOM is based upon Figure 1.8. The value for southern Alaska is based upon the cumulative production through 2002, 1.27 Gb, and anticipated future production before production is terminated. At the end of 2003, cumulative production in the U.S. was 187.6 Gb, 73.3% of the 256.0 Gb total.

Oil and Gas Moratoria in the U.S.

Over the years, coastal states and local communities along coastlines have sought moratoria to offshore oil and gas activity because of concerns over their impact. The first federal offshore oil and gas leasing moratorium was imposed in 1982 by an act of Congress. It placed a moratorium on 736 acres off the northern and central California coast. In June 1990, President George H.W. Bush withdrew further offshore acreage from central California to the Washington/Canada border, southwest Florida, north Atlantic and eastern Gulf of Mexico until 2000. A prohibition to leasing and drilling also occurred off the North Carolina coast in 1990 as part of the Oil Pollution Control Act of 1990, although the drilling ban has since been repealed.

President Clinton extended Bush's moratorium until 2012 and expanded moratorium acreage in the eastern Gulf of Mexico from ~20 million acres to ~70 million acres, expanded acreage off the Atlantic coast and included acreage in the North Aleutian Basin (Alaska). In the Gulf of Mexico, the moratorium area includes federal water within 15 miles of the

Alabama coast and within 1000 miles of the Florida coast. President George W. Bush has since withdrawn an area approximately 20 miles by 90 miles along the western boundary of the eastern planning area in the GOM, south of the Alabama/Florida border.

In Pacific federal offshore waters, there is presently oil development in the Santa Maria-Partington Basin, Santa Barbara–Ventura Basin and the Los Angeles Basin off south and central California. Oil companies are interested in opening protected acreage off the California coast but further oil exploration and development is unlikely in the foreseeable future because of strong public opposition. It appears that the Santa Barbara oil blowout of 1969 is still reasonably fresh in the minds of many Californians. The moratorium acreage of the Atlantic, Pacific from Washington to northern California and the North Aleutian Basin has so little oil that it is unlikely that oil development would occur even if the moratorium were removed. The eastern GOM also is expected to provide very little oil, although the amount of gas may be significant.

The MMS estimates 24.9 Gb of technically recoverable oil from Alaskan federal waters, see Table 1.6.[54] The Expected Recovery Volume is 10.5 Gb. Based upon the MMS assessment, most of the 24.9 Gb would come from the Beaufort and Chuchi Seas off northern Alaska. Presently the Northstar field, just off the coast, is producing oil. Since 1970, over 99,000,000 acres of the Beaufort and Chuchi Seas has been offered in oil and gas lease sales and presently there are active leases on over 140,000 acres.[55] There has been no stampede to explore and develop oil and gas resources off the north coast of Alaska and no stampede looks imminent due to the brutal condition in the Arctic Ocean and the exceptional expenses involved. Colin Campbell expects the Arctic Ocean, off northern Alaska, to be gas prone rather than oil prone. It's quite likely that the 10.5 Gb Expected Recovery Volume is far higher than what will ever be produced from those waters.

U.S. Oil Imports

As U.S. oil production has declined and consumption has increased, oil imports have risen significantly (see Figure 1.21).

In 2003, the U.S. oil importation rate was 9.65 mb/d while production was 5.73 mb/d.[56] Imports represented 62.7% of U.S. demand. The decline in imports during 2002 can be attributed to the impact of the 9/11 terrorist attack and the economic downturn. It should be viewed as a temporary situation.

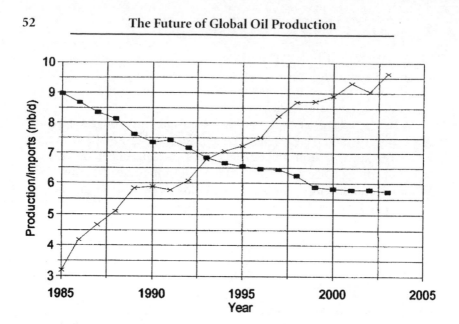

Figure 1.21— U.S. oil production [rectangles] and imports [X] (Data from the US DOE/EIA).

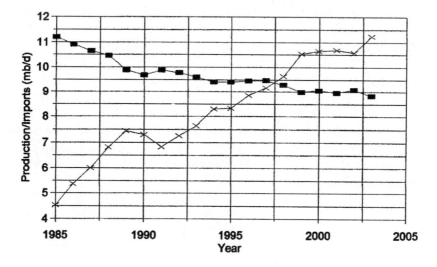

Figure 1.22 — U.S. total liquid hydrocarbons production [rectangles] and imports [X] (Data from the US DOE/EIA).

In terms of total liquid hydrocarbons, the situation appears slightly better in as much as the production rate was 8.84 mb/d and the importation rate was 11.2 mb/d in 2003.[57] Imports represented 55.9% of demand (see Figure 1.22).

To place 11.2 mb/d in perspective, the world's second highest consuming country of TLHs in 2003 was China, at 5.63 mb/d.[58] U.S. imports will grow substantially in the future even if the U.S. exploits the last of its untapped regions. How quickly U.S. oil imports grow will largely be determined by how fast consumption increases. The US DOE/EIA is projecting that U.S. total liquid hydrocarbons demand will increase by 9.4 mb/d over the period from 2000 to 2025.[59] That and more would have to come from imports. A global oil supply crisis, causing significantly higher prices, would reduce the expected increase in demand. Also, a serious effort to reduce U.S. oil consumption could significantly reduce the increase in oil imports. There is no reason to expect that in the near future.

2

Oil Production in Western Europe

Historically Western Europe had not been a significant oil-producing region until production started in the North Sea during the middle 1970s following discoveries beginning in 1968. Today, Western Europe's production represents nearly 9 percent of the world's total.[1] Most of that production occurs in the North and Norwegian Seas. Figure 2.1 shows the North and Norwegian Seas.

Western Europe's main oil producing countries are the United Kingdom (U.K.), Norway and Denmark. After the OPEC oil embargo in 1973, rapid development of many non-OPEC producing regions occurred, most notably the North Sea, Alaska and Mexico. In the U.K., oil production rose to more than 2 mb/d within 10 year after North Sea production started. In Norway, initial development was slower with the 2 mb/d level reached in ~15 years after North Sea production started. Denmark produces significantly less oil than the U.K. and Norway, ~368,000 b/d in 2003, but much more than any other West European nation.

Oil Production in the United Kingdom

The first giant field developed in the U.K. was the Forties field. Production started in 1976 and rose quickly to a maximum production rate of 523,000 b/d in 1980.[2] As Figure 2.2 illustrates, production has declined significantly since then. In 2002, Forties field production was 54,277 b/d, about 1/9th the maximum production rate. The production profile for the Forties field is indicative of field production for older fields throughout the North and Norwegian Seas. Production rises rapidly with maximum production generally occurring within 6 years after initial production.

Figure 2.1— The North and Norwegian Seas. The Norwegian Sea is north of the line that runs through Oslo (U.S. Department of Energy/Energy Information Administration).

Production typically declines at an average rate of 10–20 percent/year after maximum production has been reached. Often a production plateau occurs when the production rate reaches approximately 1/10th maximum production, as secondary extraction methods are used to extend the life of the field. After the plateau, production declines to a point where it is no longer economically feasible to maintain the field and production is terminated. Several North Sea fields have been shut down including Maureen, Argyll, Albuskjell, Cod, Edda and Yme, but their demise was little noticed.

Figure 2.3 is a graph of annual production versus cumulative production for the Forties field. The ultimate recovery from the Forties field will be ~2.5 Gb. It appears that only the Ekofisk and Statfjord fields will produce more than the Forties field in the North and Norwegian Seas.

Figure 2.4 is the summed production for the three largest U.K. fields after the Forties field: Brent, Piper and Ninian. Summed production for the three fields peaked in 1983 at 862,733 b/d. In 2002 summed produc-

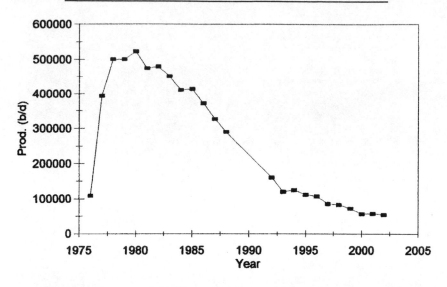

Figure 2.2 — Forties field oil production (Data from *Oil & Gas Journal*)

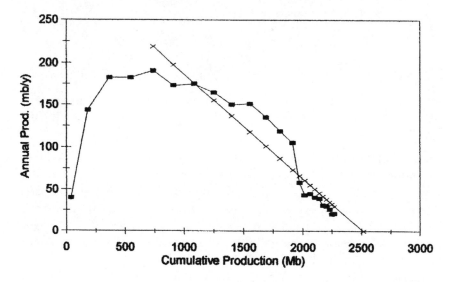

Figure 2.3 — Annual production versus cumulative production for Forties field oil production [rectangles] and best-line line to x-axis [X] (Data from *Oil & Gas Journal*).

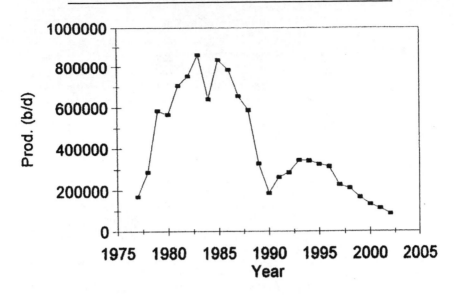

Figure 2.4 — Summed oil production for the Brent, Piper and Ninian fields (Data from *Oil & Gas Journal*).

tion was 87,869 b/d, 10.2 percent of the 1983 production level. The significantly lower production level during the 1989–1991 period was due to the Piper field fire that led to an extended shutdown of the field.

A large and growing list of U.K. fields are now in decline (see Table 2.1). Table 2.1 only includes fields that had a maximum production rate of at least 25,000 b/d and that have been in decline for at least 3 years.

The average decline rate for the 52 fields listed in Table 2.1 was 15.4 percent for 2000–2001. To counteract the rapid decline of mature fields, new but smaller fields are being brought on-line at an accelerating rate. Figure 2.5 shows the exponential increase in the number of active U.K. fields.

In 2002, there were over 260 U.K. fields in production with 84 fields under development.[3] The fields that are now being brought on-line start production at or near their maximum production rates. Many will probably have lifetimes of less than 10 years. In an extreme example of small fields having short lifetimes, the Durward and Dauntless fields were brought on-line in August 1997 and terminated in April 1999.

Several points can be made concerning the data in Table 2.1. First, the application of modern technology in the extraction of oil has not prevented rapid production declines in U.K. oil fields. Modern technology actually creates high decline rates by accelerating extraction rates in the early phase of extraction which leads to high decline rates after the pro-

U.K. Oil Fields in Decline
(Data from *Oil & Gas Journal*)

Field	On-line Date	Peak Year	Max. Prod. (b/d)	2000 Prod. (b/d)	2001 Prod. (b/d)	Abs. Decline (b/d)	% Abs. Decline	2000–2001 % Chge
1. Auk	1976	1977	58,690	11,470	8,066	50,624	86.3	-29.7
2. Piper	1977	1979	276,758	23,651	19,743	257,015	92.9	-16.5
3. Forties	1976	1980	523,000	56,541	58,000	465,000	88.9	2.6
4. Thistle	1978	1982	129,662	5,916	7,000	122,662	94.6	18.3
5. Ninian	1979	1982	304,806	35,157	36,392	268,414	88.1	3.5
6. Heather	1979	1982	37,767	3,818	4,580	33,187	87.9	20.0
7. Maureen	1984	1984	85,374	-	-	85,374	100.0	-
8. Claymore	1978	1984	103,600	30,911	29,109	74,491	71.9	-5.8
9. Murchison	1981	1984	109,145	11,127	8,479	100,666	92.2	-23.8
10. Brent	1977	1985	439,843	75,943	58,651	381,192	86.7	-22.8
11. Beatrice A&B	1982	1985	57,649	2,840	2,001	55,648	96.5	-29.5
12. Buchan	1981	1985	39,000	7,200	7,943	31,057	79.6	10.3
13. South Brae	1984	1986	97,879	5,977	5,738	92,141	94.1	-4.00
14. Fulmar	1982	1986	156,962	4,762	3,548	153,414	97.7	-25.49
15. N. Cormorant	1982	1986	100,998	28,923	30,326	70,672	70.0	4.85
16. N.W. Hutton	1983	1986	52,785	1,711	400	52,385	99.2	-76.62
17. Dunlin	1979	1987	103,273	10,600	11,842	91,431	88.5	11.72
18. Tartan	1981	1987	35,110	4,896	3,652	31,458	89.6	-25.41
19. Statfjord	1980	1987	114,623	24,695	16,442	98,181	85.7	-33.42
20. Clyde	1987	1988	51,443	9,171	8,252	43,191	84.0	-10.02
21. Hutton	1985	1988	63,012	8,365	3,033	59,979	95.2	-63.74
22. S&C Cormorant	1980	1988	122,400	18,766	12,914	109,486	89.4	-31.18
23. Eider	1988	1990	40,548	7,290	4,992	35,556	87.7	-31.52
24. North Brae	1988	1990	80,400	9,330	6,524	73,876	91.9	-30.08
25. North Alwyn	1988	1991	92,058	19,246	16,710	75,348	81.8	-13.18
26. Balmoral	1992	1992	28,050	5,732	5,656	22,394	79.8	-1.33
27. Arbroath	1990	1992	35,478	19,794	2,200	33,278	93.8	-88.89
28. Scapa	1986	1992	28,128	8,892	7,633	20,495	72.9	-14.16
29. Magnus	1984	1992	155,400	60,203	44,000	111,400	71.7	-26.91
30. Beryl	1977	1993	110,849	33,677	31,791	79,058	71.3	-5.60
31. Osprey	1991	1993	33,000	5,923	9,284	23,716	71.9	56.74
32. Tern	1990	1994	75,270	37,090	34,679	40,591	53.9	-6.50
33. Bruce	1993	1994	47,930	38,170	38,000	9,930	20.7	-0.45
34. Scott	1993	1995	179,940	57,636	44,602	135,338	75.2	-22.61
35. Gryphon	1993	1995	45,227	16,844	19,846	25,381	56.1	17.82
36. East Brae	1993	1995	74,178	22,718	13,395	60,783	81.9	-41.04
37. Strathspey	1994	1995	34,644	9,462	7,688	26,956	77.8	-18.75
38. Miller	1992	1996	135,299	42,360	29,000	106,299	78.6	-31.54
39. Wytch Farm	1986	1996	100,293	61,800	54,000	46,293	46.2	-12.62
40. Nelson	1994	1996	144,096	86,128	60,096	84,000	58.3	-30.22
41. Dunbar	1994	1996	52,479	34,973	29,707	22,772	43.4	-15.06
42. Alba	1994	1997	90,841	77,788	79,428	11,413	12.6	2.11
43. Fife	1995	1996	33,301	12,043	9,263	24,038	72.2	-23.08
44. Hudson	1993	1995	36,310	24,689	20,238	16,072	44.3	-18.03
45. Bruce	1993	1994	47,930	38,170	38,000	9,930	20.7	-0.45

Field	On-line Date	Peak Year	Max. Prod. (b/d)	2000 Prod. (b/d)	2001 Prod. (b/d)	Abs. Decline (b/d)	% Abs. Decline	2000–2001 % Chge
46. Pelican	1996	1996	31,570	14,694	9,531	22,039	69.8	-35.14
47. Thelma	1996	1997	27,570	16,370	14,431	13,139	47.7	-11.84
48. Douglas	1990	1997	34,559	17,959	23,064	11,495	33.3	28.43
49. Harding	1988	1998	86,304	80,635	66,000	20,304	23.5	-18.15
50. MacCulloch	1990	1998	41,033	28,127	22,425	18,608	45.3	-20.27
51. Joanne	1981	1998	30,827	14,229	9,877	20,950	68.0	-30.59
52. Gannett A	1978	1996	28,184	15,240	11,408	16,776	59.5	-25.14

duction peak. Second, not all oil fields decline at the same rate due to a variety of factors, but all fields in Table 2.1 that have been in decline for at least 6 years declined more than 50 percent from their maximum production rates.

As a growing number of larger U.K. fields have experienced declining production, the rapid introduction of smaller fields has not prevented U.K.'s oil production from declining since 1999 (see Figure 2.6).

In Figure 2.6, data points after 2002 are estimated based upon an EUR of 36 Gb. The U.K.'s production rate rose rapidly after 1975, reaching a peak in 1987 at 2.60 mb/d. The Piper field fire in 1987 lead to a retrenchment in U.K. production, which reached a low point of ~1.7 mb/d in 1990. Production increased again after 1992 to a second peak of 2.68 mb/d in 1999. In 2003, U.K.'s oil production averaged 2.07 mb/d, a decline of 22.8 percent from the 1999 production peak.[4]

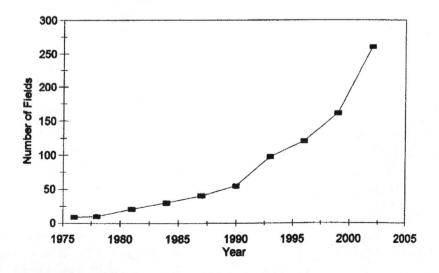

Figure 2.5 — Number of U.K. oil fields versus year (Data from *Oil & Gas Journal*)

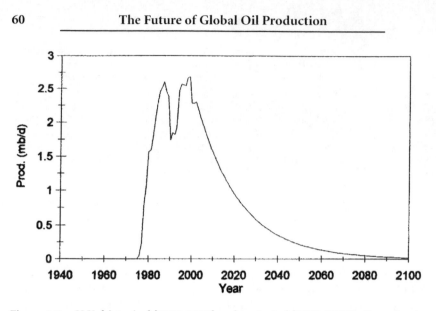

Figure 2.6 — U.K. historical [1950–2002] and projected [2003–2100] oil production assuming an ultimate recovery of 36 Gb (Historical data from the US DOE/EIA).

C.D. Masters et al. of the USGS had estimated U.K.'s ultimate oil recovery at ~36 Gb back in 1994.[5] One method of estimating EUR values for a large area containing many oil fields is with a creaming curve. A creaming curve is a plot of cumulative oil discovery versus the cumulative number of wildcat wells. Once the favorable region for oil fields is determined, the discovery rate is high since the larger fields are relatively easy to find. As an oil province becomes more extensively explored, there are fewer places to search for new fields and the fields that are discovered get smaller. Consequently, the oil discovery rate declines with time. The creaming curve for the U.K. (see Figure 2.7) suggests that 36 Gb may be a bit high but a reasonable estimate for the U.K.'s ultimate recovery.

The U.K.'s peak production rate occurred in 1999 when cumulative production was ~18 Gb, adding further weight to the belief that the U.K.'s ultimate recovery will be ~36 Gb. The production curve after 2002, Figure 2.6, assumes that the production decline will be steady. The total area under the curve represents 36 Gb and the average decline rate after the 1999 peak is 4.8 percent/year. Cumulative production at the end of 2002 was 20.3 Gb.

In their International Energy Outlook 2003 (IEO2003), the US DOE/EIA is considerably more optimistic concerning future U.K. production, although considerably less optimistic than their IEO2001.[6] The International Energy Outlook's include NGLs and refinery gain in their estimates of future oil production. Since 1995, the U.K.'s refinery gain and NGLs total

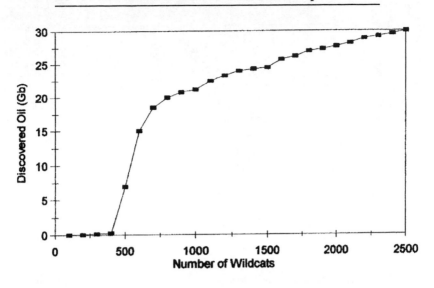

Figure 2.7 — Creaming curve for the U.K. (Data from Jean Laherrere)

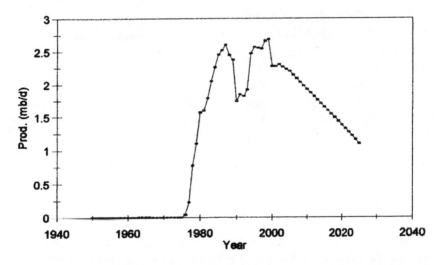

Figure 2.8 — U.K. historical [1950–2002] and projected [2003–2025] oil production using the US DOE/EIA's IEO2003 projection through 2025 (Historical data from the US DOE/EIA).

has been ~300,000 b/d. If future NGLs and refinery gain production is assumed to be constant at 300,000 b/d and that is subtracted from the US DOE/EIA's future projection of oil production, Figure 2.8 is the result. Based upon Figure 2.8, the U.K.'s 2025 oil production rate would be ~1.1 mb/d whereas in Figure 2.6, it would be ~0.74 mb/d.

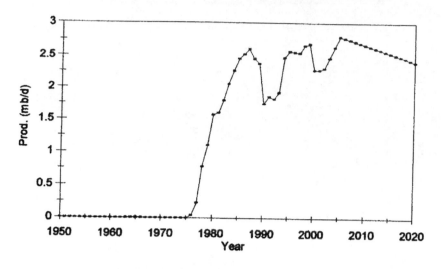

Figure 2.9 — U.K. historical [1950–2002] and projected [2003–2020] oil production based upon the US DOE/EIA's IEO2001 (Historical data from the US DOE/EIA).

The US DOE/EIA was far more optimistic in their IEO2001 in which they stated, "The United Kingdom is expected to produce about 3.1 million barrels/day by the middle of this decade, followed by a decline to 2.7 mb/d by 2020."[7]

Subtracting 300,000 b/d for NGLs and refinery gain would give 2.8 mb/d of oil production by the middle of the decade and 2.4 mb/d in 2020. The resulting graph is shown in Figure 2.9. Cumulative production through 2020 would be 36.6 Gb and the production rate would still be 2.4 mb/d. Apparently the US DOE/EIA is finally recognizing the limits of the U.K.'s oil resource although their forecast is still rosy.

Oil Production in Norway

Norway's oil production started in the 1970s with most of the oil coming from the Ekofisk and West Ekofisk fields. In 1978, those two fields produced nearly 350,000 b/d, over 99 percent of Norway's total oil production.[8] The Ekofisk field is a giant field that is ultimately expected to produce ~3.5 Gb of oil.[9] In the middle 1980s, three other giant fields started producing oil: Statfjord, Gullfaks, and Oseberg. With production coming mainly from giant fields, Norway's oil output grew through the 1980s and 1990s to over 3 mb/d. By the late 1990s, production was declining rapidly from the Statfjord, Gullfaks and Oseberg fields. Summed production for the three fields is shown in Figure 2.10.

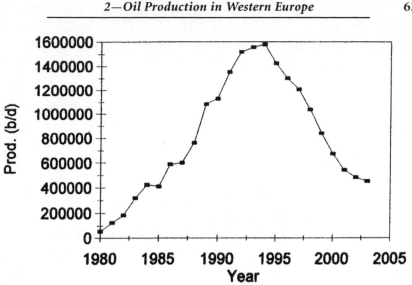

Figure 2.10 — Summed oil production for the Statfjord, Oseberg and Gullfaks fields (Data from the Norwegian Petroleum Directorate, NPD).

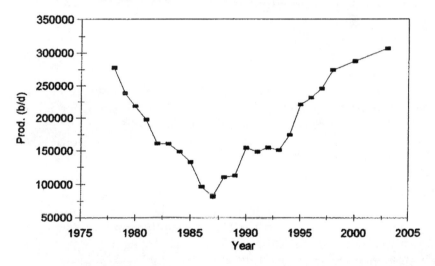

Figure 2.11— Ekofisk field crude oil production (Data from the NPD)

Summed production from Statfjord, Oseberg and Gullfaks peaked in 1994 at 1,579,594 b/d. By 2003, summed production from the three fields had declined to 455,777 b/d, 28.8 percent of the 1994 production level.

The Ekofisk field has had an unusual production profile (see Figure 2.11). The increasing production from the Ekofisk field in recent years has been due to the Ekofisk II development, which was completed in 1998.

Table 2.2 — Norway's Oil Fields in Decline
(Data from *Oil & Gas Journal*)

Field	On-line Date	Peak Year	Max. Prod. (b/d)	2001 Prod. (b/d)	2002 Prod. (b/d)	Abs. Decline (b/d)	% Abs. Decline	2001– 2002% Change
1. Tor	1978	1979	80,361	4,426	3,525	76,836	95.6	-20.4
2. Eldfisk	1979	1980	118,166	34,395	42,588	75,578	64.0	23.8
3. Murchison	1981	1985	37,646	2,406	1,815	35,831	95.2	-24.6
4. Statfjord	1980	1991	646,000	174,588	152,960	493,040	76.3	-12.4
5. Hod	1990	1991	28,000	6,498	6,412	21,588	77.1	-1.3
6. Ula	1986	1992	133,000	22,791	21,435	111,565	83.9	-5.9
7. Gyda	1990	1992	68,000	19,226	12,038	55,962	82.3	-37.4
8. Gullfaks	1988	1994	530,000	181,597	158,853	371,147	70.0	-12.5
9. Oseberg	1988	1994	502,644	189,140	174,351	328,293	65.3	-7.8
10. Veslefrikk	1989	1995	76,819	34,077	28,354	48,465	63.1	-16.8
11. Brage	1993	1996	110,337	38,428	36,942	73,395	66.5	-3.9
12. Heidrun	1995	1997	231,219	174,223	174,679	56,540	24.5	0.3
13. Statfjord East	1994	1998	73,013	37,880	33,059	39,954	54.7	-12.7
14. Valhall	1983	1999	91,554	75,159	72,075	19,479	21.3	-4.1

Production from the field declined slightly in 2003 and is expected to decline to ~80,000 b/d by 2010.[10]

As in the case of the U.K., an increasing number of large Norwegian oil fields are declining (see Table 2.2).

Table 2.2 only contains data for fields that had maximum production rates of greater than 25,000 b/d and that have been declining for at least 3 years. The average decline rate for the 14 fields was 7.6 percent/year for 2001–2002. Like the U.K., the number of producing fields has grown exponentially with time. The increasing number of active fields did not prevent a sizeable decline in Norway's oil production in 2002, 98,344 b/d.[11] It could be argued that the production decline was due to an agreement Norway made with OPEC, and several other non-OPEC producers, to limit production in the first half of 2002. The problem with the argument is that there was a substantially greater decline during the second half of the year compared to the first half of the year. Table 2.3 provides a comparison of Norway's production in 2001 and 2002.

There are still 6 major fields yet to come on-line in Norway with a summed EUR of ~960 Mb (see Table 2.4). To place 960 Mb in perspective, 7 major Norwegian fields were brought on-line in 1999 with a summed EUR of ~1,700 Mb.[12] The introduction of those fields raised Norway's oil production only slightly over the course of several years. Without the rapid introduction of major fields in the last few years, Norway's oil production has been declining and will continue to decline in the future.

Table 2.3 — Norway's Oil Production (2001–2002)
Data from the US DOE/EIA

Period	Oil Production (b/d)
2001-First Half	3,213,776
2002-First Half	3,171,150
First Half Difference	
2002–2001	-42,626
2001-Second Half	3,283,099
2002-Second Half	3,130,083
Second Half Difference	
2002–2001	-153,016
2001 Yearly Production	3,248,740
2002 Yearly Production	3,150,396
2002–2001 Difference	-98,344

Table 2.4 — Norway's Major Fields not yet On-Line
Data from the Norwegian Petroleum Directorate

Field	Anticipated On-Line Date	EUR (Mb)
1. Kristin	2005	218
2. Snohvit	2005	113
3. Ormen Lange	unknown	139
4. Skarv	unknown	131
5. Tyrihans South	unknown	138
6. Ellida	unknown	220

At an accelerating rate, small fields are being brought on-line to maintain Norway's production at the highest possible level. Production rates for smaller Norwegian fields start at or near peak production and decline rapidly soon after production starts (see Figures 12).

Figure 2.13 is a creaming curve for Norway. The creaming curve suggests that the EUR for Norway will be ~28 Gb. On average, EUR values for Norwegian fields have increased somewhat with time so an ultimate recovery of 30 Gb appears to be a reasonable estimate. Norway's peak production occurred when cumulative production was ~15 Gb, adding further weight to the belief that Norway's EUR will be ~30 Gb.

Figure 2.14 is a graph of Norway's historical and projected oil production assuming an ultimate recovery of 30 Gb. Norway's oil production had a peak in 1997 (3.15 mb/d), a valley and then a second peak in 2001 (3.25 mb/d). The valley was the result of insufficient new oil coming on-line to make up for the decline of older fields. The introduction of 7 major fields in 1999 raised Norway's oil production for a few years before it started declining again in 2002. In 2003, the production rate was 3.07 mb/d, a decline of 180,000 b/d from the 2001 average. In Figure 2.14, the decline

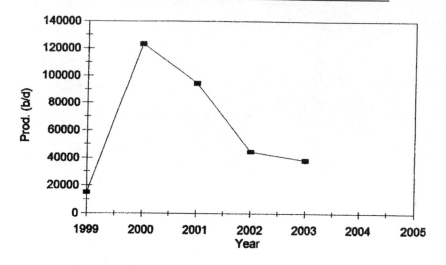

Figure 2.12 — Jotun field crude oil production (Data from the NPD)

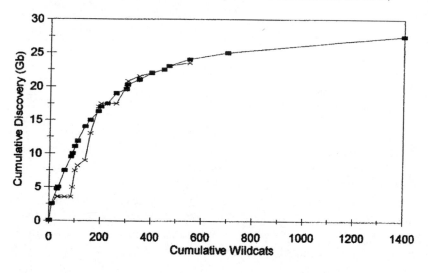

Figure 2.13 — Creaming curve for Norway, theoretical curve [rectangles] and actual discovery rate [X] (Data from Colin Campbell).

rate after 2002 is projected to be 7.2 percent/year and the oil production rate in 2020 is projected to be ~0.75 mb/d. The area under the curve is 30 Gb. Through 2002, Norway's cumulative oil production was 16.4 Gb.[13]

    Figure 2.15 is a production projection for Norway based upon data from the US DOE/EIA's IEO2003.

    The US DOE/EIA's oil production forecast from their IEO2003

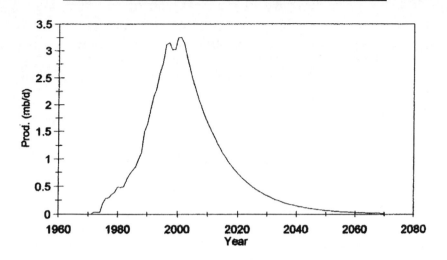

Figure 2.14 — Norway's historical [1970–2002] and projected [2003–2070] oil pro-duction assuming an ultimate recovery of 30 Gb (Historical data from the NPD).

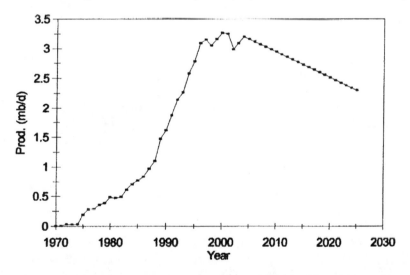

Figure 2.15 — Norway's historical [1970–2002] and projected [2003–2025] oil pro-duction with the projection based upon the IEO2003 (Historical data from the US DOE/EIA).

includes NGLs and refinery gain. Norway's NGLs production was ~180,000 b/d in 2002 and refinery gain production was essentially zero.[14] In Figure 2.15, NGLs and refinery gain production is assumed to be constant over the forecast period at 0.20 mb/d, 200,000 b/d. That has been subtracted from the IEO2003 oil production projection for Norway. In Figure 2.15,

Norway's oil production would be ~2.3 mb/d in 2025. In Figure 2.14, Norway's oil production would be ~0.50 mb/d in 2025. Based upon Figure 2.15, cumulative production through 2025 would be 39.5 Gb.

The US DOE/EIA makes the following interesting statement in their IEO2003:

> In the IEO2003 forecast, the decline in North Sea production is slowed as a result of substantial improvement in field recovery rates. Production from Norway, Western Europe's largest producer, is expected to peak at about 3.4 million barrels per day in 2004 and then gradually decline to about 2.5 million barrels per day by the end of the forecast period *with the maturing of some of its larger and older fields*. [emphasis added].[15]

As Figure 2.10 and Table 2.2 illustrate, the statement suggests that the US DOE/EIA isn't aware of what's happening in Norway's oil fields, and quite likely, fields throughout the world. Decline rates for many Norwegian fields are comparable to U.K. fields, 10–20 percent/year. The Statfjord field has declined at an average rate of 12.1 percent/year since 1992, the Gullfaks field 13.5 percent/year since 1994 and the Oseberg field 11.9 percent/year since 1994. The US DOE/EIA makes their projections of future oil production rates based upon the global petroleum assessments by the USGS. If the future production profile shown in Figure 2.14 is reasonably accurate, the unusually high forecast by the US DOE/EIA suggests a serious flaw in the USGS assessment for Norway and possibly the world. Based upon data from 2002 and 2003, it appears likely that the IEO2003 will be ~500,000 b/d high for the estimate of Norway's TLHs production in 2004.[16,17]

Oil Production in Denmark

Denmark's oil production has risen steadily since 1980, reaching a rate of ~370,000 b/d in 2000. It has largely paralleled production from Denmark's largest field, the Dan field (see Figure 2.16), which reached a peak of nearly 120,000 b/d in 2001 before declining to ~100,000 b/d in 2003. The Dan field is a field in decline.

In 1999, the Halfdan field was brought on-line (see Figure 2.17). The Danish Energy Authority, DEA, is projecting that the Halfdan field will peak in 2004 at ~105,000 b/d before declining to ~91,000 b/d in 2007.[18]

The decline of an increasing number of older fields ensures that Denmark's oil production (see Figure 2.18) will soon start to decline because there are no large fields to replace their declining production. The DEA is projecting that Denmark's oil production will peak in 2004 at ~414,000

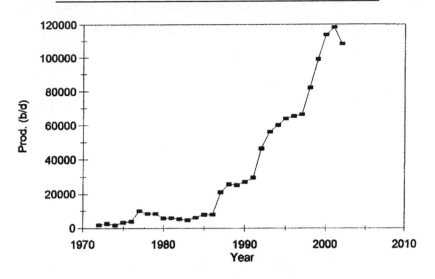

Figure 2.16 — Dan field oil production (Data from the Danish Energy Authority)

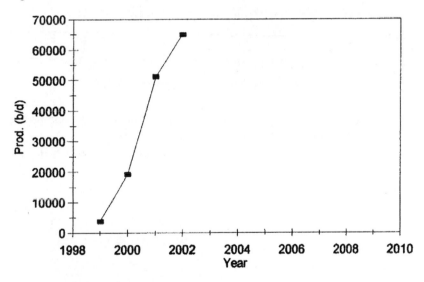

Figure 2.17 — Halfdan field oil production (Data from the DEA)

b/d. Estimates of Denmark's EUR are on the order of 2–3 Gb.[19,20] Denmark's cumulative production was 1.33 Gb at the end of 2002, over half of 2 Gb and nearly half of 3 Gb. In their 20 year forecast, the DEA projects that Denmark will be producing ~60,000 b/d in 2022.[21] The dip in production in 2001 was due to the Gorm field fire, which shut down several fields for an extended period.

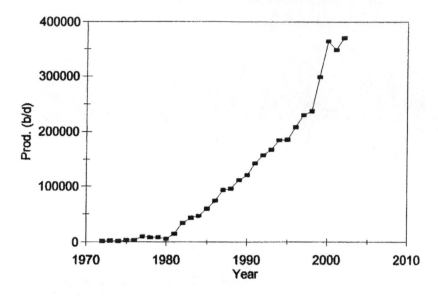

Figure 2.18 — Denmark's oil production (Data from the DEA)

Oil Production in the
Rest of Western Europe[22]

No other West European nation produces as much as 100,000 b/d of oil, although Italy produced 112,000 b/d in 1997. The largest oil producer's beyond the U.K., Norway and Denmark are Italy at 78,000 b/d and Germany at 65,000 b/d, as of 2001. Oil production from West European nations beyond the U.K., Norway and Denmark reached a maximum of 512,000 b/d in 1988, but had declined to 338,000 b/d in 2002 (see Figure 2.19).[23]

Oil production for all of Western Europe is shown in Figure 2.20. Western Europe's oil production reached its highest level in 1999 at 6.33 mb/d, but declined to 5.99 mb/d in 2002.[24]

Conclusion

Oil production in the North and Norwegian Seas is declining rapidly. In 2003, production was 349,000 b/d lower than in 2002 and 639,000 b/d lower than in 1999.[25] Developing smaller and smaller fields can only slow the inexorable decline.

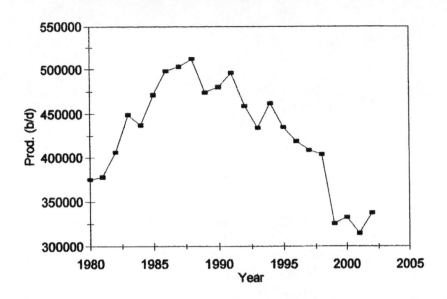

Figure 2.19 — Oil production for Western Europe excluding the U.K., Norway and Denmark (Data from the US DOE/EIA).

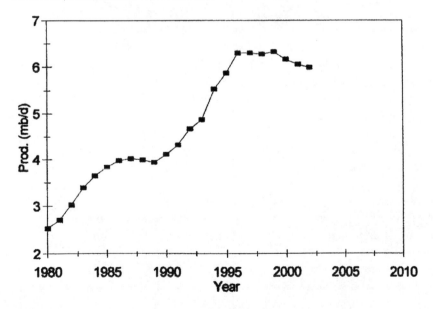

Figure 2.20 — Oil production for Western Europe (Data from the US DOE/EIA)

3

Oil Production in Mexico and Canada

In 2003, Mexico and Canada were both among the top 10 oil producing nations of the world with Mexico number 6 at 3.37 mb/d and Canada number 10 at 2.31 mb/d. Mexico was the number 2 oil exporter to the U.S., supplying 1.59 mb/d while Canada was number 3, supplying 1.55 mb/d.[1]

Oil Production in Mexico

The main oil-producing region in Mexico is the Bay of Campeche (Gulf of Mexico), between the Yucatan Peninsula and the main body of Mexico. Oil production also occurs onshore, south of the Bay of Campeche in the state of Tabasco and in the "Golden Lane" south of Tampico, on the Gulf of Mexico coast (see Figure 3.1).

The Mexican oil industry dates back to 1901 when the English based company Mexican Eagle, under the leadership of Sir Weetman Pearson, and the U.S. based company Pan American, under the leadership of Edward Doheny, began exploring for Mexican oil in earnest. It was nine years before Mexican Eagle made the first major strike at the Potrero del Llano 4 well in 1910. The well was near Tampico in a region that became known as the "Golden Lane." The Golden Lane extends south from Tampico for approximately 70 miles. The initial flow of oil from the well was 110,000 b/d, the highest flowing well in the world at the time. The initial strike led to a series of discoveries with well flow rates of 70,000–100,000 b/d per well being common.[2]

During World War I, Mexico became a critical source of oil for the U.S. and by 1920 it was providing 20% of U.S. demand. From 1919 through

Figure 3.1— Map of Mexico (Courtesy of the University Libraries, The University of Texas at Austin).

1926, Mexico had the second highest oil production rate of any country in the world. At its high point in 1921, Mexico had an annual output of 193 Mb, about 530,000 b/d.[3]

In the early 1900s, Mexican President Porfirio Diaz had established rules that were attractive to foreign oil companies, but he was overthrown in 1911. That led to an extended period of social disorder in Mexico. A new constitution was written in 1917 and Article 27 stipulated that subsurface rights belonged to the government rather than to private interests. An intense dispute ensued between the government and oil companies, particularly U.S. companies, which caused the companies to reduce their investment in the Mexican oil industry, ultimately leading to a decline in production. In the early 1920s, production was ~500,000 b/d but by the early 1930s, it had declined to ~100,000 b/d.[4]

In 1938, the Mexican oil industry was nationalized and the national oil company Petroleos Mexicanos, Pemex, was formed. Since its formation, Pemex has retained exclusive rights to oil exploration and production within Mexico.

During the 1950s and 1960s, Mexico's oil production was constrained by the belief that oil resources were limited and that they should be used as wisely as possible. After World War II, economic growth led to a significant increase in oil consumption, which required Mexico to import oil after 1957.[5] Concerns over imports led to an expansion of exploration in the 1960s and 1970s. In 1972, oil was discovered in the state of Tabasco. Further exploration in the adjacent Bay of Campeche ultimately led to the discovery of the supergiant Cantarell complex in 1976, as well as other prolific offshore oil fields including Abkatun, Ku, Pol and Chuc. The newly

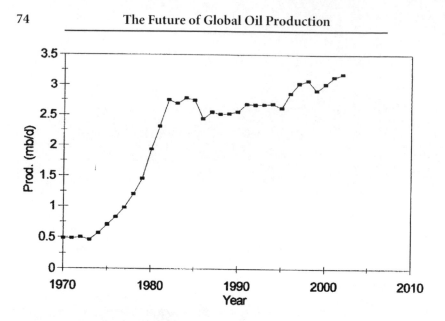

Figure 3.2 — Mexico's oil production (Data from Colin Campbell [1930–1959] and the US DOE/EIA [1960–2002]).

discovered oil came at an opportune time due to Mexico's severe economic problems and the high price of oil after the 1973 oil crisis.

Figure 3.2 is a graph of Mexico's oil production. Production increased dramatically during the late 1970s/early 1980s, from less than 500,000 b/d in 1973 to 2.75 mb/d in 1982.[6] The increase was due mainly to developments in the Bay of Campeche, most notably the Cantarell complex.

Approximately 75% of Mexico's oil production comes from the Bay of Campeche.[7] Production from the bay has increased nearly 600,000 b/d for the period 1999–2002 due to a nitrogen injection project at the Cantarell complex.[8]

The Cantarell complex is located about 80 miles from the Mexican coast. It consists of five fields: Akal, Nohoch, Chac, Kutz and Sihil but it is typically referred to as if it were one field. The Akal field is by far the largest of the four fields with ~93% of the existing proven reserves.[9] In 2002, Cantarell had the second highest production rate of any oil field or complex in the world and it has produced over 900,000 b/d through most of its productive history.[10] The high production rate through the early years of its history was made possible by the high reservoir pressure. By the middle 1990s, the reservoir pressure was declining. In order to maintain production at its historically high rate, Pemex decided on a project to inject nitrogen into the reservoir, which began in 1997 and was completed in November 2001. By 2002, Cantarell's oil production had increased to

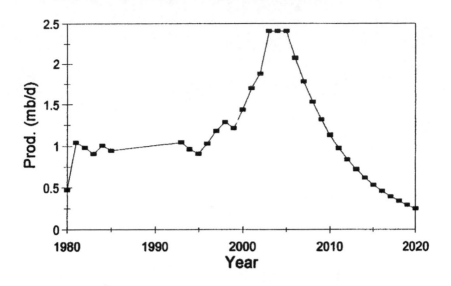

Figure 3.3 — Cantarell's historical [1980–2002] and projected [2003–2020] oil production (Historical data from *Oil & Gas Journal*).

1,851,000 b/d, ~400,000 b/d above the 2000 average. It represented nearly 60% of Mexico's total oil production.[11]

According to a recent article, the director general of exploration and production for Pemex, Luis Ramirez Corzo, expects Cantarell's production to start declining at 14%/year starting in 2006 after a projected peak production of 2.41 mb/d.[12] Decline rates of 10%/year and higher are being experienced in giant and supergiant fields such as Prudhoe Bay (10.1%/year since 1989), Statfjord (12.1%/year since 1992), Gullfaks (13.8 %/year since 1994) and Oseberg (11.9%/year since 1994).[13,14] Figure 3.3 is a graph of Cantarell's historical production [1980–2002] and projected production [2003–2020] using Corzo's forecast for projected production. Pemex did not provide field level oil production data to *Oil & Gas Journal* from 1986 through 1992 which explains the missing data points for that period in Figure 3.3 and succeeding graphs for Mexican oil fields.

At the end of 2002, Cantarell's cumulative production was ~9.2 Gb.[15,16] If production declines as Corzo states, cumulative production at the end of 2050 would be 17.15 Gb. According to a Simmons & Company International report, the fields that make up the Cantarell complex have proven reserves of 9.8 Gb, presumably at the end of 2002, which would make Cantarell's EUR at least ~19 Gb.[17] Jean Laherrere has estimated that Cantarell's EUR is ~19 Gb.[18] An average decline rate of 10.5%/year after 2005 gives an ultimate recovery of 19 Gb, assuming that the production

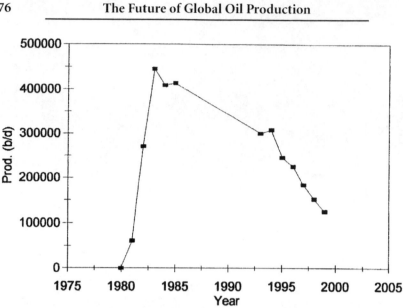

Figure 3.4 — Abkatun field oil production (Data from *Oil & Gas Journal*)

rate is 2.41 mb/d for the period 2003–2005. That may mean that either Corzo's projection is too high or the EUR is estimated too high.

Two other Mexican fields have achieved a production rate of at least 200,000 b/d: Abkatun and Ku. Figure 3.4 is a production graph for the Abkatun field. The Ku field will be discussed later.

The Abkatun field reached peak production in 1983 at 444,477 b/d. By 2002, production had decline to 79,709 b/d, a decline of 364,768 b/d (82.1%) from the peak production rate.[19]

There are 5 onshore fields in southern Mexico that achieved a production rate of > 100,000 b/d since 1971: Samaria, Cunduacan, Cactus, Jujo and Cardenas. Samaria, Cunduacan and Cactus were brought on-line in the early 1970s, while Jujo and Cardenas were brought on-line in the early 1980s. Figure 3.5 is a graph of the summed production for the 5 fields.

Summed production for the 5 fields peaked in 1978 at 604,355 b/d. In 1998, summed production was 219,720 b/d, 36.4% of peak summed peak production. *Oil & Gas Journal* has Mexican oil field data for 2002 but doesn't have data for the Sumaria field. The summed production for the other 4 fields declined from 138,229 b/d in 1998 to 102,893 b/d in 2002.[20]

Three other offshore fields have achieved a production level >100,000 b/d since 1971: Pol, Caan and Chuc. All three fields are beyond their peak production rates. Caan produced 192,488 b/d in 1998 and 132,778 b/d in

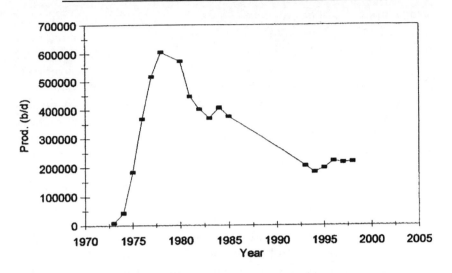

Figure 3.5 — Summed production from Samaria, Cunduacan, Cactus, Jujo and Cardenas (Data from Oil & Gas Journal).

2002. Chuc produced 146,146 b/d in 1999 and 107,167 b/d in 2002. Pol produced 164,999 b/d in 1993 and 42,073 b/d in 2002.[21]

The Cantarell complex produces heavy oil while other Mexican fields produce light and extra-light grades of oil. Production of light and extra-light Mexican oil has been declining in recent years. While Cantarell's production rose rapidly from 1995 through 2002 (850,000 b/d), oil production for Mexican fields outside of the Cantarell complex declined by 30% during the same time period. That decline significantly reduced the impact of the large production increase from the Cantarell complex such that Mexico's oil production only increased 410,000 b/d.[22]

During the 1980s and 1990s, Mexico consistently claimed oil reserves of 60 Gb and more.[23] In recent years, Mexico's oil reserves have been dramatically lowered as the Mexican government complied with U.S. Securities and Exchange Commission guidelines for determining oil reserves. In September 2002, Pemex revised its oil reserves downward again to 12.6 Gb.[24] The Mexican experience in dealing with oil reserves illustrates the problem with reported figures. Countries find it easy to exaggerate.

Pemex had hoped to increase Mexico's oil production to 4.0 mb/d in 2004 but that is not going to happen (the average production rate through the first 9 months was ~3.4 mb/d). A major new development is the Ku-Zaap-Maloob complex, also in the Bay of Campeche. Pemex is expecting to spend $4.3 billion over the next 8 years developing the complex. According to Pemex, this complex is projected to produce ~260,000 b/d in 2003,

~445,000 b/d in 2006 and ~800,000 b/d in 2011.[25] That would be an increase of 540,000 b/d from 2003 through 2011 while the Cantarell complex may decline ~1.4 mb/d from 2003 through 2011. For Mexico to hold future oil production near its present level, it would have to develop substantial production capacity outside of the Ku-Zaap-Maloob complex.

Over the years, the Mexican government has relied heavily on revenues from Pemex for funding social services. That has limited Pemex's exploration and production (E & P) efforts in the past, but the government has decided that Pemex requires more money. In 1995, the E & P budget was under $2 billion. By the late 1990s, it had risen to over $5 billion. In 2003, the E & P budget was expected to exceed $11 billion. The number of offshore drilling rigs has increased from 5 in 2001 to an expected 25 in 2003 and 40–45 in 2004.[26] Clearly the Mexican government is making a concerted effort to increase Mexico's oil production.

Spending money on oil exploration does not ensure finding large quantities of oil, as the U.S. experience during the late 1970s/early 1980s proved. Some analysts make the case that ~90% of Mexico's GOM has not been explored and that with exploration, large quantities of oil will be discovered. Geologically, Mexico's GOM consists of two distinct regions: the southern GOM and the northern GOM. The southern GOM is where the Cantarell complex, the Ku-Zaap-Maloob complex and other prolific offshore fields are located and where almost all of the Mexican GOM oil has been discovered. Presumably the region has been sufficiently explored so that most or all of the major fields have been discovered. The reservoirs in the southern GOM consist of carbonate reef structures. In Mexico's northern GOM, the rock that could conceivably contain reservoirs is sandstone. The sandstone is not as thick and uniform as farther north, in the U.S. GOM, and the rock quality is not considered good. Some experts feel that good reservoirs are unlikely in this region and that prospects for significant oil discoveries are poor. To date there have not been any significant exploration successes in this region.[27]

In their IEO2003, the US DOE/EIA states: "Mexico is expected to adopt energy policies that will encourage the efficient development of its resource base. Expected production volumes in Mexico exceed 4.2 million barrels per day by the end of the decade and remain near that level through 2025."[28]

It appears that the US DOE/EIA fails to appreciate the impact that declining oil field production will have on future Mexican production. Declining production from the Cantarell complex will strongly influence Mexico's future oil production since Cantarell produces such a large percentage of Mexico's oil. If production from the Cantarell complex starts declining in 2006, it's realistic to expect Mexico's oil production to decline as well. The situation would be comparable to Alaska when the Prudhoe Bay field started declining. The Ku-Zaap-Maloob development, and possibly others, will slow the decline of Mexican oil production but it's unrealistic to assume, as the US DOE/EIA does, that production can increase until 2010 and remain near that level through 2025. If Mexico's oil production were to increase to 4.2 mb/d in 2010 and remain fairly steady through 2025, Mexico's cumulative production from 2003 through 2025 would be ~33.7 Gb. That would be more than the sum of the undiscovered Mexican reserves (20.6 Gb), estimated by the USGS in their WPA2000, and the present proven reserves (12.6 Gb), 33.2 Gb.[29] Apparently the US DOE/EIA expects a lot of reserve growth in Mexican oil fields.

Colin Campbell estimates that the ultimate oil recovery for Mexico will be 55 Gb.[30] Mexico's cumulative production at the end of 2002 was 30.07 Gb.[31] Based upon the US DOE/EIA's forecast, cumulative production at the end of 2025 (~63.7 Gb) would be more than Campbell's EUR and production would still be ~4.2 mb/d. The US DOE/EIA does include NGLs and refinery gain in their forecasts but those components do not explain the wide discrepancy between their forecast and that of Campbell. If Campbell's EUR is close to the mark, Mexico's oil production should start declining soon.

Richard Duncan does include NGLs in his forecasts and he projects a significant decline in Mexico's oil + NGLs production in coming years (see Figure 3.6).

Duncan projected that Mexico's oil + NGLs production would peak in 2001 at 3.62 mb/d, decline to 1.34 mb/d in 2025 and 0.460 mb/d in 2039.[32] Mexico's TLHs production, mostly oil + NGLs, was 3.62 mb/d in 2001 but increased to 3.80 mb/d in the first 3 quarters of 2003.[33] The 2003 data suggest that Duncan could be a little pessimistic about Mexico's production capability, or the data could mean that the rapid rise in Cantarell complex production now will be compensated by lower production in the future.

Figure 3.7 is Colin Campbell's forecast for Mexico's oil production. Campbell projects that Mexico's oil production will peak in 2002 at 3.18 mb/d, decline to 1.12 mb/d in 2025 and 0.575 mb/d in 2040.[34] In 2002, Mexico's oil production was 3.18 mb/d but in 2003, it averaged 3.37 mb/d.[35] As in the case of Duncan, Campbell could be a little pessimistic about Mexico's production capability or it could mean that the rapid rise in Cantarell complex production now will be compensated by lower production in the future. Clearly both Duncan and Campbell are not as optimistic about Mexico's future oil production as the US DOE/EIA.

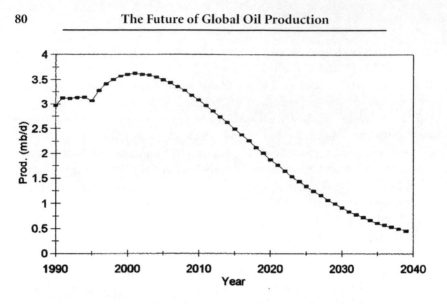

Figure 3.6 — Duncan's forecast for Mexico's oil + NGLs production

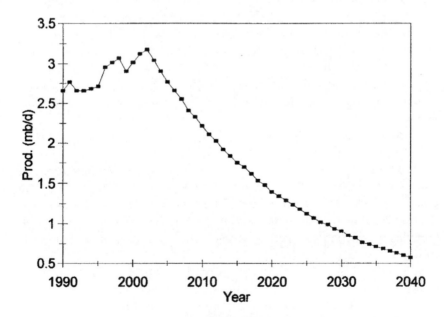

Figure 3.7 — Campbell's forecast for Mexico's oil production

Figure 3.8— Map of Canada (Courtesy of the University Libraries, The University of Texas at Austin).

Oil Production in Canada

The important oil producing provinces and territories in Canada are Alberta, Saskatchewan, British Columbia, the Northwest Territories (including Nunavut) and offshore Newfoundland/Labrador (see Figure 3.8).[36] Oil production outside of those provinces and territories is insignificant.

Oil Production in Alberta

Canada's oil production was insignificant prior to the late 1940s when major discoveries were made in the province of Alberta. Most Canadian oil production occurs in the Western Canadian Sedimentary Basin (WCSB) along the eastern side of the Canadian Rocky Mountains in Alberta, Saskatchewan and to a small extent, Northwest Territories. During the last 50 years, oil production from the WCSB has been the overwhelming

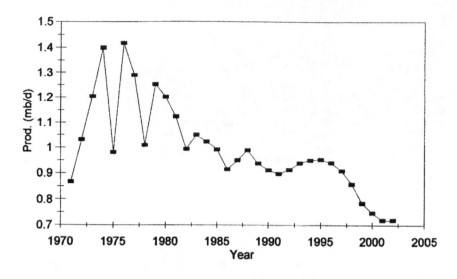

Figure 3.9 — Alberta's conventional oil production (Data from *Oil & Gas Journal*)

source of Canada's oil production. Figure 3.9 is a graph of Alberta's conventional oil production.

During the period from 1971 through 1984, Alberta's conventional oil production generally was above 1 mb/d. Since 1985, it has not exceeded 1 mb/d. From 1995 through 2002, conventional oil production declined at an average rate of 3.93%/year. The total production decline during the period was 235,532 b/d, 24.7%. About 75% of Canada's cumulative conventional oil production through 2001 came from Alberta. In 2002, the percentage of Canada's conventional oil production that Alberta produced was only ~50%.[37] Alberta has over 34,000 oil wells, but 17,700 of those wells produce an average of only 6.5 b/d.[38] Alberta's oil wells are not very productive and they're getting progressively less productive. Concerning oil production in Alberta, Raymond Chan, chief financial officer of Baytex Energy Ltd., stated, "The fact of the matter is that the [WCSB] basin is maturing and all the low-hanging fruit has been picked. What's left is the [oil sands] megaprojects."[39]

Alberta's cumulative conventional oil production through 2002 was 14.76 Gb.[40]

Figure 3.10 is an oil production graph for Alberta's oil fields that achieved a production rate > 100,000 b/d since 1971: Provost, Pembina, Swan Hills and Redwater.

Summed production from the Provost, Pembina, Swan Hills and Redwater fields was 389,139 b/d in 1972. By 2002, summed production from

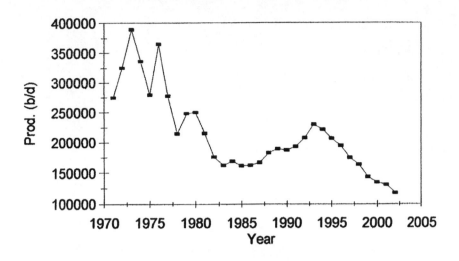

Figure 3.10 — Summed field production for the Provost, Pembina, Swan Hills and Redwater fields (Data from *Oil & Gas Journal*).

the four fields had declined to 117,771 b/d, 30.3% of the 1972 production level.[41]

Oil Production in Saskatchewan, British Columbia and the Northwest Territories

Figure 3.11 is a graph of the summed oil production from Saskatchewan, British Columbia and the Northwest Territories. (Throughout the book data presented for the Northwest Territories includes the Nunavut Territory.) The summed production rose rapidly during the 1990s due to rapidly increasing production from Saskatchewan. In recent years, the summed production has remained relatively flat at ~485,000 b/d as Saskatchewan's oil production has reached a plateau. In the near future, the summed production will start to decline as production declines in Saskatchewan. Cumulative oil production from Saskatchewan, British Columbia and the Northwest Territories was 4.93 Gb at the end of 2002.[42]

According to the US DOE/EIA the Queen Charlotte Basin, off the west coast of Canada, could contain as much as 10 Gb of oil.[43] That figure is probably an inflated oil-in-place value, in which case the amount of extract oil would be considerably less. In their World Petroleum Assessment 2000, the USGS concluded that Canada has 1.796 Gb of undiscovered offshore reserves.[44] Their assessment calls the US DOE/EIA estimate

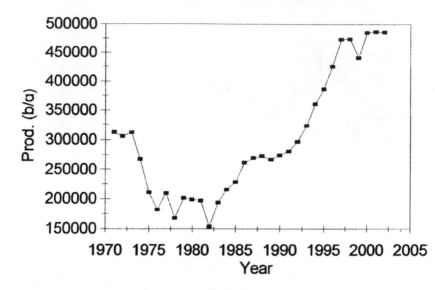

Figure 3.11— Summed oil production for Saskatchewan, the Northwest Territories and British Columbia (Data from *Oil & Gas Journal*).

for the Queen Charlotte Basin into question. The British Columbian government is pushing to lift a 30-year ban on oil exploration off the British Columbian coast.

Oil Production in Atlantic Canada

Atlantic Canada's oil production began in the early 1990s but it did not become a significant component of Canada's oil production until the Hibernia field came on-line in November 1997. In 2002, the Terra Nova field was brought on-line adding a second major source of oil to Atlantic Canada's production. In 2003, the summed production rate for the Hibernia and Terra Nova fields was 337,000 b/d. That is considerably higher than the 2001 average of 149,000 b/d and the 2002 average of 285,000 b/d. In 2005/2006, the White Rose field will add a third major source of oil to Atlantic Canada's production but by then production from Hibernia and Terra Nova could be declining. Cumulative production for Atlantic Canada was 444.4 Mb through 2003.[45]

The Hibernia field was discovered in 1979 in the Jeanne d'Arc Basin, underlying the Grand Banks. It was not developed until the 1990s due to high costs and the rigorous technological demands of producing oil from the northern Atlantic Ocean. The Hibernia field is the fifth largest field ever discovered in Canada with an EUR of 884 Mb.[46] It actually consists of two reservoirs: Hibernia and Ben Nevis-Avalon. Oil production from the Hibernia field was 149,000 b/d in 2001, 180,000 in 2002 and 203,000 b/d in 2003. In March 2003, the Hibernia field operator was allowed to increase the average daily production rate to 220,000 b/d, or 80 Mb/year. Cumulative production through 2003 was 314 Mb, 35.5 percent of the field's EUR.[47] If production is maintained at ~220,000 b/d through 2005, over half (~480 Mb) of Hibernia's original endowment will have been produced by the end of 2005. Production from Hibernia was initially projected to be terminated 18 years after first oil,[48] although the field's lifetime should be shortened due to the accelerated rate of extraction.

The Terra Nova field came on-line in 2002 and caused Atlantic Canada's oil production to increase 92 percent over the 2001 average. The field's production rate was 105,000 b/d in 2002 and 134,000 b/d in 2003. The 2003 average exceeds the originally expected plateau production rate of ~115,000 b/d. In March 2003, the Terra Nova field operator was permitted to maintain an average production rate of 150,000 b/d or 55 Mb/year.[49] If the Terra Nova field's oil production rate is maintained at 150,000 b/d during 2004–2005, approximately half of the field's original endowment of oil will be extracted by the end of 2005. The EUR for the field is 370–470 Mb.[50,51]

The third major field in Atlantic Canada is the White Rose field, discovered in 1984. It has an EUR of 200–250 Mb.[52] Oil production is expected to begin in 2005/2006 with an estimated peak production rate of 92,000 b/d.[53] The maximum summed production from Hibernia, Terra Nova and White Rose fields should be 400,000–450,000 b/d, which should occur not long after production starts from the White Rose field. Clearly Atlantic Canada's oil will not be wasted on future generations.

Hibernia, Terra Nova and White Rose fields may be the end of the line for Atlantic Canada's oil production. In February 2003, Chevron Canada Resources, ExxonMobil, Norsk Hydro and Petro-Canada announced that they would terminate exploration in the Hebron/Ben-Nevis fields for financial reasons and because of problems associated with developing scattered deposits. PetroCanada, Encana and Norsk Hydro have been exploring the Flemish Pass Basin, off the East Coast, but to date have not found commercial quantities of oil.[54]

Figure 3.12 is a graph of Atlantic Canada's oil production.

Conventional Oil Production in Canada

Figure 3.13 is a graph of Canada's conventional oil production. In 2002, the production rate was 1.51 mb/d.[55] Although production is declin-

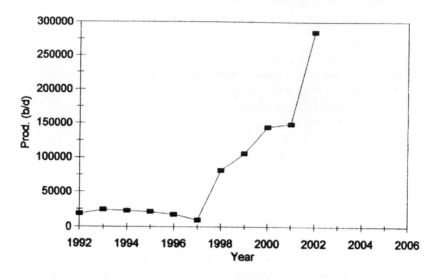

Figure 3.12 — Atlantic Canada's offshore oil production (Data from *Oil & Gas Journal* [1992–2001] and the Newfoundland & Labrador Statistics Agency [2002–2003]).

ing in Alberta and the Northwest Territories, increasing production in Atlantic Canada has prevented a decline in Canada's conventional oil production.

Oil Production from the Athabasca Oil Sands

A major source of Canada's oil production in recent years has been the Athabasca Oil Sands, located in northern Alberta. Proven reserves of oil for the Athabasca Oil Sands has been reported to be 174.4 Gb as of Jan. 2004.[56]

Oil sands are a mixture of sand, clay, water and a hydrocarbon called bitumen. Bitumen is a solid or semi-solid hydrocarbon that cannot be pumped out of the ground. Oil sands can be dug up and processed or an "in situ" procedure can be used to obtain the oil. According to the Alberta Ministry of Energy, roughly 2 tons of oil sands are required to produce 1 barrel of oil.[57]

Surface mining can only be used for ~20 percent of Alberta's oil sands at today's oil prices.[58] Surface mining involves excavating the oil sands, transporting it to a processing plant and processing the oil sands to separate the bitumen from the sand, clay and water. After separation, bitumen is heated or mixed with lighter hydrocarbons to allow the bitumen

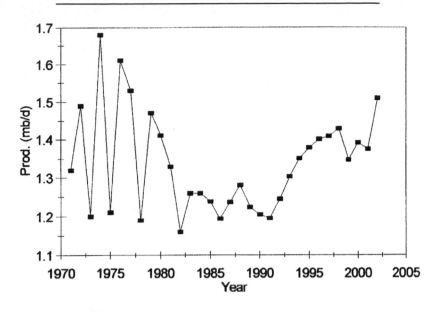

Figure 3.13 — Canada's conventional oil production (Data from *Oil & Gas Journal*)

to flow. The largest use of condensate and natural gas liquids in western Canada is as a diluent in the blending of heavy oil and bitumen to facilitate its transport to market by pipelines. Typically bitumen requires the addition of approximately 40 percent diluents while conventional heavy oil requires about 7 percent.[59] After separation, the bitumen is transferred to a refinery where it is upgraded. "In situ" extraction is used when the bitumen is too deep for surface mining. Steam is injected into the ground which allows the bitumen to flow and separate from the clay and sand. According to *Oil & Gas Journal*, "in situ" bitumen production was 302,750 b/d in 2002.[60]

Both methods of extracting oil from oil sands are energy intensive. According to Walter Youngquist, the energy profit ratio for oil production from oil sands is only 1.5.[61] That means it takes the energy equivalent of 2 barrels of oil to produce 3 barrels of oil from oil sands. Much of the energy used in the extraction and processing of oil sands comes from burning natural gas. Natural gas is used to generate electrical energy for mining and processing facilities and to create steam for "in situ" extraction. Approximately 20 percent of Canada's natural gas supply is used for oil sands extraction and processing.[62] In 2003, the price of natural gas in North America averaged approximately 3 times the price during the 1990s.[63] The increased price of natural gas has made the economics of oil sands development less favorable. Natural gas production in western Canada appears to be in long-term decline and this could have serious implication for future oil sands development. Atomic Energy of Canada Ltd. has commissioned the Canadian Energy Research Institute to study the feasibility of using nuclear power as an energy source for oil sands extraction and processing as a substitute for natural gas.[64]

The Kyoto Protocol agreement, which Canada ratified in 2002, also has possible implications for oil sands development. It requires countries to limit emissions of carbon dioxide in an effort to reduce greenhouse gas warming of the earth. The agreement may require companies producing oil from oil sands to invest in CO_2 emissions reduction technology or acquire carbon credits to offset emissions associated with oil production.

Another problem that may affect oil sands development involves the impact of natural gas production in the oil sands region on "in situ" oil extraction. According to ConocoPhillips, steam pressure is not contained within rock layers if natural gas is removed from oil sands.[65] The pressure within the oil sands can become too low to extract bitumen using existing technology rendering large amounts of bitumen inaccessible. According to Neil McCrank, Alberta Energy and Utility Board (EUB), "There is an immediate and continued risk to bitumen recovery from the production of natural gas [within the Athabasca Oil Sands region]."[66]

Because of the concern over natural gas production affecting bitumen recovery, 938 natural gas wells were shut down during 2003 in the oil sands region.[67]

The high development costs of oil sands projects and the increasing price of natural gas used for extraction and processing have already resulted in TrueNorth Energy, Canadian Natural Resources and Petro-Canada delaying projects. In the case of Petro-Canada, they decided in spring 2003 to defer an upgrader expansion, budgeted at $5.8 billion, until it can find a way to cut costs. Shell Oil's Athabasca Oilsands project was originally projected to cost $3.8 billion but ultimately cost $5.7 billion. Syncrude Canada Ltd. reported that their latest oil sands expansion will cost $7.6 billion, nearly twice the original estimate. Suncor's Millennium project increased in cost from $2 billion to $3.4 billion.[68] According to a recent article in *The Toronto Globe and Mail*, the era of the oil sands mega-project may be coming to an end due to large cost overruns.[69]

With that said, there are oil sands projects that have recently been completed and projects that are still going forward. In 2001, Suncor completed Project Millennium, which has a production capacity of 225,000 b/d.

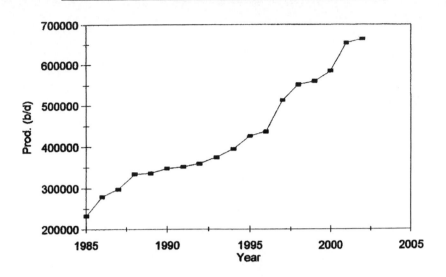

Figure 3.14 — Oil production from oil sands projects (Data calculated from Canada's total oil production [US DOE/EIA] minus Canada's conventional oil production [*Oil & Gas Journal*]).

A second Suncor project, the Voyageur Project, is expected to produce 500,000–550,000 b/d by 2012. A third Suncor project, the Firebag Project, is an "in situ" project that is projected to produce ~35,000 b/d beginning in 2004. The Athabasca Oil Sands Project, a joint venture of Shell Canada Ltd.; Chevron Canada Ltd. and Western Oil Sands Inc., is expected to produce 155,000 b/d of diluted bitumen in the near future with plans to ultimately increase production to 525,000 b/d. Encana Inc. has two projects under development. The Christina Lake Thermal Project is expected to produce 70,000 b/d and the Foster Creek Project is expected to produce 20,000 b/d initially, with a possible production increase to 100,000 b/d by 2007.[70] Canadian studies have indicated that the maximum potential production rate of oil from oil sands could be ~3.0 mb/d from 15–24 processing plants.[71]

Figure 3.14 is a graph of oil production from oil sands projects. In 2002, production was 660,000 b/d.[72,73]

Figure 3.15 is a graph of Canada's total oil production, including both conventional and unconventional oil.

Canada's total oil production in 2003 was 2.31 mb/d, while cumulative production at the end of 2003 was 24.5 Gb.[74] Whether Canada's future production rate increases or decreases will depend largely upon how rapidly production can be increased from the Athabasca Oil Sands. A slow rise in Canada's production appears likely, at least in the near future, due to

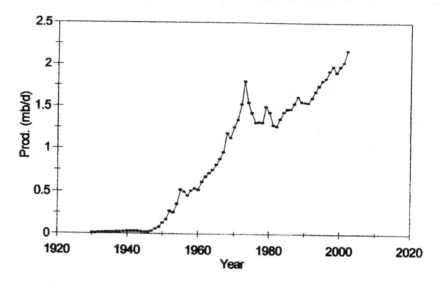

Figure 3.15 — Canada's total oil production (Data from Colin Campbell [1930–1959] and US DOE/EIA [1960–2002]).

unconventional oil production increasing more rapidly than the decline in conventional oil production. If cost problems hamper oil sands development, Canada's production could decline.

Future Oil Production in Canada

The US DOE/EIA's IEO2003 states the following concerning Canada's near term oil production:

> Canada's conventional oil output is expected to increase by more than 200,000 barrels per day over the next 2 years, mainly from Newfoundland's Hibernia oil project, which could produce more than 155,000 barrels per day at its peak sometime in the next several years. Canada is projected to add an additional 500,000 barrels per day in output from a combination of frontier area offshore projects and oil from tar sands."[75]

It's assumed that the US DOE/EIA is forecasting production for 2003–2005 relative to the 2002 oil production average. If the Hibernia field produces 220,000 b/d and the Terra Nova field produces 150,000 b/d in 2005, the combined production increase for those two fields would be 85,000 b/d from 2002 to 2005. Countering increasing production from Atlantic Canada is declining conventional oil production from Alberta and the Northwest Territories. Alberta's conventional oil production declined at an average rate of 3.93 percent from 1996 through 2002.[76] If that average decline rate continues from 2002 through 2005, Alberta's conventional oil production would decline ~81,500 b/d. If the Northwest Territories average decline rate for 1993–2002 continues from 2002 through 2005, its oil production would decline ~2,200 b/d. The summed decline for Alberta and the Northwest Territories would be ~83,700 b/d and Canada's conventional oil production would increase by only ~1,300 b/d. Conventional oil production from Saskatchewan and British Columbia could also decline during 2002–2005 causing a decrease in Canada's conventional oil production. The 200,000 b/d increase for Canada's conventional oil production that the US DOE/EIA forecast predicts appears to be based upon wishful thinking.

In the case of oil sands development, it's possible that projects in the planning stage or under development may be delayed or terminated so it's impossible to accurately assess how quickly production may increase. The US DOE/EIA is projecting that Canada's oil production will increase by ~700,000 b/d, presumably from 2002 to 2005. Looking back at the period 1999–2002, Canada's oil production increased 260,000 b/d. That increase was made possible by the rapid production increases from Hibernia and Terra Nova fields as well as production increases from oil sands development. The production increases from Hibernia and Terra Nova fields will not be nearly so large from 2002 to 2005. Canada's oil production increase for 2003 was ~95,000 b/d over the 2002 average. Production would have to increase ~600,000 b/d in 2004/2005 to make the US DOE/EIA projection valid. That appears unlikely unless unconventional production can grow at a much higher rate than it has historically grown.

Figure 3.16 is a graph of Richard Duncan's forecast for Canada's oil + NGLs production. His forecast includes unconventional oil production from oil sands projects.

Duncan projects that Canada's oil + NGLs production will reach its highest rate in 2010 at 2.93 mb/d, decline to 2.23 mb/d in 2025 and to 1.27 mb/d in 2039.[77]

Figure 3.17 is Colin Campbell's forecast for Canada's conventional oil production. His forecast does not include unconventional oil production from oil sands projects but it illustrates how quickly he expects Canada's conventional oil production to decline.

Campbell projected that Canada's conventional oil production would be 1.07 mb/d in 2000, decline to 0.274 mb/d in 2025 and 0.110 mb/d in 2040.[78] Since conventional oil production was 1.51 mb/d in 2002, it appears

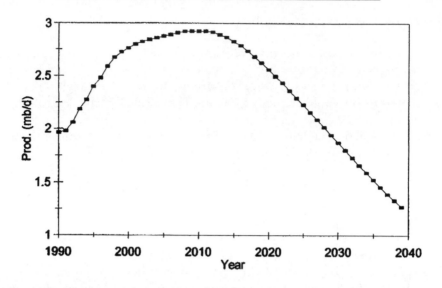

Figure 3.16 — Duncan's forecast for Canada's oil + NGLs production

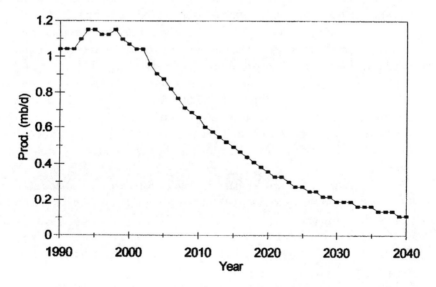

Figure 3.17 — Campbell's forecast for Canada's conventional oil production

that Campbell may have under-estimated Canada's production potential or that production will be lower in the future due to higher production now. Canada's cumulative conventional oil production at the end of 2002 was 19.6 Gb.[79] Campbell's EUR for Canada's conventional oil production is 25 Gb, which would leave ~5.4 Gb of oil to be produced after 2002.[80]

Conclusion

In conclusion, there are good reasons to expect that Mexico's oil production will peak in 2003 or soon thereafter. Production from the Cantarell complex, which produces ~60 percent of Mexico's oil, can not be sustained at the 2003 production rate for much longer. As production declines from the Cantarell complex, Mexico's production will as well.

Canada's oil production will increase slowly in coming years if unconventional oil production increases faster than the decline of conventional oil production. If cost problems delay or terminate oil sands projects, Canada's oil production could start declining in the near future.

4

Oil Production in South and Central America

Oil production in South and Central America started during the early 1900s. Prior to 1950, most of that production originated from Venezuela. Today, most production from the region, ~95 percent, comes from 5 countries: Venezuela, Brazil, Colombia, Ecuador and Argentina (see Figure 4.1). All 5 countries produce more than 350,000 b/d.

The most important oil producer among the 5 nations is Venezuela, which was a founding member of the Organization of Petroleum Exporting Countries (OPEC). Because of Venezuela's membership within OPEC, its oil production has been based upon OPEC's production quotas over much of the period since the 1978/1979 oil crisis. Venezuela has by far the largest oil resource of any country in South and Central America.

Beyond Venezuela, the other four significant oil producing nations in South and Central America are in various stages of production. Since 1995, Brazil's oil production has risen rapidly due to intense development of the deep-water Campos Basin. Colombia's oil production rose rapidly from 1985 to 1999, due largely to development of the Cano Limon, Cusiana and Cupiagua fields. Colombia's oil production has declined rapidly since 1999, paralleling the rapid decline of those 3 fields. Argentina has been producing oil for a long time and is now in long-term decline. Ecuador's oil production could increase in the next few years due to recent developments but after that, production is likely to decline.

A noteworthy aspect of oil production in South and Central America is that historically it has not been as intense as that of the U.S. and North Sea. The intensity of development has increased in the last 15 years, particularly in the Campos Basin of Brazil and the large fields of Colombia. Colombia's oil production has declined rapidly since 1999 and intense

Figure 4.1— Map of South America (Courtesy of the University Libraries, The University of Texas at Austin).

development of the Campos Basin will lead to a rapid production decline in Brazil after the production peak.

Figure 4.2 is a graph of oil production from South and Central America since 1980. Production rose from 3.65 mb/d in 1980 to 6.60 mb/d in 2000 before declining to 6.12 mb/d in 2002.[1]

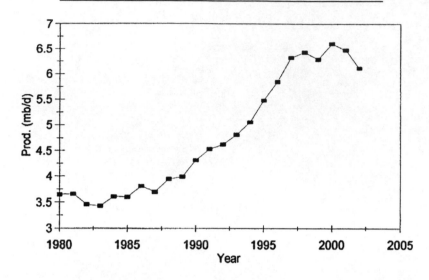

Figure 4.2 — Oil production in South and Central America (Data from the US DOE/EIA).

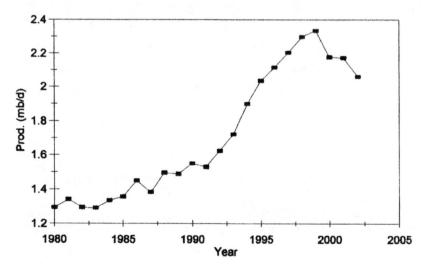

Figure 4.3 — Oil production in South and Central America, excluding Brazil and Venezuela (Data from the US DOE/EIA).

If oil production from Brazil and Venezuela is subtracted from that of South and Central America, it appears that production from the remainder of South and Central America has entered long-term decline (see Figure 4.3).

Production rose from 1.30 mb/d in 1980 to 2.34 mb/d in 1999 before declining to 2.06 mb/d in 2002, a decline of 280,000 b/d (~12 percent) from the 1999 value.[2]

Oil production in Venezuela, Brazil, Colombia, Ecuador and Argentina will be covered individually and the remainder of South and Central America will be covered as a whole in this chapter.

Oil Production in Venezuela

Like the United States, Venezuela has had a long oil production history. Over much of its production history, Venezuela has been among the top oil producing nations of the world. In the early 1960s it was the second leading oil producing nation behind the U.S. In 2002, it ranked number 8 in the world for oil production.[3]

Venezuela's oil exploration started in the early 1900s, stimulated by the passage of the 1905 Mining Law which opened the country to exploration. Extra heavy oil was discovered in eastern Venezuela in 1912, but the first major commercial development of conventional oil was the Mene Grande field, located east of Lake Maracaibo, which was discovered in 1914. Major oil discoveries were made along the eastern margin of Lake Maracaibo between 1917 and 1922, the fields becoming known as the Bolivar Coastal fields.[4] During the 1930s, oil derricks were placed in Lake Maracaibo.

During the 1940s, 36 oil fields were discovered in eastern Venezuela.[5] During the 1950s, further discoveries were made in eastern Venezuela and the Maracaibo Basin. Also during the 1950s, the Orinoco Oil Belt, containing extra heavy oil, was delineated.

Venezuela was a founding member of OPEC when it was formed in 1960. Venezuela nationalized its oil industry in August 1975, creating the state oil company Petroleos de Venezuela SA (PDVSA). PDVSA must hold at least a 51 percent share of any oil exploration and production in Venezuela.

As stated in the introduction, OPEC countries increased their reported oil reserves during the late 1980s to increase their production quotas within OPEC. Venezuela was the first to increase its reserves by adding some Orinoco extra heavy oil in 1987. The increase by Venezuela stimulated other OPEC members to increase their reserves to balance the addition made by Venezuela.

Venezuela has 10 fields with EUR values over 1.5 Gb, shown in Table 4.1.

Venezuela's oil production has come mainly from the fields in Table

Table 4.1— Venezuela's Ten Largest Oil Fields*

Fields	Reported EUR Value (Gb)	Cumulative Production at the end of 1996 (Gb)	Highest Prod. Rate for 1971-1996 (b/d)	Estimated 2000 Prod. Rate (b/d)$$	% Produced Based Upon Reported EUR
Lagunillas†	14.0	11.8	940,070 (1971)	200,000	84.3
Bachequero†	8.0	7.2	738,853 (1971)	260,000	90.0
Tia Juana†	5.0	4.6	373,025 (1971)	100,000	92.0
Carito	4.5	0.13	61,271 (1991)	<100,000	2.9
Lama†	4.0	3.0	320,246 (1971)	<100,000	75.0
El Furrial	3.5	0.62	277,737 (1993)	100,000	17.7
Boscan	2.5	0.91	78,870 (1992)	<100,000	36.4
Pueblo Viejo†	2.0	Unknown	0	<100,000	
Centro	2.0	1.2	189,396 (1993)	100,000	60.0
Lamar	1.75	1.4	146,187 (1973)	100,000	80.0
Total§	45.2	30.9			68.4

* Data from "Country Assessment Series-Venezuela" by The Association for the Study of Peak Oil, Newsletter 22
† Part of the Bolivar Coastal field complex
§ Not including the Pueblo Viejo field
$$ Estimates from Simmons & Company International

4.1. Most of the fields have cumulative production values well over 50 percent of their reported EUR values and are in a serious state of depletion. The summed EUR for the fields in Table 4.1 is 45.2 Gb, excluding Pueblo Viejo. Approximately 30.9 Gb of oil from the Table 4.1 fields, 68.4 percent, had been produced by the end of 1996.

Figure 4.4 is a graph of the summed production for Venezuela's fields that achieved production rates of at least 300,000 b/d after 1970: Lagonillas, Bachaquero, Lama and Tia Juana. Summed production from the Lagonillas, Bachaquero, Lama and Tia Juana fields was 2.37 mb/d in 1971. By 1996, summed production for the four fields was 1.01 mb/d, 42.6 percent of the 1971 production level. OPEC production quotas were a factor in reduced production after 1973, but the declines of the fields are a significant factor in the much lower production level of the 1990s.

Since 1971, 5 other Venezuelan fields achieved a production rate of at least 100,000 b/d: Lamar, Centro, El Furial, Mulata and Santa Barbara. Figure 4.5 is a graph of the summed production for the 5 fields.

From 1971 through 1986, only the Lamar and Centro fields were producing oil and their production rates generally declined during the period. Summed production from the 5 fields started increasing in 1987 with the introduction of the El Furial field and a spurt in production from the Centro field. In 1989, production started from the Santa Barbara field and in 1991, production started from the Mulata field. Production increases from

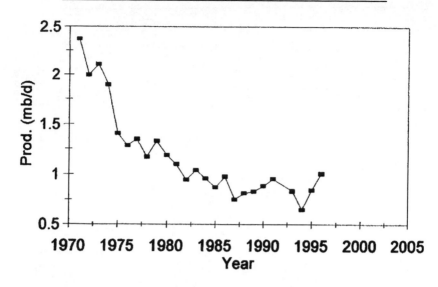

Figure 4.4 — Summed oil production for Lagonillas, Bachaquero, Lama and Tia Juana fields (Data from *Oil & Gas Journal*).

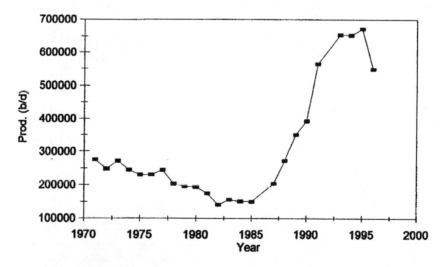

Figure 4.5 — Summed oil production from Lamar, Centro, El Furial, Mulata and Santa Barbara fields (Data from *Oil & Gas Journal*).

the El Furial, Santa Barbara and Mulata fields are responsible for the summed production increase from 1987 to 1995. The decrease in production in 1996 is due to a large production decline from the El Furial field, possibly due to technical problems.

Figure 4.6 is a graph of Venezuela's oil production. Venezuela's oil pro-

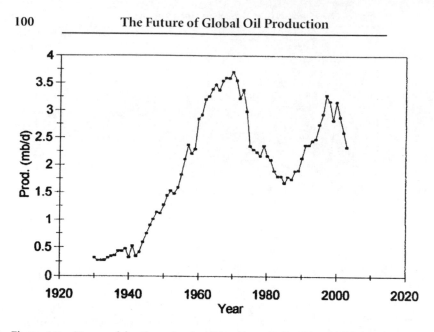

Figure 4.6 — Venezuela's oil production (Data from Colin Campbell [1930–1959] and US DOE/EIA [1960–2002]).

duction reached its highest rate in 1970 at 3.71 mb/d. The dip in production following that peak, which hit a low in 1985 at 1.68 mb/d,[6] was the result of reduced demand for OPEC oil as non-OPEC nations increased their production after the oil crises of the 1970s. Production reached a second peak of 3.28 mb/d in 1997. In recent years, the number of producing fields in Venezuela has increased substantially: from 68 in 1979, to 88 in 1989, to 240 in 1999.[7] The increasing number of fields is an indication of production problems at the older, larger oil fields. In spite of the rapidly increasing number of fields, Venezuela's oil production has been declining since 2000.

There was a sharp decline in Venezuela's oil production during the first few months of 2003 due to a strike by PDVSA workers that started in December 2002. The strike was an effort by PDVSA employees, and others, to force President Hugo Chavez to resign or hold early elections. The strike caused oil production to drop from 2.97 mb/d in November 2002 to 0.63 mb/d in January 2003. Venezuela's oil production crept up after January as the strike petered out. By May 2003, production was 2.66 mb/d.[8] The increasing oil production through the early part of 2003 masks underlying problems with Venezuela's oil production that has been exacerbated by the strike.

More than a third of PDVSA employees were terminated as a result of the strike and new employees have taken their place.[9] Some oil industry sources in Venezuela claim that the lack of experience by new employees is causing maintenance and reservoir management problems. One source stated, "There is a perception that production is heavily declining now. That reality is sinking in and they [PDVSA] are having serious problems with maintenance which in turn impacts production."[10]

According to Fernando Delgado, executive director of the Zulia state branch of Venezuela's national oil chamber, there is a natural 20 percent annual decline in Venezuela's oil fields and poor maintenance will exacerbate future oil production.[11] Some analysts estimate that production from the Lake Maracaibo region has declined by up to 350,000 b/d due to poor well maintenance.[12] PDVSA may have overproduced some fields after the strike and an industry source stated, "That is always a bad industry practice because when you overproduce you will never reach optimum economic recovery."[13]

It has been reported that there is a reduced number of active wells in the western Lake Maracaibo region and a reduced level of drilling.[14] According to Gero Farruggio, senior consultant for the oil consulting firm Wood MacKenzie,

> We believe the current level of production cannot be maintained. History has shown that Venezuelan oil fields have critical needs. [Fields operated by PDVSA] are likely to exhibit the strong decline levels experienced in recent years as a result of under investment.[15]

Luke Parker of Wood MacKenzie stated that,

> Some of the production deficit will be picked up by IOC (international oil companies) fields which have enjoyed a relaxation of their OPEC quotas (since the strike). However, this will be limited to a 10 percent increase from current IOC production by 2005. It is unlikely that new discoveries such as the [Ceuta] Tomoporo field, which PDVSA intends to tender under terms of the new hydrocarbon law, will come on-stream before 2008.[16]

PDVSA has a plan to spend $45 billion on oil exploration and development by awarding joint venture contracts to Venezuelan and foreign oil companies, but international oil companies are wary of investing in Venezuela because of the country's political problems. PDVSA wants to increase Venezuela's oil production to 5.1 mb/d by 2008. It's questionable whether such an increase in production is possible.

According to a Wood MacKenzie consultant,

> It's hard to see where the necessary investment levels will emerge to maintain Venezuela's current production capacity. A continuation of the status quo would see Venezuela struggle to supply its current market share and could result in production levels falling to a new low of 2.5 mb/d by 2008.[17]

Venezuela's conventional oil production averaged 2.3 mb/d in October 2003 while extra heavy oil production from the Orinoco Oil Belt averaged 0.37 mb/d.[18] Extra heavy oil is used as a boiler fuel, called Orimulsion, or as a low grade crude oil that is upgraded in special refineries. Orimulsion consists of ~70 percent natural bitumen, ~30 percent water and less than 1 percent surfactants. Bitumen is a solid or semi-solid hydrocarbon. There are presently 4 joint venture extra heavy oil projects under development or in production.[19]

1. The Petrozuata development, by ConocoPhillips, which is currently producing up to 120,000 b/d.
2. The Cerro Negro extra heavy oil field, by ExxonMobil, which started production in 2001 and is currently producing up to 120,000 b/d.
3. The Sincor project, by TotalFinaElf and Statoil, which began production in February 2002. It is presently producing up to 160,000 b/d with maximum production expected to be 200,000 b/d.
4. The Hamaca project, by ConoccoPhillips and ChevronTexaco, which started in November 2001. It is currently producing up to 30,000 b/d with maximum production expected to be 190,000 b/d after completion of the Hamaca upgrader in late 2004.

Estimates of economically recoverable extra heavy oil and bitumen in the Orinoco Oil Belt range from 100 to 270 Gb. According to the U.S. DOE/EIA, conventional "proven" oil reserves in Venezuela, as of January 2003, were 77.8 Gb, which isn't supposed to include extra heavy oil and bitumen.[20] The Venezuelan government added Orinoco extra heavy oil to their reserves estimate back in 1987, so the 77.8 Gb figure presumably includes extra heavy oil. As stated in the introduction, oil reserves figures are flawed, especially those for members of OPEC, and it's not wise to put much stock into the oil reserves estimate for Venezuela.

The US DOE/EIA projects that Venezuela's TLHs production capacity will increase steadily from 3.2 mb/d in 2001 to 5.6 mb/d in 2025.[21] That forecast appears unlikely to be met because approximately half of Venezuela's conventional oil has been produced. Excluding the production problems of late 2002/early 2003, Venezuela's oil production has been declining since 2000. For the April through September period, Venezuela's oil production was 2.867 mb/d in 2001, 2.741 mb/d in 2002 and 2.630 mb/d in 2003. That's a decline of 237,000 b/d for the specified period from 2001 to 2003. In 2000, Venezuela's oil production for the year was 3.155 mb/d,[22] suggesting that production has declined consistently since 2000 if the domestic problems that started in Dec. 2002 are excluded. Venezuela's unconventional oil production is likely to increase in the future, but the

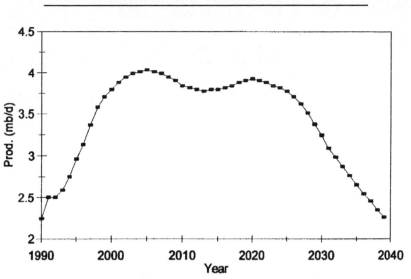

Figure 4.7 — Duncan's forecast for Venezuela's oil + NGLs production

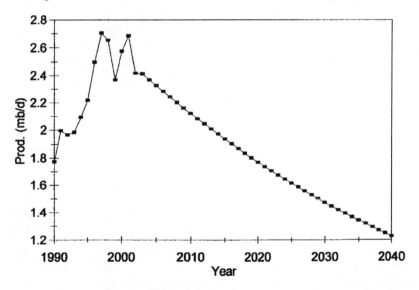

Figure 4.8 — Campbell's forecast for Venezuela's oil production

increase will be largely or totally negated by the decline of conventional oil production.

Figure 4.7 is Richard Duncan's forecast for Venezuela's oil + NGLs production. Duncan projects that Venezuela's oil + NGLs production will remain relatively flat at 3.5 — 4.1 mb/d between 1998 and 2028, followed by a decline to 2.26 mb/d in 2039.[23] In 2003, THLs production averaged 2.34 mb/d but it was influenced by the PDVSA strike in the early part of the year. In no year from 1998 through 2003 has TLHs production been as high as 3.5 mb/d.

Figure 4.8 is Colin Campbell's forecast for Venezuela's oil production. Campbell projects a decline in Venezuela's conventional oil production from 2.69 mb/d in 2001 to 1.60 mb/d in 2025 and 1.23 mb/d in 2040. A key difference between the forecasts of Duncan and Campbell is that Campbell does not include unconventional oil production from the Orinoco Oil Belt in his forecast. Campbell estimates that cumulative production of conventional oil at the end of 2075 will be 95 Gb.[24] At the end of 2001, 46 Gb of conventional oil had been produced, 48 percent of 95 Gb.[25]

Oil Production in Brazil

Brazil's oil production began in the early 1950s from both onshore and shallow-water (<1000 feet) offshore fields concentrated along the Atlantic coast. Much of the onshore portion of Brazil is underlain with the Brazilian and Guayana Shields, basement rock, so the geologically favorable onshore area is limited, as well as potential production. Figure 4.9 is a graph of Brazil's oil production, excluding production from the deep-water (>1000 feet) Campos Basin.

The production rate from the region is about 250,000 b/d. Brazil's onshore oil production rate is slightly over 200,000 b/d and has been creeping up slowly in recent years. Oil production from the shallow-water offshore portion of Brazil reached its highest rate in 1984 at over 60,000 b/d. It has since declined to approximately 30,000 b/d.[26]

When Brazil's oil imports soared in the 1970s, the state oil company, Petrobras, started exploring the deep-water Campos Basin, located >60 miles from Brazil's coastline, leading to the discovery of approximately 12.5 Gb of oil from the 1970s through 1990s.[27] Brazil's oil production has risen rapidly in recent years due to intense development of the basin (see Figure 4.10). In 2002, oil production from the Campos Basin represented 82.6 percent of Brazil's total oil production.[28] Brazil's future production will largely depend on what happens in the Campos and Santos Basins.

Campos Basin production is concentrated in 7 large fields: Marlim, Marlim Leste, Marlim Sul, Barracuda, Caratinga, Albacora and Voador. Another field, Roncador, was producing oil until 3 explosions in 2001 sunk the P-36 oil platform which produced the oil. The field was expected to

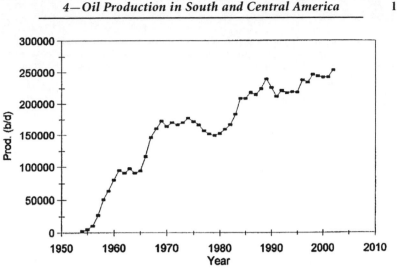

Figure 4.9 — Oil production in Brazil, excluding the Campos Basin (Data from the state oil company Petrobras).

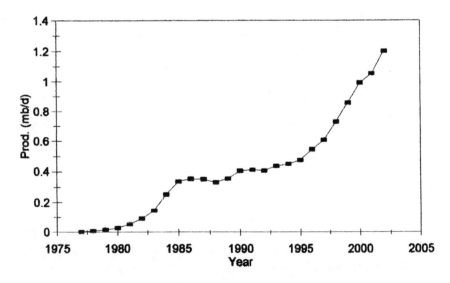

Figure 4.10 — Oil production from the Campos Basin (Data from the state oil company Petrobras).

start producing oil again in late 2002 from a new platform, with production expanded in early 2004 after completion of a second platform. At the end of 2002, cumulative production from the basin was 3.98 Gb.[29]

Table 4.2 contains publicly available oil reserves data for several Campos Basin fields.

Table 4.2 — Published Reserves for Campos Basin Fields

(Data from "Wood Mackenzie Believes Deepwater Brazil Stands at the Crossroads," *http://www.woodmac.com/news_e_30.htm* and *http://www.offshore-technology.com/projects/marlimpetro/*)

Field	Reserves (Gb)
Marlim	1.7
Barracuda-Caratinga	1.1
Albacora	1
Roncador	2
Marlim Sul	Possibly 1.2

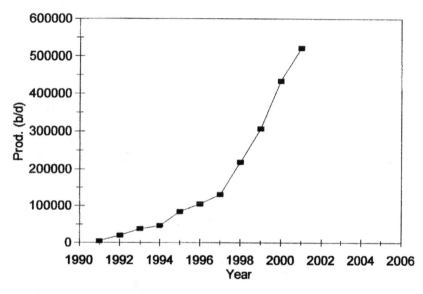

Figure 4.11 — Marlim field oil production (Data from Jean Laherrere)

The Marlim field has the highest production rate of any field in the Campos Basin (see Figure 4.11). The field was discovered in 1985 in over 2000 feet of water, approximately 70 miles offshore. There are 147 wells planned for the field, at least 95 of which had been drilled by Jan. 1, 2003. Most wells will be for oil extraction but some will be for water or gas injection.

In 2001, the oil production rate from the Marlim field averaged ~520,000 b/d.[30] Cumulative production at the end of 2001 was 0.70 Gb. If the EUR for the field is 1.7 Gb, cumulative production should have reached 50 percent of the EUR in 2002, suggesting that production should start declining soon, if it hasn't already.

The Roncador field was discovered in 1996 in over 4000 feet of water, approximately 125 miles offshore. At the time of the sinking of the P-36

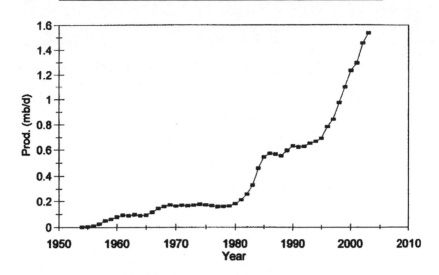

Figure 4.12 — Brazil's oil production (Data from Petrobras [1954–2002] and US DOE/EIA [2003]).

platform in 2001, production from the field was 83,000 b/d and the production capacity was 180,000 b/d. Peak production from the two new platforms is expected to be 180,000 b/d.

Figure 4.12 is a graph of oil production for all of Brazil. Brazil's oil production has risen from 693,000 b/d in 1995 to 1,550,000 b/d in 2003, an increase of 857,000 b/d.[31]

Until 1998, Petrobras had monopoly rights over oil exploration, production, refining and distribute in Brazil. In 1998, the Brazilian National Petroleum Agency opened up 92 percent of the acreage in the nations sedimentary basins to independent oil companies. Since then, large independent oil companies have been actively exploring for oil in Brazil.

The USGS provides some impressive estimates of undiscovered oil volumes off Brazil's coast in their World Petroleum Assessment 2000. They estimated that the Campos Basin had a mean undiscovered oil resource of 16.3 Gb and the Santos Basin, south of the Campos Basin, had 23.2 Gb as of January 1, 1999. For Brazil as a whole, the USGS estimated a mean undiscovered oil resource of approximately 47 Gb (see Figure 4.13).[32]

Actual exploration results in the Campos Basin have not been nearly as rosy as the USGS assessment. According to the oil consulting firm Wood McKenzie, international oil companies drilled 32 deep-water wildcat wells in the Campos Basin since the discovery of the Roncador field in 1996 without any large discoveries. Only 7 wells have the possibility of commercialization. During the same period, Petrobras drilled 113 wildcat wells

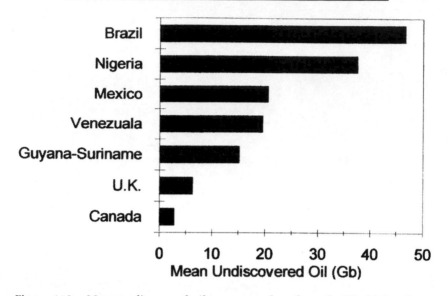

Figure 4.13 — Mean undiscovered oil resource values from the World Petroleum Assessment 2000.

with only two fields, Jubarte and Cachalote, being discovered. Both fields are in block BC-60, where most of the other commercial Campos Basin fields have been discovered. If large oil discoveries aren't made soon, Wood McKenzie expects Brazil's oil production to peak in 2007 at ~2.1 mb/d and decline to ~1.6 mb/d in 2010.[33]

In their IEO2003, the U.S. DOE/EIA states, "Brazil's [oil] production is expected to rise throughout the forecast period and to top 3.9 million barrels per day by 2025."[34] The difference between the US DOE/EIA forecast and that of Wood McKenzie couldn't be much greater.

The Brazilian government is giving oil companies every opportunity to discover the oil that the USGS assessment claims is in the Campos and Santos Basins. In 1999, the government offered 12 blocks for leasing, each block being about 1800 miles square. Foreign oil companies involved in winning bids included Unocal, Texaco, Amerada Hess, ExxonMobil, BP-Amoco, Agip and Repsol YPF. In 2000, the government offered 23 blocks for leasing, mostly smaller blocks to appeal to small oil companies. Acreage in the Campos and Santos Basins generated the most interest. In 2001, the government offered 53 blocks for leasing, 43 of the blocks being offshore in deep water. ExxonMobil, Royal Dutch/Shell, TotalFinaElf and Statoil had winning bids in the 2001 exploration license auction. In 2002, the government offered 39 blocks for leasing.[35] Another exploration license auction was set for August 2003 but there was little interest by international oil companies. Explanations for the lack of interest include the high tax rate associated with oil production, the high costs associated with producing the heavy oil that is found in most Campos Basin fields and better exploration opportunities in other regions of the world.

The lack of significant commercial discoveries since the discovery of the Roncador field certainly plays an important part in the recent disinterest in Brazilian oil exploration. Since 1998, TotalFinaElf, BPAmoco and ConocoPhillips have not found any commercially viable oil fields. Discoveries that have been made are small, located in deep water and consist of extremely viscous oil. TotalFinaElf has announced plans to scale back exploration activities in Brazil. Petrobras has not given up hope for further large deep-water discoveries. In May 2003, they announced plans to invest $34 billion over the next 4 years, mainly in exploration.[36] The poor discovery results since 1996 suggest that the Campos and Santos assessment volumes in the World Petroleum Assessment 2000 may be unrealistically high.

In the Santos Basin, Chevron has teamed up with Petrobras to explore a block ~2500 miles square, while Amerada Hess acquired 2 exploration blocks in 1999. Petrobras made a 40 Mb discovery in the Santos Basin during 2001. That is a far cry from the >1 Gb discoveries of the Campos Basin. Petrobras also made a recent discovery that was reported to be 0.8–1.0 Gb, probably oil-in-place.

Figure 4.14 is Richard Duncan's forecast for Brazil's oil + NGLs production.

Duncan projects that Brazil's oil + NGLs production will peak in 2007 at 1.06 mb/d, decline to 0.684 mb/d in 2025 and 0.400 mb/d in 2039.[37] Since Brazil's production rate was 1.55 mb/d in 2003, his assessment for the early years of this decade are below the actual production rate. It may mean that Duncan has not accurately assessed the oil resource of the Campos Basin.

Figure 4.15 is Colin Campbell's forecast for Brazil's oil production.

Campbell projects that Brazil's oil production will rise to ~2.25 mb/d in ~2007 and remain at that level for approximately 5 years before declining to near zero in 2040. Campbell estimates that Brazil's cumulative oil production at the end of 2075 will be 22.5 Gb, essentially its EUR.[38] At the end of 2002, Brazil had a cumulative production of 6.88 Gb, 31 percent of 22.5 Gb.[39]

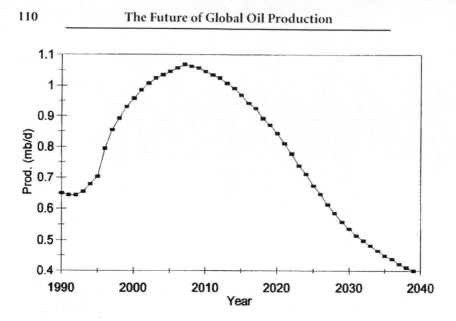

Figure 4.14 — Duncan's forecast for Brazil's oil + NGLs production

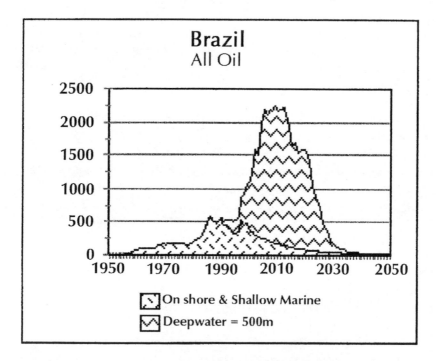

Figure 4.15 — Campbell's forecast for Brazil's oil production

Oil Production in Colombia

Colombia's oil production started after the discovery of the Orito field, east of the Andes Mountains, in 1962 by Texaco and Gulf Oil Companies. The Orito field is in an advanced state of depletion but as of 2000, the field was still producing about 4,200 b/d.[40]

In the early 1980s, concerns about the need for possible future oil imports motivated the government to relax laws dealing with oil exploration and development by foreign oil companies. Between 1970 and 1986, Colombia's oil production generally hovered in the 100,000–200,000 b/d range.[41] The government's stimulus to international oil companies was rewarded with 3 major discoveries in the 1980s: Cano Limon, Cusiana and Cupaigua, all in the Llanos Basin.

The Cano Limon field has a reported EUR of 1.3 Gb. According to Occidental Petroleum, oil production peaked in 1990 at 208,000 b/d and cumulative production is 0.91 Gb (date unknown).[42] Oil production data for the Cano Limon field are inconsistent in *Oil & Gas Journal*; it appears that production from the Cano Limon field was occasionally credited to the La Yuca and Matanegra fields. Because of the inconsistency, Figure 4.16 is a graph of summed production from the Cano Limon, La Yuca and Matanegra fields.

What is apparent from Figure 4.16 is that summed production for the

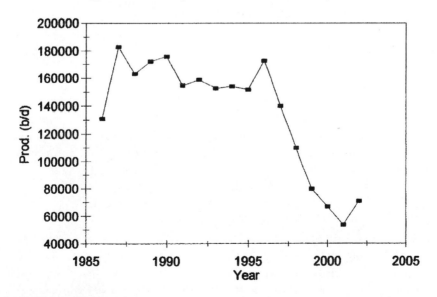

Figure 4.16 — Oil production from the Cano Limon/La Yuca/Matanegra fields (Data from *Oil & Gas Journal*).

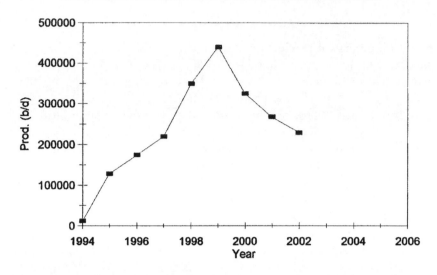

Figure 4.17 — Summed production from the Cusiana/Cupiagua fields (Data from *Oil & Gas Journal*).

three fields has declined substantially in recent years. In 1996, summed production was 172,554 b/d, but it declined to 70,764 b/d in 2002, a decline of ~102,000 b/d (~59 percent) over 6 years.[43]

The second major oil field discovery in the 1980s was the Cusiana field, with a reported EUR of 1.5 Gb. The Cusiana discovery was quickly followed by the discovery of the Cupiagua field, with a reported EUR of 0.5 Gb.[44] Figure 4.17 is a graph of summed production from the Cusiana and Cupiagua fields.

Summed production from the fields peaked in 1999 at 440,000 b/d. Summed production declined to 230,153 b/d in 2002, a decline of ~210,000 b/d (~48 percent) in the course of 3 years. At the end of 2002, cumulative production from the two fields was 0.785 Gb.[45] Since production is declining rapidly from the two fields, it may indicate that the EUR values are overestimated.

In 2000, the Cano Limon, Cusiana and Cupiagua fields produced ~55 percent of Colombia's total oil production.[46] As these fields have declined, so has Colombia's oil production (see Figure 4.18).

Colombia's oil production peaked in 1999 at 816,000 b/d, declined to 577,000 b/d in 2002 and to 538,000 b/d in 2003.[47] In their July 2003 Oil Market Report, the International Energy Agency (IEA) projected that Colombia's oil production would decline 49,000 b/d in 2004.[48]

In their IEO2003, the US DOE/EIA states that "Colombia's current economic downturn and civil unrest have delayed development of its

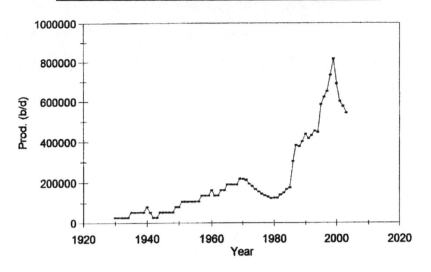

Figure 4.18 — Colombia's oil production (Data from the US DOE/EIA)

upstream sector, but its output is expected to top 650,000 b/d within the decade then show a modest decline for the remainder of the forecast period."[49]

The IEO2003 forecast is a significant departure from the IEO2001 forecast which projected that Colombia's oil production would surpass 1 mb/d by 2010.[50] The IEO2001 forecast didn't make any sense and the IEO2003 forecast still appears excessively optimistic. It seems illogical that an economic downturn in Colombia would delay production development if international oil companies are doing the work. Furthermore, the oil could be sold in the international marketplace to make Colombia money.

For the period 1999–2002, an average of almost 20 exploration contracts per year were signed by independent oil companies and the Colombian government, but there have not been any significant discoveries as a result of those contracts. In 2003, there were only 2 exploration contracts signed as of July.[51] Reasons given for the low level of interest by independent oil companies include the guerrilla war, high drilling costs and most importantly, a shortage of good prospects.

There are considerable problems in Colombia that could hinder oil development by international oil companies. The Cano Limon pipeline was bombed 170 times by guerillas in 2001, holding back more than 24 million barrels of crude oil according to the state oil company Ecopetrol. In 2002, the Cano Limon pipeline was only bombed 41 times but Colombia's oil production stilled declined from the 2001 level.[52] The Cusiana/Cupiagua complex and associated Ocensa pipeline have not been a frequent tar-

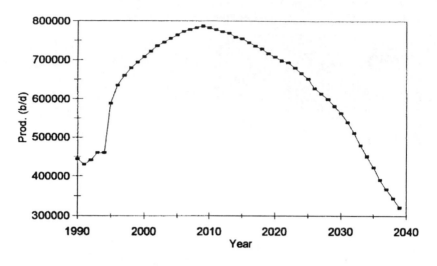

Figure 4.19 — Duncan's forecast for Colombia's oil + NGLs production

get of bombings because most of the pipeline is underground making it a more difficult target for bombing.

In 2002, two Colombian oil fields were brought on-line: Suroriente and Guado. The Suroriente field is expected to have a peak production rate of 6,000 b/d, while the Guado field is expected to have a peak production rate of 20,000–30,000 b/d. In March 2003, Ecopetrol announced the discovery of a field with estimated reserves of ~200 Mb.[53] More recent analysis indicated that the reservoir contains mainly water and Occidental Petroleum has turned the field over to the Colombian government, apparently finding it unworthy of development.

Figure 4.19 is Richard Duncan's forecast for Colombia's oil + NGLs production.

Duncan projects that Colombia's oil + NGLs production will peak in 2009 at ~787,000 b/d, decline to ~652,000 b/d in 2025 and ~321,000 b/d in 2039.[54] Duncan underestimated Colombia's oil + NGLs production prior to 2001 and appears to have overestimated it from 2001 on. About 98 percent of Colombia's TLHs production during the period 1999–2001 was due to oil, so TLHs production has followed oil production closely.[55]

Figure 4.20 is Colin Campbell's forecast for Colombia's oil production.

Campbell projected that Colombia's oil production would peak in 1999 at 822,000 b/d, decline to 192,000 b/d in 2025 and 82,000 b/d in 2040. His forecast from 1999 through 2003 is very close to the actual production values. Campbell estimates that Colombia's cumulative production at the

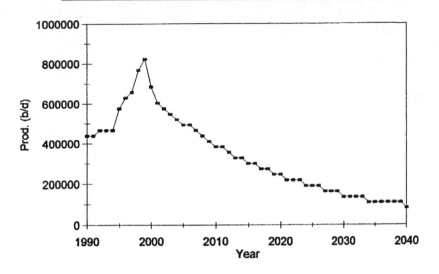

Figure 4.20 — Campbell's forecast for Colombia's oil production

end of 2075 will be 10 Gb, essentially its EUR.[56] At the end of 2002, cumulative production was 6.24 Gb, 62 percent of 10 Gb.[57]

Oil Production in Argentina

Argentina's oil exploration started during the early 1900s, although production didn't exceed 100,000 b/d until 1959.[58] Production rose rapidly through the 1960s to over 400,000 b/d by 1971 and remained in the 400,000–500,000 b/d range until the early 1990s. Production then climbed to a peak of 847,000 b/d in 1998. In 2003, production was 741,000 b/d, a decline of 106,000 b/d (12.5 percent) since 1998.[59] Figure 4.21 is a graph of Argentina's oil production.

Argentina has been extensively explored with ~4000 wildcat wells having been drilled.[60] Most of Argentina's oil fields are relatively small and located onshore. There was hope that oil exploration offshore near the Malvinas Islands would provide further reserves, but results have been disappointing.

In their IEO2003, the US DOE/EIA makes an interesting statement concerning Argentina:

> Argentina is expected to increase its production volumes by at least 150,000 barrels per day over the next two years, and by the middle of the decade it is capable of becoming a million barrel per day producer.[61]

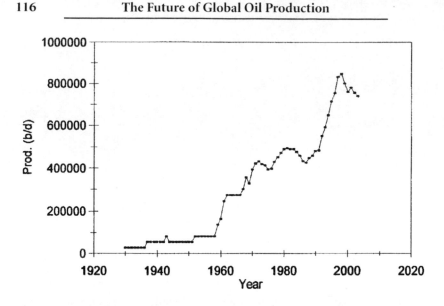

Figure 4.21— Argentina's oil production (Data from Colin Campbell [1930–1969] and US DOE/EIA [1970–2003]).

How the US DOE/EIA reached that conclusion is uncertain, but recent production data do not support the US DOE/EIA's claim. In 2003, Argentina's oil production rate declined 16,000 b/d from the 2002 average.[62] That is not a good start to the 150,000 b/d increase that the US DOE/EIA projects over the next 2 years. Meanwhile, the International Energy Agency projects that Argentina's oil production will continue to decline in 2004.[63]

According to Platts Global Energy, there is little interest by foreign oil companies to explore for oil in Argentina because there are few, if any, promising exploration targets. Even Argentina's oil companies are looking elsewhere for oil.[64]

Figure 4.22 is Richard Duncan's forecast for Argentina's oil + NGLs production. Duncan projected that Argentina's oil + NGLs production would peak in 2001 at ~911,000 b/d, decline to ~278,000 b/d in 2025 and ~134,000 b/d in 2039.[65] Argentina's TLHs production peaked in 1998 at 902,000 b/d and had declined to 834,000 b/d by 2001. Argentina's NGLs and refinery gain production averaged about 55,000 b/d for the period 1999–2001. Oil production represented 93.7 percent of TLHs production during the period.[66]

Figure 4.23 is Colin Campbell's forecast for Argentina's oil production. Campbell projected that Argentina's oil production would peak in 1998 at ~849,000 b/d, decline to ~137,000 b/d in 2025 and ~55,000 b/d in

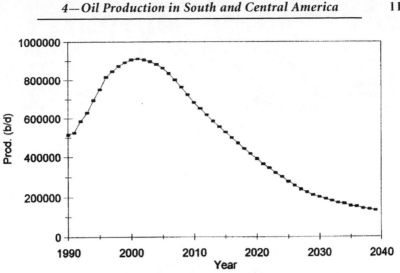

Figure 4.22 — Duncan's forecast for Argentina's oil + NGLs production

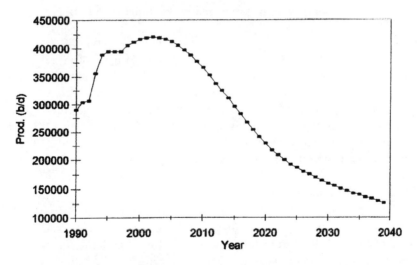

Figure 4.23 — Campbell's forecast for Argentina's oil production

2040. Campbell has estimated that Argentina's cumulative production at the end of 2075 will be 12 Gb, essentially its EUR.[67] At the end of 2002, cumulative production was 8.88 Gb, 74 percent of 12 Gb.[68]

Oil Production in Ecuador

Ecuador's first oil discovery occurred during the 1970s east of the Andes Mountains. Further exploration in the region led to a series of dis-

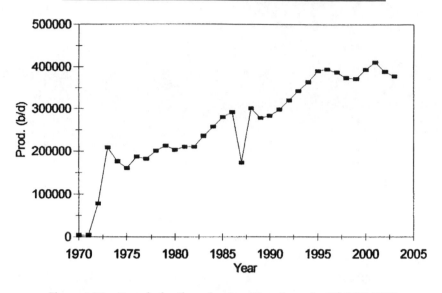

Figure 4.24 — Ecuador's oil production (Data from the US DOE/EIA)

coveries. Much of Ecuador's oil production comes from 6 fields: Shushu-findi, Sacha, Cononaco, Cuyabeno, Lago Agrio, and Auca although there were 70 field listed in *Oil & Gas Journal* for 2002.[69] Several other fields are expected to come on-line in the near future: Palo Azul and Eden-Yuturi with summed peak production of ~55,000 b/d. The Ishpingo, Tambo-cocha and Tiputini (ITT) oilfields have a reported 2 Gb of heavy oil with a potential peak production of 200,000 b/d.[70] The state oil company, Petroe-cuador, is interested in getting independent oil companies involved in the development of the ITT fields, and to cover the estimated $3.5 billion expense, but development is presently on hold.[71]

Figure 4.24 is a graph of Ecuador's oil production. Ecuador's highest oil production rate was in 2001 at 412,000 b/d. In 2003, the production rate averaged 403,000 b/d but in November, after completion of the OCP oil pipeline, the production rate was 497,000 b/d.[72]

The US DOE/EIA states, "Although the current political situation in Ecuador is in transition, there is still optimism that Ecuador will increase production by more than 350,000 barrels per day within the next few years."[73]

The main constraint to higher oil production is the limitation of pipelines to carry the oil. The OCP (Oleoducto de Crudos Pesados) pipe-line apparently started transporting heavy oil in September 2003 but there are questions about whether oil production can be raised enough to fill the pipeline. According to a Petroecuador source, "They built the OCP saying that the companies that were building it would produce enough crude to fill the pipeline, but the fields operated by private companies are declining at a faster rate than [state oil company] Petroecuador's fields."[74]

The source further added:

> After all the seismic studies they have done on these fields, the only one that might be able to increase production before the pipeline starts up is Occidental['s] and maybe Repsol YPF['s], but even then they will only have about 250,000 barrels a day [to put in the pipeline].[75]

According to the US DOE/EIA, the pipeline has a maximum capacity of 518,000 b/d. Due to the OCP pipeline, the US DOE/EIA states, "Ecuador's oil transport capacity could increase to as much as 850,000 bbl/d, allowing for significant increases in oil production and export capacity."[76]

The US DOE/EIA assumes that 160,000 b/d of oil that is transported by the SOTE pipeline will be shifted to the OCP pipeline but the Petroecuador source states, "Why would we pay US$2 a barrel [for transport through the OCP pipeline] when we could pay 30 cents a barrel using our own [SOTE] pipeline — it doesn't make sense."[77]

Ecuador's September 2003 production rate (477,00 b/d) was 97,000 b/d higher than the August rate (380,000 b/d), suggesting the pipeline has started carrying oil.[78] The International Energy Agency is projecting that Ecuador could increase its production rate by 100,000 b/d in 2004.[79]

Ecuador reports 4.6 Gb of "proven" reserves, suggesting that a higher production rate is possible.[80] Two Gb of that oil is in ITT fields, which will be brought on-line sometime in the future. In their World Petroleum Assessment 2000, the USGS assessed Ecuador's mean undiscovered oil reserves at 0.970 Gb, indicating that there isn't too much more oil to find in Ecuador.[81]

Figure 4.25 is a graph of Richard Duncan's forecast for Ecuador's oil + NGLs production. Duncan projected that Ecuador's oil + NGLs production would peak in 2002, at ~421,000 b/d, decline to ~186,000 b/d in 2025 and ~126,000 b/d in 2039.[82]

Figure 4.26 is Colin Campbell's forecast for Ecuador's oil production. Campbell projects that Ecuador's oil production will be ~410,000 b/d from 2000–2007, decline to ~219,000 b/d in 2025 and ~110,000 b/d in 2040. Campbell estimates that Ecuador's cumulative production at the end of 2075 will be 8.5 Gb, essentially its EUR.[83] At the end of 2002, cumulative production was 3.13 Gb, ~37 percent of 8.5 Gb.[84]

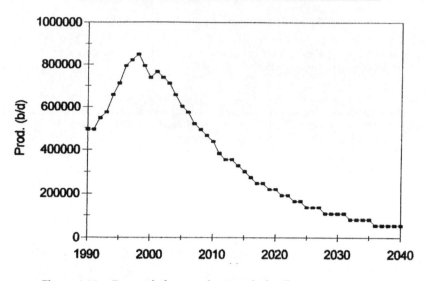

Figure 4.25 — Duncan's forecast for Ecuador's oil + NGLs production

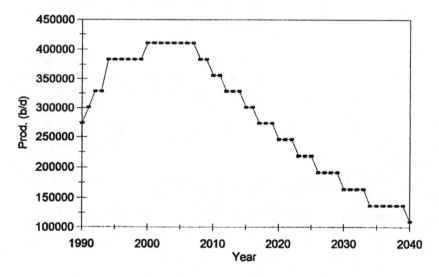

Figure 4.26 — Campbell's forecast for Ecuador's oil production

Oil Production in the Rest of South and Central America

Figure 4.27 is a graph of oil production for South and Central America, excluding the 5 countries covered previously. Oil production from this region has never been particularly high. In 1981, production reached its

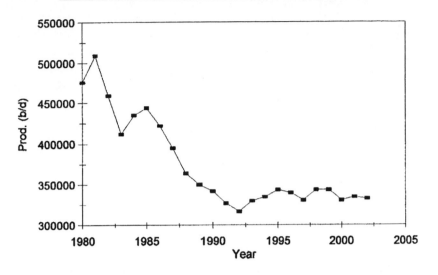

Figure 4.27 — Oil production for South and Central America, excluding the 5 countries covered previously (Data from the US DOE/EIA).

highest rate at 500,000 b/d. It then declined to the 300,000–350,000 b/d range where it has been for the last decade.[85]

A few noteworthy areas within this region merit mention. The first is the Suriname-Guyana Basin, off the coast of Suriname and Guyana. In their World Petroleum Assessment 2000, the USGS estimated that this basin has a mean undiscovered oil resource of 15.2 Gb. They state that the 15.2 Gb will be found in 117 fields ranging in size from 1 Mb to 4 Gb, with more than 30 fields containing more than 100 Mb. They project that 6 will contain more than 500 Mb.[86]

Up to 2003, there had been little exploration of this basin. CGX Energy Inc. of Canada has been the only oil company to have completed an offshore oil well during the period 1990–2000. Presently there is a territorial dispute between Suriname and Guyana concerning the location of the offshore border. In July 2000, the Surinamese military evicted CGX Energy employees from an oil drilling rig in an offshore concession granted by Guyana. Other independent oil companies have been waiting to see how the territorial dispute will be settled before going forward with exploration.

A second area worth mentioning is the Falkland Islands. Approximately ten years ago the Falkland Islands was being billed by some as the "New Kuwait" because of its supposed "massive" amount of oil. As of 2001, none of that "massive" amount of oil had been found, let along produced. When the U.S. media reports about oil supplies for a region or country, it's typical for the report to state that the region or country has massive, huge or tremendous amounts of oil without providing quantitative amounts. In 1997, Amerada Hess, Shell, U.K.'s Lasmo and Canada's International Petroleum Corporation acquired leases for exploration in the Falkland Islands. In the late 1990s, 6 wildcat wells were drilled but no commercially exploitable amounts of oil were discovered.[87] That doesn't mean there isn't exploitable amounts of oil in the Falkland Islands, but it has tempered the excitement that existed in the 1990s.

The USGS's World Petroleum Assessment 2000 estimates a mean oil resource of 5.83 Gb for the Falkland Islands.[88] Clearly the Falkland Islands is not the "New Kuwait" of oil. Any possible oil would be located offshore in the North Falklands Basin, north of the islands.

Conclusion

Figure 4.28 is a graph of summed oil production for the top 5 oil producing nations in South and Central America that produce approximately 95 percent of the regions oil: Venezuela, Brazil, Colombia, Ecuador and Argentina.

Summed oil production from the 5 nations reached its highest rate in 2000 at 6.27 mb/d. In 2003, the production rate averaged 5.57 mb/d, 700,000 b/d (11.1 percent) less than the 2000 average.[89] Political problems in Venezuela lead to a lower production rate during late 2002 and early 2003, but even if Venezuela's production had averaged the rate achieved during the last 6 months of 2003, summed production from the 5 countries would still have been over 400,000 b/d less than the 2000 average. Venezuela, Colombia and Argentina have production problems that are not connected to political and economic difficulties within the countries. Ecuador may be able to increase production in the near term, but long-term decline appears likely starting in the not-to-distant future. Even Brazil, in which production is rising rapidly, may see production plateau or decline starting in approximately 2007. Venezuela can increase production of extra heavy oil, but it appears that conventional oil production will continue to decline in the future. Can extra heavy oil production increase faster than the decline of conventional oil? That remains to be seen. It appears likely that summed oil production from the top 5 oil producing nations in South and Central America will never again reach the level obtained in 2000.

Figure 4.29 is the US DOE/EIA's forecast of TLHs production capacity for South and Central America in their IEO2003.

The US DOE/EIA projects that TLHs production capacity for South

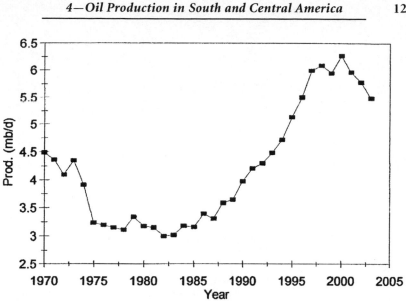

Figure 4.28 — Oil production from the top 5 oil producing nations in South and Central America (Data from the US DOE/EIA).

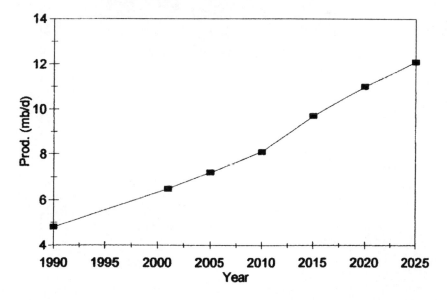

Figure 4.29 — The US DOE/EIA's forecast for South and Central America's TLHs production capacity.

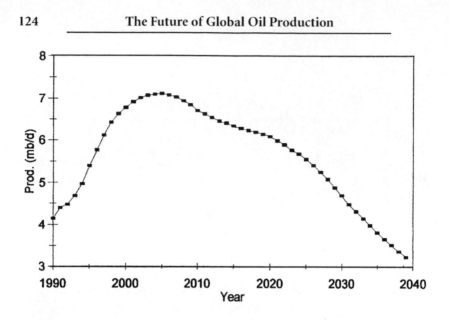

Figure 4.30 — Duncan's forecast for summed oil + NGLs production from the top 5 oil producing nations in South and Central America.

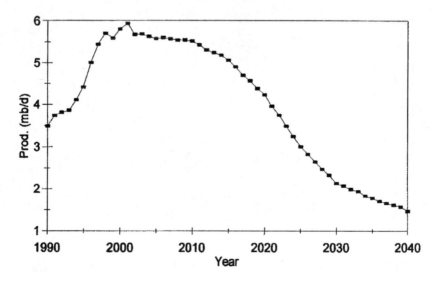

Figure 4.31— Campbell's forecast for summed oil production from South and Central America's top 5 oil producing nations.

and Central America will increase from 6.5 mb/d in 2001 to 12.1 mb/d in 2025.[90] The declining production rate for the top 5 producing nations in the region during the last 3 years calls into question the forecast by the US DOE/EIA.

Figure 4.30 is Richard Duncan's forecast for summed oil + NGLs production from the top 5 oil producing nations in South and Central America.

Duncan projects that summed oil + NGLs production from the 5 countries will peak in 2005 at 7.12 mb/d, decline to 5.56 mb/d in 2025 and 3.24 mb/d in 2039.[91] His forecast includes production from Venezuela's Orinoco Oil Belt.

Figure 4.31 is Colin Campbell's forecast for summed oil production from the top 5 oil producing nations in South and Central America.

Campbell projected that summed oil production from the 5 countries would peak in 2001 at 5.94 mb/d, decline to 3.01 mb/d in 2025 and 1.47 mb/d in 2040.[92] Campbell does not include extra heavy oil production from the Orinoco Oil Belt in his forecast.

5

Oil Production in Asia

Asia is a significant oil producing region and an increasingly important oil consuming region. Excluding the Asian portion of the Former Soviet Union, Asia produced 7.49 mb/d of oil in 2001, 11.0 percent of the world's total. The Asian countries that produce at least 200,000 b/d of oil, as of 2001, include China (3,300,000 b/d), Indonesia (1,369,000 b/d), Australia (657,000 b/d), Malaysia (654,000 b/d), India (642,000 b/d) and Vietnam (357,000 b/d). The top 6 Asian oil producing countries accounted for 93.2 percent of Asia's total production in 2001.[1] This chapter will analyzes the 6 countries mentioned above separately and treat the remainder of Asia as a unit (see Figure 5.1).

Figure 5.2 is a graph of Asia's TLHs production and imports. The bulk of Asia's TLHs imports is oil, 92.6 percent in 2001. From 1980 to 2001, Asia's TLHs production increased from 5.08 mb/d to 8.09 mb/d, a production increase of 3.01 mb/d. Asia's oil production increased from 4.85 mb/d in 1980 to 7.49 mb/d in 2001, an increase of 2.64 mb/d. The oil production increase was the result of increases in many countries, most notably China, which increased its production by 1.19 mb/d from 1980 to 2001.[2] That represents ~45 percent of Asia's total oil production increase during the period.

The intensity of Asia's oil and gas development increased substantially from 1980 to 2001. Asia's new oil fields are generally being brought on-line at or near peak production and declines begin within a few years after initial production. Increasingly the oil exploration and production effort has moved offshore. For the period 1993–2002, 79.1 percent of China's oil production increase came from offshore developments.[3] Most oil production in Australia, Malaysia, India and Vietnam comes from offshore fields.

Asia's TLHs demand is growing rapidly, lead principally by China. In 2001, that demand was 21.22 mb/d while production was 8.09 mb/d. Imports of 13.13 mb/d met 61.9 percent of Asia's TLHs demand.[4]

126

Figure 5.1— Map of Asia (Courtesy of the University Libraries, The University of Texas at Austin).

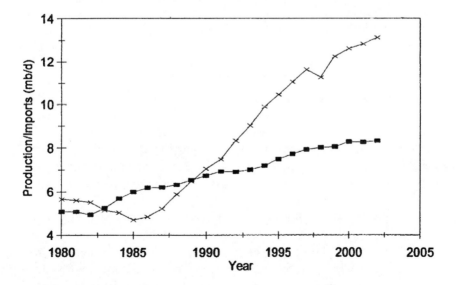

Figure 5.2 — Asia's TLHs production [rectangles] and imports [X] (Data from the US DOE/EIA).

Figure 5.3 — Map of Australia (Courtesy of the University Libraries, The University of Texas at Austin).

Oil Production in Australia

The most important oil producing regions within Australia include the Timor Sea, the Indian Ocean off northwest Australia and the Bass Straits between Australia and Tasmania (see Figure 5.3).

The Timor Sea and Indian Ocean off northwest Australia are more prone to contain gas and condensate, rather than crude oil, because much of the source rock in the region dipped below the oil window causing cracking of larger hydrocarbon molecules. In spite of that, some >50 Mb crude oil fields have been found in the region including Laminaria, Corallina, Buffalo, Challis, Cassini, Wanaea and Jabiru. Exploration in the region started in the 1970s and has progressively moved to deeper water, further from the Australian coast. Several oil companies are planning to explore The Great Australian Bight, off southern Australia, and the outer Otway Basin between Victoria and Tasmania although oil prospects aren't particularly good.[5]

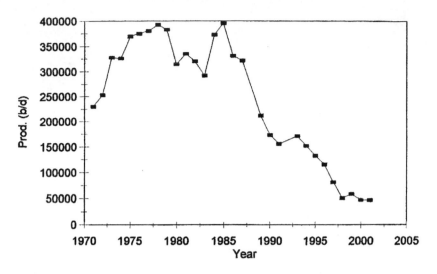

Figure 5.4 — Summed oil production from the Kingfish, Halibut, Mackerel, Fortescue and West Kingfish fields (Data from *Oil & Gas Journal*).

Australia's first oil discovery occurred in 1900 when a crew drilling for water surprisingly struck oil. By 1930, at least 157 onshore wildcat wells had been drilled. Oil drilling was sporadic until 1953 when the Rough Range field was discovered in Western Australia. The Rough Range discovery was followed by the discovery of the Moonie field, as well as fields on Barrow Island, off the west coast of Australia. Offshore oil exploration began in 1959 and Bass Straits' exploration started in 1967. Major oil discoveries were made in the Bass Straits during the late 1960s and 1970s including the Kingfish field (EUR 1,200 Mb), Halibut field (EUR 850 Mb), Mackerel field (EUR 450 Mb), Fortescue field (EUR unknown) and the West Kingfish field (EUR unknown).[6]

Figure 5.4 is a graph of the summed oil production for the 5 fields in the Bass Straits that achieved production rates of at least 50,000 b/d: Kingfish, Halibut, Mackerel, Fortescue and West Kingfish.

Oil production from the Fortescue and West Kingfish fields didn't start until 1984 so the production rate of 392,763 b/d in 1978 was due to summed production from the Kingfish, Halibut and Mackerel fields. The addition of the Fortescue and West Kingfish fields led to a peak in 1985 at 395,762 b/d. By 2001, summed production from the 5 fields had declined to 46,883 b/d, a decline of 348,879 b/d (88.2 percent) from the 1985 peak. The average decline rate for the 5 fields from 1985 through 2001 was 12.9 percent/year. Bass Straits' oil production by Esso-BHP, which produces from the 5 fields, peaked in 1985 at 474,129 b/d. By 2001, production had

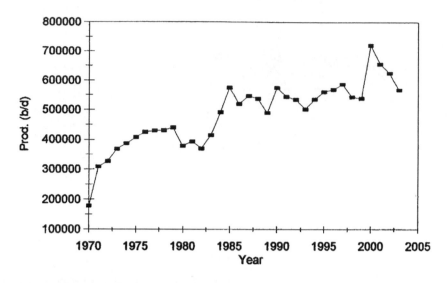

Figure 5.5 — Australia's oil production (Data from the US DOE/EIA)

declined to 160,335 b/d, a decline of 313,794 b/d (66.2 percent) from the 1985 peak.[7]

In 1995, oil production from the Carnarvon Basin, off northwest Australia, overtook Bass Straits' production. Carnarvon Basin crude oil production reportedly peaked in 1996 and is expected to decline to less than 25 percent of the peak rate by 2008, although condensate production is expected to remain relatively constant during the period.[8] Today, oil production from the Timor Sea and Indian Ocean, off northwestern Australia, provides the bulk of Australia's oil.

In the last decade, much of the oil exploration and development effort in Australia has been in the Timor Sea. In 1994/1995 two large fields, Laminaria and Corallina, were discovered there. The fields came on-line in November 1999 at a reported production rate of 142,500 b/d and were expected to reach a peak production rate of 180,000 b/d. The two fields have a combined EUR of 198 Mb.[9] The start-up of the Laminaria/Corallina fields, as well as significant production increases from several other fields, caused a pronounced increase in Australia's oil production in 2000 (see Figure 5.5).

In 1999, Australia's oil production rate averaged 539,000 b/d. In 2000, the rate increased to 722,000 b/d.[10] Because the summed EUR of the Laminaria/Corallina fields is relatively low and the early production rate was very high, it didn't take long before production started declining from the two fields. The production rate averaged 136,673 b/d in 2000 and 117,500 b/d in 2001.[11] By the time Phase 2 of the Laminaria/Corallina development was brought on-line in June 2002, summed production from the two fields was reportedly only 73,000 b/d. Phase II brought 2 new wells on-line, Wells 7 and 8. Well 7 had a reported initial production rate of 20,000 b/d and Well 8 had a rate of 50,000 b/d.[12] It appears that Phase II of the Laminaria/Corallina development didn't have a significant positive effect on Australia's oil production rate because it declined 4.72 percent in 2002 relative to 2001. In 2003, Australia's oil production rate declined to 579,000 b/d, a decline of 143,000 b/d (21.3 percent) from the 2000 average.[13]

Australia and East Timor are in a dispute concerning the boundary between the two countries, where several significant oil and gas discoveries have been made. Many of those discoveries including Laminaria (oil), Corallina (oil), Sunrise (gas) and Bayu-Undan (mainly gas) are much closer to East Timor than Australia. The boundary was established in 1972 as a result of an agreement between Indonesia and Australia. Since then, East Timor has become an independent nation. Whatever results from the dispute, in terms of boundary changes, both countries have expressed an interest that the dispute not impact oil and gas exploration and production in the disputed region.

The US DOE/EIA's IEO2003 states, "Australia has made significant recent additions to its proved reserves and it is possible that Australia will become a one million barrel per day producer by the middle of this decade."[14]

When the US DOE/EIA makes statements concerning oil, they are referring to total liquid hydrocarbons. In 2001, Australia produced 744,000 b/d of TLHs, 657,000 b/d of that was oil (88.2 percent).[15] Assuming that percentage remains constant through 2005, Australia would have to produce 883,000 b/d of oil in 2005 for Australia to produce 1 mb/d of TLHs. There is no possibility that Australia will produce 883,000 b/d of oil in 2005. It's more likely that Australia will produce closer to 500,000 b/d of oil in 2005 as increasing production from new fields is negated by declining production from old fields. Again, the US DOE/EIA ignores the decline of mature fields when projecting future oil production.

Figure 5.6 is a graph of Richard Duncan's forecast for Australia's oil + NGLs production.

Duncan projected that Australia's oil + NGLs production would reach a peak of ~762,000 b/d in 2003 before gradually declining to ~82,000 b/d in 2039.[16] It appears that Australia's oil production peaked in 2000. Since oil makes up the bulk of Australia's oil + NGLs production, oil + NGLs production may have peaked in 2000 as well. Australia's TLHs production declined 61,000 b/d from 2000 to 2001.[17]

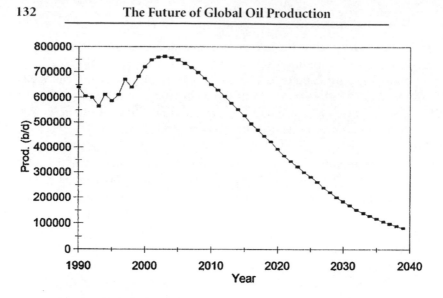

Figure 5.6 — Duncan's forecast for Australia's oil + NGLs production

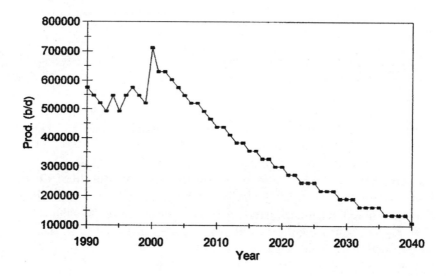

Figure 5.7 — Campbell's forecast for Australia's oil production

Figure 5.7 is a graph of Colin Campbell's forecast for Australia's oil production. Campbell projected that Australia's oil production would peak in 2000 at ~700,000 b/d, decline to ~240,000 b/d in 2025 and ~110,000 b/d in 2040. Campbell estimates that Australia's cumulative oil production at the end of 2075 will be 11 Gb, essentially its EUR.[18] Cumulative production at the end of 2002 was 5.65 Gb, 51 percent of 11 Gb.[19]

Oil Production in China

China's oil production is located mainly in east and northeastern China, northwestern China and offshore in the Bohai Sea and the mouth of the Pearl River. China's first oil discovery was made on Taiwan in 1878. Further discoveries were made on mainland China starting in 1907. China's largest oil field before 1950 was the Yuman field which began producing oil in 1939, but significant production didn't occur in China until after 1950.

In 1952, the Ministry of Geology and Mineral Resources (MGMR) was established. Joint survey teams of Chinese and Russian geologists were sent to explore northwestern China, including the Xinjiang Autonomous Region. That region has since become a major source of oil for China. In 1954, Li Siguang, director of the MGMR, led a strategic oil investigation of China that culminated in the discovery of the Daqing, Shengli and Liaohe Oil Regions. Those 3 oil regions, in eastern and northeastern China, produced 57.8 percent of China's oil in 2000.

The Daqing Oil Region is located in northeastern China and covers an area of approximately 1 million acres. The impression given from data sources and articles dealing with Daqing is that it represents one field. In actuality, PetroChina produced oil from 19 fields in the Daqing region and the summed production is published in *Oil & Gas Journal* and other data outlets. Annual production from the region reached 1 mb/d in 1976 and remained above 1 mb/d until 2003.[20,21] The region presently produces about 30 percent of China's oil.[22] Figure 5.8 is a graph of oil production from the region. Production data for China's oil fields and oil regions have only been supplied to *Oil & Gas Journal* since 1990, which is the reason that data only date back to 1990 in Figures 8–14.

The region's oil production started to noticeably decline after 1999. It was 1,108,000 b/d in 1999 but was expected to average only 970,000 b/d in 2003, a decline of 138,000 b/d (12.5 percent) from the 1999 average.[23] It has been estimated that about 77 percent of Daqing's recoverable oil reserves, ~15 Gb, have been extracted.[24] If that figure is correct, the Daqing Oil Region should ultimately produce ~20 Gb.

The Shengli Oil Region is located in eastern China and was discovered in 1961. In the early 1990s, the region's production rate was over 670,000 b/d but it declined rapidly during the middle 1990s. Since 1997, the decline rate has slowed. The production rate was 534,302 b/d in 2002.[25] Figure 5.9 is a graph of oil production from the Shengli Oil Region.

At the end of 2002, the Shengli Oil Region had produced 5.67 Gb of oil from 65 fields containing about 21,000 wells. The average water

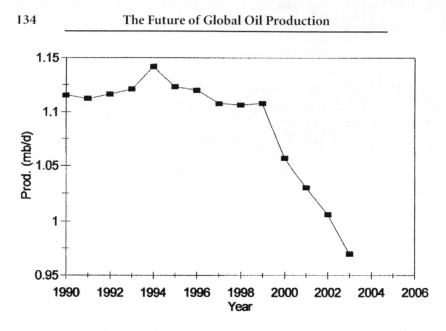

Figure 5.8 — The Daqing Oil Region's oil production (Data from *Oil & Gas Journal* [1990–2001] and *Alexander's Gas and Oil Connections* [2002–2003]).

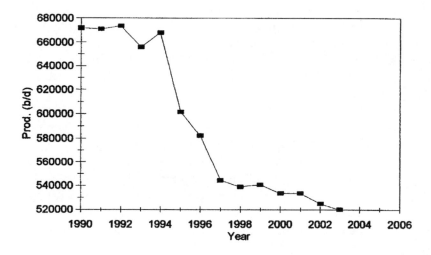

Figure 5.9 — The Shengli Oil Region's oil production (Data from *Oil & Gas Journal*)

cut, the percentage of water extracted in the production of oil, is ~90 percent indicating that the Shengli Oil Region is in a serious state of depletion.[26]

Oil was discovered in the Liaohe Oil Region in 1968 and production started in 1971. The region covers 580,000 acres in northeastern China and

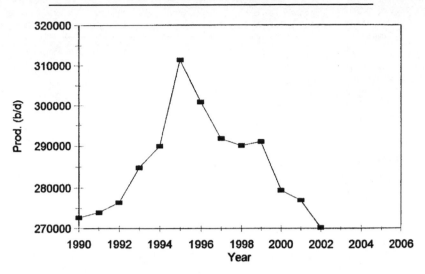

Figure 5.10 — The Liaohe Oil Region's oil production (Data from *Oil & Gas Journal*)

is China's third largest oil-producing region.[27] Figure 5.10 is a graph of oil production from the region.

The region's oil production rate peaked in 1995 at 311,313 b/d. In 2001, the rate had declined to 277,002 b/d, a decline of 34,311 b/d (11.0 percent) from the 1995 average.[28]

Two other oil regions worth noting are Zhongyuan, in eastern China, and Huabei, in northern China. Figure 5.11 is a graph of the summed production for the two oil regions.

The summed oil production rate for the two regions was 233,638 b/d in 1990 but it declined to 157,178 b/d in 2001, a decline of 76,460 b/d (32.7 percent) since 1990.[29]

What Figures 8–11 illustrate is that China's oil production in the eastern half of the country has been declining, excluding offshore production. The summed production rate for Daqing, Shengli, Liaohe, Zhongyuan and Huabei declined 333,626 b/d (14.5 percent) from 1994 to 2002.[30] China's production has increased slowly in recent years because increasing production from western China and offshore areas has been greater than the decline in production from eastern and northeastern China. How long can that continue?

The main oil-producing region in western China is the Xinjiang Oil Region, covering an area of 901,420 acres.[31] Figure 5.12 is a graph of oil production from the region.

For the period 1990 to 2001, oil production in the region increased from 136,373 b/d to 193,660 b/d, an increase of 57,287 b/d.[32] Claims have

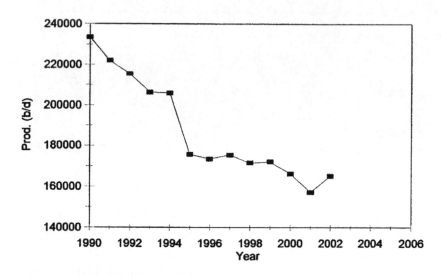

Figure 5.11— The summed oil production for the Zhongyuan and Huabei Oil Regions (Data from *Oil & Gas Journal*).

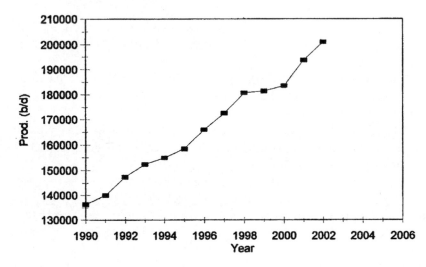

Figure 5.12 — The Xinjiang Oil Region's oil production (Data from *Oil & Gas Journal*).

been made that oil production in the region will increase to ~470,000 b/d in 2005.[33] The Chinese government is hoping that the region will produce 1 mb/d by 2008.[34] Achieving either of those production goals will require a much more rapid production increase than has occurred in the past.

Figure 5.13 is a graph of China's onshore oil production. China's

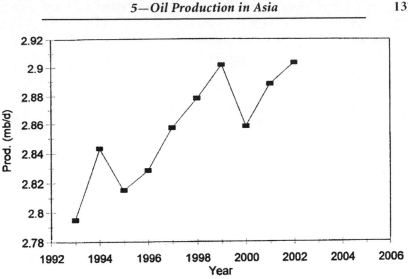

Figure 5.13 — China's onshore oil production (Data from *Oil & Gas Journal*)

onshore oil production reached its highest rate in 2002 at a little over 2.9 mb/d, essentially the same as in 1999.[35] For onshore oil production to increase in the future, production in western China would have to increase at a faster rate than the production decline in eastern China. An increasing level of onshore oil exploration is occurring in 2 basins of northwestern China: Tarim and Bohaiwan. In their World Petroleum Assessment 2000, the USGS estimates that the most likely undiscovered oil reserves for the two basins is ~9.3 Gb.[36] How valid that estimate is will only be determined with time. PetroChina Ltd claims that the Tarim Basin could hold as much as 73 Gb, but Western analysts say that estimate could be as much as 100 times too high.[37] According to a Beijing-based consultant, "There could be a bit of misunderstanding because China often looks at in-place reserves rather than those that may be commercially recoverable and actually utilized."[38] He further stated, "I'm not sure how much of an energy hope the Tarim is because of the costs involved. You need large-scale infrastructure like the West-to-East pipeline (an $8 billion gas pipeline from the basin) to actually transport oil and gas to demand centers."[39]

Figure 5.14 is a graph of China's offshore oil production. China's offshore oil production increased from 92,954 b/d in 1993 to 502,500 b/d in 2002, an increase of 409,546 b/d during the period. Over the same period, China's oil production increased 517,780 b/d. The offshore production increase represents 79.1 percent of China's production increase from 1993 to 2002.[40]

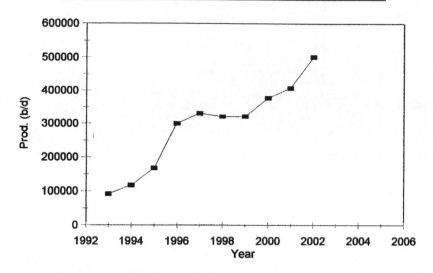

Figure 5.14 — China's offshore oil production (Data from *Oil & Gas Journal*)

Several large offshore projects are in various stages of development. Phillips Petroleum brought the Peng Lai field on-line in 2002 with an expected peak production rate of 100,000 b/d in 2004. ChevronTexaco made an agreement with the Chinese National Offshore Oil Corporation (CNOOC) for the development of the Bozhong field in the Bohai Sea. Reserves of the Bozhong field have been estimated at 1.3 Gb,[41] but that may be oil-in-place in which case the actual amount of extractable oil would be considerably less.

Figure 5.15 is a graph of China's total oil production. The production rate has risen fairly steadily from 0.600 mb/d in 1970 to 3.409 mb/d in 2003.[42] In the January 2004 Oil Market Report, the International Energy Agency (IEA) is projecting that China's oil production rate will decline 20,000 b/d in 2004.[43] The decline may represent the start of a long-term decline for China's oil production.

Figure 5.16 is the US DOE/EIA's forecast for China's TLHs production, in their IEO2003. The US DOE/EIA projects that China's TLHs production will reach a peak of 3.60 mb/d in 2010 and only decline to 3.4 mb/d in 2025.[44]

Figure 5.17 is a graph of Richard Duncan's forecast for China's oil + NGLs production. Duncan projected that China's oil + NGLs production would peak in 2002 at ~3.4 mb/d, decline to ~2.2 mb/d in 2025 and ~1.3 mb/d in 2039.[45] The difference between Duncan's forecast and that of the US DOE/EIA can't be explained by refinery gain.

Figure 5.18 is a graph of Colin Campbell's forecast for China's oil pro-

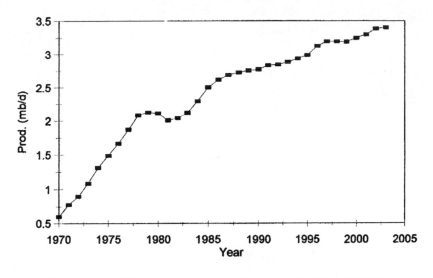

Figure 5.15 — China's oil production (Data from the US DOE/EIA)

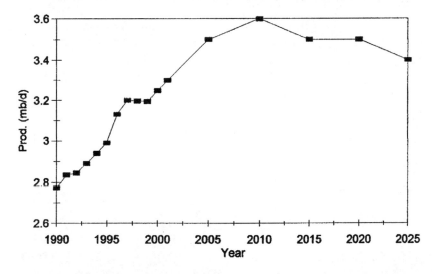

Figure 5.16 — The US DOE/EIA's forecast for China's TLHs production (Historical data [1990–2002] from the US DOE/EIA).

duction. Campbell projected that China's oil production would peak in 2002 at ~3.4 mb/d, decline to ~1.3 mb/d in 2025 and ~0.66 mb/d in 2040. Campbell estimates that China's cumulative production at the end of 2075 will be 57 Gb, essentially its EUR.[46] At the end of 2002, China's cumulative production was 28.2 Gb, 49.5 percent of 57 Gb.[47]

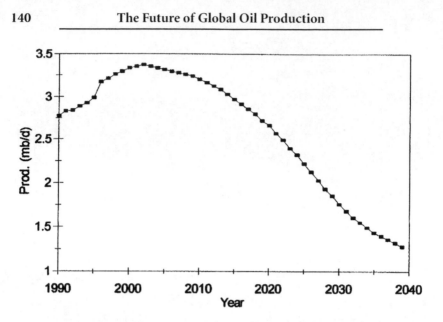

Figure 17 — Duncan's forecast for China's oil + NGLs production

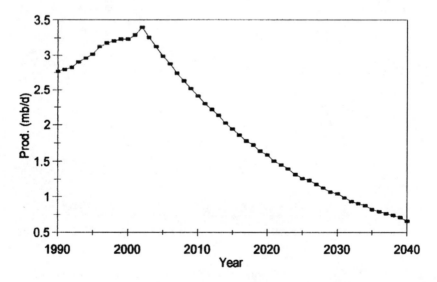

Figure 5.18 — Campbell's forecast for China's oil production

China's TLHs consumption has been rising much more rapidly than its TLHs production (see Figure 5.19). In 2003, it became the world's second largest consumer of TLHs behind the U.S.[48]

In 2002, China's TLHs imports represented 35.9 percent of total consumption, up from near zero in 1993.[49] The consumption and import

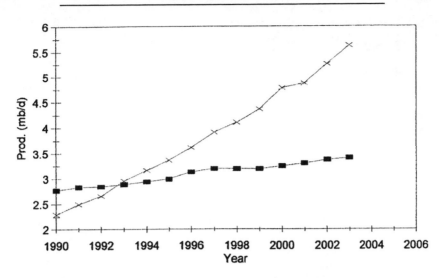

Figure 5.19 — China's TLHs production [rectangles] and consumption [X] (Data from the US DOE/EIA).

trends will continue in the future barring a catastrophic economic downturn. The US DOE/EIA projects that China's TLHs consumption will grow from 4.8 mb/d in 2001 to 10.9 mb/d in 2025 (3.3 percent/year).[50] That consumption rate increase would be considerably lower than it was for the period 1990–2002 (7.18 percent/year). The Chinese Academy of Geological Sciences estimates that TLHs consumption will reach 14.0 mb/d by 2020.[51] Whatever the actual growth rate is for China's TLHs consumption in the future, TLHs imports will grow rapidly. The growth of TLHs imports has serious geopolitical implication as the U.S. and China increasingly compete for Middle East oil.

Oil Production in India

India is an oil poor country largely underlain with basement rock. Most of its production occurs in west coast offshore waters, most notably from the Bombay High field. There is also production in northwestern India and the Palk Straits south of Pondicherry. In 1993, the New Exploration Licensing Policy (NELP) was established to permit foreign involvement in exploration with the objective of increasing India's oil production. There has been little interest by international oil companies for exploring in India and no major discoveries have been made in recent years.

India's first oil discovery was made in the state of Assam in 1889. Pro-

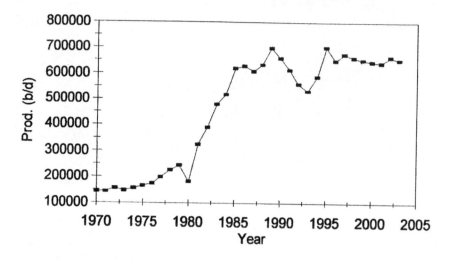

Figure 5.20 — India's oil production (Data from the US DOE/EIA)

duction was trivial prior to the 1960s and even now it is not impressive by global standards. In 1974, the Oil and Natural Gas Commission of India discovered the Bombay High field. Production from the field was responsible for a sharp increase in India's oil production from 1980 to 1985. Figure 5.20 is a graph of India's oil production.

India's oil production rate reached 700,000 b/d in 1989, 420,000 b/d of that was from the Bombay High field.[52] After 1989, there was a decline in production because some offshore wells were shut down due to poor production practices. The production increase from 1993 to 1995 was largely due to the introduction of the South Heera field. Since 1995, India's oil production rate has remained fairly constant between 650,000 b/d and 700,000 b/d.[53,54]

Since 1985, there has been a significant increase in the number of producing oil fields in India (see Figure 5.21).

The number of oil fields increased from 19 in 1985 to 53 in 2000,[55] but that led to essentially no increase in India's oil production rate. That suggests the production from the small fields that are being added is just replacing the declining production from older fields.

Figure 5.22 is a graph of oil production from the Bombay High field.

The field reached its highest production rate in 1989 at 420,179 b/d, but it gradually declined to 202,355 b/d in 2002, an average decline rate of 8.33 percent/year.[56] The Bombay High field is actually made up of two reservoirs: Bombay High North and Bombay High South. Phase II development of the field was launched in 2001, at an estimated cost of $1.5 bil-

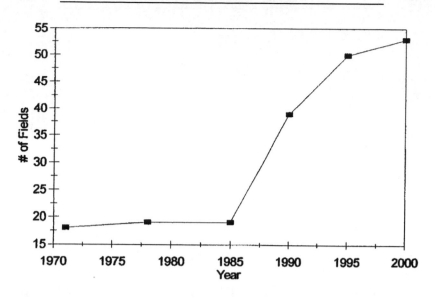

Figure 5.21— The number of producing oil fields in India (Data from *Oil & Gas Journal*).

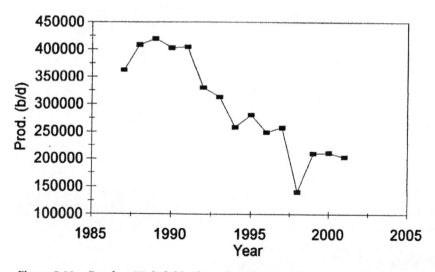

Figure 5.22 — Bombay High field oil production (Data from *Oil & Gas Journal*)

lion.[57] The objective of the development is to increase oil recovery from 28 percent to 40 percent, an increase corresponding to more than 400 Mb of oil. Cumulative production from the Bombay High field was ~2.13 Gb at the end of 2001.[58]

Four other fields in India had peak production rates of at least 35,000

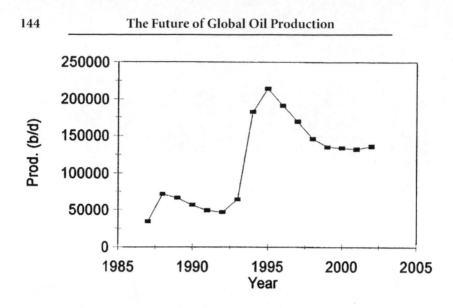

Figure 5.23 — Summed oil production for the Lakwa-Lakhmani, Gandhar, Neelam and Heera/South Heera fields (Data from *Oil & Gas Journal*).

b/d: Lakwa-Lakhmani, Gandhar, Neelam and Heera/South Heera. Figure 5.23 is a graph of the summed production for the four fields.

Summed production for the four fields peaked in 1995 at 214,400 b/d. By 2002, summed production had declined to 136,420 b/d, 63.6 percent of the 1994 production level.[59]

The Indian government hopes that deepwater discoveries will lead to an increase in India's oil production. The directorate general of the governments upstream oil agency, Avinash Chandra, claims that India can triple its oil production over the next 10 years, a rather far fetched claim.[60] There is little reason to believe that India's oil production can increase, let alone triple, in the next 10 years.

Concerning India's oil production, the US DOE/EIA states in their IEO2003: "India is expected to show some modest production increase early in this decade and only a modest decline in output thereafter."[61]

Considering the poor oil discovery rate in recent years and the decline of major fields, a modest production increase followed by a modest decline appears optimistic.

Figure 5.24 is a graph of Richard Duncan's forecast for India's oil + NGLs production.

Duncan projected that India's oil + NGLs production would reach a maximum rate of ~850,000 b/d in 2003, decline to ~350,000 b/d in 2025 and ~220,000 b/d in 2039.[62] India's TLHs production peaked in 1997 at 764,000 b/d, but it declined every year through 2001 when it was down to

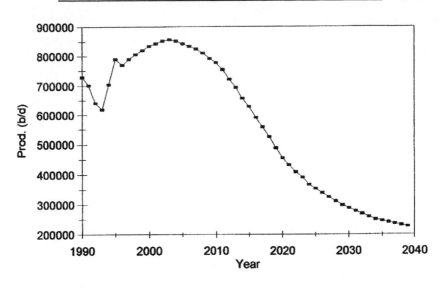

Figure 5.24 — Duncan's forecast for India's oil + NGLs production

736,000 b/d.[63] Since India's oil production rate has remained relatively flat from 2001 to 2003, it doesn't appear possible that India's oil + NGLs production will come close to 850,000 b/d in 2003.

Figure 5.25 is a graph of Colin Campbell's forecast for India's oil production. Campbell projects that India's oil production will decline from ~658,000 b/d in 2004 to ~274,000 b/d in 2025 and ~164,000 b/d in 2040. Clearly Duncan and Campbell are not as optimistic about India's future oil production as the US DOE/EIA. Campbell estimates that India's cumulative oil production through 2075 will be 12 Gb, essentially its EUR.[64] At the end of 2002, cumulative production was 5.8 Gb, 48.3 percent of 12 Gb.[65]

Oil Production in Indonesia

A large portion of Indonesia's oil production comes from two fields, Duri and Minas, located in central Sumatra. There is also oil production offshore from northwestern Java, off East Kalimantan and in the Natuna Sea.

Indonesia is the birthplace of the Royal Dutch Company, a result of an oil discovery on Borneo in 1883. The Royal Dutch Company merged with the Shell Transport and Trading Company in 1907 to form Royal Dutch/Shell. Prior to and during WWII numerous fields were discovered on Sumatra including Duri and Minas.

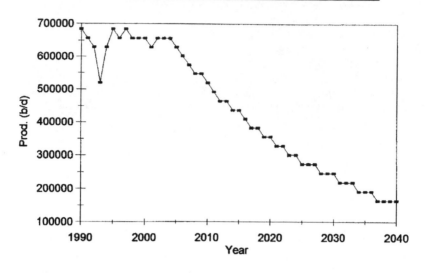

Figure 5.25 — Campbell's forecast for India's oil production

The Minas field was discovered in 1944 but production didn't start until 1952. It is the largest field ever discovered in Southeast Asia. Figure 5.26 is a graph of oil production from the Minas field.

In 1974, the Minas field produced 420,356 b/d. By 2001, the production rate had declined to 126,316 b/d, a decline of 294,040 b/d (70.0 percent) from the 1974 production level.[66] Recently Caltex Pacific Indonesia (CPI), owned by ChevronTexaco, spent $800 million on Light Oil Steam Flood (LOSF) technology to coax the remaining extractable oil out of the field. The technology is energy intensive, lowering the net energy yield for the field, but it will extend the field's life. According to ChevronTexaco, cumulative production from the Minas field was ~4 Gb at the end of 2002.[67]

The Duri field was discovered in 1941 but didn't start producing oil until 1958. The field's oil is highly viscous making it difficult to extract. As early as 1960 water flooding was used to coax oil out of the reservoir. In 1967, a technique known as cyclic steam injection was used to enhance recovery. The cyclic steam technique involves injecting steam into production wells to make the oil flow more easily. The oil was pumped out after the injection of steam. Wells are cycled between injecting steam and pumping oil, an inefficient method of extraction. In 1985, a steam-flooding project was initiated. The process involves continuous steam injection into 6 peripheral wells while oil is pumped out of a central well. The field has been divided into 12 regions. To date, steam flooding has been completed for 8 regions. It has been reported that this technique will allow 60–65 percent of the in-place oil to be extracted. The project uses a

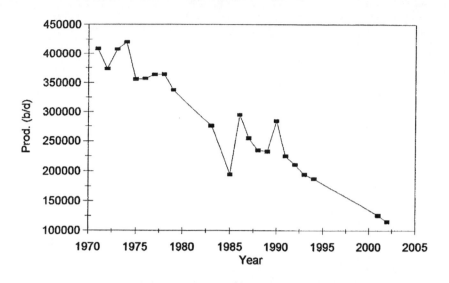

Figure 5.26 — Minas field oil production (Data from *Oil & Gas Journal*)

reported 340,000 tons of water/day and considerable energy to create the steam for the process.[68] In the southern part of the project area, at least 60,000 b/d of oil are used for heating water to make steam.[69] Recently a 300 MW natural gas fired power plant was completed to supply power and steam to the northern half of the project area.[70] The Duri field also requires a massive amount of human effort and resources to maintain and expand production. A ChevronTexaco factsheet states, "In Duri, for example, a given week may see 10 to 15 wells being drilled, another 100 wells being serviced and improved, and some eight miles of pipelines being installed."[71]

The project has cost at least $2 billion so far and will cost considerably more when it is completed later this decade.[72]

Figure 5.27 is a graph of oil production from the Duri field. According to ChevronTexaco, the Duri field had produced 1.3 Gb of oil by the end of 2002. The reported EUR for the field is 3.1 Gb.[73]

Seven other Indonesian oil fields achieved production rates of greater than 100,000 b/d since 1971: Bekasap, Bangko, Ardjuna, Attaka, Handil, Arun and Widuri. The Handil field reached a peak production rate of 174,570 b/d in 1977, but declined to 37,934 b/d by 1994. The Widuri field produced 119,189 b/d in 1991, but declined to 68,566 b/d by 1994.[74] Recent data are not available for Handil and Widuri. Figure 5.28 is a graph of summed production for the Bekasap, Bangko, Ardjuna, Arun and Attaka fields.

The summed production rate for the 5 fields reached a maximum in 1976 of 347,368 b/d and was still over 300,000 b/d in 1994, largely due to

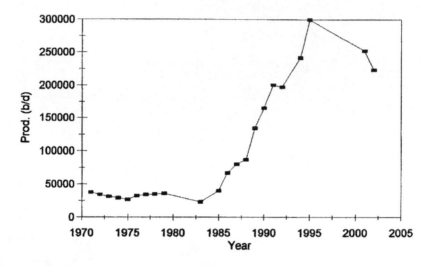

Figure 5.27 — Duri field oil production (Data from *Oil & Gas Journal* except for 1995, from ChevronTexaco).

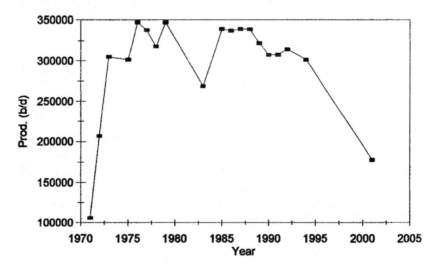

Figure 5.28 — Summed oil production for the Bekasap, Bangko, Ardjuna, Arun and Attaka fields (Data from *Oil & Gas Journal*).

the introduction of the Arun field in 1978. In 2001, the summed production rate had declined to 177,732 b/d, and that figure includes production from several additional fields near the Ardjuna and Arun fields. The summed production rate for the 5 fields declined 169,636 b/d (48.8 percent) between 1976 and 2001.[75]

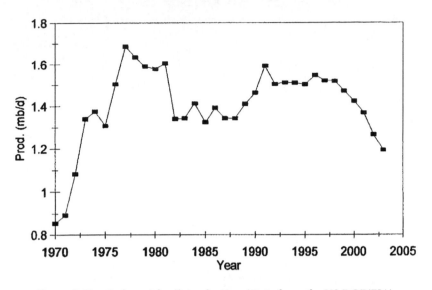

Figure 5.29 — Indonesia's oil production (Data from the US DOE/EIA)

Figure 5.29 is a graph of Indonesia's oil production. Indonesia's oil production reached its highest rate in 1977 at 1.69 mb/d. Because Indonesia is a member of OPEC, with OPEC quotas applied to its production, it hasn't necessarily produced up to its capacity over much of the period after the oil crisis of the late 1978/early 1980s. Since 1996, the production rate has declined 380,000 b/d (24.5 percent) from 1.55 mb/d to 1.17 mb/d in 2003.[76] The number of producing oil fields in Indonesia increased dramatically from 1976 to 1995 (see Figure 5.30), but that has not prevented the steep decline in production from occurring.

The number of producing fields increased from 76 in 1976 to 280 in 1990 to 354 fields in 2000.[77] The small increase in the number of producing fields from 1995 to 2000 probably means there are not many fields left worth developing.

Indonesia's petroleum prospects are limited to a few sedimentary basins located in Sumatra, the Java Sea, southeast Borneo and Irian Jaya. Because the central and western regions of the country have been extensively explored and developed, further exploration is concentrated in eastern Indonesia. There have been two recently reported discoveries in southern Sumatra, both of which were reported to contain 230 Mb of oil. That may be oil-in-place in which case the amount of recoverable oil would be considerably less. Three new projects are expected to begin production before 2004. The West Seno field, located offshore near East Kalimatan, is expected to produce 40,000 b/d by May 2003 and eventually peak at 60,000

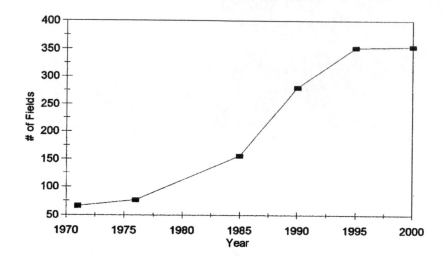

Figure 5.30 — The number of producing oil fields in Indonesia (Data from *Oil & Gas Journal*).

b/d. Conoco's Belanek Project is expected to add 100,000 b/d to production in the West Natuna region by 2004.[78] ExxonMobil's Banyu Urip offshore field is expected to come on-line in 2004 and ultimately reach a peak production rate of 165,000 b/d.[79] Even with this flurry of development Indonesia's oil production rate is not expected to increase significantly due to the decline of older fields. It just may continue to decline.

Unfortunately the US DOE/EIA doesn't provide an individual assessment for Indonesia in their IEO2003, but it notes that "oil producers in the Pacific Rim are expected to increase their production volumes significantly as a result of enhanced exploration and extraction."[80]

Figure 5.31 is a graph of Richard Duncan's forecast for Indonesia's oil + NGLs production. Duncan projects that Indonesia's oil + NGLs production will decline from 1.61 mb/d in 2002 to 1.1 mb/d in 2025 and 0.518 mb/d in 2039. Comparing his 2000 and 2001 estimates with actual TLHs production shows that he was high by 70,000 b/d in 2000 and 130,000 b/d in 2001.[81,82] That may suggest that Duncan's projection for Indonesia is more optimistic than is warranted.

Figure 5.32 is a graph of Colin Campbell's forecast for Indonesia's oil production. Campbell projects that Indonesia's oil production will decline steadily after 1995 from 1.51 mb/d to ~0.49 mb/d in 2025 to ~0.27 mb/d in 2040. The production trend in recent years lends support to Campbell's projection. Campbell estimates that Indonesia's cumulative production at

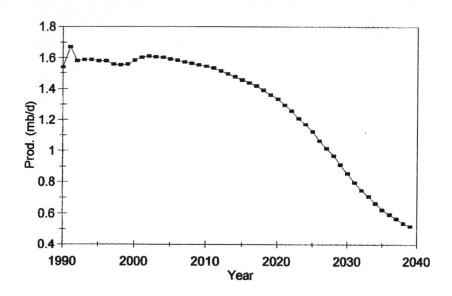

Figure 5.31— Duncan's forecast for Indonesia's oil + NGLs production

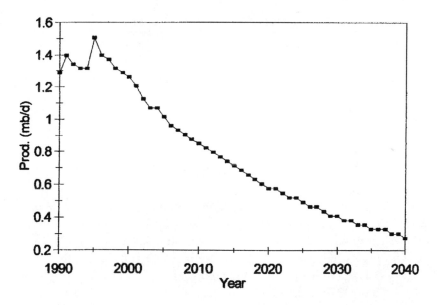

Figure 5.32 — Campbell's forecast for Indonesia's oil production

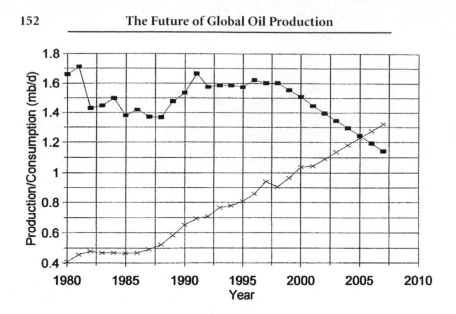

Figure 5.33 — Indonesia's historical and projected TLHs production [rectangles] and consumption [X]. Historical data are from 1980 through 2001 (Data from the US DOE/EIA).

the end of 2075 will be 31 Gb, essentially its EUR.[83] At the end of 2002, cumulative production was 20.5 Gb, 66 percent of 31 Gb.[84]

Figure 5.33 is a graph of Indonesia's historical and projected TLHs production and consumption.[85,86] The graph illustrates the narrowing gap between production and consumption. If the 1998–2001 trends continue, Indonesia's TLHs consumption will surpass production in 2006. It clearly won't be long before Indonesia is a net importer of TLHs.

Oil Production in Malaysia

Malaysia's oil production occurs offshore, primarily near the Malaysian Peninsula. Malaysia's oil history dates back to 1910 when Royal Dutch/Shell discovered minor quantities of oil in the country. It became a significant oil producer only after oil was discovered offshore in the 1960s. In 1970, Malaysia only produced 18,000 b/d of oil,[87] but further discoveries through the 1970s and 1980s lead to a steady production increase. Most of Malaysia's presently active oil fields date back to the 1970s and 1980s.

Approximately 30 percent of Malaysia's oil production in 2000 came from 3 fields: Guntong, Seligi and Tapis. Production data for Malaysia's oil fields are sparse but it appears that the largest fields are in decline. The Guntong field, with the highest production rate of any field in Malaysia,

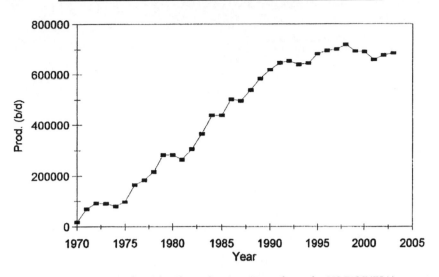

Figure 5.34 — Malaysia's oil production (Data from the US DOE/EIA)

was producing 108,700 b/d in 1999 but declined to 97,000 b/d in 2000. The field with the second highest production rate, the Seligi field, declined from 84,700 b/d in 1999 to 68,000 b/d in 2000.[88]

Figure 5.34 is a graph of Malaysia's oil production. Malaysia's oil production reached its highest rate in 1998 at 720,000 b/d. In 2003, the average rate was 696,000 b/d.[89] In recent years there has been a lack of new discoveries and it appears Malaysia's oil production is poised to decline. Because of the lack of new discoveries, the state oil company, Petronas, is concentrating on investing in overseas operations, aiming to derive 30 percent of its revenues from overseas operations by 2005, up from <5 percent in 1996.[90]

There have been numerous recent oil developments in Malaysia. The Seligi F platform, the 7th completed production platform for the Seligi field, came on-line in March 1998 and was expected to reach a production rate of greater than 20,000 b/d before declining.[91] The Seligi H platform, part of the Satellite Fields Development Project, came on-line in 2001. It was the first of 5 platforms to be installed over 6 fields. The last of the platforms for the project was expected to come on-line in early 2003. The EUR for the fields associated with the project is reported to be 90 Mb. Peak production from the project is expected to be 40,000 b/d.[92]

In other developments, the Angsi field started producing oil in December 2001 at 15,000 b/d. The Angsi C and E platforms are expected to come on-line in 2004 with an expected peak production rate of 65,000 b/d.[93] Production began from the Larut field (EUR = 72 Mb) in January 2003.[94] The projected peak production rate for the field is 33,000 b/d. The

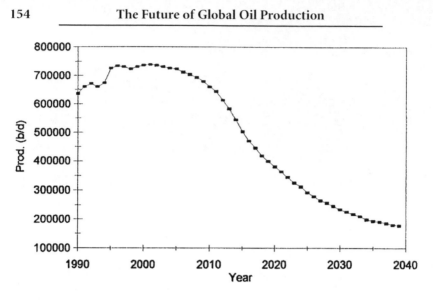

Figure 5.35 — Duncan's forecast for Malaysia's oil + NGLs production

US DOE/EIA claims that the Larut field is expected to reach a peak production rate of 140,000 b/d, but that must be incorrect if the EUR is only 72 Mb. Lastly, the Bunga Kekwa Project came on-line in April 2001 at a production rate of 18,000 b/d. It is expected to have a peak production rate of 40,000 b/d.[95]

Concerning Malaysia's future oil production, the US DOE/EIA states in their IEO2003: "Malaysia shows little potential for any significant new finds, and its output is expected to peak at around 800,000 barrels per day early in this decade and then gradually decline to 680,000 barrels per day by 2025."[96]

As stated previously, when the US DOE/EIA makes a reference to oil, it actually represents TLHs. It doesn't appear that Malaysia's TLHs production rate can increase to 800,000 b/d during this decade. The highest TLHs production rate Malaysia achieved was in 1998 at 811,000 b/d. In 2001, the TLHs production rate was only 730,000 b/d.[97] It is implausible that Malaysia's TLHs production rate would only decline to 680,000 b/d in 2025 considering the lack of new fields to bring on-line between now and 2025.

Figure 5.35 is a graph of Richard Duncan's forecast for Malaysia's oil + NGLs production. Duncan projected that Malaysia's oil + NGLs production would peak in 2001 at 739,000 b/d, decline to 293,000 b/d in 2025 and 178,000 b/d in 2039.[98] Duncan's estimate for 2025 is only 43 percent of the US DOE/EIA's estimate for TLHs production.

Figure 5.36 is a graph of Colin Campbell's forecast for Malaysia's oil

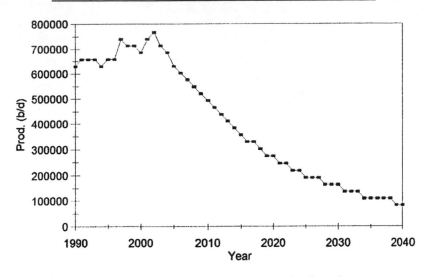

Figure 5.36 — Campbell's forecast for Malaysia's oil production

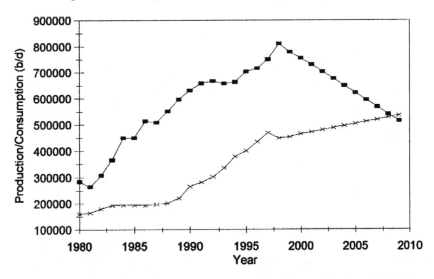

Figure 5.37 — Malaysia's historical and projected TLHs production [rectangles] and consumption [X]. Historical data are from 1980 through 2001 (Data from the US DOE/EIA).

production. Campbell projected that Malaysia's oil production would peak in 2002 at ~767,000 b/d, decline to ~192,000 b/d in 2025 and ~82,000 b/d in 2040. Campbell estimates that Malaysia's cumulative oil production at the end of 2075 will be 10 Gb, essentially its EUR.[99] At the end of 2002, cumulative production was 5.5 Gb, 55 percent of 10 Gb.[100]

Figure 5.37 is a graph of Malaysia's historical and projected TLHs production and consumption.[101,102] The production and consumption trends for 1998–2001 are extended to 2010 to obtain an approximate date when Malaysia will become a net importer of TLHs. Based upon the graph, that will occur in 2009.

Oil Production in Vietnam

Vietnam's oil production is a relatively new development (see Figure 5.38).

Production rose steadily from its beginning in 1986 to 357,000 b/d in 2001 but declined to 339,000 b/d in 2002.[103] In recent developments, production from the Rang Dong field was expected to reach 65,000 b/d with the completion of two new offshore platforms in November 2002. In 2002, the Ca Ngu Vang (Golden Tuna) and Voi Trang (White Elephant) fields were discovered. Fields in the Golden Tuna area are reported to have reserves of 250 Mb. A discovery in the Cuu Long Basin was reported to have recoverable reserves of 400 Mb. Production was scheduled to start in 2003 at 38,000 b/d and increase to 70,000 b/d by 2005. The Su Tu Den field was expected to come on-line by the end of 2003 and reach a peak production rate of over 25,000 b/d.[104]

Concerning Vietnam, the US DOE/EIA states in their IEO2003: "Vietnam is still viewed with considerable optimism regarding long-term production potential, although exploration activity has been slower than originally hoped. Output levels from Vietnamese fields are expected to exceed 415,000 barrels per day by 2025."[105]

The statement above doesn't make it clear whether the US DOE/EIA expects Vietnam's oil production to reach a peak between now and 2025 or just continue to increase through 2025. An increase to 415,000 b/d would not be very much above the current production rate. For Vietnam to have that rate in 2025 assumes that there is considerable oil remaining to be found, which does not appear to be the case. In their World Petroleum Assessment 2000, the USGS estimates that the most likely undiscovered amount of oil in Vietnam is 40 Mb, which is pretty paltry.[106]

Figure 5.39 is Richard Duncan's forecast for Vietnam's oil + NGLs production. Duncan projects that Vietnam's oil + NGLs production will peak in 2005 at ~244,000 b/d, decline to ~96,000 b/d in 2025 and ~44,000 b/d in 2039.[107] He is obviously low for his estimates of the early years for the forecast period, but that may mean that peak production will come before 2005 and that the decline will be steeper than he predicts.

Figure 5.40 is a graph of Colin Campbell's forecast for Vietnam's oil

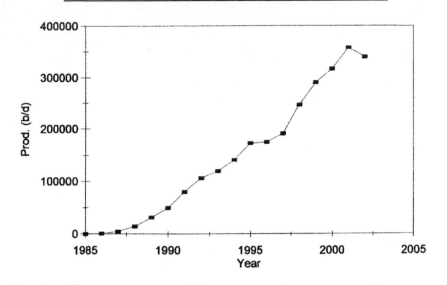

Figure 5.38 — Vietnam's oil production (Data from the US DOE/EIA)

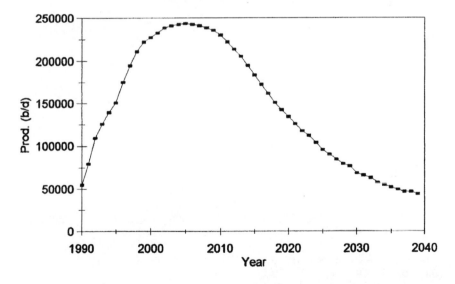

Figure 5.39 — Duncan's forecast for Vietnam's oil + NGLs production

production. Campbell projects that Vietnam's oil production will plateau from 1999 through 2009 at ~301,000 b/d, decline to ~110,000 b/d in 2025 and ~27,000 in 2040. He estimates that Vietnam's cumulative production at the end of 2075 will be 3.3 Gb, essentially its EUR.[108] At the end of 2001, cumulative production was 0.9 Gb, 27 percent of 3.3 Gb.[109]

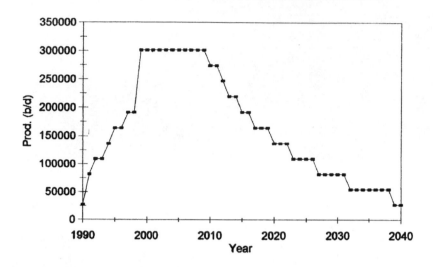

Figure 5.40 — Campbell's forecast for Vietnam's oil production

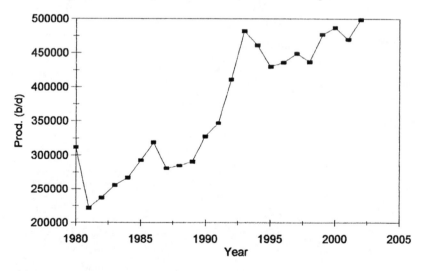

Figure 5.41— Asia's oil production, excluding the top 6 producing nations in Asia (Data from US DOE/EIA).

Oil Production in the Rest of Asia

Figure 5.41 is a graph of Asia's oil production, excluding the 6 nations covered previously. In 2002, the production rate in this region was 499,000 b/d. Most of that production came from Brunei (163,000 b/d), Thailand (127,200 b/d), Papua New Guinea (55,200 b/d) and Pakistan (50,300 b/d).[110]

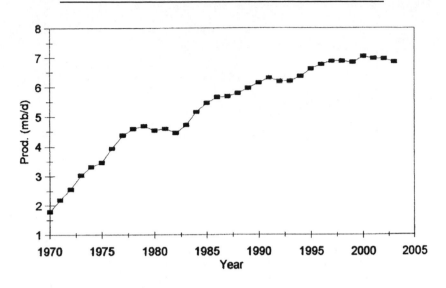

Figure 5.42 — Oil production from Asia's 6 major oil producers (Data from the US DOE/EIA).

Production in Brunei and Thailand is increasing while production in Papua New Guinea is declining. Production in Pakistan has held reasonably stable over the last decade.

Conclusion

Even though the US DOE/EIA is optimistic about Asia's future oil production, there is a strong basis for believing that oil production has probably already peaked. Figure 5.402 is a graph of oil production from the 6 major Asian oil producers that produce 93.2 percent of Asia's oil: China, Indonesia, Australia, Malaysia, India and Vietnam.

Oil production reached its highest rate for Asia's 6 major oil producers in 2000 at 7.05 mb/d. In 2003, the production rate was 6.87 mb/d, a decline of 180,000 b/d.[111]

Oil production from Australia and Indonesia has been declining in recent years and it appears likely that it will continue to decline in the future. In the January 2004 Oil Market Report, the International Energy Agency (IEA) projected that oil production from India and Malaysia would increase ~20,000 b/d each in 2004,[112] but production from both countries is likely to start declining soon after that.

China's oil production has been rising slowly in recent years because

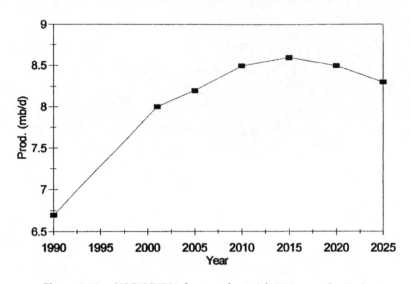

Figure 5.43 — US DOE/EIA forecast for Asia's TLHs production

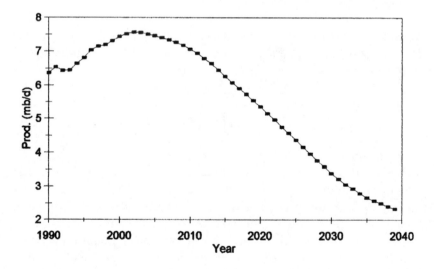

Figure 5.44 — Duncan's forecast for oil + NGLs production from Asia's 6 major producing nations.

the increase in production from western China and offshore areas has been greater than the decline in production from eastern and northeastern China. The IEA is projecting a 20,000 b/d decline for China's oil production in 2004, which may be the start of a long-term decline. China's oil consumption and imports will continue to rise rapidly unless there is a

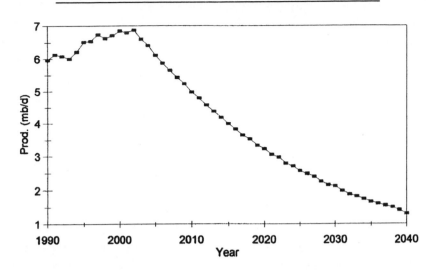

Figure 5.45 — Campbell's forecast for oil production from Asia's 6 major oil pro-ducing nations.

severe economic slowdown, possibly creating serious geopolitical problems in the future.

Vietnam's oil production has risen rapidly since 1990 and the IEA is projecting a further increase in 2004.[113] Due to the limited oil resource in Vietnam, production is likely to peak in the near future.

Figure 5.43 is a graph of the US DOE/EIA's forecast for Asia's TLHs production from their IEO2003.

The US DOE/EIA projects that Asia's TLHs production will remain above 8 mb/d from 2001 through 2025, with maximum production occurring in 2015.[114]

Figure 5.44 is Richard Duncan's forecast for oil + NGLs production from Asia's 6 major oil producing nations.

Duncan projected that oil + NGLs production from Asia's 6 major producing nations would peak in 2002 at 7.57 mb/d, decline to 4.37 mb/d in 2025 and 2.34 mb/d in 2040.[115]

Figure 5.45 is Colin Campbell's forecast for oil production from Asia's 6 major oil-producing nations. Campbell projected that oil production from Asia's 6 major oil producing nations would peak in 2002 at 6.88 mb/d, decline to 2.58 mb/d in 2025 and 1.32 mb/d in 2040.[116]

6

Oil Production in the Middle East

The Middle East is the most important oil producing region globally, containing the world's largest resource base. The Middle East's important oil producing nations are Saudi Arabia, Iraq, Iran, Kuwait, United Arab Emirates (UAE), Qatar, Oman, Yemen and Syria. Those 9 countries produce essentially all of the Middle East's oil (see Figure 6.1).

The Middle East has been a major oil producing region since the 1950s. Most Middle East oil producing nations are members of the Organization of Petroleum Exporting Countries (OPEC). The member of OPEC with the highest production rate is Saudi Arabia. Because of its large production capacity, Saudi Arabia has taken on the roll of swing producer within OPEC, lowering production when oil prices are low and raising production when prices are high, thereby maintaining a more stable world price. Through the 1980s and 1990s, members of OPEC did not produce oil at the rate they were capable of because globally there was excess oil production capacity. In the case of Saudi Arabia, oil production declined from 9.90 mb/d in 1980 to 3.39 mb/d in 1985 and still hasn't returned to the 1980 level.[1]

Figure 6.2 is a graph of oil production from the Persian Gulf nations. Production reached its highest rate in 1977 at 21.73 mb/d. After the oil crisis of the late 1970s/early 1980s, production declined significantly reaching a low of 9.63 mb/d in 1985. Since 1985, production has crept up, reaching 19.23 mb/d in 2003.[2]

In this chapter, oil production from Bahrain will not be covered in detail because Bahrain is an insignificant producing nation that is in decline. Bahrain's oil production rate was 48,000 b/d in 1980 but in 2001, it was only 35,000 b/d.[3]

The Middle East has many of the world's largest oil fields including

162

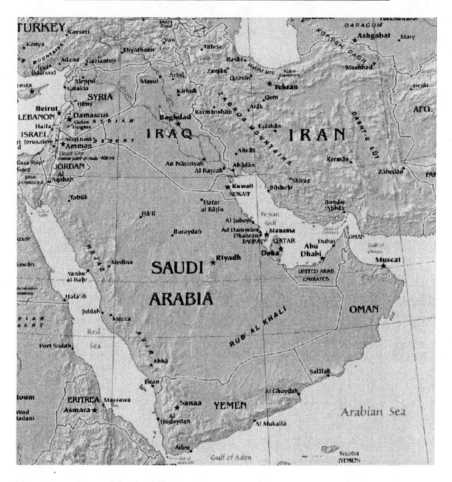

Figure 6.1— Map of the Middle East (Courtesy of the University Libraries, The University of Texas at Austin).

Ghawar (Saudi Arabia), Safaniya (Saudi Arabia), Berri (Saudi Arabia), Abqaiq (Saudi Arabia), Burgan (Kuwait), Kirkuk (Iraq), Rumaila (Iraq), Gachsarin (Iran) and Agha Jari (Iran).

Production data supplied to the US DOE/EIA by Middle East members of OPEC do not distinguish between oil and TLHs production; the production values for those two quantities are the same. For Qatar, and possibly other Middle East members of OPEC, NGLs production is becoming a sizeable component of TLHs production and it will grow in the future.

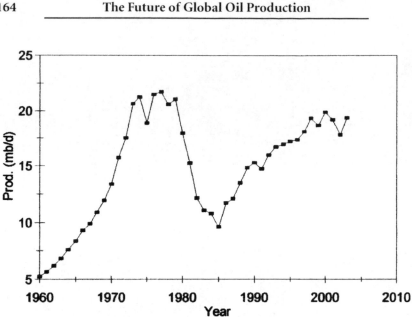

Figure 6.2 — Oil production from Persian Gulf nations (Data from the US DOE/EIA — Persian Gulf nations include Bahrain, Iran, Iraq, Kuwait, Qatar, Saudi Arabia and United Arab Emirates).

Oil Production in Saudi Arabia

Interest in Saudi Arabian oil exploration perked up in 1932 when Standard Oil of California (Socal) discovered oil in Bahrain, a few miles off the coast of Saudi Arabia. Not long after that, May 1933, Socal signed an oil concession with Saudi Arabia allowing them to explore and develop oil in Saudi Arabia. Exploration started at a site called the Damman Dome, thought to be a sure bet for oil because of its structural similarity to the oil containing structure in Bahrain. Drilling started in the summer of 1934. After six dry wells, the seventh was successful some 4 years after drilling commenced. Because of the immensity of the exploration and development task in Saudi Arabia, Socal brought the Texaco Oil Company in as a partner, forming the Arabian-American Oil Company, Aramco. Soon after the first oil discovery, a pipeline was built to Ras Tanura, a marine terminal. The first shipment of oil was made in April 1939. In 1940, production reached a high of 20,000 b/d but WWII brought exploration and development to a halt. A skeleton crew maintained production at 12,000–15,000 b/d during the war.[4]

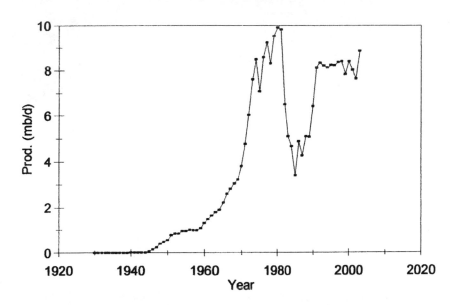

Figure 6.3 — Saudi Arabia's oil production (Data from Colin Campbell [1930–1959] and the US DOE/EIA [1960–2003]).

During the 1940s, the precursors of the Exxon and Mobil Oil Companies were also brought into Aramco to provide added capital, international expertise and markets. Adding the two American companies also kept the concession in American hands. After WWII, the world's largest oil field, Ghawar, was discovered in Saudi Arabia. Later, a field in the same structural uplift, Safaniya, was discovered offshore. Approximately half of all the oil ever discovered in Saudi Arabia was originally contained in those two fields.[5]

Since 1970, Saudi Arabia has been among the top three oil producing nations and through most of the 1990s it was the world's top oil producer. Figure 6.3 is a graph of Saudi Arabia's oil production.

Saudi Arabia's oil production reached its highest rate in 1980 at 9.90 mb/d. In 2003, the production rate was 8.85 mb/d.[6]

Saudi Arabia will probably have an ultimate recovery of ~300 Gb.[7] According to the US DOE/EIA, Saudi Arabia contains 264.2 Gb of known reserves with up to 1,000 Gb of ultimately recoverable reserves.[8] The idea that Saudi Arabia could contain 1,000 Gb of oil appears far-fetched. Saudi Arabia has been extensively explored, enough to ensure that most, if not all, of its large fields (>1 Gb) have been discovered. As Matthew Simmons has pointed out, there have been no major exploration successes in Saudi Arabia since the 1960s.[9] Almost all of Saudi Arabia's oil production comes from old fields which are increasingly showing their age. Saudi Arabia can

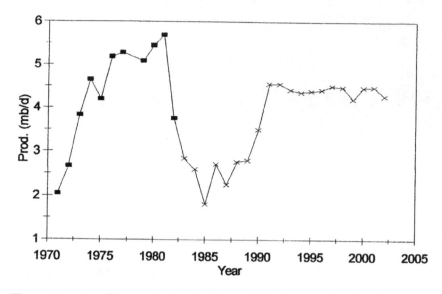

Figure 6.4 — Actual [rectangles] and estimated [X] oil production for the Ghawar field (Actual data from *Oil & Gas Journal*).

increase its oil production by developing smaller fields, as well as further development of a few large fields, but there is a limit to how much Saudi Arabia can increase its production.

Middle East members of OPEC have generally not made production data for individual fields available since the early 1980s, including Saudi Arabia. Prior to 1983, Saudi Arabia provided production data for individual fields so it's possible to get some idea of the cumulative production from its older oil fields. Figure 6.4 is a graph of actual (1971–1982) and estimated (1983–2002) oil production for the Ghawar field.

The estimated production in Figure 6.4, after 1982, assumes that the ratio of Ghawar production/Saudi Arabian production after 1982 was the average of 1980–1982, 0.561. The highest production rate reached during 1971–1982 was 5.69 mb/d. At the end of 1982, cumulative production from the field was 24.69 Gb.[10] Using the estimated production values from Figure 6.4, cumulative production for 1983–2002 would be 27.2 Gb and total cumulative production would be 51.9 Gb. According to Matthew Simmons, Ghawar's production reached 6.3 mb/d in the 1990s before production was reduced due to reservoir damage, but no other source of information has been found to confirm that. If the Ghawar field did reach a production rate of 6.3 mb/d in the 1990s, cumulative production would be somewhat higher than 51.9 Gb. According to Simmons, production in 2000 was 4.5 mb/d, close to the estimated value of 4.48 mb/d.[11]

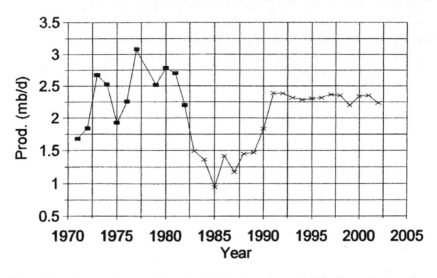

Figure 6.5 — Summed actual [rectangles] and estimated [X] oil production for Safaniya, Abqaiq and Berri fields (Actual data from *Oil & Gas Journal*).

There have been various estimates of Ghawar's EUR, ranging from 60–120 Gb.[12,13] The cumulative production estimate of 51.9 Gb suggests that possibly well over half to somewhat less than half of Ghawar's oil has been produced. It has been reported that the southern end of the field is totally infiltrated with water, that a high level of infill drilling is necessary to maintain the present production rate and that 7 mb/d of seawater is pumped into the Ghawar reservoir to maintain reservoir pressure.[14] Those bits of information suggest that all is not well with the Ghawar field.

Safaniya, Abqaiq and Berri are also Saudi Arabian oil fields in the supergiant category that have been producing oil for extended periods. Figure 6.5 is a graph of actual (1971–1982) and estimated (1983–2002) summed oil production for the three fields. Estimated production for the Safaniya, Abqaiq and Berri fields were obtained in the same manner as that for the Ghawar field.

Based upon Figure 6.5, the summed cumulative production for Safaniya, Abqaiq and Berri fields was 29.7 Gb at the end of 2002.[15] The summed EUR values for the three fields is reported to be 54 Gb.[16] According to Matthew Simmons, the Safaniya field was producing over 1 mb/d in 1990 but production had declined to ~500,000 b/d by 2000.[17] That would mean the cumulative production for the Safaniya field at the end of 2002 would probably be ~12 Gb, compared to 14.4 Gb based upon Figure 6.5. A decline in production from the Safaniya field after 1990 possibly means that over half of its ultimate recovery has been produced.

The Abqaiq field's highest production rate after 1970 was 1.09 mb/d in 1973.[18] In 2000, the estimated production rate was 600,000 b/d, the same as what Matthew Simmons reports.[19] Based upon Figure 6.5, cumulative production from the Abqaiq field at the end of 2002 was ~10.4 Gb. The EUR for the field has been reported to be 12 Gb.[20]

The highest production rate that the Berri field achieved during 1971–1982 was 807,557 b/d in 1976.[21] The estimated production rate for 2000 was 433,000 b/d. According to Matthew Simmons, the Berri field was producing ~400,000 b/d in 2000 so the estimated value is close.[22] Based upon Figure 6.5, the Berri field had a cumulative production of 4.9 Gb at the end of 2002. The EUR for the Berri field has been reported to be 12 Gb.[23]

There are several other large fields (>1 Gb) in Saudi Arabia: Zuluf, Shayba, Faroozan/Marjan, Khurais, Qatif and Manifa. According to Matthew Simmons, Zuluf was producing ~500,000 b/d in 2000, Shayba ~600,000 b/d and Faroozan/Marjan ~250,000 b/d.[24] The Faroozan/Marjan fields have a reported EUR of 10 Gb and the Manifa field 11 Gb.[25] EUR values for the other fields are unknown. The Khurais field was mothballed in the late 1970s, but there are plans to resuscitate production in the not-to-distant future to possibly 800,000 b/d. In March 2002, Saudi Arabia reportedly awarded contracts to expand the production capacity at the Qatif field to 800,000 b/d by 2005.[26]

The US DOE/EIA doesn't provide estimates of future oil production for individual Persian Gulf countries in their IEO2003, but it does provide estimates of oil production capacity for individual countries and total Persian Gulf production. From that, it's possible to estimate what the US DOE/EIA expects for future oil production from individual Persian Gulf countries. Table 6.1 provides US DOE/EIA estimates of future oil production capacity for Saudi Arabia and the Persian Gulf, the ratio of those production capacities (Ratio A/B) and the US DOE/EIA's estimate of future Persian Gulf oil production. Estimates of future oil production for Saudi Arabia are calculated by multiplying the Ratio A/B by the estimated Persian Gulf oil production values.

Using the US DOE/EIA based projection, Saudi Arabia's cumulative oil production would be ~213 Gb at the end of 2025, and production would still be rising. Assuming that Saudi Arabia has an ultimate recovery of ~300 Gb, production should start declining not long after ~150 Gb of oil has been produced. That would occur in ~2016 using the US DOE/EIA based projection.

Figure 6.6 is a graph of Richard Duncan's forecast for Saudi Arabia's oil + NGLs production. Duncan projects that Saudi Arabia's future oil +

Table 6.1— US DOE/EIA Estimates for Saudi Arabia*

	2005	2010	2015	2020	2025
A. Saudi Arabia's Oil Production Capacity (mb/d)	11.1	13.6	15.7	19.5	23.8
B. Persian Gulf Oil Production Capacity (mb/d)	24.5	28.7	33.0	38.9	45.2
Ratio A/B	0.453	0.474	0.476	0.501	0.527
Persian Gulf Oil Production (mb/d)	21.7	24.8	29.2	34.6	40.5
Saudi Arabia's Estimated Oil Production (mb/d)†	9.83	11.8	13.9	17.3	21.3

* From the International Energy Outlook 2003 by the US DOE/EIA
  † For most Middle East oil producing nations, US DOE/EIA production data are the same for oil production and TLHs production and are assumed to be the same in the future.

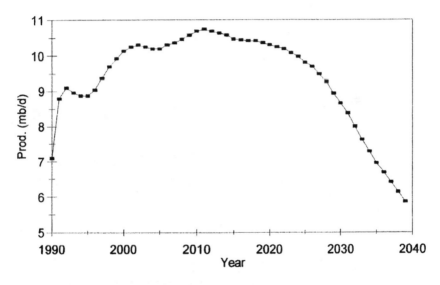

Figure 6.6 — Duncan's forecast for Saudi Arabia's oil + NGLs production

NGLs production will peak in 2011 at 10.74 mb/d, decline to 9.81 mb/d in 2025 and 5.86 mb/d in 2039.[27]

Figure 6.7 is a graph of Colin Campbell's forecast for Saudi Arabia's oil production. Campbell projects that Saudi Arabia's future oil production will peak in 2013 at 9.73 mb/d, decline to 8.84 mb/d in 2025 and 7.25 mb/d in 2040. Campbell estimates that Saudi Arabia's cumulative oil production at the end of 2075 will be 300 Gb, essentially its EUR.[28] At the end of 2002, Saudi Arabia's cumulative production was 95.2 Gb, 31.7 percent of 300 Gb.[29]

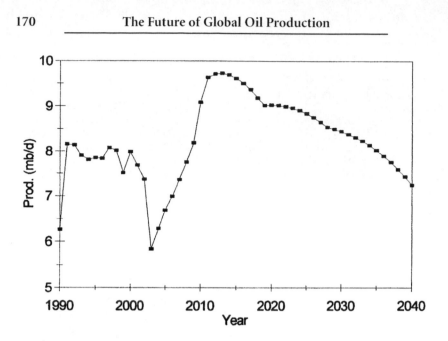

Figure 6.7 — Campbell's forecast for Saudi Arabia's oil production

Oil Production in Kuwait

Kuwait's oil production started after the discovery of the megagiant Burgan field, the world's second largest oil field, in the 1930s. The Greater Burgan fields, consisting of Burgan, Magwa and Ahmadi, have a reported EUR of ~70 Gb.[30,31] Production data for Kuwait's oil fields are scant, with data only published once in *Oil & Gas Journal* since 1971, in 1977. In that year, the Burgan field produced 1,036,587 b/d, Magwa 181,878 b/d and Ahmadi 161,540 b/d. Summed production from the three fields represented 82.60 percent of Kuwait's oil production in 1977. Summed cumulative production from the three fields was 15.67 Gb at the end of 1977, 87.20 percent of Kuwait's total.[32] Assuming that the ratio of Greater Burgan production/Kuwait production has remained constant since 1977, the Greater Burgan fields would have a cumulative production of 27.8 Gb at the end of 2002. An unknown amount of oil from the Greater Burgan fields was burned during the Persian Gulf War of 1990/1991 and will be ignored. Assuming that the ~70 Gb EUR value for the Greater Burgan fields is accurate, about 40 percent of the oil had been produced by the end of 2002. Today, the Greater Burgan fields are producing 1.35–1.6 mb/d.[33,34] Based upon the ratio of Greater Burgan production/Kuwait production, production from the area would be 1.33 mb/d.

Beyond the Greater Burgan area, there are 3 other giant/supergiant fields in Kuwait: Raudhatain (EUR = 6 Gb), Sabriya (EUR = 3.8 Gb) and Minagish (EUR = 2 Gb).[35] The Roudhatain field, in northern Kuwait, is the only other field in Kuwait that was producing greater than 100,000 b/d in 1977.[36] It's presently producing ~225,000 b/d. Another northern field, Sabriya, is producing ~95,000 b/d. The southern fields of Minagish and UmmGudair are producing at a summed production rate of ~140,000 b/d,[37] while Kuwait's share of the Neutral Zone is producing ~150,000 b/d.[38]

The US DOE/EIA reports that the South Magwa field, discovered in 1984, holds at least 25 Gb of oil.[39] That must be oil-in-place rather than recoverable oil. In November 2000, Kuwait announced the discovery of a significant amount of light oil near Sabriya, although an estimated volume was not given.

According to the US DOE/EIA, Kuwait has proven reserves of 96.5 Gb. That is probably inflated with political reserves. Kuwait's share of the Neutral Zone, located between Kuwait and Saudi Arabia, has a reported 5 Gb of proven reserves.[40]

Figure 6.8 is a graph of Kuwait's oil production. Kuwait reached its highest oil production rate in 1972 at 3.28 mb/d. Since then, Kuwait's oil production has been influenced by the OPEC oil embargo, OPEC production quotas and the Persian Gulf War in 1990/1991. In 2003, Kuwait's oil production rate averaged 2.18 mb/d.[41] In recent years Kuwait has suffered from production problems due to explosions, oil spills and equipment shutdowns. Analysts have blamed the problems on a lack of maintenance, insufficient technical expertise and poorly-trained low-paid foreign workers. Some of Kuwait's oil infrastructure was never repaired after the 1990/1991 Persian Gulf War.

The Kuwaiti government is pushing a project known as "Project Kuwait," a $7 billion 25-year plan, formulated in 1997, to increase Kuwait's oil production and address declining production in mature oil fields. The Kuwaiti government is considering permitting foreign oil companies to invest in production, reversing 2 decades of Kuwaiti policy. During the 1990/1991 Persian Gulf War, all of Kuwait's oil gathering stations were damaged or destroyed. Since then, most have been restored and 2 new stations have been built. "Project Kuwait" would require more gathering stations to further expand oil production capacity to 3 mb/d by 2005 and 3.5 mb/d by 2010. Much of the anticipated production increase would occur in the northern and western oil fields. The plan is to increase production from ~450,000 b/d to 900,000 b/d in the northern fields and from ~120,000 b/d to over 500,000 b/d in the western oil fields during the next 10 years.[42]

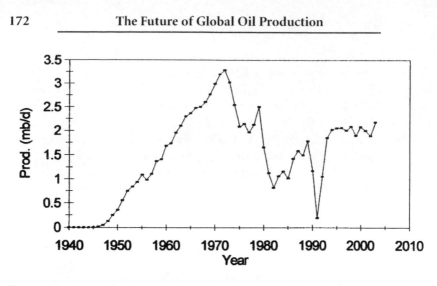

Figure 6.8 — Kuwait's oil production (Data from Colin Campbell [1940–1959] and the US DOE/EIA [1960–2002]).

Table 6.2 — US DOE/EIA Estimates for Kuwait*

	2005	2010	2015	2020	2025
A. Kuwait's Oil Production Capacity (mb/d)	2.8	3.3	3.9	4.5	5.1
B. Persian Gulf Oil Production Capacity (mb/d)	24.5	28.7	33.0	38.9	45.2
Ratio A/B	0.114	0.115	0.118	0.116	0.113
Persian Gulf Oil Production (mb/d)	21.7	24.8	29.2	34.6	40.5
Kuwait's Estimated Oil Production (mb/d)†	2.47	2.85	3.45	4.01	4.58

From the International Energy Outlook 2003, US DOE/EIA
  † For most Middle East oil producing nations, US DOE/EIA production data are the same for oil production and TLHs production and are assumed to be the same in the future

Applying the same procedure to Kuwait as was applied to Saudi Arabia in Table 6.1, gives the data and results of Table 6.2.

Based upon the US DOE/EIA projection, cumulative oil production at the end of 2025 would be 60.7 Gb. Adding the ~2 Gb burned in the 1990/1991 Persian Gulf War brings the total to ~63 Gb. Colin Campbell estimates Kuwait's EUR to be ~90 Gb.[43] If that estimate is in the ballpark, Kuwait's oil production should start declining after ~45 Gb of oil has been removed from Kuwait's oil fields, which would occur in ~2013 based upon the US DOE/EIA projection.

Figure 6.9 is a graph of Richard Duncan's forecast for Kuwait's oil + NGLs production. Duncan projects that Kuwait's future oil + NGLs production will peak in 2018 at 4.68 mb/d, decline to 4.47 mb/d in 2025 and 2.79 mb/d in 2040.[44]

Figure 6.10 is Colin Campbell's forecast for Kuwait's oil production.

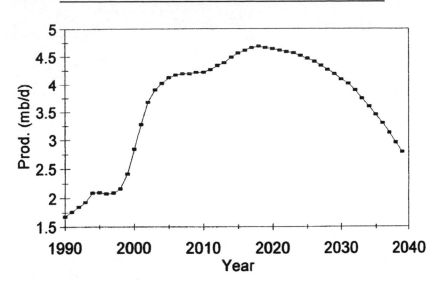

Figure 6.9 — Duncan's forecast for Kuwait's oil + NGLs production

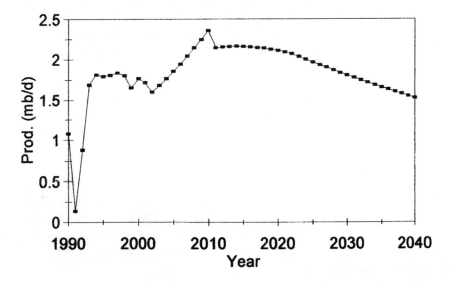

Figure 6.10 — Campbell's forecast for Kuwait's oil production

Campbell projects that Kuwait's future oil production will peak in 2010 at 2.36 mb/d, decline to 1.97 mb/d in 2025 and 1.52 mb/d in 2040. Campbell estimates that Kuwait's cumulative production at the end of 2075 will be 90 Gb, essentially its EUR.[45] At the end of 2002, Kuwait's cumulative production was 32.6 Gb, 36.2 percent of 90 Gb.[46]

Oil Production in the Neutral Zone

The Neutral Zone is a region located between Saudi Arabia and Kuwait that is jointly controlled by the two countries. The Neutral Zone was created in 1922 by the British High Commissioner because of disputes between Ibn Saud, ruler of Saudi Arabia, and the Amir of Kuwait. Another objective of the creation was to accommodate the Bedouins who wandered between Kuwait and Saudi Arabia grazing their flocks.

Kuwait's original oil concession in the Neutral Zone (1947) went to a group of American independent oil companies that included Phillips, Ashland and Sinclair. The consortium was called Aminoil. Saudi Arabia's original oil concession in the Neutral Zone (1948) went to Pacific Western, owned by J. Paul Getty.

The concessionaires had to combine operations to a large extent because Kuwait and Saudi Arabia split oil revenues from the Neutral Zone. After 5 dry holes, oil was discovered in March 1953 at a field called Wafra, a discovery that Fortune magazine described as "somewhere between colossal and history making." That appears to be a bit of an exaggeration, although the Wafra field is indeed large. In 1992, the Wafra, S. Fuwaris and S. Umm Gudair fields had a summed cumulative production of ~1.8 Gb.[47] Oil production from the Neutral Zone helped make J. Paul Getty the richest person in the world in 1957.

The Neutral Zone field with the highest production rate during the 1970s was the Khafji field, which was producing over 300,000 b/d in the early years of that decade. At the end of 1992, the Khafji and Hout fields had a summed cumulative production of 3.07 Gb.[48] According to Matthew Simmons, the Khafji field was still producing approximately 300,000 b/d in 2000.[49]

Figure 6.11 is a graph of Neutral Zone oil production. Production reached its highest rate in 2000 at 630,000 b/d. In 2002, the production rate had declined to 538,000 b/d.[50] The US DOE/EIA makes no mention of the Neutral Zone in their IEO2003. Likewise, Richard Duncan has no forecast for Neutral Zone oil production. Figure 6.12 is a graph of Colin Campbell's forecast for Neutral Zone oil production.

Campbell projected that Neutral Zone oil production would peak in 2000 at 630,000 b/d, decline to 356,000 b/d in 2025 and 247,000 b/d in 2040. He estimates that the Neutral Zone will have a cumulative production of 16 Gb at the end of 2075, essentially its EUR.[51] At the end of 2001, cumulative production was 6.6 Gb, 41 percent of 16 Gb.[52]

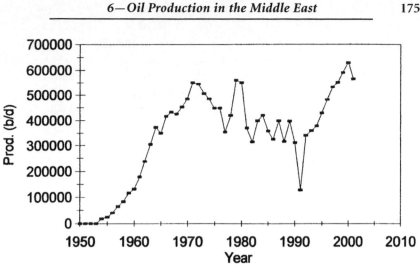

Figure 6.11— The Neutral Zone's oil production (Data from Colin Campbell)

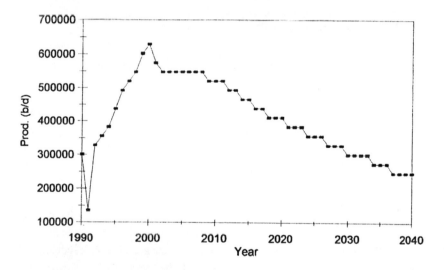

Figure 6.12 — Campbell's forecast for Neutral Zone oil production

Oil Production in Iran

Iran's oil exploration started in the early 1900s when a British entre-preneur, William Knox D'Arcy, signed a 60-year concession, in 1901, to explore and develop oil. Oil seeps in the Zargros foothills of southwest-ern Iran had long been known about and by 1901 there had been decades of oil production in the Baku area near the Caspian Sea, not far from Iran.

After seven discouraging years, oil was discovered in May 1908 at Masjid-I-Sulaiman. In 1914, the British government acquired a 51 percent stake in D'Arcy's enterprise, forming the Anglo-Persian Oil Company. Later Anglo-Persian became the British Petroleum Corporation, BP.

In 1951, Prime Minister Mohammad Mossaddeg nationalized BP's exclusive concession, ultimately leading other countries to following suit. The British government didn't take the takeover well. With the aid of the U.S. government, through the Central Intelligence Agency (CIA), the British government was successful in having Mossaddeg overthrown and the Shah of Iran installed as leader of Iran. Because of the assistance of the U.S. government, via the CIA, the Shah gave a consortium of American oil companies and BP exclusive rights to explore and develop Iranian oil.

After 1955, Iran's oil production grew rapidly, ultimately reaching a rate of ~6 mb/d in 1974.[53] In 1978, the Shah was overthrown and Ayatollah Khomeini became leader of Iran. Iran had been the second leading oil exporting nation globally prior to the regime change, but the Khomeini government terminated oil exports in December 1978. Exports resumed in March 1979 at a much lower level. The cutoff of Iranian oil exports followed by a greatly reduced export level created the second oil crisis of the 1970s, which was exacerbated by the Iran/Iraq war that started in September 1980.

Since the middle 1980s, Iran's politics have become more moderate and oil production has increased from ~2 mb/d to ~3.8 mb/d in 2003.[54] The higher production rate allows for a higher export rate and consequently a means of acquiring hard currency. Iran exports ~2.5 mb/d, mainly to Europe, Japan, China, South Korea and India. Internal consumption is ~1.3 mb/d, but it is growing rapidly.[55]

Figure 6.13 is a graph of Iran's oil production. Most Iranian oil fields are located near the Iraqi border and the Persian Gulf, a region known as the Zagros foothills. Historically, most of Iran's oil production has come from a handful of giant and supergiant fields: Ahwaz, Marun, Gachsaran, Agha Jari and Bibi Hakimeh. All of the fields had maximum production rates greater than 450,000 b/d during the 1970s and 3 of them had production rates greater than 1 mb/d. Summed production for the five fields reached a high of 4.2 mb/d in 1974 (see Figure 6.14).[56]

In 1977, the fields were producing 81.1 percent of Iran's total oil production and they had a cumulative production of 17.9 Gb.[57] Now they are experiencing serious depletion problems. Collectively they only produced ~1.1 mb/d in 2000, representing 29.8 percent of Iran's total oil production.[58] Assuming a constant production decline rate for the five fields during 1978–2000, the five fields would have a cumulative production of 37.8 Gb

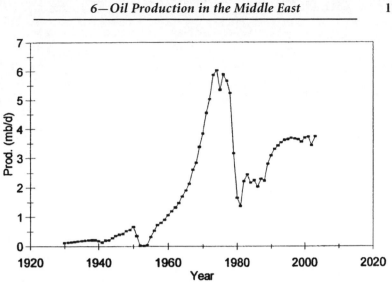

Figure 6.13 — Iran's oil production (Data from the US DOE/EIA)

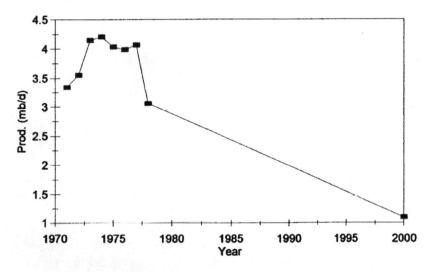

Figure 6.14 — Summed production from the Agha Jari, Bibi Hakimeh, Ahwaz, Gach-saran and Marun fields (Data from *Oil & Gas Journal* [1971–1978] and Simmons & Company International [2000]).

at the end of 2000. The summed EUR for the five fields, see Table 6.3, is ~62 Gb, so the fields may have produced ~60 percent, and possibly more, of their summed EUR. According to Iran's oil minister, oil fields in Iran are experiencing a depletion rate of 250,000–300,000 b/d per year.[59] That does not bode well for Iran's future oil production.

Table 6.3 — EUR Values for Iran's 15 Largest Oil Fields*

Field	Discovery Date	EUR (Gb)	Field	Discovery Date	EUR (Gb)
Gashsaran	1928	15	Karanj	1963	2
Ahwaz	1958	15–17	Paris	1964	2
Marun	1963	15–16	Salman	1965	2
Agha Jari	1937	14	Haft Kel	1927	2
Azedegan	1999	5	Aboozar	1961	1.5
Rag-e-Safid	1963	3	Mansuri	1963	1.5
Bibi-Hakimeh	1961	2.5	Masjid-I-Sulaiman	1908	1.5
Foroozan	1966	2.5			

* Country Assessment — Iran, Association for the Study of Peak Oil, Newsletter No 32

About 350 wildcat wells have been drilled in Iran, finding ~120 Gb of oil. Most of the oil was contained in a small number of giant and supergiant fields.[60] Table 6.3 provides data for Iran's 15 largest oil fields.

Iran has 5 main offshore fields: Doroud, Salman, Sirri, Nowruz and Soroush. Each of the fields has reached or will reach a maximum production rate of greater than 100,000 b/d. Presently Iran's offshore production rate is ~600,000 b/d.[61]

The Iranian government plans to increase Iran's oil production rate to 5.6 mb/d by 2010 and 7.3 mb/d by 2020,[62] although the feasibility of achieving those goals appears questionable. The government hopes that foreign investment will fund the expansion. Unfortunately for Iran, much of the production increase from new fields will merely replace declining production from old fields.

In October 1999, Iran announced the discovery of the Azadegan field, which the US DOE/EIA states contains up to 45 Gb of oil and has the potential to produce 300,000–400,000 b/d.[63] The 45 Gb figure is apparently oil-in-place, in which case recoverable reserves would be much less than 45 Gb. The Forties field (U.K.) with an EUR of 2.8 Gb reached a peak production rate of ~510,000 b/d, suggesting that the true size of recoverable reserves in the Azadegan field is much less than 45 Gb. According to the Association for the Study of Peak Oil, the Azedegen field was discovered at such a late date because it lies in a sensitive area near the Iraqi border. They claim that reserves have been reported to be ~5 Gb in two reservoirs but that estimates are being revised downward.[64]

In February 2001, the National Iranian Oil Company announced the discovery of an offshore field named Dasht-e Abadan that could have reserves comparable to Azadegan. Several other fields have been discovered recently including Darkhovin, Henjani and Esfandir. The Darkhovin field is projected to have a maximum production rate of 160,000 b/d.[65]

Table 6.4 — US DOE/EIA Estimates for Iran*

	2005	*2010*	*2015*	*2020*	*2025*
A. Iran's Oil Production Capacity (mb/d)	3.9	4.2	4.5	4.7	4.9
B. Persian Gulf Oil Production Capacity (mb/d)	24.5	28.7	33.0	38.9	45.2
Ratio A/B	0.159	0.146	0.136	0.121	0.108
Persian Gulf Oil Production (mb/d)	21.7	24.8	29.2	34.6	40.5
Iran's Estimated Oil Production (mb/d)†	3.45	3.62	3.97	4.19	4.37

* From the International Energy Outlook 2003, US DOE/EIA
† For most Middle East oil producing nations, US DOE/EIA production data are the same for oil production and TLHs production and are assumed to be the same in the future

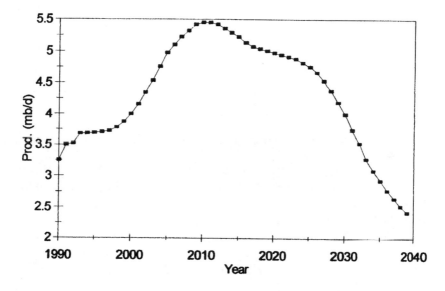

Figure 6.15 — Duncan's forecast for Iran's oil + NGLs production

Applying the same analysis to Iran as was applied to Saudi Arabia in Table 6.1, gives the data and results in Table 6.4.

Based upon the US DOE/EIA projection, Iran's cumulative oil production at the end of 2025 would be 87.46 Gb, with production still rising. Colin Campbell has estimated Iran's EUR to be 130 Gb.[66] Based upon the US DOE/EIA projection, cumulative production at the end of 2010 would be 65 Gb, half of 130 Gb.

Figure 6.15 is Richard Duncan's forecast for Iran's oil + NGLs production. Duncan projects that Iran's future oil + NGLs production will peak in 2010–2011 at 5.45 mb/d, decline to 4.76 mb/d in 2025 and 2.43 mb/d in 2039.[67]

Figure 6.16 is Colin Campbell's forecast for Iran's oil production. Campbell projects that Iran's future oil production will peak in 2009 at

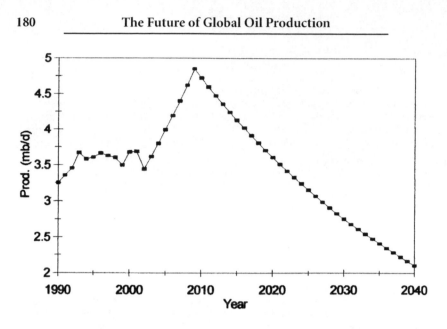

Figure 6.16 — Campbell's forecast for Iran's oil production

4.85 mb/d, decline to 3.15 mb/d in 2025 and 2.11 mb/d in 2040. Campbell estimates that Iran's cumulative oil production at the end of 2075 will be 130 Gb, essentially its EUR.[68] At the end of 2002, cumulative production was 54.9 Gb, 42.2 percent of 130 Gb.[69]

Oil Production in Iraq

The existence of oil had been known about for millennia in the region that is now Iraq. Over the ages, Middle East oil had been used in warfare, to make medicine and to make mortar in the construction of ancient cities such as Babylon. In what is now Iraq, oil exploration started in the early 20th century as a result of observed oil seeps while surveying the route for a proposed German railway to Baghdad. The Sultan of the Ottoman Empire called upon Calouste Gulbenkian to investigate the prospects for oil development and Gulbenkian concluded that the prospects were good. In 1912, Gulkenkian established the Turkish Petroleum Company but little exploration was done prior to the end of World War I. After the war, the Iraq Petroleum Company was formed consisting of the Turkish Petroleum Company and most of the world's major international oil companies.

In the 1920s, exploration was initiated and the Kirkuk oil field was discovered (1927). The Kirkuk field was an impressive discovery since it has an EUR of 16 Gb. Iraq's production rate rose through the 1930s and

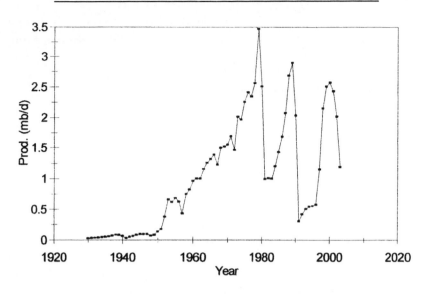

Figure 6.17 — Iraq's oil production (Data from the US DOE/EIA)

1940s, reaching 100,000 b/d in 1947. In 1953, a second supergiant field, Ramaila (EUR = 20 Gb), was discovered. A third supergiant field, East Baghdad (EUR =14), was discovered in 1976.[70] Of the ~80 fields that have been discovered in Iraq, only 20 were producing oil in 2000.

The summed EUR for Iraq's fields discovered to date is ~90 Gb. Campbell estimates that Iraq will ultimately produce 135 Gb of oil, 45 Gb of which is undiscovered.[71] The USGS estimates a median undiscovered resource of 45 Gb in their World Petroleum Assessment 2000.[72] Other organizations: Baker Institute, Center for Global Energy Studies and the Federation of American Scientists believe another 100 Gb or more of oil could be discovered in Iraq.[73]

Iraq's oil production has fluctuated wildly over the years due to wars, economic sanctions and OPEC production quotas (see Figure 6.17).

Due to the most recent war, 2003, oil production dropped precipitously again. In August 2003, Iraq was producing just under 1 mb/d. According to the U.N. Joint Logistics Center, about 60 percent of Iraq's northern production, 200,000–300,000 b/d, is re-injected into fields to maintain reservoir pressure while liquefied petroleum gas is removed for use.[74] That means that the actual production rate in August may have only been 700,000–800,000 b/d.

Prior to the 2003 war, oil industry experts generally concluded that Iraq's sustainable production capacity was no higher than 2.8–3.0 mb/d. Iraq's oil infrastructure is in a serious state of decay. According to a June

2001 report by the U.N., Iraq's oil production capacity would fall sharply unless technical and infrastructure problems were addressed soon.[75] Iraq has the oil resource capacity to have a significantly higher production rate, but an improvement in the political situation is necessary before production can be seriously increased.

Production data for Iraq's oil fields were only made available to *Oil & Gas Journal* for a few years in the 1970s. During that period, the Kirkuk field produced 0.9–1.1 mb/d. Cumulative production for the Kirkuk field was 6.76 Gb at the end of 1975. The Ramaila field produced 800,000 b/d in 1975 and cumulative production was 2.20 Gb at the end of the year. The only other fields that were producing over 100,000 b/d in 1975 were the Zubair field (200,000 b/d) and the Ramaila North field (150,000 b/d).[76]

Applying the same analysis for Iraq as was applied to Saudi Arabia in Table 6.1, gives the data and results in Table 6.5.

Based upon the US DOE/EIA projection, Iraq's cumulative oil production at the end of 2025 would be 57.95 Gb. Colin Campbell has estimated Iraq's EUR to be 135 Gb,[77] so cumulative production at the end of 2025 would still be less than half of Campbell's EUR estimate based upon the US DOE/EIA projection.

Figure 6.18 is Richard Duncan's forecast for Iraq's oil + NGLs production. Duncan projects that Iraq's oil + NGLs production will rise to ~5 mb/d in 2005 and remain between 5–5.5 mb/d through 2028, before declining to 3.15 mb/d in 2039.[78]

Figure 6.19 is Colin Campbell's forecast for Iraq's oil production. Campbell's forecast assumes that the political situation in Iraq will stabilize and conditions will be conducive to oil development. He projects that future production will peak in 2019 at 4.61 mb/d, decline to 4.32 mb/d in 2025 and 3.28 mb/d in 2040. Campbell estimates that Iraq's cumulative oil production at the end of 2075 will be 135 Gb, essentially its EUR.[79] At the end of 2002, cumulative production was 28.2 Gb, 20.9 percent of 135 Gb.[80]

Table 6.5 — US DOE/EIA Estimates for Iraq*

	2005	2010	2015	2020	2025
A. Iraq's oil Production Capacity (mb/d)	3.2	3.6	4.2	4.6	5.2
B. Persian Gulf Oil Production Capacity (mb/d)	24.5	28.7	33.0	38.9	45.2
Ratio A/B	0.131	0.125	0.127	0.118	0.115
Persian Gulf Oil Production (mb/d)	21.7	24.8	29.2	34.6	40.5
Iraq's Estimated Oil Production (mb/d)†	2.84	3.10	3.71	4.08	4.66

*From the International Energy Outlook 2003, US DOE/EIA
†For most Middle East oil producing nations, US DOE/EIA production data are the same for oil production and TLHs production and are assumed to be the same in the future

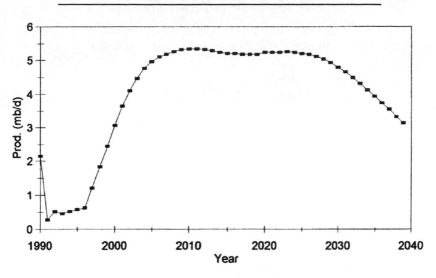

Figure 6.18 — Duncan's forecast for Iraq's oil + NGLs production

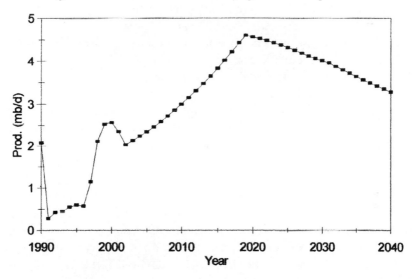

Figure 6.19 — Campbell's forecast for Iraq's oil production

Oil Production in the United Arab Emirates

The United Arab Emirates (UAE) is a federation of 7 emirates, only 3 of which are important in terms of oil production: Abu Dhabi, Dubai, and Sharjah. The most important oil emirate is Abu Dhabi, where oil was first discovered in 1958 at the onshore Bab field. Oil was discovered offshore in 1959 at the Umm Shaif field. The second most important oil emirate is Dubai, where oil was discovered offshore at the Fateh field in 1966 and the Fateh Southwest field in 1970.

Most of the oil fields in the UAE have been producing oil since the 1960s or 1970s. A total of 6 fields were producing at least 100,000 b/d during 1971–1981 when field data were published in *Oil & Gas Journal*: Bu Hasa (Adu Dhabi-onshore), Umm Shaif (Abu Dhabi-offshore), Zakum (Abu Dhabi-offshore), Asab (Abu Dhabi-onshore), Fateh (Dubai-offshore) and Fateh SW (Dubai-offshore). The Bu Hasa field was producing 680,000 b/d in 1974.[81] Matthew Simmons reports that the field was producing 450,000 b/d in 2000,[82] but the US DOE/EIA reports that the field was only producing ~100,000 b/d in 2003. The US DOE/EIA further reports that Abu Dhabi plans on spending $300 million to increase the capacity of the Bu Hasa field to 480,000 b/d.[83]

The Asab field was producing over 400,000 b/d in the 1970s,[84] but it was producing less than 300,000 b/d in 2000 according to data from Simmons.[85] Zakum actually consists of two fields: Lower Zakum and Upper Zakum. In 1977 the two fields were producing a total of 300,000 b/d.[86] Simmons reports that both fields individually were producing 400,000 b/d in 2000.[87] The Zakum fields have a reported EUR of 12 Gb. The Umm Shaif field was producing ~250,000 b/d during 1977–1981, but the present production rate is unknown. The Fateh and Fateh Southwest fields were both producing 150,000–200,000 b/d in the late 1970s/early 1980.[88] Their production rates are probably declining because Dubai's production is declining.

According to the US DOE/EIA, proven oil reserves in the UAE total 97.86 Gb, with Abu Dhabi holding 92.2 Gb (94 percent), Dubai holding 4 Gb (4 percent) and Sharjah holding 1.5 Gb (1.5 percent).[89] The 97.86 Gb figure is probably inflated with political reserves. In the case of Dubai, oil production has generally been declining since 1991, suggesting that it has passed the mid-point of its ultimate production (see Figure 6.20).

Figure 6.21 is a graph of the UAE's oil production. The UAE's oil production was insignificant until the early 1960s. Production peaked in 1977 at 2.0 mb/d followed by a decline in the 1980s to ~1.15 mb/d. Production rose to approximately 2.25 mb/d in the early 1990s and has remained relatively flat since then.[90] The current production capacity is reported to be 2.6 mb/d, 1.4 mb/d onshore and 1.2 mb/d mb/d offshore.

An objective of the UAE is to increase its oil production capacity to 3 mb/d by 2007.[91] In order to achieve that goal, expansion of capacity at the Bu Hasa field and a natural gas re-injection project for the Bab field are major components of the plan.

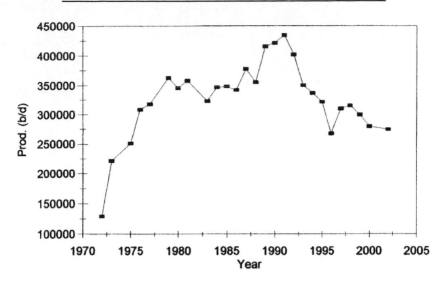

Figure 6.20 — Dubai's oil production (Data from *Oil & Gas Journal*)

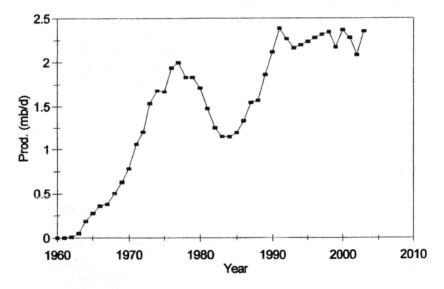

Figure 6.21— The UAE's oil production (Data from the US DOE/EIA)

Applying the same analysis for the UAE as was applied to Saudi Arabia in Table 6.1, gives the data and results in Table 6.6.

Based upon the US DOE/EIA projection, the UAE's cumulative oil production at the end of 2025 would be 50.9 Gb. Colin Campbell has estimated the UAE's ultimate recovery to be ~84 Gb.[92] The UAE's production

Table 6.6 — US DOE/EIA Estimates
for the United Arab Emirates*

	2005	2010	2015	2020	2025
A. The UAE's Oil Production Capacity (mb/d)	2.9	3.4	4.0	4.8	5.4
B. Persian Gulf Oil Production Capacity (mb/d)	24.5	28.7	33.0	38.9	45.2
Ratio A/B	0.118	0.118	0.121	0.123	0.119
Persian Gulf Oil Production (mb/d)	21.7	24.8	29.2	34.6	40.5
The UAE's Estimated Oil Production (mb/d)†	2.56	2.93	3.53	4.26	4.82

International Energy Outlook 2003, US DOE/EIA
†For most Middle East oil producing nations, US DOE/EIA production data are the same for oil production and TLHs production and are assumed to be the same in the future

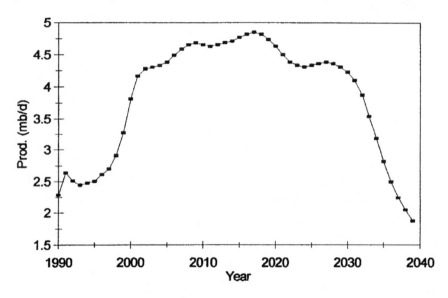

Figure 6.22 — Duncan's forecast for the UAE's oil + NGLs production

should start declining in about 2020 when cumulative production is ~42 Gb, half of 84 Gb, based upon the US DOE/EIA projection.

Figure 6.22 is Richard Duncan's forecast for the UAE's oil + NGLs production. Duncan projects that the UAE's oil + NGLs production will reach its highest rate in 2017 at 4.85 mb/d, decline to 4.33 mb/d in 2025 and 1.87 mb/d in 2039.[93]

Figure 6.23 is Colin Campbell's forecast for the UAE's oil production. Campbell projects that the UAE's oil production will peak in 2010 at 2.64 mb/d, decline to 2.19 mb/d in 2025 and 1.65 mb/d in 2040. Campbell estimates that the UAE's cumulative oil production at the end of 2075 will be 84 Gb, essentially its EUR.[94] At the end of 2002, cumulative production was 22.5 Gb, 26.8 percent of 84 Gb.[95]

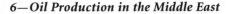

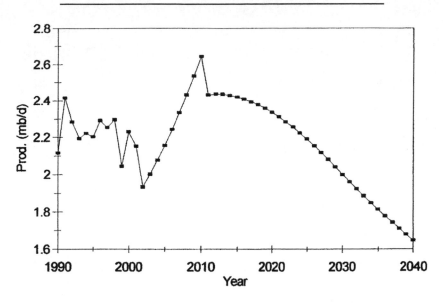

Figure 6.23 — Campbell's forecast for the UAE's oil production

Oil Production in Qatar

Qatar's oil production began in 1950, the result of production from the supergiant onshore Dukhan field, discovered in 1940. Production rose steadily through the 1950s, 1960s and early 1970s, reaching a peak in 1973 at 570,000 b/d (see Figure 6.24).[96]

Qatar is a member of OPEC and it experienced declining production like that of other OPEC nations during the late 1970s/early 1980s. In 2003, Qatar's production rate was 762,000 b/d.

Into the 1990s, Qatar was producing almost all of its oil from 4 fields: Dukhan, Bul Hanine, Maydan-Mahzam and Idd El Shargi. In 1980, nearly 80 percent of Qatar's total oil production came from only the Dukhan and Bul Hanine fields.[97] By 2002, the number of producing fields had expanded to 8 with 6 of those fields being offshore. According to the US DOE/EIA, Qatar is expected to increase its oil + NGLs production capacity to over 1 mb/d by 2006.[98]

The Dukhan field is by far the largest field in Qatar. Since 1971, the production rate for the field has generally exceeded 200,000 b/d, and in 2000 it averaged 307,397 b/d.[99] Figure 6.25 is a graph of oil production from the Dukhan field.

Production data for the Dukhan field are incomplete, but the field

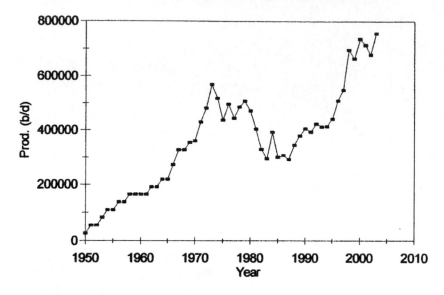

Figure 6.24 — Qatar's oil production (Data from Colin Campbell [1950–1969] and the US DOE/EIA [1970–2003]).

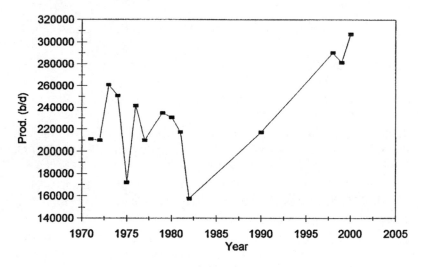

Figure 6.25 — Dukhan field oil production (Data from *Oil & Gas Journal*)

had a cumulative production of 2.65 Gb at the end of 1990.[100] If it is assumed that the Dukhan field produced at an average rate of 250,000 b/d since 1990, cumulative production would be 3.75 Gb at the end of 2002. According to the US DOE/EIA in 1997, the Dukhan field had reserves of 2.2 Gb.[101] Based upon cumulative production at the end of 1996, ~3.2 Gb,[102]

Table 6.7 — Data for Qatar's Offshore Oil Fields
(From Country Analysis Brief—Qatar, US DOE/EIA)

Field	On-line Date	Maximum Known Production (b/d)	Production in 2000 (b/d)
al Rayyan	1996	21,644 (1998)	12,055
al-Khalij	1997	23,096 (1998)	21,370
Maydan-Mahzam	1965	177,886 (1971)	51,781
Bul Hanine	1973	165,000 (1979)	75,000
al-Shaheen	Unknown	112,329 (2000)	112,329
Id al-Shargi North Dome	Unknown	124,658 (1998)	96,712

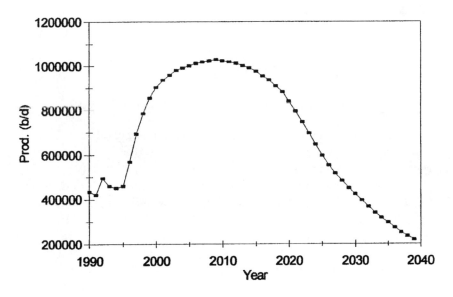

Figure 6.26 — Duncan's forecast for Qatar's oil production

the EUR for the field would be ~5.4 Gb. If that is accurate, nearly 70 per-cent of Dukhan's oil was produced by the end of 2002.

Table 6.7 provides data for Qatar's offshore oil fields. The Maydan-Mahzam and Bul Hanine fields are well past their peak production. There is insufficient data to assess the production status of the other fields in Table 6.7.

Based upon data in the IEO2003, the US DOE/EIA expects Qatar's oil production rate to increase steadily until 2020 when it reaches ~1 mb/d and then remain at that rate through 2025.[103]

Figure 6.26 is Richard Duncan's forecast for Qatar's oil + NGLs pro-duction. Duncan projects that Qatar's oil + NGLs production will peak in

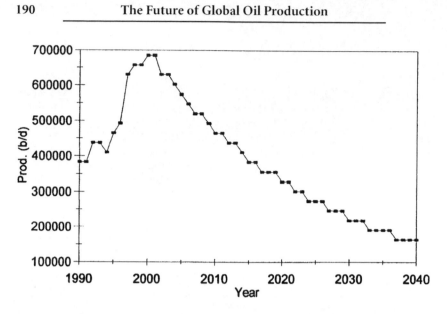

Figure 6.27 — Campbell's forecast for Qatar's oil production

2009 at 1.03 mb/d, decline to 0.597 mb/d in 2025 and 0.219 mb/d in 2039.[104] Qatar has the largest natural gas field in the world, the North field, and produces considerable quantities of NGLs from the field.

Figure 6.27 is Colin Campbell's forecast for Qatar's oil production. Campbell projected that Qatar's oil production would peak in 2000–2001 at 685,000 b/d, decline to 274,000 b/d in 2025 and 164,000 b/d in 2040. Campbell estimates that Qatar's cumulative oil production will be 13 Gb at the end of 2075, essentially its EUR.[105] At the end of 2002, cumulative production was 7.0 Gb, 54 percent of 13 Gb.[106]

Oil Production in Oman

Oman's first oil discovery was made in 1957 but most of its oil fields were discovered in the 1960s. Fields tend to be small and scattered, unlike its neighbors the UAE and Saudi Arabia. Most fields are located in the north and central part of the country. Field data are sparse but in 1997 there were 4 fields that produced over 50,000 b/d: Yibal (220,394 b/d), Nimr (91,650 b/d), Lekhwair (87,484 b/d) and Rima (75,153 b/d).[107] The Yibal field is declining rapidly and is expected to produce only 40,000–50,000 b/d in 2004. Other larger fields such as Rahud and al-Huwaisah are also in decline.[108]

Oman's oil production rate was fairly insignificant prior to 1980 but

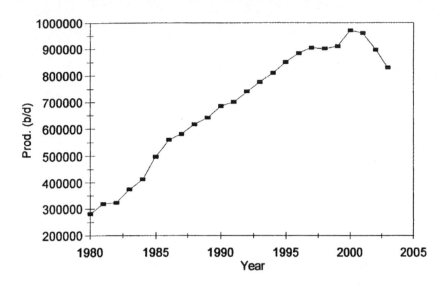

Figure 6.28 — Oman's oil production (Data from the US DOE/EIA)

it rose rapidly during the 1980s and 1990s. Production reached a peak in 2000 at 970,000 b/d. In 2003, the production rate was 822,000 b/d, a decline of 148,000 b/d (15.2 percent) from the 2000 production peak.[109] The decline has occurred in spite of heavy investment in recent years by Petroleum Development Oman (PDO), which produces ~90 percent of Oman's oil. PDO was producing over 900,000 b/d in the late 1990s but production declined to just over 700,000 b/d in October 2003.[110] Figure 6.28 is a graph of Oman's oil production.

PDO hopes to increase its oil production rate to 800,000 b/d by 2007 through the investment of $7.5 billion. The money would be used for enhanced oil recovery from mature fields and development of fields in southern Oman that the PDO claims have a maximum production potential of 100,000 b/d.[111]

In their IEO2003, the US DOE/EIA states the following concerning Oman:

> Two non-OPEC Persian Gulf producers [Oman and Yemen] are expected to increase output gradually over the first half of this decade. Enhanced recovery techniques are expected to increase output in Oman by more than 160,000 barrels per day, with only a gradual production decline anticipated after 2005.[112]

As Figure 6.28 illustrates, Oman's oil production has been declining since 2000 and will probably continue to decline in the future. All of Oman's TLHs production is due to oil, or they don't distinguish NGLs and

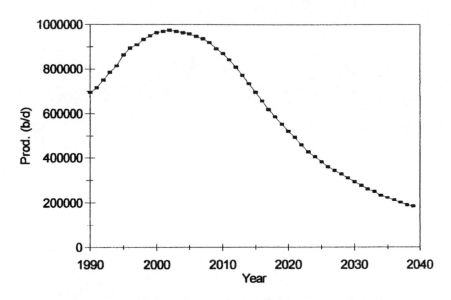

Figure 6.29 — Duncan's forecast for Oman's oil + NGLs production

refinery gain production, so a decline in oil production represents the decline in TLHs production. That calls the EIA's optimism concerning Oman's future TLHs production into question.

Figure 6.29 is Richard Duncan's forecast for Oman's oil + NGLs production. Duncan projected that Oman's oil + NGLs production would peak in 2002 at 976,000 b/d, decline to 384,000 b/d in 2025 and 186,000 b/d in 2039.[113]

Figure 6.30 is Colin Campbell's forecast for Oman's oil production. Campbell projected that Oman's oil production would peak in 2001 at 964,000 b/d, decline to 359,000 b/d in 2025 and 190,000 b/d in 2040. Based upon the recent decline of Oman's oil production, it appears that production has peaked and that the forecasts by Duncan and Campbell are close to the mark. Campbell estimates that Oman's cumulative oil production at the end of 2075 will be 15 Gb, essentially its EUR.[114] At the end of 2002, cumulative production was 7.1 Gb, 47 percent of 15 Gb.[115]

Oil Production in Yemen

Yemen's oil production got a late start, only beginning in 1986. By 2000, production had increased to 440,000 b/d (see Figure 6.31).[116] The US DOE/EIA reports that production was 443,288 b/d in 2002, indicating that it reached a temporary plateau that started in 2000. The Yemeni govern-

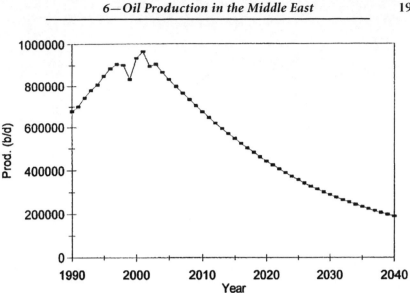

Figure 6.30 — Campbell's forecast for Oman's oil production

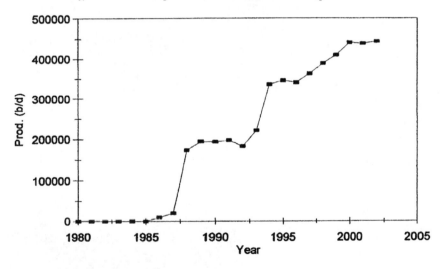

Figure 6.31— Yemen's oil production (Data from the US DOE/EIA)

ment has stated that Yemen's production capacity should reach 500,000 b/d by the end of 2003.[117]

In their IEO2003, the US DOE/EIA states, "Current oil production in Yemen is expected to increase by at least 90,000 barrels per day in the next several years, and those levels should show little decline throughout the forecast period."[118]

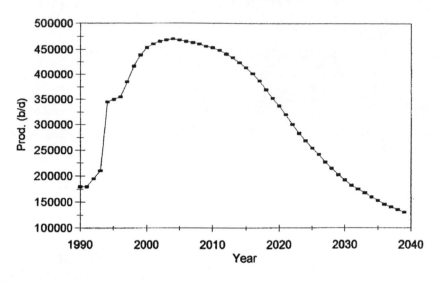

Figure 6.32 — Duncan's forecast for Yemen's oil production

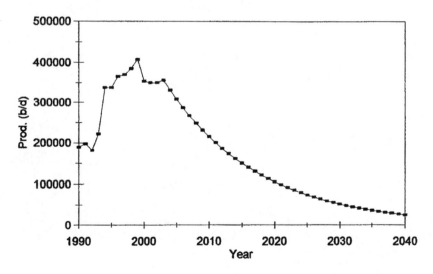

Figure 6.33 — Campbell's forecast for Yemen's oil production

Figure 6.32 is Richard Duncan's forecast for Yemen's oil + NGLs production. Duncan projects that Yemen's oil + NGLs production will peak in 2004 at 471,000 b/d, decline to 254,000 b/d in 2025 and 131,000 b/d in 2039.[119]

Figure 6.33 is Colin Campbell's forecast for Yemen's oil production.

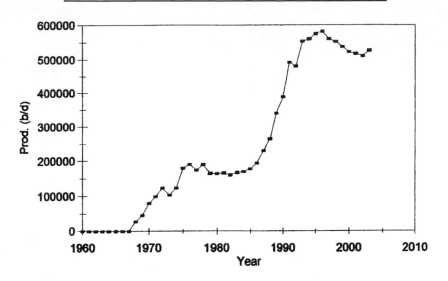

Figure 6.34 — Syria's oil production (Data from Colin Campbell [1960–1979] and the US DOE/EIA [1980–2003]).

Campbell projected that Yemen's oil production would peak in 1999 at 408,000 b/d, decline to 74,000 b/d in 2025 and 25,000 b/d in 2040. Since Yemen's oil production was ~440,000 b/d during 2000–2002, it appears that Campbell's forecast may be a bit pessimistic or that future production is being sacrificed for current production. Campbell estimates that Yemen's cumulative oil production at the end of 2075 will be 3.5 Gb, essentially its EUR.[120] At the end of 2002, Yemen's cumulative production was 1.7 Gb, 43 percent of 3.5 Gb.[121] The US DOE/EIA reports that Yemen's proven oil reserves are 4 Gb.[122]

Oil Production from Syria

Syria's first oil discovery, the Karatchuk field, was made in 1940 but further exploration was delayed until the end of World War II. After the war, Syria's most important discovery was the giant Suwaidiyah field, in 1959, with an EUR of 1.5 Gb.[123] Syria's oil production didn't begin until 1968. The production rate increased from 170,000 b/d in 1980 to 582,000 b/d in 1996 when it peaked. In 2002, the production rate averaged 510,000 b/d, but it increased to 527,000 b/d in 2003.[124] The increase in 2003 may be the result of a new field or fields coming on-line. Figure 6.34 is a graph of Syria's oil production.

The Syrian government would like to raise the production rate by

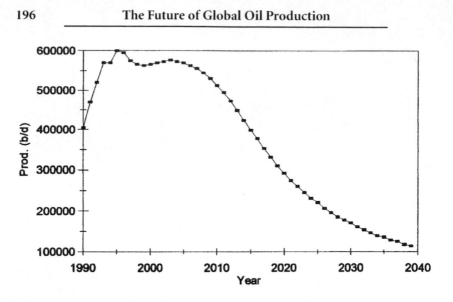

Figure 6.35 — Duncan's forecast for Syria's oil + NGLs production

intensifying exploration and production. To further exploration, the Oil and Mineral Resources Ministry has opened new exploration blocks and received bids from several international oil companies. A concern of the government is that Syria may become a net oil importer before 2010 if domestic production can't be increased.

In their IEO2003, the US DOE/EIA states the following concerning Syria: "Syria is expected to hold its production flat throughout this decade, but little in the way of new resource potential will allow anything except declining production volumes."[125]

Figure 6.35 is Richard Duncan's forecast for Syria's oil + NGLs production. Duncan projected that Syria's maximum oil + NGLs production would occur in 1995 at 600,000 b/d and that it would be followed by a production plateau during 2000–2005, a decline to 221,000 b/d in 2025 and 114,000 b/d in 2039.[126]

Figure 6.36 is Colin Campbell's forecast for Syria's oil production. Campbell projected that Syria's oil production would peak in 1995 at 605,000 b/d, decline to 82,000 b/d in 2025 and 25,600 b/d in 2040. Campbell estimates that Syria's cumulative oil production at the end of 2075 will be 6 Gb, essentially its EUR.[127] At the end of 2002, cumulative production was 3.8 Gb, 63 percent of 6 Gb.[128]

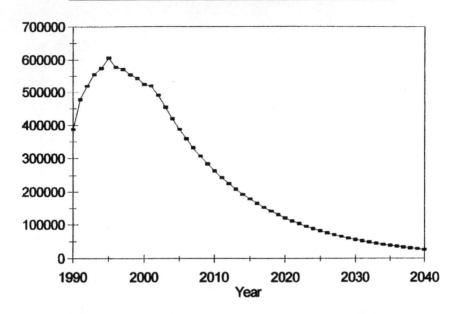

Figure 6.36 — Campbell's forecast for Syria's oil production

Conclusion

Of any region in the world, the Middle East is most capable of increasing oil production if the necessary infrastructure investments are made. Many of the largest Middle East fields have produced close to half of their reported EUR values, and some well over half, but there are numerous undeveloped fields in the region, some quite large.

The US DOE/EIA is projecting that Persian Gulf oil production will increase from 19.9 mb/d in 2000 to 40.5 mb/d in 2025 (see Figure 6.37).[129] The US DOE/EIA forecast ignores the limitations of oil resources in the Persian Gulf. Saudi Arabia, Kuwait and Iraq will probably have future oil production peaks occurring after 2010, while Iran and the UAE should have future peaks around 2010.

Peak timing will depend on how rapidly each country increases production. If global oil supplies get severely tight prior to 2010, there will be tremendous pressure on Middle East countries to increase production to meet world demand.

Outside of Saudi Arabia, Kuwait, Iraq, Iran and the UAE, the remaining Middle East producers are either beyond their peak production rates or close to their peaks. Oman and Syria have experienced

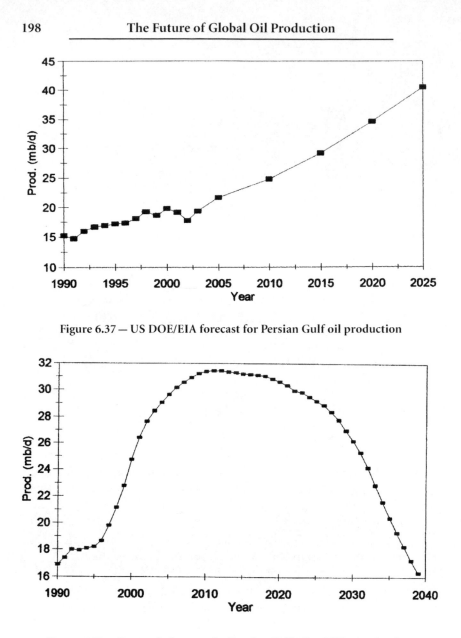

Figure 6.37 — US DOE/EIA forecast for Persian Gulf oil production

Figure 6.38 — Duncan's forecast for Persian Gulf oil + NGLs production

declining production in recent years and that trend is likely to continue. Production in Qatar, Yemen and the Neutral Zone appears to be close to peak.

Figure 6.38 is Richard Duncan's forecast for Persian Gulf oil + NGLs production. Duncan projects that Persian Gulf oil + NGLs production will

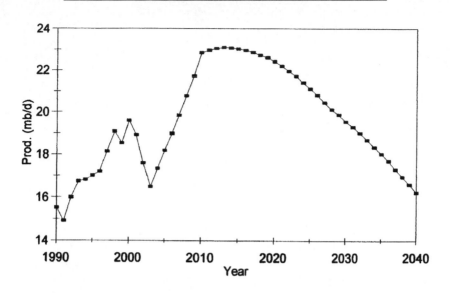

Figure 6.39 — Campbell's forecast for Persian Gulf oil production

be 31 to 32 mb/d from 2009 through 2018 and then decline to 29.2 mb/d in 2025 and 16.3 mb/d in 2039.[130]

Figure 6.39 is Colin Campbell's forecast for Persian Gulf oil production. Campbell projects that Persian Gulf oil production will be 22 to 24 mb/d from 2010 through 2021 and then decline to ~16 mb/d in 2040.[131]

7

Oil Production in the Former Soviet Union

The region that is now the Former Soviet Union (FSU) has had a long oil production history. During the period 1885–1905, the region produced oil at a rate comparable to the U.S. at the time. After 1905, the region experienced an extended period during which production was much less than that for the U.S. Production then rose rapidly from 1960 to 1980. For the period 1974–1991, the Soviet Union was the world's top oil producing nation, producing 3–4 mb/d more than the U.S. during the late 1980s.[1] After the fall of the Soviet Union, oil production declined to approximately half of what it had been in the late 1980s. Since the late 1990s, oil production has surged in the FSU, mainly from Russia. Figure 7.1 is a map of the Former Soviet Union.

The main oil producing regions in the FSU are located in western Siberia, the northern Ural Mountains region, just east of the Ural Mountains and the Caspian Sea region. The Caspian Sea region was the first area in what became the Soviet Union in which oil was extensively exploited. For many centuries oil seeps had been known to exist in the region. Marco Polo had reported hearing about an oil spring near Baku, on the coast of the Caspian Sea, back in the 13th Century. By 1829, there were 82 hand-dug pits for the collection of oil near Baku. Beginning in about 1870, the Russian government opened the area to competitive private enterprise for the development of oil resources. The first wells were drilled in 1871–72 and by 1873, more than 20 small refineries were in operation. By the early 1880s, oil production in the Baku area reached 10.8 mb/year, about 1/3rd that of U.S. production.[2]

Oil development in the Baku region was characterized by its numerous oil gushers. One gusher, "Droozba" (Friendship), flowed for 5 months at ~43,000 b/d. Unfortunately most of the oil was wasted. Russian oil pro-

Figure 7.1— Map of the Former Soviet Union (Courtesy of the University Libraries, The University of Texas at Austin).

duction rose tenfold between 1879 and 1888, reaching 23 mb/year, about 4/5ths that of U.S. production.[3]

In 1905, a violent upheaval involving political, racial and ethnic problems enveloped the Baku area leading to the torching of a majority of the wells and derricks in the region. Fully 2/3rds of all the wells were destroyed. Along with social and political problems in the region, poor drilling and production practices damaged fields contributing to the decline of production. For the period 1904–1913, Russia's share of world petroleum exports dropped from 31 percent to 9 percent, although the Baku region remained an important oil producing area. During WWII, a central goal of Germany's Russian campaign was to capture the Baku oil fields. Hitler considered oil a vital commodity for an industrial society and Germany was severely deficient in oil. After the war, Albert Speer, the German Minister for Armaments and War Production, stated that, "the need for oil certainly was a prime motive" in the decision to invade Russia.[4] Germany never made it to the Baku oil fields.

The rapid increase in the Soviet Union's oil production from 1960 to 1980 was due to a surge in production from western Siberia and Ural Mountains region. Production peaked in 1987/1988 at 12.05 mb/d. After the collapse of the Soviet Union in the early 1990s, oil production went into steep decline, ultimately reaching a low of 6.73 mb/d for the FSU in 1996.[5] Since 1998, there has been a rapid increase in the FSU's oil production, mostly from Russia. Figure 7.2 is a graph of the FSU's oil production.

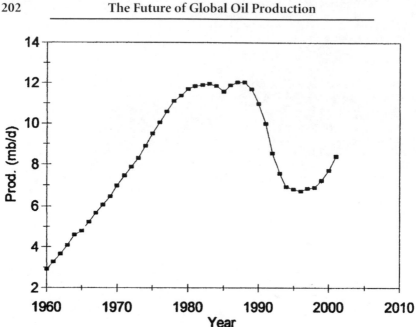

Figure 7.2 — The FSU's oil production (Data from the U.S. DOE/EIA)

Oil Production in Russia

Russia's oil production increase since the late 1990s is mostly due to the application of advanced production technology techniques to previously developed oil fields. In 1998, Russia's oil production rate was 5.85 mb/d. In 2003, the production rate was 8.18 mb/d, an increase of 2.33 mb/d over the 1998 rate.[6] The Russian Oil Ministry is projecting that Russia's oil production will average 8.8 mb/d in 2004.[7] Russia's oil production increase since 1999 has made up the bulk of the non-OPEC production increase since then, as Table 7.1 illustrates.

The West Siberian Basin produces ~75 percent of all Russian oil and natural gas.[8] It is the richest oil and gas bearing basin in Russian territory and the second richest basin in the world behind the Middle East.[9] Initial exploration for oil and gas in the basin dates back to the 1950s with oil initially coming on-line in 1964. In 1980, the West Siberian Basin was producing over 6 mb/d. By the middle 1980s, over drilling and the high rate of production were causing reservoir damage and rising water levels in fields. Poor well maintenance led to the shutdown of many wells. In 1985, 2,500 wells were idled and the first decline in production from the basin occurred, ~250,000 b/d. A comprehensive development plan was created

Table 7.1— Russian and Non-OPEC Oil
Production Increases Since 1999
(International Petroleum Production Data, U.S. DOE/EIA)

Year Increment	Russia's Oil Production Increase (b/d)	Non-OPEC Production Increase (b/d)	Russia's % of non-OPEC Production Increase
1999–2000	400,000	811,000	49.3
2000–2001	570,000	660,000	86.4
2001–2002	359,000	732,000	49.0
2002–2003	774,000	953,000	81.2
Sum/Average	2,103,000	3,156,000	66.6

to deal with problems such as idled wells. Advanced secondary recovery was widely applied as part of the development plan, which led to a production increase of ~500,000 b/d in 1986 and further increases in the late 1980s.[10]

The West Siberian Basin has a large number of giant and supergiant oil fields including Samotlor, Mamontovo, Fedorovo, Priob, Krasnoleninsk and Tevlin. The largest field is the Samotlor field, discovered in 1965. It is the 7th largest oil field ever discovered globally.[11] Figure 7.3 is a graph of annual production from the Samotlor field versus cumulative production.

The field reached its highest production rate in the 1980s when it produced ~3.5 mb/d. Since the late 1980s, there has been a rapid production decline and it now produces only ~0.32 mb/d, 1/10th of peak production.[12] Based upon Figure 7.3, ultimate production from the Samotlor field will be ~20 Gb. In recent years, the Haliburton Corporation has become involved in production at the field. They plan on installing ~4,600 new wells between 1999 and 2020, with ~2,300 being horizontal wells.[13] It appears that the new wells will only manage to maintain production near the currently much lower production rate for awhile before production declines further.

The second most productive oil basin in Russia is the Volga-Ural Basin. It has been extensively developed and seriously depleted. Figure 7.4 is a graph of oil production from the Romashkino field, the second largest field in Russia with an EUR of ~15 Gb. Peak production occurred during the late 1960s and early 1970s at ~1.65 mb/d. Production had declined to ~275,000 b/d by the late 1990s.[14]

The 3rd most productive oil basin in Russia is the Timan Pechora Basin of north-central Russia. The Timan Pechora Basin attracted interest for its oil back in the 1930s after several discoveries were made.[15] After WWII, extensive exploration of the basin was initiated. By the late 1960s,

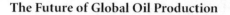

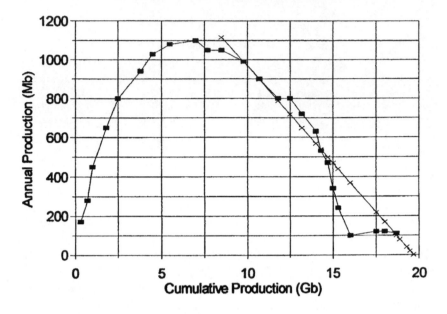

Figure 7.3 — Samotlor field annual production versus cumulative production [rectangles] and best-fit line to x-axis [X] (Data from Jean Laherrere).

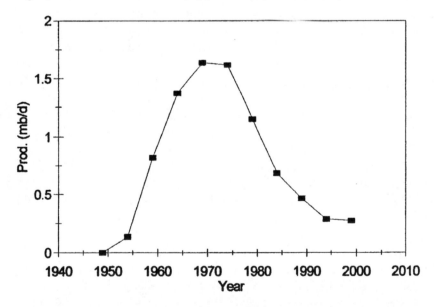

Figure 7.4 — Romanshkino field oil production (Data from Simmons & Co. International).

exploration activities extended north of the Arctic Circle, indicating that the area has been extensively explored. Oil exploration in the Barents Sea, Arctic Ocean, began in the 1970s, with initial wildcat drilling starting in the early 1980s.

At this time there are ~180 known oil and gas fields in the basin but only ~20 are producing oil and/or gas because most of the fields are small.[16] The largest undeveloped field in the basin is the Prirazlomnoye field (EUR = 600 Mb), located 60 km off the north coast in the Barents Sea. The field is expected to come on-line in 2005 and have a peak production rate of 150,000 b/d. The basin contains areas that have received relatively little exploration attention, probably for good reason, so there is considerable interest by international oil companies to explore those relatively unexplored areas.

One area in Russia that has attracted a lot of interest by international oil companies is the Sakhalin Island area in the Sea of Okhotsk, off the east coast of Siberia. International oil companies plan on spending at least $45 billion in coming years to explore and develop oil and gas.[17] Sakhalin Island is a 600 mile long island north of Japan. Oil and gas fields are situated north of the island with gas predominating. Presently there are 2 projects under development, Sakhalin I and Sakhalin II. The companies involved in the Sakhalin I project expect to spend $12 billion to develop oil and gas.[18] Recoverable reserves of oil are reported to be ~2.3 Gb in 3 fields, with first oil expected in 2005. Companies involved with the Sakhalin II project expect to spend at least $9 billion to recover both oil and natural gas. Recoverable oil reserves are reported to be ~1 Gb.[19] Oil production started in 1999 but only occurs in the summer months because the sea is covered with ice during the winter.

In 2000, there were 9 oil fields in Russia that were producing at least 100,000 b/d (see Table 7.2).

Presently the rate of oil extraction is greatly exceeding the rate of oil discovery in Russia. In order to increase Russia's oil production in coming years, large amounts of capital will be needed to develop new fields and extend the life of existing fields. Foreign capital has been instrumental in increasing Russia's oil production since 1996. In July 1996, there were 106 oil and gas joint ventures between foreign oil companies and Russian oil companies. In February 2003, BP-Amoco announced it would pay $6.75 billion to merge with the Alfa Group and Access Renova (AAR) to create Russia's 3rd largest oil and gas company.

Russia's cumulative oil production at the end of 2002 was 121 Gb. Colin Campbell estimates that the ultimate oil recovery will be ~200 Gb.[20]

Table 7.2 — Russian Oil Fields Producing at Least 100,000 b/d
(From "The World's Giant Oilfields," Simmons & Company International)

Field	Year 2000 Production (b/d)
1). Samotlor	320,000
2). Romashkino	300,000
3). Tevlin-Russkin	200,000
4). Vatyegan	200,000
5). Lyantor	160,000
6). Fedorov	150,000
7). Mamontov	125,000
8). Sutormin	100,000
9). Povkhov	100,000

Oil Production in the Caspian Sea Region

Over the last decade, various sources, including agencies of the U.S. government, have claimed that recoverable oil reserves in the Caspian Sea region were comparable to those of the Middle East. Several years ago the US DOE/EIA downgraded previous U.S. government estimates of possible oil reserves in the region but were still reporting 233 Gb, as were other organizations.[21,22] Even that estimate appears to be greatly exaggerated. The US DOE/EIA is now stating that the region has 17–33 Gb of proven reserves.[23]

Some people in the oil industry claim that recoverable oil reserves are even less than that. Gian Maria Gros-Pietro, Chairman of Italy's Eni Oil Company, when speaking at the Eurasian Economic Summit in 2002 stated that the Caspian region contains 7.8 Gb of what apparently is recoverable oil, 70 percent of which is in Kazakhstan. He estimates that in 2010 the Caspian Sea region will produce ~3.8 mb/d, which would be comparable to what Iran presently produces.[24] Gros-Pietro may be underestimating recoverable reserves in the region, but it appears clear that claims of over 100 Gb of recoverable reserves is highly unlikely.

Table 7.3 provides data for several oil development projects in the region. Most of the oil in the Caspian Sea region is in the northern half of the Caspian Sea or surrounding onshore areas. In May 2003, the countries of the northern Caspian Sea region: Russia, Azerbaijan and Kazakhstan, divided the northern 64 percent of the Caspian Sea into 3 unequal parts giving Kazakhstan 27 percent, Russia 19 percent and Azerbaijan 18 percent. With the agreement, oil developments should move forward.

Table 7.3 — Oil Development Projects in the Caspian Sea Region*

Country	Project	Reported Proven Reserves (Gb)	2002 Production (b/d)	Projected 2003, 2005 or 2006 Production (b/d)	Projected 2008 or beyond Production (b/d)
Azerbaijan	ACG Megastructure	5.4	125,000	460,000 (2005)	1,000,000 (2008/2009)
Kazakhstan	Tengiz	6–9	285,000	450,000 (2006)	700,000 (2010)
	Karachaganak	2.4	100,000		240,000 (2008)
	Kashagan	7–9		100,000 (2005)	1,200,000†
Turkmenistan	Cheleken	0.6	10,000	11,000 (2003)	
	Nebit Dag	0.1	10,000	12,000 (2003)	
Uzbekistan	Central Ustyurt and Southwest Gissar	unknown		2,600 (2006)	

From Country Analysis Brief-Caspian Sea Region, US DOE/EIA
†*From "Oil field mega projects 2004," Chris Skrebowski*

Oil Production in Kazakhstan

Kazakhstan claims most of the Caspian Sea's largest fields with total proven reserves of 9–17.6 Gb, according to the US DOE/EIA. In 2002, Kazakhstan's TLHs production was 939,000 b/d. The government hopes that Kazakhstan will produce 2.4 mb/d by 2010 and 3.6 mb/d by 2015.[25] Most of the production will come from the Tengiz, Kashagan and Karachaganak fields.

The Tengiz field is located onshore along the northeast coast of the Caspian Sea. ChevronTexaco estimates recoverable reserves at 6–9 Gb. Field development by the consortium of companies involved with the field started in 1993. By 2002, production had reached 285,000 b/d. In 2003, the consortium started a $3 billion expansion project to increase production to ~450,000 b/d by 2006. According to ChevronTexaco, Tengiz could potentially produce 700,000 b/d by the end of the decade.[26]

The Kashagan field was discovered in 2000 and is located off the northern coast of the Caspian Sea near the city of Atyrau. The consortium developing the field estimates recoverable reserves at 7–9 Gb of oil equivalent with further potential to 9–13 Gb. Production from Phase I development is expected to start in 2005 and ultimately reach ~100,000 b/d.[27] The oil from the Kashagan field is a high sulfur, low quality oil.

The Karachaganak field, containing oil and condensate, is located in northern Kazakhstan, just south of Russia. According to British Gas, a member of the consortium developing the field, reserves are >2.4 Gb. In 2002, production was ~100,000 b/d. The consortium plans to increase production to ~140,000 b/d in 2003 and 240,000 b/d by 2008.[28]

Pipelines are necessary to transport oil from the Caspian Sea region to world markets. In November 2001 the Caspian Pipeline Consortium (CPC) pipeline was completed, connecting Kazakhstan's Caspian Sea area oil with Russia's Black Sea port of Novorossiysk. The initial pipeline capacity was 560,000 b/d, with expected expansion to 1.34 mb/d. In 2002, the CPC pipeline carried ~260,000 b/d, mostly from the Tengiz field. By the end of 2003, the pipeline is expected to carry 350,000–415,000 b/d.[29] Oil from the Caspian Sea region also flows north through Russia's Atyrau-Samara pipeline system. A pipeline to China and a connection to the Baku-Tiblisi-Ceyhan pipeline are under consideration. The Baku-Tiblisi-Ceyhan pipeline will connect the Caspian Sea city of Baku with the Mediterranean port of Ceyhan. The pipeline is scheduled to be completed in 2004 with first oil flowing in 2005. It is projected to carry ~1 mb/d.[30]

Oil Production in Azerbaijan

Azerbaijan has proven oil reserves of 7–13 Gb, according to the US DOE/EIA, mostly in the Azeri, Chirag and deep-water Gunashli fields. The ACG project is developing those three fields. Phase I of the project is expected to reach a production rate of 400,000 b/d by 2005. Phase II is projected to raise production to ~1 mb/d by 2008–2009.[31] Phase III involves full field development and is currently under investigation. At this point in time, production is constrained by pipeline limitations but the completion of the Baku-Tablisi-Ceyhan pipeline should eliminate the constraint.

Conclusion

Figure 7.5 is a graph of the US DOE/EIA's forecast for the FSU's total liquid hydrocarbons production. Based upon the US DOE/EIA's forecast, TLHs production for the FSU would increase from 8.8 mb/d in 2001 to 15.9 mb/d in 2025.[32] A production rate of 15.9 mb/d would exceed the previous peak for the Soviet Union (12.05 mb/d in 1988) by 3.25 mb/d. The previous peak occurred when the West Siberian and other Russian oil

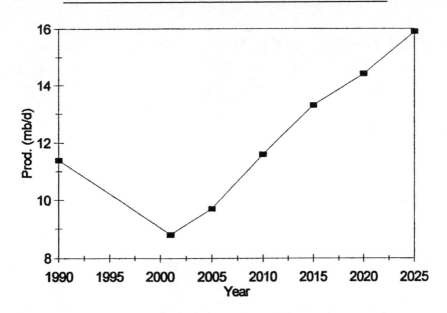

Figure 7.5 — US DOE/EIA's forecast for the FSU's total liquid hydrocarbons production (Data from the US DOE/EIA).

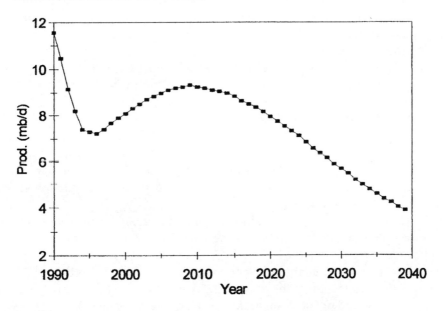

Figure 7.6 — Richard Duncan's forecast for the FSU's oil + NGLs production

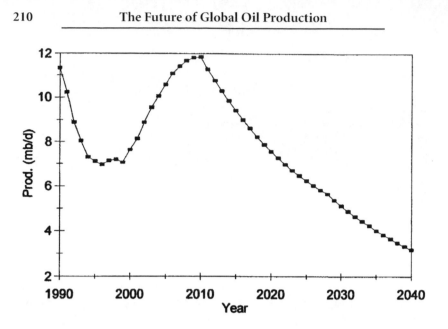

Figure 7.7 — Colin Campbell's forecast for the FSU's oil production

basins were relatively young. By 2025, the Russian oil basins will be old and most fields seriously depleted. There will be production growth in the Caspian Sea region but it's implausible that FSU production can come close to 15.9 mb/d in 2025.

Figure 7.6 is a graph of Richard Duncan's forecast for the FSU's oil + NGLs production. Duncan projects that the FSU's oil + NGLs production will increase from the late 1990s to 2009 when production reaches 9.32 mb/d. He predicts that production will decline to 6.85 mb/d in 2025 and 3.90 mb/d in 2039.[33] The 6.85 mb/d estimate for 2025 is only 43 percent that of the US DOE/EIA's forecast. The FSU's total liquid hydrocarbons production in 2003 was 10.30 mb/d suggesting that Duncan has underestimated the FSU's production potential or that present production is sacrificing future production.

Figure 7.7 is a graph of Colin Campbell's forecast for the FSU's oil production. Campbell projects that the FSU will experience a secondary oil production peak of 11.85 mb/d in 2010 followed by a decline to 6.25 mb/d in 2025 and 3.18 mb/d in 2040.[34] Campbell estimates that the FSU's cumulative production at the end of 2075 will be ~300 Gb, essentially its EUR.[35] At the end of 2001, cumulative production was 141.5 Gb, 47.2 percent of 300 Gb.[36]

8

Oil Production in Africa

The bulk of Africa's oil production is concentrated in a small group of countries. Only 3 countries have achieved a production rate above 1 mb/d: Algeria, Libya and Nigeria. Only 2 other countries have achieved a production rate above 0.5 mb/d: Egypt and Angola. Only 3 other countries have achieved a production rate greater than 0.2 mb/d: Congo, Gabon and Sudan. Figure 8.1 is a map of Africa showing the location of the major oil producing countries.

In 2001, 94.7 percent of Africa's oil production came from the 8 countries with production rates above 0.20 mb/d.[1] This chapter will separately deal with those 8 countries: Algeria, Angola, Congo, Egypt, Gabon, Libya, Nigeria and Sudan. The rest of Africa will be treated as a unit.

Figure 8.2 is a graph of Africa's oil production. Africa's reduced oil production during the 1980s was due to reduced production in Libya, Nigeria and Algeria, all OPEC nations. For the period 1982–2002, the production rate increased from 4.73 mb/d to 7.44 mb/d due to broad based production increases. Some African oil producing nations are in decline: Egypt, Gabon, Congo, Cameroon and Tunisia. Libya will never again produce as much oil as it once did although production should be able to rise above the current rate over the next few years. In 1970, Libya produced 3.38 mb/d, considerably more than the 1.42 mb/d produced in 2003.[2] Algeria has the capacity to increase production somewhat over its present rate as well. In recent years there has been an oil boom in the deep-water off the coast of West Africa, with production starting several years ago. Angola and Nigeria will be able to increase their production rates due to deep-water production even though on-shore and shallow-water production will decrease.

Map of Africa (Courtesy of the University Libraries, The University of Texas at Austin).

Oil Production in Algeria

Algeria's first oil discovery occurred in 1949, but it was several discoveries in 1956 by the French state oil company that made Algeria an important oil producing nation: Hassi Messaoud North and Hassi Messaoud South. The French looked upon the discoveries as a secure source of oil for France, providing freedom from foreign oil suppliers. It also encouraged them to explore further for African oil. Oil production from the discoveries started in 1958. Most of Algeria's large oil fields were discovered during the late 1950s and 1960s. Figure 8.3 is a graph of Algeria's oil production.

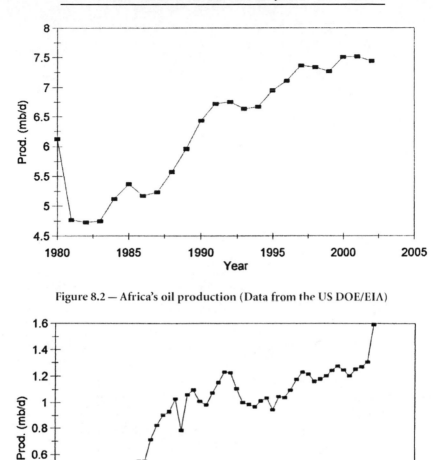

Figure 8.2 — Africa's oil production (Data from the US DOE/EIA)

Figure 8.3 — Algeria's oil production (Data from Colin Campbell [1950–1979] and the U.S. DOE/EIA [1980–2003])

By far, Algeria's largest oil fields are Hassi Messaoud North and Hassi Messaoud South, located in south central Algeria. In the early 1980s, half of Algeria's oil production came from the Hassi Messaoud fields. By 1999, the fields had declined significantly and they were producing only 28 percent of Algeria's oil (see Figure 8.4).[3]

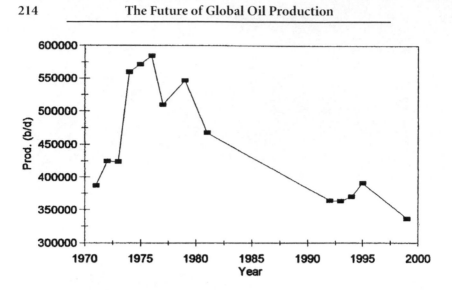

Figure 8.4 — Oil production from the Hassi Messaoud fields (Data from *Oil & Gas Journal*).

The better days of the Hassi Messaoud fields are behind them. In 1976, the fields produced 585,000 b/d but by 1999, the last year of available data in *Oil & Gas Journal*, the production rate had declined to 336,000 b/d.[4] The Halliburton Corporation has an 8 year contract to employ enhanced oil recovery techniques to the fields in an attempt to prevent a further decline in production.

Several other Algerian oil fields achieved production rates of 100,000 b/d or greater during 1971–1999. The Zarataine field, discovered in 1957, was producing 100,000 b/d in the middle to late 1970s. In 1999, the production rate had declined to 27,000 b/d. The Hassi R-Mel field, discovered in 1979, was producing 322,000 b/d in 1992, but declined to 273,000 b/d in 1995. Unfortunately the 1999 production rate for the field was listed as 9,973 b/d in *Oil & Gas Journal*, an apparent mistake.[5]

The Algerian National Council of Energy believes that the country contains large quantities of undiscovered hydrocarbons. The government is employing international oil companies to help explore and develop the remaining oil. Algeria plans to raise its crude oil production capacity from 1.1 mb/d in 2002 to 1.5 mb/d by 2004 and 2 mb/d within 10 years. In January 2003, the state oil company, Sonatrach, announced that it had brought the 1 Gb Ourhoud oil field on-line with an initial production rate of 75,000 b/d. A peak production rate of 230,000 b/d was expected by March 2003.[6] Algeria's oil production increase in 2003 may be largely due to the introduction of the Ourhoud field.

Algeria's oil production has a large condensate component. In 2002, the crude oil production rate was ~840,000 b/d while the condensate production rate was ~430,000 b/d. About 70 percent of Algeria's oil production takes place in the Hassi Messaoud area, but other areas are receiving increasing attention.[7]

BHP Corporation plans to spend $190 million for the "ROD" integrated oil development project in the Berkine Basin of eastern Algeria. Oil production from the project will come on-line in 2004 and reach a peak production rate of 80,000 b/d. In July 2000, several companies announced that they would develop the MLN field, in the Berkine Basin, which is expected to have a peak production rate of 35,000–40,000 b/d. Several oil companies have a joint venture in the Hassi Berkine South oil field. Production started in 1998 and averaged ~26,000 b/d in 2000. The field's production capacity was reported to be 285,000 b/d in the middle of 2002. Amerada Hess Corporation plans to spend $500 million over 5 years to enhance recovery from the el-Gassi, el-Agreb and Zotti fields, increasing the production rate for the fields from 30,000 b/d to 45,000 b/d.[8]

Algeria's largest field after the Hassi Messaoud fields is the Rhourde El Baguel field. It was discovered in 1962 and has a reported EUR of 3 Gb. This field has been producing oil for decades, but foreign investment is reportedly going to increase the production rate from 27,000 b/d at present to 125,000 b/d by 2010.[9]

Concerning Algeria, the US DOE/EIA say, "Increased optimism about the production potential of Algeria, Libya, and Venezuela supports the possibility that the growth in world dependence on Persian Gulf oil will slow."[10]

The US DOE/EIA's optimism concerning Algeria is not shared by Richard Duncan and Colin Campbell. Figure 8.5 is a graph of Richard Duncan's forecast for Algeria's oil + NGLs production.

Duncan projected that Algeria's oil + NGLs production would peak in 2002 at 1.59 mb/d, decline to 0.55 mb/d in 2025 and 0.29 mb/d in 2039.[11]

Figure 8.6 is Colin Campbell's forecast for Algeria's crude oil production. Campbell's forecast only applies to crude oil production, rather than crude oil + condensate. He projects that crude oil production will plateau from 2001 through 2008 at 849,000 b/d, decline to 575,000 b/d in 2025 and 411,000 b/d in 2040. At the end of 2002, cumulative oil production was 12.7 Gb.[12]

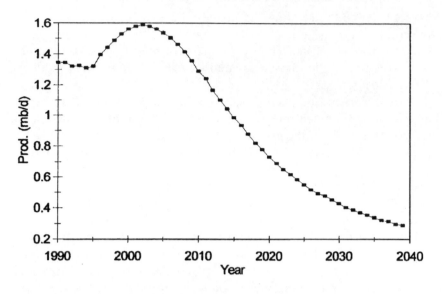

Figure 8.5 — Duncan's forecast for Algeria's oil + NGLs production

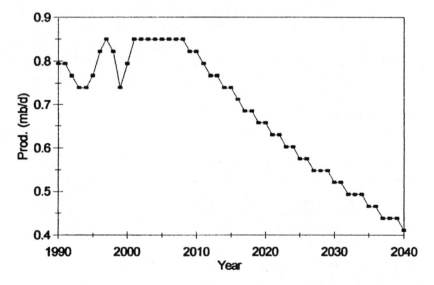

Figure 8.6 — Campbell's forecast for Algeria's crude oil production

Oil Production in Angola

Angola's oil exploration started in the early 1950s when the Belgian oil company, Fina Oil, secured explorations rights in the country. The first discovery occurred in 1955. The onshore portion of Angola had limited oil potential, which stimulated exploration offshore starting in 1966. That exploration led to the discovery of numerous offshore fields from which Angola obtains most of its oil. In the 1990s, exploration began in the deep-water region off Angola, which has led to the discovery of ~10 Gb of deep-water oil. In the last few years, only minor discoveries have been made in the deep-water region, suggesting that the bulk of the deep-water oil has been discovered.[13]

Figure 8.7 is a graph of Angola's oil production. Angola's oil production rate didn't exceed 200,000 b/d until 1984, but it climbed to over 900,000 b/d in 2003.[14] Several deep-water fields have come on-line in the last few years and numerous others will come on-line in the next few years. The new deep-water fields should greatly increase Angola's oil production over the next decade.

Angola had only 1 field that achieved a production rate greater than 100,000 b/d prior to 2000, the Takula field (see Figure 8.8).

The Takula field reached its highest production rate in 1995 at 156,730 b/d. In 2002, the production rate had declined to 102,506 b/d, a decline of 54,224 b/d (34.6 percent) from the 1995 peak. Cumulative production through 2002 was 823 Mb.[15] It appears that the Takula field is in long-term decline. Declining production is common for many of Angola's older onshore and shallow-water fields.

International oil companies have been responsible for the oil development in Angola's deep-water region. The production profiles for Angola's deep-water fields will be similar to North Sea fields, where production rates have generally peaked within 6 years of initial production and then declined rapidly. A difference between North Sea fields and Angola's deep-water fields is that the largest discoveries in the North Sea are substantially bigger than the largest discoveries to date in Angola. The largest North Sea field is the Statfjord field, EUR = ~4.2 Gb.[16] The largest discoveries in Angola's deep-water region are Girassol (EUR = ~0.66 Gb), Dalia (EUR = ~0.8 Gb) and Rosa (EUR = ~0.7 Gb).[17]

Angola's first deep-water field to come on-line is the Kuito field, discovered in 1997. Production started in 1999 and the rate was projected to reach a peak of 100,000 b/d in 2000.[18] As of 2002, the production rate had only reached ~66,000 b/d.[19]

The Girassol field was projected to come on-line in 2000 and reach

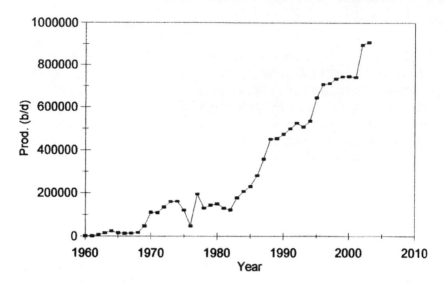

Figure 8.7 — Angola's oil production (Data from Colin Campbell [1960–1979] and the US DOE/EIA [1980–2003]).

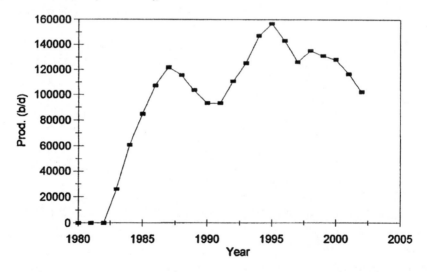

Figure 8.8 — Takula field oil production (Data from *Oil & Gas Journal*)

a peak production rate of 200,000 b/d.[20] Production didn't start until January 2002, but the production rate did average 200,000 b/d in 2002 according to *Oil & Gas Journal*.[21] A production rate of 200,000 b/d corresponds to 73 Mb/y. The high production rate ensures that the rate will start declining in less than 6 years unless problems delay the decline.

There are several other fields in the vicinity of Girassol including Dalia, Rosa, Lirio, Tulipa, Orquidea, Cravo, Camelia and Jasmin 1. All of these fields were discovered during 1997–2000. The Dalia field is projected to come on-line in late 2004.

Numerous other deep-water discoveries have been made including Xikomba, Belize, Benguela, Tomboco and Tombua. The Xikomba field was discovered in 1999 and has an EUR of ~100 Mb. Production is expected to start in late 2003 with a peak production rate of ~80,000 b/d. The Belize, Benguela, Tomboco and Tombua fields are expected to come on-line in 2005 with a summed initial production rate of 140,000 b/d and a summed peak production rate of ~200,000 b/d.[22] Production from the deep-water region of Angola should rise rapidly baring development and production problems, but the decline of many older Angolan fields, such as the Takula field, will negate some portion of that increasing production.

Concerning Angola, the US DOE/EIA states in their IEO2003: "Angola is expected to become a million barrel per day producer early in this decade. Given the excellent exploration results, Angola could produce volumes of up to 3.2 million barrels per day well into the later years of the forecast period."[23]

At this point in time, it appears likely that Angola's oil production rate should increase above 1 mb/d in the next few years, but the 3.2 mb/d projection appears based upon wishful thinking.

Figure 8.9 is Richard Duncan's forecast for Angola's oil + NGLs production. Duncan projected that Angola's oil + NGLs production would peak in 2003 at 828,000 b/d, decline to 272,000 b/d in 2025 and 145,000 b/d in 2039.[24] It appears that he has not included deep-water oil production in his forecast and has underestimated Angola's potential production. Angola's production rate in 2003 averaged 923,000 b/d.[25]

Figure 8.10 is Colin Campbell's forecast for Angola's oil production. Campbell projects that Angola's oil production will peak in 2020 at ~1.8 mb/d before declining rapidly to 180,000 b/d in 2040. Campbell estimates that Angola's cumulative oil production at the end of 2075 will be 20 Gb, including deep-water production, essentially its EUR.[26] At the end of 2002, cumulative production was 4.57 Gb, 23 percent of 20 Gb.[27]

Oil Production in Congo (Brazzaville)

Congo's first oil discovery was the Pointe Indienne field, in 1951. Production from the field started in 1957. Most of Congo's oil fields date back to the 1970s and 1980s, with fields generally being small. In 1980, Congo's

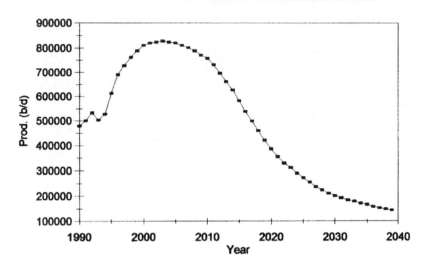

Figure 8.9 — Duncan's forecast for Angola's oil + NGLs production

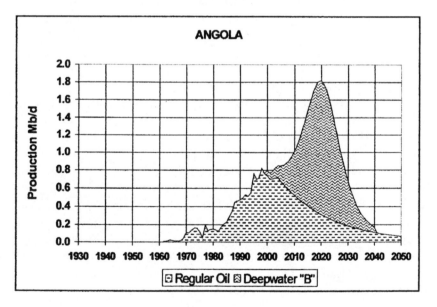

Figure 8.10 — Campbell's forecast for Angola's oil production

oil production rate was only ~65,000 b/d, but it quadrupled between 1980 and 2000 as off-shore fields were discovered and developed.[28] By 2000, many of the fields had started declining and consequently, Congo's production rate has declined every year since then (see Figure 8.11).

Congo's largest field is the N'Kossa field, with a reported EUR of ~500

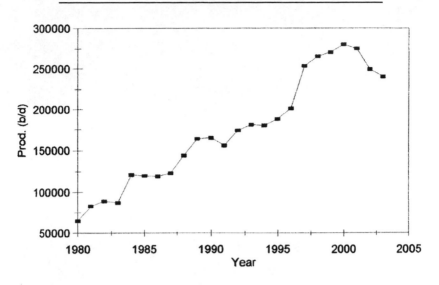

Figure 8.11— Congo's oil production (Data from the US DOE/EIA)

Mb. The field was brought on-line in 1996 and was expected to achieve a peak production rate of 100,000–110,000 b/d. In the first quarter of 2003 it was only producing 34,000 b/d of crude oil and 10,000 b/d of liquefied gas. Congo's field with the highest production rate is the Kitina field, discovered in 1991. It had a production rate of ~60,000 b/d, or 21.9 Mb/y, in 2003. The Kitina field has a reported EUR of ~145 Mb, so it can't maintain a production rate of ~60,000 b/d for too long.[29]

Several fields are expected to be brought on-line in the near future including Libondo, Tchibeli, Litanzi and Yanga-Sud. The introduction of those fields should slow the rate of Congo's production decline.

The US DOE/EIA states the following concerning Congo in their IEO2003:

> Several West African producers (Angola, Cameroon, Chad, **Congo**, Gabon, and Ivory Coast) are expected to reap the benefits of substantial exploration activity, especially considering the recent rebound in oil prices. The other West African producers [beyond Angola] with offshore tracts are expected to increase output by up to 1 million barrels per day for the duration of the forecast.[30]

Although some offshore fields have been discovered in recent years, they appear to be relatively small and do not justify a belief that Congo's production rate can increase by 1 mb/d.

Figure 8.12 is Richard Duncan's forecast for Congo's oil + NGLs production. Duncan projected that Congo's oil + NGLs production would

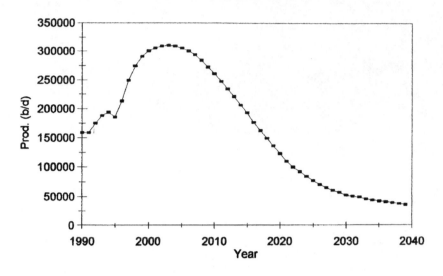

Figure 8.12 — Duncan's forecast for Congo's oil + NGLs production

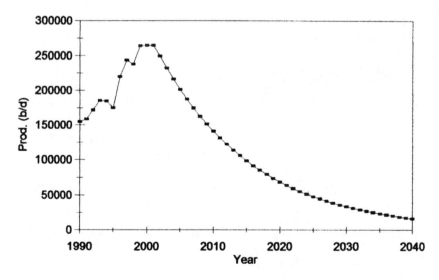

Figure 8.13 — Campbell's forecast for Congo's oil production

peak in 2003 at 311,000 b/d, decline to 77,000 b/d in 2025 and 36,000 b/d in 2039.[31]

Figure 8.13 is Colin Campbell's forecast for Congo's oil production. Campbell projected that Congo's oil production would peak in 2000 at 265,000 b/d, decline to 48,000 b/d in 2025 and 17,000 b/d in 2040. Production appears to have peaked in 2000 at 280,000 b/d. Campbell estimates that Congo's cumulative oil production at the end of 2075 will be 2.86 Gb, essentially its EUR.[32] At the end of 2002, cumulative production was 1.54 Gb, 53.8 percent of 2.86 Gb.[33]

Oil Production in Egypt

Egypt's oil exploration started in the 1920s and resulted in the discovery of a few small on-shore oil fields. It wasn't until the 1960s, with the discovery of oil in the Gulf of Suez, that significant amounts of oil were found. The first large discovery in the gulf was the El Morgan field, with an EUR > 1 Gb, discovered in 1965.[34] During the late 1960s and 1970s several other large fields were discovered in the gulf: October, July, Ramadan and Belayim Marine. Egypt's oil production rate didn't exceed 100,000 b/d until 1963 and 200,000 b/d until 1969.[35] Production rose rapidly from 1974 through 1987 due to the development of the large Gulf of Suez fields. In recent years, Egypt's oil production has been declining (see Figure 8.14).

Production reached its highest rate in 1996 at 922,000 b/d. In 2003, the production rate was 618,000 b/d, 304,000 b/d (~33 percent) less than the 1996 maximum.[36]

Egypt's oil production comes from 2 main regions: the Gulf of Suez region and the El Alemein region of western Egypt. About 60 percent of Egypt's oil production originates from the gulf region. Oil production from the gulf region started in the 1960s, but it is now declining in spite of considerable efforts to prevent the decline. British Petroleum is in the process of investing $450 million to enhance oil recovery from field's in the gulf.[37] Petrobel, Egypt's second largest oil company, is also investing large sums of money to address declining production from the Belayim field, near the gulf.

The El Morgan field achieved the highest production rate of any field in Egypt during 1971–2002. The field actually consists of 2 reservoirs: El Kareem and El Belayim, but it is typically characterized as one field. Figure 8.15 is a graph of oil production from the El Morgan field.

The oil production rate for the El Morgan field was 260,868 b/d in 1971. By 1998, the last year of available data, the rate had declined to 40,586 b/d, 220,282 b/d (84.4 percent) less than in 1971.[38] The field had a short-term production increase during the late 1970s/early 1980s, but the rate has declined almost every year since 1985.

Several other Egyptian fields have also achieved production rates of 100,000 b/d or higher: October, July, Ramadan and Belayim Marine. Figure 8.16 is a graph of the summed production rate for the 4 fields.

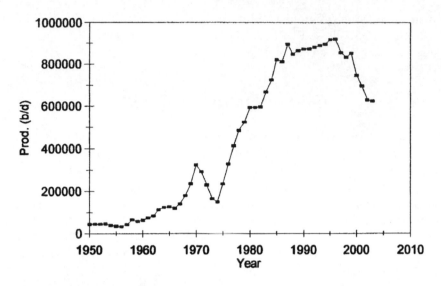

Figure 8.14 — Egypt's oil production (Data from Colin Campbell [1950–1979] and the US DOE/EIA [1980–2003]).

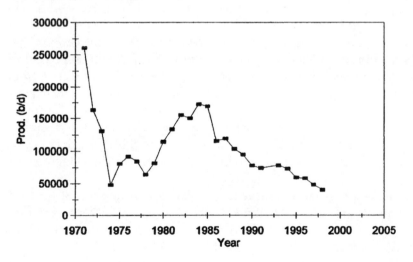

Figure 8.15 — Oil production from the El Morgan field (Data from *Oil & Gas Journal*).

The maximum summed production rate for the 4 fields occurred in 1990 at 409,728 b/d. By 1998, the last year of available data, the summed production rate had declined to 251,599 b/d, 158,129 b/d (38.6 percent) less than in 1990. In 1990, summed production for the 4 fields represented nearly 47 percent of Egypt's total oil production. By 1998, the summed pro-

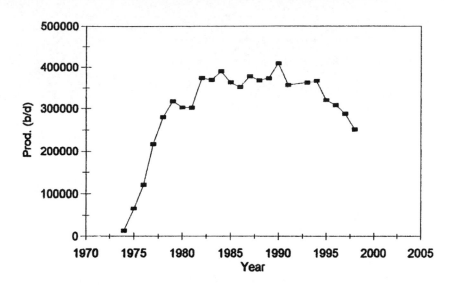

Figure 8.16 — Summed production rate for October, July, Ramadan and Belayim Marine fields (Data from *Oil & Gas Journal*).

duction for the 4 fields only represented about 30 percent of Egypt's total oil production.[39] Clearly the decline of Egypt's large oil fields is dragging its production down.

Egypt does not have a lot of geologically favorable unexplored frontier area from which to make new discoveries. One area that hasn't been explored extensively is Egypt's portion of the Mediterranean Sea. The area is now being explored, but the Mediterranean shelf is narrow, steep and unlikely to offer more than modest potential.

In the IEO2003, the US DOE/EIA states, "North African producers Egypt and Tunisia produce mainly from mature fields and show little promise of adding to their reserve posture. As a result, their production volumes are expected to decline gradually throughout the forecast."[40]

It's encouraging that the US DOE/EIA recognizes that Egypt's oil production rate will decline in the future.

Figure 8.17 is Richard Duncan's forecast for Egypt's oil + NGLs production. Duncan projects that Egypt's oil + NGLs production will decline to 282,000 b/d in 2025 and 173,000 b/d in 2039.[41]

Figure 8.18 is Colin Campbell's forecast for Egypt's oil production. Campbell projects that Egypt's oil production will decline to 192,000 b/d in 2025 and 82,000 b/d in 2040. Campbell estimates that Egypt's cumulative production at the end of 2075 will be 13 Gb, essentially its EUR.[42] At the end of 2002, cumulative production was 8.91 Gb, 68.5 percent of 13 Gb.[43]

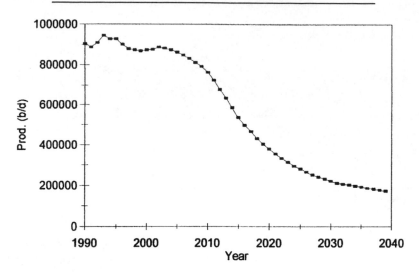

Figure 8.17 — Duncan's forecast for Egypt's oil + NGLs production

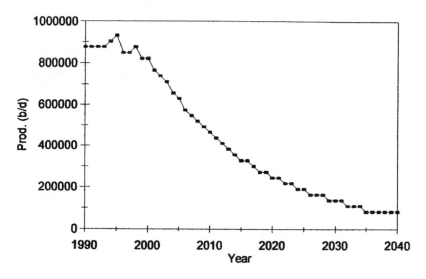

Figure 8.18 — Campbell's forecast for Egypt's oil production

Oil Production in Gabon

Gabon's oil exploration dates back to the middle 1950s with the first discovery occurring in 1957. As is the case with other West African oil producing nations, much of Gabon's production occurs offshore. Gabon is a

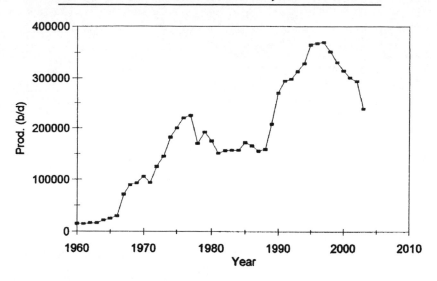

Figure 8.19 — Gabon's oil production (Data from Colin Campbell [1960–1979] and the US DOE/EIA [1980–2003]).

relatively minor oil producing nation with a declining production rate. The rate peaked in 1997 at 370,000 b/d, but it declined to 241,000 b/d in 2003, 129,000 b/d (34.9 percent) less than in 1997.[44] Figure 8.19 is a graph of Gabon's oil production.

The decline in Gabon's oil production rate is largely due to the rapid decline of the largest oil field, Rabi-Koungu, which has a reported EUR of ~850 Mb. The production rate for the field has declined from 217,000 b/d in 1997 to ~55,000 b/d in early 2003.[45] A gas injection project, Rabi Phase III, is being employed in an attempt to boost and prolong production.

In spite of Gabon's significant production decline since 1997, the government has revised its oil reserves upward from 1.3 Gb in 1996 to 2.5 Gb in 2002. In 2000/2001, Gabon made 27 exploration blocks available to international oil companies: 13 onshore, 5 shallow-water offshore and 9 deep-water offshore.[46] The government is attempting to stem the declining production rate. Oil companies were not overly enthusiastic about the exploration license sale.

The US DOE/EIA states, "Several West African producers (Angola, Cameroon, Chad, Congo, Gabon, and Ivory Coast) are expected to reap the benefits of substantial exploration activity, especially considering the recent rebound in oil prices. The other West African producers [beyond Angola] with offshore tracts are expected to increase output by up to 1 million barrels per day for the duration of the forecast."[47]

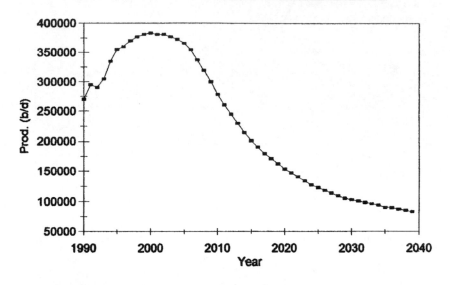

Figure 8.20 — Duncan's forecast for Gabon's oil + NGLs production

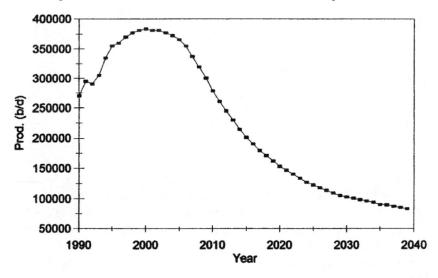

Figure 8.20 — Duncan's forecast for Gabon's oil + NGLs production

At this point in time, it's questionable whether Gabon can stop its declining oil production rate, let alone increase the rate by up to 1 mb/d. There have not been any major deep-water discoveries in Gabon to justify the belief that Gabon can significantly increase its production.

Figure 8.20 is Richard Duncan's forecast for Gabon's oil + NGLs production. Duncan projected that Gabon's oil + NGLs production would

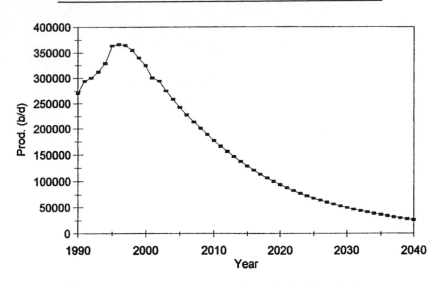

Figure 8.21— Campbell's forecast for Gabon's oil production

peak in 2000 at 384,000 b/d, decline to 123,000 b/d in 2025 and 83,000 b/d in 2039.[48]

Figure 8.21 is Colin Campbell's forecast for Gabon's oil production. Campbell projects that Gabon's oil production will decline to 68,000 b/d in 2025 and 26,000 b/d in 2040. He estimates that Gabon's cumulative production at the end of 2075 will be 4.5 Gb, essentially its EUR.[49] At the end of 2002, cumulative production was 2.83 Gb, 63 percent of 4.5 Gb.[50]

Oil Production in Libya

Libya's first oil exploration success occurred in 1957 with a minor discovery in the Sirte Basin. That was followed by a string of major discoveries, listed in Table 8.1.

Oil production started in 1961 and reached a peak rate of 3.32 mb/d in 1970, as the fields discovered in the 1950s and 1960s were intensively exploited. After 1970, the production rate declined rapidly due to political events in Libya and the OPEC oil embargo of 1973. Production remained at a reduced level after that due to the oil crisis of the late 1970s/early 1980s, OPEC production quotas, declining production from old fields and the lack of advanced exploration and production technology. In 2003, Libya's production rate was 1.42 mb/d.[51] Figure 8.22 is a graph of Libya's oil production.

Table 8.1— Major Libyan Oil Discoveries*

Field (Discovery Date)	EUR (Gb)	Maximum Production Rate since 1971 (b/d), (Year)†	Field (Discovery Date)	EUR (Gb)	Maximum Production Rate Since 1971 (b/d), (Year)
Amal (1959)	4.5	162,408 (1971)	Sarir (1961)	6.0	440,269 (1971)
Beda (1959)	1.0	Unavailable	Waha (1961)	1.0	146,381 (1973)
Nasser (1959)	2.0	357,903 (1971)	Angila-Nafoora (1965)	2.0	282,654 (1972)
Defa (1960)	2.0	212,269 (1980)	Intisar (1967)	2.25	581,067 (1971)
Gialo (1961)	3.5	359,408 (1971)	Bu Attifel (1968)	1.5	180,695 (1991)

*Data from "Country Assessment — Libya," Association for the Study of Peak Oil, Newsletter No 34
†Based upon data from Oil & Gas Journal

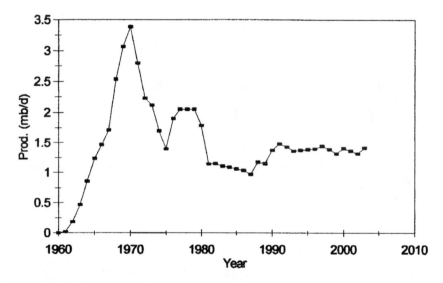

Figure 8.22 — Libya's oil production (Data from the US DOE/EIA)

The oil fields discovered in the 1950s and 1960s are aging, with state operated fields reportedly declining at 7–8 percent/year. Future increases in Libyan oil production will probably have to rely on more recent discoveries. The El Sharara field in the Murzuq Basin, discovered in 1988, was brought on-line in 1996. It was projected to have a maximum production rate of 200,000 b/d by 1998, but various problems have delayed reaching that rate. A consortium of companies announced a 1997 discovery in the Murzuq Basin of ~700 Mb. The field was given the name Elephant, apparently to suggest how large it is, but compared to the early Libyan discoveries the Elephant field is not very large. It was due to come on-line in 2000 at ~50,000 b/d but the start-up was delayed. Even with

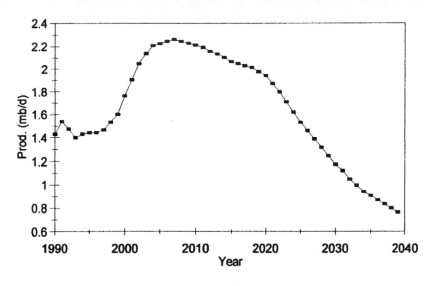

Figure 8.23 — Duncan's forecast for Libya's oil + NGLs production

the delay, the field is expected to reach a production rate of 200,000 b/d in 2004.[52]

Regarding Libya, the US DOE/EIA states, "Increased optimism about the production potential of Algeria, Libya, and Venezuela supports the possibility that the growth in world dependence on Persian Gulf oil will slow."[53]

Libya's oil production rate can probably increase somewhat due to rapid development of more recent oil discoveries, but the increase will be limited.

Figure 8.23 is Richard Duncan's forecast for Libya's oil + NGLs production. Duncan projects that Libya's oil + NGLs production will reach 2.26 mb/d in 2007 before declining to 1.53 mb/d in 2025 and 0.77 mb/d in 2039.[54]

Figure 8.24 is Colin Campbell's forecast for Libya's oil production. Campbell projects that Libya's oil production will plateau from 2003 through 2011 at 1.37 mb/d, decline to 1.06 mb/d in 2025 and 0.81 mb/d in 2040. He estimates that Libya's cumulative production at the end of 2075 will be 55 Gb, essentially its EUR.[55] At the end of 2002, cumulative production was 23.6 Gb, 43 percent of 55 Gb.[56]

Oil Production in Nigeria

Nigeria's oil exploration started in the late 1930s, but it was interrupted by World War II so that the first oil discovery didn't occur until 1957. Initial exploration took place in the Niger Delta, suggesting that early

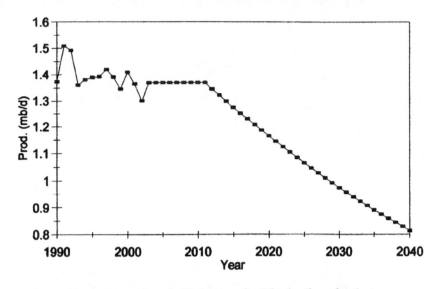

Figure 8.24 — Campbell's forecast for Libya's oil production

oil explorers knew where to look. Most of Nigeria's current oil production occurs in the Niger Delta, both onshore and offshore, from approximately 250 producing fields.[57]

In recent years, exploration has moved into the deep-water region of
Nigeria where numerous significant discoveries have been made includ-
ing Erha, Agbami, Bonga, Bonga South West, EA, Abo, Akpo, Ukot and
Usan fields. Table 8.2 contains data for these deep-water fields.

Along with the numerous deep-water fields, there are several shallow-
water fields that were expected to come on-line in 2003/2004: Yohi, Ame-
nam and Kpono. The Yohi field started up in February 2003 at 90,000 b/d
and was expected to peak at 150,000 b/d in late 2004. The Amenam/Kpono
fields are expected to come on-line by July 2004 and have a peak production rate of 125,000 b/d.[58]

Beyond the large deep-water fields listed in Table 8.2, Nigeria has 13
giant fields listed in Table 8.3.

Figure 8.25 is a graph of Nigeria's oil production. Nigeria's production rate rose rapidly in the late 1960s/early 1970s due to production from
fields discovered in the late 1950s and 1960s. Nigeria, being a member of
OPEC, had a dip in production through the 1980s. In 2003, the production rate was 2.24 mb/d.[59]

The US DOE/EIA assesses Nigeria's situation in their IEO2003:

OPEC members outside the Persian Gulf are expected to increase their production potential substantially, despite their higher capacity expansion costs. There

Table 8.2 — Deep-Water Discoveries in Nigeria*

Field	Discovery Date	EUR (Gb)	Expected On-Line Date	Estimated Peak Production Rate (b/d)†
Erha	1991	0.60	2005	150,000
Agbami	1998	0.80	2006	225,000
Bonga	1996	1.10	2004	225,000
Bonga South West	2001	1.40	2005	unknown
EA	unknown	0.35	2002	125,000
Abo	unknown	unknown	2003	30,000
Akpo	2000	unknown	unknown	unknown
Ukot/Usan	1999/2002	unknown	2006	unknown

* From "Country Assessment — Nigeria," Association for the Study of Peak Oil, Newsletter No 27
†From "Country Analysis Brief — Nigeria," US DOE/EIA, March 2003

Table 8.3 — Giant Fields in Nigeria Excluding Deep-Water Fields*

Field	Discovery Date	EUR (Gb)	Field	Discovery Date	EUR (Gb)
Nembe Creek	1973	1.00	Bomu	1958	0.70
Forcados Yokri	1968	1.00	Obagi	1964	0.60
Imo River	1959	0.90	Ekulama	1958	0.55
Edop	1981	0.85	Okan	1964	0.55
Cowthorne Channel	1963	0.75	Amenom	1990	0.50
Jones Creek	1967	0.75	Kokari	1961	0.50
Meren	1965	0.70			

* From "Country Assessment — Nigeria," Association for the Study of Peak Oil, Newsletter No 27

is much optimism regarding Nigeria's offshore production potential, although it is unlikely to be developed until the middle to late part of this decade.[60]

The US DOE/EIA forecasts that Nigeria will steadily increase its production capacity from 2.2 mb/d in 2001 to 4.6 mb/d in 2025.[61] Nigeria clearly has the potential to significantly increase its production, but the magnitude of the US DOE/EIA forecast appears unrealistic.

Figure 8.26 is Richard Duncan's forecast for Nigeria's oil + NGLs production. Duncan projects that Nigeria's oil + NGLs production will be relatively stable from 2000 through 2010 at ~2.5–2.6 mb/d, decline to 1.38 mb/d in 2025 and 0.85 mb/d in 2039.[62] In the first 3 quarters of 2003, Nigeria's TLHs production averaged 2.18 mb/d.[63]

Figure 8.27 is a graph of Colin Campbell's forecast for Nigeria's oil production. Campbell projects that Nigeria's oil production will peak at ~3.1 mb/d in 2009, decline to ~1.7 mb/d in 2025 and ~0.9 mb/d in 2040. Campbell estimates that Nigeria's cumulative production at the end of 2075 will be 62.5 Gb, essentially its EUR.[64] At the end of 2002, cumulative production was 22.71 Gb, 36.3 percent of 62.5 Gb.[65]

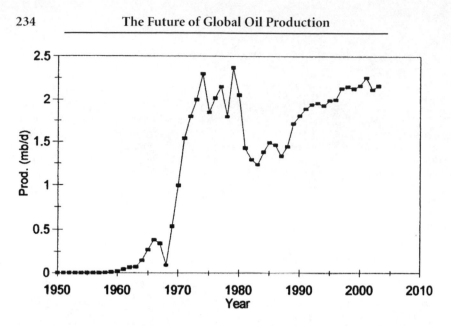

Figure 8.25 — Nigeria's oil production (Data from the US DOE/EIA)

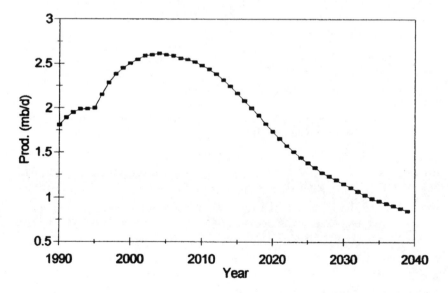

Figure 8.26 — Duncan's forecast for Nigeria's oil + NGLs production

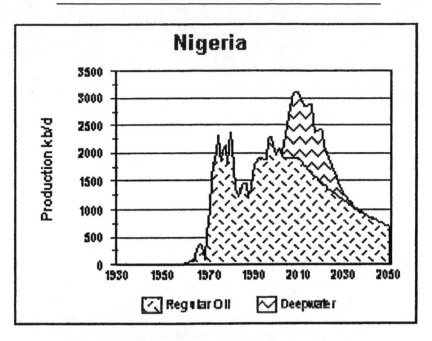

Figure 8.27 — Campbell's forecast for Nigeria's oil production

Oil Production in Sudan

Sudan's oil exploration began in the early 1960s with the effort concentrated in the Red Sea. Despite extensive exploration, no significant quantities of oil were discovered in that area. Exploration also took place in southern Sudan where several fields were discovered, namely the Heglig and Unity fields. Due to civil unrest, the discoveries were not developed until the 1990s. Production started in 1996. Those two fields have a reported combined EUR of 0.66–1.2 Gb. It wasn't until the Greater Nile Oil Pipeline was completed in 1999 that significant quantities of oil were produced. The pipeline has a current capacity of 250,000 b/d and can be expanded to 450,000 b/d. In 2002, Sudan's oil production rate reached 227,500 b/d.[66]

Most of Sudan's oil exploration to date has been in southern, central and western Sudan, as well as the Red Sea. The Sudanese government is making exploration acreage available throughout Sudan in the hopes of increasing production. Several fields in the Mujlad Basin of western Sudan were expected to start producing oil in 2002, although problems with militants have hampered production increases throughout Sudan. The government

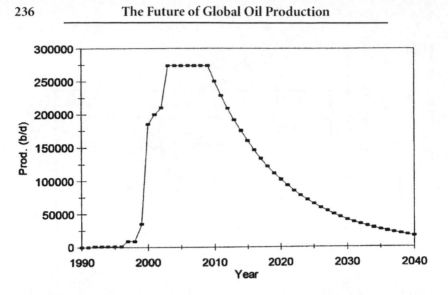

Figure 8.28 — Campbell's forecast for Sudan's oil production

hopes to increase production to 300,000 b/d in 2003 and 450,000 b/d in 2005.[67] The feasibility of attaining those production rates remains to be seen.

Says the US DOE/EIA, "Sudan and Equatorial Guinea are expected to produce significant volumes [of oil] by the middle of this decade. Both could approach 500,000 barrels per day."[68]

Expecting Sudan to produce 500,000 b/d by the middle of this decade may be optimistic. Equatorial Guinea has a similar oil production profile to that of Sudan. Production started in the early 1990s and reached 181,000 b/d in 2001.[69] Neither Richard Duncan nor Colin Campbell have forecasts for Equatorial Guinea's oil production, reflecting their belief that it will never be more than a minor oil producing nation.

Richard Duncan has not made a forecast for Sudan's oil + NGLs production. Figure 8.28 is Colin Campbell's forecast for Sudan's oil production.

Campbell projects that Sudan's oil production will plateau from 2003 through 2009 at 274,000 b/d, decline to 64,000 b/d in 2025 and 17,000 b/d in 2040. He estimates that Sudan's cumulative production at the end of 2075 will be 2 Gb, essential its EUR.[70] At the end of 2002, cumulative production was 0.2 Gb, 10 percent of 2 Gb.[71]

Oil Production in the Rest of Africa

Oil production in the remainder of Africa, beyond the top 8 producing nations covered previous, comes mostly from 3 nations: Tunisia, Cameroon

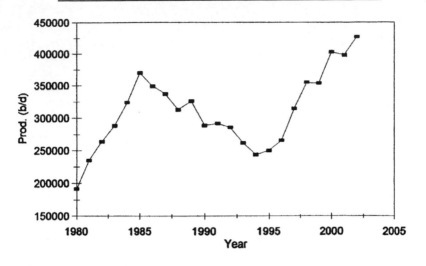

Figure 8.29 — Oil production from Africa, excluding the top 8 producing nations (Data from the US DOE/EIA).

and Equatorial Guinea. Those 3 nations produced 82.4 percent of the oil from this region in 2001. Oil production in Tunisia and Cameroon has been declining for many years. In 1980, Tunisia's oil production rate was 120,000 b/d. The production rate has declined steadily since then and was 70,000 b/d in 2001. Cameroon's oil production rate increased until 1985 when it reached 185,000 b/d. After 1985, the rate declined steadily so that in 2001 it was only 77,000 b/d. Equatorial Guinea's oil production rate increased rapidly after 1991, when it was zero, to 181,000 b/d in 2001.[72] Numerous offshore fields have been discovered in Equatorial Guinea which will allow further growth in its production rate. Figure 8.29 is a graph of oil production from this region.

In the 1980s, the oil production rate rose rapidly due to increasing production from Cameroon. When production from Cameroon started declining, production from the region declined. The rise in the production rate after 1994 has been due to the rapid rise in Equatorial Guinea's oil production. In 2002, the production rate from the region was 427,000 b/d.[73] Once Equatorial Guinea's production rate starts declining, production from the region will decline.

Conclusion

Africa's oil production rate can be increased due to developments in Angola, Nigeria, Algeria, Libya and Sudan. While those areas experience production increases, production is likely to decline in Egypt, Gabon, Tunisia and Cameroon.

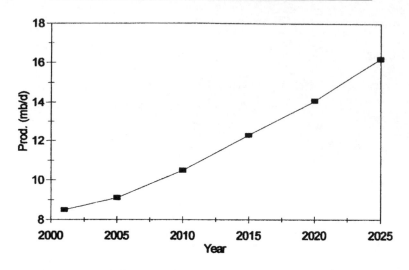

Figure 8.30 — US DOE/EIA forecast for Africa's production capacity

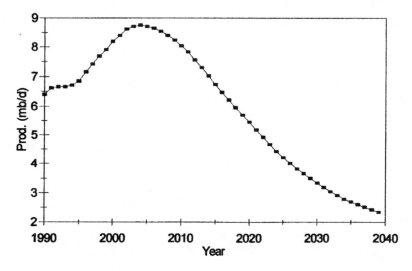

Figure 8.31— Duncan's oil production forecast for Africa's top 7 oil producing nations.

Figure 8.30 is the US DOE/EIA's forecast for Africa's oil production capacity. They project that capacity, and presumably production, will increase from 8.5 mb/d in 2001 to 16.2 mb/d in 2025.[74]

Richard Duncan and Colin Campbell are less optimistic about Africa's oil production future. Figure 8.31 is Duncan's forecast for oil + NGLs production from Africa's top 7 oil producing nations.[75]

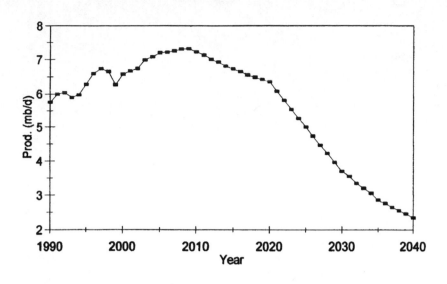

Figure 8.32 — Campbell's oil production forecast for Africa's top 8 producing countries.

Duncan projects that oil + NGLs production from Africa's top 7 oil producing nations will peak in 2004 at 8.77 mb/d, decline to 4.22 mb/d in 2025 and 2.34 mb/d in 2039.[76]

Figure 8.32 is Colin Campbell's forecast for oil production from Africa's top 8 oil producing nations. Campbell projects that oil production from these nations, including deep-water areas, will peak at 7.32 mb/d in 2009, decline to 5.00 mb/d in 2025 and 2.34 mb/d in 2040.[77]

9

Global Oil Production

There is a wide variation of estimates for the date of peak global oil production. The US DOE/EIA is extremely optimistic, projecting that peak TLHs production will not occur before 2025. Figure 9.1 is a graph of historical TLHs production and the US DOE/EIA's forecast.

The US DOE/EIA projects that TLHs production will increase from ~78 mb/d in 2000 to 118.8 mb/d in 2025.[1] Since oil makes up the bulk of TLHs production and will in the future, oil production will have to increase significantly as well. In 1990–1991, oil made up 90.6 percent of global TLHs production, while in 2001–2002, oil made up 88.0 percent of global TLHs production.[2] In spite of that percentage decline, global oil production increased 6.3 mb/d from 1990 to 2002.

At the end of 2003, cumulative global oil production was ~955 Gb.[3] Assuming that oil production makes up 85 percent of TLHs production through 2025, cumulative oil production at the end of 2025 would be ~1630 Gb using the US DOE/EIA forecast. The US DOE/EIA is basing their forecast upon the USGS World Petroleum Assessment 2000 which projects a global EUR of ~3200 Gb.[4] If the actual EUR is ~2000 Gb, as most petroleum geologists predict, the US DOE/EIA forecast can not be valid.

Richard Duncan estimates that global peak oil + NGLs production will occur in 2006 at ~82 mb/d (see Figure 9.2). To place 82 mb/d in perspective, global TLHs production in 2003 was 79.2 mb/d. He projects that global oil + NGLs production will decline to ~67 mb/d in 2020 and ~29 mb/d in 2040.[5] As Figure 9.2 illustrates, he projects that OPEC oil production will exceed non-OPEC oil production after 2008.

Figure 9.3 is Colin Campbell's forecast for global conventional oil production, excluding deepwater and polar oil. Campbell projected that global oil production, excluding deepwater and polar oil, would peak around 2000 at ~64 mb/d, decline to ~47 mb/d in 2020 and ~22 mb/d in

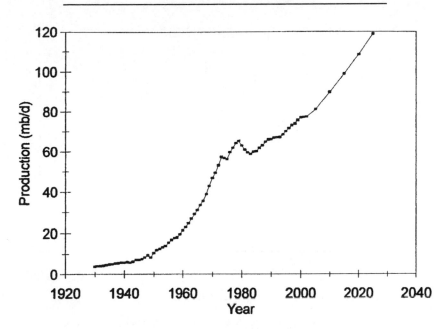

Figure 9.1— Historical TLHs production [1930–2002] and the US DOE/EIA forecast through 2025 [2003–2025].

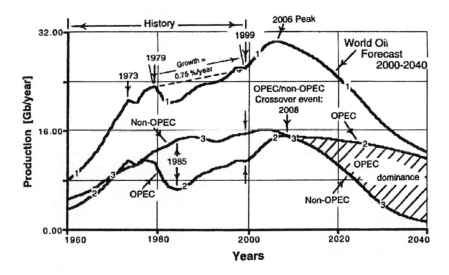

Figure 9.2 — Duncan's forecast for global oil + NGLs production

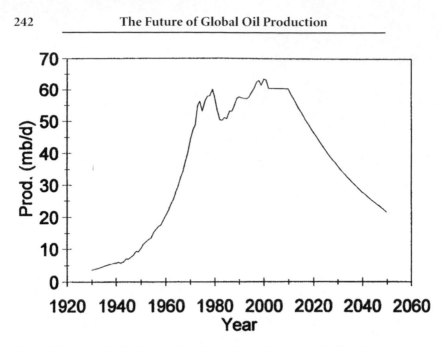

Figure 9.3 — Campbell's forecast for global oil production, excluding deepwater and polar oil.

2050. He is now projecting that global oil production, including deepwater and polar oil will peak in 2008.[6]

Global oil production has been rising in recent years, but most of the increase has come from Russia and OPEC. Non-OPEC production outside of Russia has been increasing only slowly since 1997 (see Figure 9.4).

For the 6-year period from 1992 through 1997, non-OPEC production, excluding Russia, increased 3.88 mb/d. For the 6-year period from 1997 through 2002, it increased 1.01 mb/d. For 2003, non-OPEC oil production, excluding Russia, increased 179,000 b/d over the 2002 average.[7] There has been an intense effort by international oil companies to explore and develop non-OPEC oil since 1997. During 2003, there were major oil developments in Brazil, Mexico, deep-water Gulf of Guinea, deep-water Gulf of Mexico, Canada, Ecuador and the Caspian Sea region that led to increases in production in those areas. The reason that non-OPEC production, outside of Russia, did not increased significantly in 2003 is due to declines in production for countries such as Norway, the U.K., Colombia, Oman, Australia and others which largely negated the production increases.

Figure 9.5 is a graph of non-OPEC total liquid hydrocarbons production since 1992, excluding the Former Soviet Union (FSU). For the 6-year period from 1992 through 1997, non-OPEC total liquid hydrocarbons

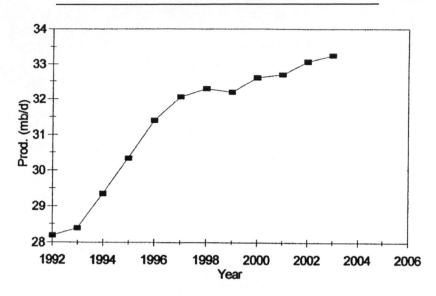

Figure 9.4 — Non-OPEC oil production, excluding Russia (Data from the US DOE/EIA).

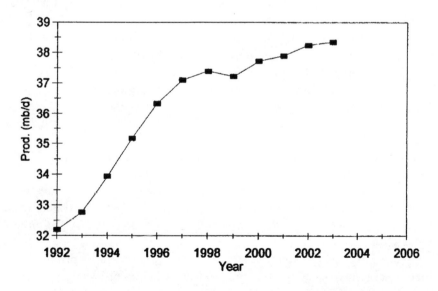

Figure 9.5 — Non-OPEC total liquid hydrocarbons production, excluding the FSU (Data from the US DOE/EIA).

production, excluding the FSU, increased 4.91 mb/d. For the 6-year period from 1997 through 2002, the increase was 1.14 mb/d. For 2003, non-OPEC total liquid hydrocarbons production, excluding the FSU, increased by 110,000 b/d.[8] It's getting increasingly difficult to increase TLHs production outside of OPEC and the FSU.

Even within OPEC, several countries are having serious problems with declining production. Indonesia's oil production declined from 1.52 mb/d in 1998 to 1.17 mb/d in 2003, a decline of 347,000 b/d (22.8 percent) in the course of 5 years. There has also been a significant decline in Venezuela's oil production. It's important to recognize that in Venezuela, domestic problems led to a reduction in production for the last month of 2002 and first 3 months of 2003. For the April through September period, Venezuela's oil production was 2.87 mb/d in 2001, 2.74 mb/d in 2002 and 2.63 mb/d in 2003. That's a decline of 237,000 b/d (8.25 percent) for the specified period from 2001 to 2003. In 2000, Venezuela's oil production for the year was 3.16 mb/d, suggesting that production has declined consistently since 2000 if the domestic problems that started in Dec. 2002 are excluded.[9]

Concerning future non-OPEC oil production growth, the US DOE/EIA says, "In the *IEO2003* reference case, non-OPEC supply from proved reserves is expected to increase steadily, from 46.7 million barrels per day in 2001 to 62.8 million barrels per day in 2025."[10]

That production increase seems implausible considering that most of the non-OPEC production growth over the last 5 years has come from Russia. Russia's oil production will increase in coming years, but the rate of increase will decline. In 2003, Russia's oil production increased 10.4 percent over 2002.[11] Russia's Deputy Energy Minister, Oleg Gordeyev, projects that production will increase 3.0–7.6 percent in 2004. Troika Dialog projects that Russia's oil production will grow less than 7.0 percent in 2004 even without major production constraints.[12] Constraints would involve a higher taxation rate on oil production and problems between the Kremlin and oil giant Yukos. Russia's oil production is likely to start declining before 2010.

In non-OPEC countries outside of Russia, there will be production increases in the Caspian Sea region, the deep-water off of West Africa, the deep-water Gulf of Mexico and the deep-water Campos Basin. Beyond that, most non-OPEC countries that have experienced increasing production in recent years are likely to experience declining production within the next 5 years.

Mexico's oil production increased 465,000 b/d from 1999 to 2003, but production is likely to start declining in the near future. Brazil's production increased 418,000 b/d from 1999 to 2003, but probably won't grow much after 2007. Canada's oil production has been increasing in recent years due to developments in Atlantic Canada and the Athabasca Oil Sands region. Atlantic Canada's oil production is likely to peak and start declining within the next 5 years. After that, any increases in Canada's oil production will be due to oil sands production increases being larger than conventional oil production decreases.

The IEO2003 states the following concerning future OPEC oil production:

> The reference case projects that about 61 percent of the increase in petroleum demand over the next two decades will be met by an increase in production by members of OPEC rather than by non-OPEC suppliers. OPEC production in 2025 is projected to be more than 25 million barrels per day higher than it was in 2001.[13]

The US DOE/EIA projects that OPEC oil production will nearly double from 30.3 mb/d in 2001 to 55 mb/d in 2025. Considering the current problems in many of the giant OPEC oil fields, that appears implausible. Members of OPEC, particularly those in the Middle East, have undeveloped fields, but as their giant fields decline the production from new fields will only partially negate the decline of old fields.

A recent report concerning major oil projects under development has concluded that there will be a significant production increase from those projects over the next 3 years as they come on-line, but that there is a lack of projects coming on-line after that to meet growing global oil demand.[14] The report analyzed all projects that involved fields with projected peak production rates greater than or equal to 100,000 b/d. Table 9.1 is a listing of the number of these mega-projects that are expected to come on-line during the 2004–2008 period.

Most of the mega-projects listed in Table 9.1 are offshore developments, most in deep-water. They tend to reach high peak or plateau production rates within a year or two after start-up. Once they start declining, the decline is rapid. Based upon the author's assessment, global oil production will not keep up with global oil demand after 2007.[16] Table 9.2 provides detailed information concerning the mega-projects expected to come on-line through 2009.

A point to be made is that actual peak production doesn't necessarily meet expected peak production. Angola's Kuito field was projected to reach a production rate of 100,000 b/d in 2000.[18,19] As of 2002, it had only achieved a production rate of 66,000 b/d.[20] Congo's N'Kossa field, which came on-line in 1996, was projected to have a peak production

Table 9.1 — Number of Mega-projects Planned Through 2008[15]

Year	Number of Projects	Summed Peak Production (mb/d)
2004	11	2.24
2005	15	3.21
2006	11	2.50
2007	3	0.47
2008	3	1.27

Mega-projects On-Line for 2004–2008[17]

Project	Location	Peak Production (b/d)	Reported EUR (Gb)
On-line 2004			
Albacora Leste	Brazil (offshore)	180,000	1.507*
Banyu Urip	Indonesia (offshore)	165,000	2.00 (in block)
Bayu-Undan	Timor Sea (offshore)	200,000	
Bonga	Nigeria (offshore)	225,000	0.600
Caofedian	China (offshore)	100,000	
Elephant	Libya (onshore)	150,000	0.760
Kizomba	Angola (offshore)	250,000	1.000*
Marco Polo	U.S. GOM (offshore)	100,000	0.180
Marlim Sul II	Brazil (offshore)	180,000	2.679*
Priobskoye	Russia (onshore)	550,000	4.000
Roncador II	Brazil (offshore)	140,000	2.000*
On-line 2005			
ACG Megastructure	Caspian Sea (offshore)	1,000,000	5.300
Barracuda-Caratinga	Brazil (offshore)	273,000	1.778*
Bonga South	Nigeria (offshore)	250,000	1.000
Erha	Nigeria (offshore)	150,000	0.500
Frade	Brazil (offshore)	110,000	0.836*
Holstein	U.S. GOM (offshore)	100,000	0.500–1.000*
Mad Dog	U.S. GOM (offshore)	100,000	Up to 0.800
Marlim Leste	Brazil (offshore)	100,000	
NEAD project	Abu Dhabi (onshore)	110,000	
Prirazlomnoye	Russia (offshore)	150,000	0.600
Roncador III	Brazil (offshore)	145,000	2.000*
Sakhalin I	Russia (offshore)	250,000	2.300
Salym fields	Russia (onshore)	120,000	0.600
Thunder Horse	U.S. GOM (offshore)	250,000	1.500*
White Rose	Canada (offshore)	100,000	0.230
On-line 2006			
Atlantis	U.S. GOM (offshore)	150,000	0.875
Agbami	Nigeria (offshore)	225,000	1.000
Benguela-Belize	Angola (offshore)	100,000	0.400
Bu Hasa	Abu Dhabi (onshore)	250,000	
Buzzard	United Kingdom (offshore)	180,000	0.400
Dalia	Angola (offshore)	240,000	1.600
Enfield	Australia (offshore)	100,000	0.363

Project	Location	Peak Production (b/d)	Reported EUR (Gb)
Kashagan Phase I	Caspian Sea (offshore)	450,000	9.000
Kizomba B	Angola (offshore)	250,000	1.000
Marlim Sul III	Brazil (offshore)	100,000	2.679*
Tengiz Expansion On-line 2007	Kazakhstan (onshore)	200,000–450,000	7.000
Lobito-Tombuco	Angola (offshore)	100,000	0.400
Platina/Plutonio	Angola (offshore)	220,000	0.800
Tahiti On-line 2008	U.S. GOM (offshore)	150,000	0.700*
Kizomba C	Angola (offshore)	250,000	1.000
Marlim Sul IV	Brazil (offshore)	120,000	2.679
Kashagan Phase II	Caspian Sea (offshore)	900,000	9.000

*Barrels of oil equivalence

Table 9.3 — Potential Mega-Projects[22]

Potential Project	Location	Peak Production (b/d)	Reported EUR (Gb)
Karachaganak Phase III & IV	Kazakhstan (onshore)		
Kashagan Phase III	Caspian Sea (offshore)	1,200,000	9.000
Ahwaz (Bangestan Development)	Iran (onshore)	350,000	
Akpo	Nigeria (offshore)		0.625*
Arash	Iran (offshore)		0.683
Azadegan	Iran (onshore)	100,000	2.5–3.5
Block 09–03	Vietnam (offshore)	100,000+	0.300–0.400
Ghawar Haradh Phase II	Saudi Arabia (onshore)	300,000	
Great White	U.S. GOM (offshore)		0.500
Kharyaga	Russia (onshore)		0.71010
Khvalynskoye	Russia (offshore)		0.627
Kirkuk Khurmala	Iraq (onshore)	100,000	
Kushk	Iran		1.000*
Lungu	China (onshore)		0.500
Majnoon	Iraq (onshore)	360,000	
Northern Fields	Kuwait (onshore)	400,000	
Northern Territories	Russia (onshore)		1.000
Qatif Field Expansion	Saudi Arabia (onshore)	500,000	
Talanskoye	Russia (onshore)		0.832
Val Gamburtsev	Russia (onshore)		0.600
Vankorskoye	Russia (onshore)		0.900
Verkhnechonsknoye	Russia (onshore)		1.500
Yuri Korchagin	Russia (offshore)		0.879
Yuzhno-Shapinskoye	Russia (onshore)		0.500
West Qurna Phase II	Iraq (onshore)	650,000	

rate of 100,000 —110,000 b/d. It never came close to the projected production level and in the first quarter of 2003, it was only producing 34,000 b/d.[21]

Table 9.4 — Number of Discoveries >= 500 Mb[23]

Year	Number of Discoveries
2000	13
2001	6
2002	2

There are projects beyond those listed in Table 9.2 that will potentially be developed at a later date (see Table 9.3).

Related to the decline in the number of mega-projects coming on-line after 2006 is the fact that the rate of +500 Mb field discoveries has steadily declined in recent years (see Table 9.4).

Economic growth will play a part in determining when global oil production peaks. From 1999 to the first three quarters of 2003, global TLHs consumption increased 2.75 mb/d,[24] so even with a downturn in the U.S. economy and major problems in the Japanese economy, there was an average annual increase in TLHs consumption of ~688,000 b/d during the period. If the Chinese economy continues on its torrid growth rate, China alone will create a significant rise in global oil consumption. It appears increasingly likely that global oil production will peak around 2010, if not before.

10

Evaluation of Alternatives to Conventional Oil

There have been innumerable claims that we can easily replace oil with alternatives or reduce consumption markedly through fuel efficiency and conservation measures. The U.S. reduced oil consumption by ~3 mb/d in the late 1970s and early 1980s in response to the oil crises of the 1970s so we can easily do it again, can't we?

The reduction of oil consumption during the late 1970/early 1980s was achieved by dramatically reducing oil consumption for electrical generation, fuel switching for space heating, applying fuel efficiency standards to motor vehicles, lowering highway speed limits and consumer purchasing of more fuel-efficient motor vehicles.

A few of those measures can be used again to reduce oil consumption, but for several of those measures it will be more difficult to achieve the savings of the past. In the case of reducing oil consumption for electrical generation, far less savings could be achieved because much less electrical generation comes from burning oil. The data in Table 10.1 illustrate the point.

As of 2001, the U.S. was only using about 30 percent of the oil it used for electrical generation in 1978. In 1978, electrical generation consumed 3.38 percent of total oil use. In 2001, it consumed 0.99 percent of total oil use. On the other side of the ledger, coal use for electrical generation more than doubled from 1978 to 2001.

Much less space heating is now accomplished with oil compared to the 1970s, as the data in Table 10.2 illustrate.

In 2001, consumption of distillate fuel oil and kerosene for residential and commercial uses was only about 52 percent the consumption level of 1978. The reduction in oil use for electrical generation and space heating during the late 1970s/early 1980s presumably involved eliminating the

Table 10.1— Use of Oil and Coal for Electrical Generation*

Year	Distillate and Residual Fuel Oil (mb/d)	Coal (millions of short tons/year)
1978	0.636	451
1985	0.173	694
2001	0.195	976

* US DOE/EIA, http://www.eia.doe.gov/

Table 10.2 — Residential and Commercial Use of Distillate Fuel Oil and Kerosene*

Year	Distillate Fuel Oil + Kerosene Consumption (mb/d)
1978	1.33
1985	0.856
2001	0.695

* US DOE/EIA, http://www.eia.doe.gov/

most easily eliminated uses. Further reductions in oil use for those applications would probably be more difficult. In the last few years, the relative price of natural gas has been higher than that for oil in North America. If that remains the case for an extended period, any fuel switching between natural gas and oil will be towards oil.

There has been a vigorous debate in the U.S. concerning the high level of sport utility vehicle (SUV) and light truck use, the relatively low fuel mileage of those vehicles and the high level of oil imports into the U.S. that are made larger due to those vehicles. What makes SUVs and light trucks affordable is the relatively high level of personal income in the U.S. and the relatively low price of gasoline and diesel fuel, although many Americans wouldn't agree that fuel prices are low. Approximately 50 percent of personal motor vehicles in the U.S. are SUVs and light trucks.[1]

There have been several suggestions for discouraging the use of SUVs and light trucks or reducing their fuel consumption. The most common suggestions involve higher fuel taxes and higher fuel efficiency standards. At this point in time there is essentially no possibility that any meaningful measures along those lines could pass the U.S. Congress. A meaningful fuel tax increase to reduce oil consumption would have to be at least $1.00/gallon and probably much more. No politician who wants to get reelected is going to push for a $1.00/gallon fuel tax increase. There have been efforts to establish higher fuel efficiency standards for SUVs and light trucks, but strong opposition by auto companies and consumers of the vehicles precludes the possibility that meaningful legislation will be enacted any time soon. SUVs and light trucks provide auto companies with their largest profits per vehicle so they will strongly oppose any legislation that could impact sales of those vehicles.

The U.S. will not do anything meaningful to reduce oil consumption until there is no alternative. That will only come when there is a serious oil crisis. If global oil supply starts declining in ~2010, it's reasonable to expect that prices would escalate dramatically, creating a crisis. If that occurs, several measures would be taken in the U.S., just as in the case of the 1970s crises. First, there would be a push to open up all U.S. territory to oil and gas development. Unfortunately there is a lot less oil in protected areas than promoters suggest. The best that could be hoped for is that it would slow the decline of U.S. oil production for awhile. Oil companies might profit handsomely from future oil developments in presently protected areas, but those developments would not prevent the continuing decline of U.S. oil production.

Along with opening up protected areas to oil and gas development, Congress would pass some conservation and fuel efficiency measures. How serious those measures might be would depend on the magnitude and duration of the oil crisis. Based upon present ideology the Republican Party, in general, would like to do as little as possible along those lines. Conservation is not something conservatives apparently believe in, except as it applies to personal virtue.

Discussions concerning the reduction of oil consumption in the U.S. center on reducing its use in motor vehicles. Airlines have been improving aviation fuel efficiency for some time and industries using oil-based machinery have an incentive to be as efficient as possible. The reduction in oil consumption would probably have to come mainly from personal motor vehicles. Personal motor vehicles use ~10 mb/d of oil distillates.[2] It's appears reasonable that the U.S. could reduce oil consumption by 2–3 mb/d without too much pain by switching to more fuel efficient vehicles. The problem with switching to more fuel efficient vehicles is that most Americans aren't interested in owning fuel efficient vehicles. People who purchase SUVs and light trucks buy them for a reason. It may be to impress their friends and neighbors, the ability to carry heavy loads or the ability to haul heavy equipment such as boats and trailers. Could owners of SUVs and light trucks live with a Toyota Prius? They could but most would not be happy with the change and many would be looking for someone to blame if forced into purchasing a highly fuel-efficient vehicle. No doubt environmentalists would top the list of those being blamed. Such a move would be considered a significant step down. A sizeable portion of the U.S. population is wealthy enough that substantially higher oil prices would not encourage a change in their vehicle purchasing. Beyond 2–3 mb/d, an increasing level of sacrifice, or pain, would be necessary.

The importance of oil is that it is an exceptional fuel for transportation purposes and for heavy equipment used in construction, farming, logging, etc. It's easy to claim that alternatives such as hydrogen, natural gas, electricity, etc. could replace oil for those uses but there are significant problems with the alternatives. Over the years there has been considerable research into the use of alternative energy sources for replacing conventional oil. Numerous government initiatives involving alternative energy have also been instituted, but essentially no change has come about from the research and initiatives.

In 1974, the Nixon administration put forth an energy initiative called Project Independence to end America's reliance on foreign oil. One of the objectives of the initiative was to develop hydrogen-fueled vehicles. The technology was projected to be ready by 1990. Little came out of Project Independence based upon the fact that the U.S. is far more dependent on oil imports now compared to 1974. In terms of hydrogen-powered vehicles, there are no such vehicles on the roads in 2003 except for a few prototypes.

During the Carter administration, there was a big push to develop oil shale as a source of oil, a result of the Energy Security Act of 1980. Carter said it would "encourage production of 2 mb/d of synthetic fuel by the year 1992."[3] Billions of dollars were spent on oil shale development. At this point in time, there is no oil production from oil shale in the U.S.

Those two examples of governmental efforts to develop alternatives to conventional oil illustrate the problems with alternatives. The alternatives can involve major technical challenges and/or be extremely expensive to develop. There are those who argue that the government just didn't follow through with the efforts, but it's likely that the projects didn't make technical and/or economic sense.

The remainder of this chapter involves an evaluation of the alternatives that have been tried or suggested for replacing conventional oil. One of the most talked about alternatives is the use of hydrogen in fuel-cell vehicles.

Fuel-Cell Powered Vehicles

The fuel cell concept dates back to 1839 with the English physicist Sir William Grove. Serious development of fuel cells didn't begin until the 1930s and use of fuel cells didn't take place until their application in the space program during the 1960s. In recent years there has been consider-able research into the use of fuel cells for motor vehicles.

The type of fuel cell used in prototype fuel-cell vehicles is called a Proton Exchange Membrane or Polymer Electrolyte Membrane (PEM) fuel cell. The PEM fuel cell was invented in the early 1960s by researchers at General Electric Corporation.[4] PEM technology was used in NASA's Gemini Project during the 1960s and has been used for other applications since then.

In a PEM fuel cell, the following chemical reactions take place at an anode and a cathode.

$$\text{Anode Reaction: } 2\ H_2(g) \rightarrow 4\ H^+(aq) + 4\ e^-$$
$$\text{Cathode Reaction: } O_2(g) + 4\ H^+ + 4\ e^- \rightarrow 2\ H_2O$$
$$\overline{\text{Overall Reaction: } 2\ H_2(g) + O_2(g) \rightarrow 2\ H_2O}$$

Hydrogen gas flows through channels in the anode where the hydro-gen is converted to hydrogen ions plus electrons. The electrons flow from the anode through an external circuit to power an electric motor. The elec-trons continue on to the cathode where they take part in the cathode reac-tion that forms water. The hydrogen ions migrate through a membrane separating the anode and cathode so they can react at the cathode. What could be easier than a fuel cell for powering a motor vehicle? Why haven't auto companies started mass producing fuel-cell vehicles yet?

Well, the overall reaction of the fuel cell shown above produces an output voltage of 0.70 volts. That's not quite enough to power a motor vehicle. Actually it takes about 300 volts to power an automobile. It requires many fuel cells stacked together in series to create what is terms a fuel cell stack. The Ford P2000 prototype fuel-cell vehicle has a stack of 400 cells and provides an output of 100 horsepower.[5]

The advantages of a fuel-cell stack to power a motor vehicle are that it is more efficient than an internal combustion engine and it creates essen-tially no pollution, at least not from the fuel cell stack itself. Theoretically, a fuel cell is ~80 percent efficient but that is only if no current is drawn from the cell. When electrical current is drawn, resistances within the fuel cell reduce the efficiency. Higher operational temperatures reduce the resis-tances and many fuel cells are designed for high temperature operation.

In the case of a PEM fuel cell, the cell membrane is incompatible with high temperatures so they typically operate at ~80°C. The efficiency of a PEM fuel cell is lower than that for other types of fuel cells because of the low operating temperature, which requires the use of a platinum catalyst on the surfaces of both electrodes to increase reaction rates.

The membrane used in a PEM fuel cell is a thin fluorocarbon polymer with covalently attached sulfonate (SO_3-) groups. The sulfonate groups form a network of water-filled channels through which protons pass easily while anions are repelled. Because of the high proton conductivity, a PEM fuel cell starts up quickly, has a high power density and output can vary quickly to meet shifts in power demand. A PEM fuel cell engine can approach 60 percent efficiency compared to 20–25 percent for a gasoline engine and ~35 percent for a modern diesel engine.[6]

In larger PEM fuel cells, such as those used in motor vehicles, the gases going into the fuel cell are generally pressurized to increase the chemical reaction rates. Air compression at ~3 atm or higher must be used for the fuel cell to have a reasonable power density. That adds complexity and cost to the fuel cell as well as causing a loss of efficiency. Heating losses also lower efficiency. When all factors are considered, a fuel-cell vehicle is probably about 40 percent efficient.[7] That's still more efficient than internal combustion engines but a long way from the theoretical limit of efficiency. To be accurately compared, the efficiency associated with producing the H_2, used in fuel-cell vehicles, should be compared to the efficiency of making oil distillates. When the efficiencies involved with making the fuels are included, a fuel-cell vehicle is probably no better than that of a gasoline engine vehicle and possibly worse.

There are four major problems with PEM fuel-cell vehicles: cost, range, hydrogen supply and the average operational lifetime of the fuel cells. In terms of cost, experts suggest that a fuel cell stack necessary to power a motor vehicle would cost >\$100,000.[8] Today's fuel cells cost \$1500–10,000/KW. The cost would have to come down to \$50–100/KW to be competitive with internal combustion engines.[9] PEM fuel cells have been in development and use for ~40 years and the unsubsidized cost for a vehicle compatible fuel cell has not dropped significantly. It's unwise to assume that there will be huge cost savings coming in the future. Also adding to the cost of fuel-cell vehicles would be the probable necessity of using ultra-light and expensive materials in the body of the vehicles. The argument put forward in assuming that fuel-cell vehicles will become widely available in the future is that with mass production, the cost of fuel-cell vehicles will decrease significantly. How much the cost might decrease is unknown, but there won't be mass production of fuel-cell vehicles until costs are reduced dramatically.

More than 90 percent of the H_2 manufactured in the U.S. is made thermochemically by a process called steam reforming.[10] Steam reforming of methane involves reacting methane with steam at high temperatures (800–1700°C):

$$CH_4 + H_2O \rightarrow CO + 3\,H_2$$
$$CO + H_2O \rightarrow CO_2 + H_2$$
$$\overline{CH_4 + H_2O \rightarrow CO_2 + 4\,H_2}$$

H_2 prepared from natural gas has been reported to be ~4 times more expensive to produce than gasoline containing the same energy content, but that depends on the price of natural gas.[11] In the last year, the price of natural gas in the U.S. has been at least twice the average price during the 1990s and for a while, greater than 5 times. Natural gas supply problems in North America suggest that prices will be considerably higher in the future compared to the 1990s so the times 4 factor is probably low for North America. As an aside, it would be more logical to burn methane, or natural gas, directly in vehicles rather than converting it to H_2 to avoid energy losses in the conversion process, but logic doesn't always rule the world. H_2 can also be prepared from water by electrolysis, but that can be up to 4 times more expensive than reforming natural gas.[12] Whatever the process used to prepare H_2, it will have a negative net energy yield and can be expected to be expensive relative to oil, which at this time has a relatively high positive net energy yield.

The fuel used in a PEM fuel cell has to be ultra-pure because the platinum catalyst is easily poisoned by impurities, particularly carbon monoxide (CO). The limit of carbon monoxide concentration in the H_2 fuel has to be less than 10 ppm. If natural gas is used to produce the H_2, carbon monoxide is an inevitable byproduct of the production process and would have to be removed. Sulfur compounds would have to be removed from the natural gas used in the reformation process to a concentration less than 0.1 ppm.[13] Avoidance of membrane fouling requires ultra-clean air. The high purity H_2 and O_2 necessary for PEM fuel cells would add to the cost of operating a fuel-cell vehicle.

There has been research into the use of on-board generators of H_2 from methanol or hydrocarbons. The problem with on-board reformers is that they add complexity and cost to the vehicle and probably would suffer from the problem of platinum catalyst poisoning. A number of auto companies are touting on-board reformers, but the cost alone would probably prohibit their use.

Presently, compressed H_2 is used in almost all fuel-cell prototypes, pressurized to 5000 psi using a carbon fiber wrapped cylinder. Even at that pressure, the range of a fuel-cell vehicle is far lower than that of a gasoline powered vehicle. As an example, the Toyota prototype has a range of 186 miles.[14] Quantum Technology, of Germany, has built a cylinder that can handle H_2 to 10,000 psi but that entails a more expensive tank and the vehicle range would still be less than a typical gasoline powered vehicle.[15]

Another problem with compressed H_2 is that it would probably have to be transported long distances from source to consumer. Some promoters of a hydrogen economy claim that a decentralized system could be used but that would eliminate the advantages of economy of scale and entail serious safety concerns. As pointed out in the introduction, hydrogen has a low energy density relative to natural gas and other fuels. The low energy density means that more H_2 would have to be pumped through a pipeline compared to natural gas to transfer the same amount of energy. This would require higher flow rates for the same diameter pipe. Higher flow rates lead to higher flow resistances and the requirement of more energy to pump the H_2. It requires about 4.6 times more energy to move H_2 through a pipeline compared to natural gas of the same energy content using the same diameter pipe.[16] That adds further to the cost of the H_2.

As Mark Sadella points out,

> Hydrogen's low energy density makes it exceedingly inefficient to transport. To illustrate this, consider that a 40-ton tanker truck loaded with gasoline contains nearly 20 times the energy of a 40-ton truck loaded with compressed hydrogen. If both trucks deliver fuel to a filling station 800 miles away, the gasoline truck consumes about three percent of the energy in its payload to make the roundtrip. But the hydrogen truck traveling the same route would consume all of the energy in its payload. Put another way, if you tried to run the hydrogen delivery truck on hydrogen, it would consume its entire payload making the trip, and have no fuel to deliver.[17]

An alternative to compressed gas is liquid H_2. Liquid H_2 has a boiling point temperature of (-423°F). Preparing and maintaining H_2 as a liquid requires a lot of energy, a major expense. Another drawback of liquid H_2 storage systems is that they lose significant amounts of H_2 due to boiling and up to 30 percent during the filling process. Liquefied H_2 is not suitable for normal vehicle use.

There has been research in the area of using metal hydrides as a storage method for H_2. In such a fuel system, H_2 gas is pumped into a fuel tank that contains an appropriate metal alloy and the gas is held between the atoms of the alloy. The metal hydride is heated to release the H_2. Metal hydride fuel tanks suffer from adding too much weight for most vehicle uses and not being able to store enough H_2 under the right conditions to be viable.

There has also been research into using carbon nanotubes as potential H_2 absorption storage devices. In a 2001 review of carbon nanotube H_2 storage devices, sponsored by the German Federal Ministry for Education and Research, they concluded:

In view of today's knowledge, it is unlikely that carbon nanostructures can store the required amount of hydrogen gas [to make them viable]. In any case, this [research assessment] calls into doubt whether carbon nanostructures would have any advantages over high-pressure tank storage.[18]

A recent article stated that the average operational lifetime of the latest generation PEM fuel cell used in motor vehicles is 200 hours under normal driving conditions.[19] That would represent less than a years worth of driving for most vehicles.

The use of hydrogen in motor vehicles dates back to the 1930s.[20] The first fuel-cell powered motor vehicle was built by General Motors back in 1966 and was called the Electrovan.[21] The Electrovan never made it in the marketplace but that hasn't stopped GM and other auto manufacturers from further efforts to make a commercially viable fuel-cell vehicle. Presently, it's common to hear that fuel-cell vehicles will be in mass production by 2010 or sooner. It's instructive to note that Daimler-Benz was stating back in 1997 that they would produce 100,000 fuel-cell vehicles by 2004. In late 2003, it appears that Daimler-Chrysler will produce no more than a few prototype fuel-cell vehicles in 2004.

Hydrogen can be used in an internal combustion engine rather than a fuel cell. Such vehicles suffer from the problems of range and hydrogen supply that PEM fuel-cell vehicles suffer from.

Concerning the general concept of a hydrogen economy, Dr. Gerd Eisenbeiss, coordinator of the Helmholtz Energy Research Programme, Germany, stated at a recent International Energy Authority conference on hydrogen:

> Many people think of hydrogen as a glorious ultimate solution. Prophets elucidate that abundant water resources are the basis of a 'hydrogen economy' but they are deceiving the public about physical facts and tremendous costs. There may be a compelling logic for hydrogen in the end, but not now, or in the near future.[22]

According to Brian Steel, University of London and Angelika Heinzel, University of Duisberg-Essen, Germany, "Unless there is a breakthrough in the production of H_2 and the development of new H_2-storage materials, the concept of a 'hydrogen economy' will remain an unlikely scenario."[23]

Environmentalists like to talk about using solar and wind to generate H_2. Nuclear promoters like to talk about using nuclear energy to make H_2. The economic practicality of using solar, wind or nuclear power to make H_2 has not been demonstrated and it's unwise to assume that it will be practical.

It's easy to dismiss the technical and economic problems associated with the use of hydrogen and PEM fuel cells as hydrogen promoters do, but the problems are real. Research can't necessarily solve technical problems or provide economically viable solutions. It takes more than naive optimism of technology to make something work. Don't be surprised if it takes far longer than promoter's and auto company's state to bring fuel-cell vehicles to market or that they never make it in the marketplace in any appreciable numbers.

Electric Powered Vehicles

Inventors in France and England were the first to develop electric vehicles in approximately 1890. The vehicles made it to America in about 1895 and by 1897, a fleet of New York City taxis ran on electricity. In 1899 and 1900, electric vehicles outsold gasoline and steam powered vehicles in the U.S. Electric vehicles enjoyed several advantages over gasoline powered vehicles in the late 1800s/early 1900s: they didn't need cranking to get started, they didn't require difficult gear shifting and they were well suited for the short distance city driving of the day. In terms of performance, the Wood's Phaeton had a range of 18 miles and a top speed of 14 mph in the early 1900s.[24]

Electric vehicles enjoyed success into the 1920s with production peaking in 1912. Several factors lead to the demise of the electric vehicle. By the 1920s, America had a better road system connecting cities which required vehicles with longer ranges. Second, the abundant supply of oil made gasoline affordable to the average consumer. Third, the invention of the electric starter in 1912 eliminated the need for hand cranking to get the motor running. Forth, mass production of gasoline powered vehicles made them much cheaper than the less efficiently produced electric vehicles. In 1912, the average electric vehicle sold for $1750 while the average gasoline powered vehicle sold for $650.[25] By 1935, electric vehicles had essentially disappeared from American roads. Between 1935 and 1960, there was no interest in electric powered vehicles in the U.S.

During the 1960s, there was renewed interest in electric vehicles. In 1964, the first Battronic electric vehicle was sold to the Potomac Edison Electric Company. It was capable of 25 mph, had a range of 62 miles and could carry 2500 pounds. During the 1960s and 1970s, Sebring-Vanguard produced over 2000 electric powered "CitiCars" with a top speed of 44 mph and a range of 50–60 miles while the Elear Corporation produced the "Elear" electric vehicle with a top speed of 45 mph and a range of 60 miles. From 1973 to 1983, Battronic worked with General Electric Corporation to produce 175 electric powered utility vans. In 1975, the U.S. Postal Service purchased 350 electric delivery jeeps from the American Motors Corporation. The jeeps had a top speed of 50 mph and a range of 40 miles at 40 mph.[26]

In more recent developments, the U.S. Electricar Company converted Chevrolet S-10 pickup trucks to electric vehicles which had a range of 60 miles and a recharging time of only 7 hours. The Solectria Corporation converted Geo Metro's to electric vehicles that had a range of 50 miles and a recharging time of less than 8 hours. In the early 1990s, the Ford Ecostar utility van, with an alternating current motor and sodium sulfur battery pack, had a top speed of 70 mph and a range of 80–100 miles.[27] Approximately 100 Ecostars were produced but they were never offered commercially. The Toyota RAV4 sport utility electric, Honda EV Plus sedan, Chrysler EPIC electric minivan and Nissan Altra EV station wagon all came out in the late 1990s. The first 3 utilized advanced nickel metal hydride batteries while the Nissan Altra EV had a lithium-ion battery pack.

General Motors created the EV1 electric vehicle in the 1990s from the ground up rather than modify existing vehicles. The EV1 was a 2-passenger sports car powered by a liquid-cooled alternating current motor and lead-acid battery pack. It had a top speed of 80 mph, a range of 80 miles and accelerated to 50 mph in less than 7 seconds. About 800 EV1s were leased before the program was terminated in 2000.[28]

The historical problems with electric vehicles still haunt recent models. Electric vehicles suffer from high cost, low range, low carrying capacity and long charging times. Electric vehicles minimally cost $30,000–40,000 and possibly much more if advanced batteries and materials are used. When the factors of low range, low carrying capacity and long charging times are taken into consideration, the price is very high relative to the capabilities of the vehicles. The typical range of an electric vehicle is 50–100 miles. It doesn't appear that advanced batteries have had a dramatic impact on range even when electric vehicles are made of ultra-light materials, which can be expensive. Charging times are measured in hours and when an electric vehicle only has a range of ~100 miles, it makes the vehicle impractical for long distance travel. Because air-conditioning, lights, windshield wipers, defrosters, radio, etc. demand electricity, their use reduces the range of the vehicle. In fact the U.S. Electricar and Solectria electric vehicles come without air-conditioning and other power accessories. The lack of power accessories wouldn't make them very appealing to most people. To achieve the highest possible range, small aerodynamic vehicles constructed of ultra-light materials are necessary. Those factors reduce the carrying capacity and increase the cost of the vehicles.

In a recent discussion on the radio concerning fuel-cell and electric vehicles, a fellow stated that a vehicle with a lithium-ion battery pack could go 300 miles/charge and only take a few minutes to charge. When something sounds too good to be true, it's a safe bet that it is too good to be true. The Ford Motor Division in Europe recently developed an electric vehicle called the e-Ka that uses a lithium-ion battery pack. According to the specifications of the vehicle, it has a range of 93–125 miles and a recharging time of 6 hours. Those specifications are a long way from 300 miles/charge and a charging time of a few minutes. The e-Ka battery pack consists of 180 cells that weighs ~70 percent less than an equivalent lead-acid battery pack.[29] The e-Ka utilizes specialized light-weight materials to reduce the mass of the car and to maximize its range.

It's safe to say that electric vehicles will never have the capabilities of internal combustion engine vehicles and will probably always be relatively expensive.

To address some of the problems of purely electric vehicles, hybrid electric vehicles (HEV) have come onto the market in the last decade, lead by the Toyota Prius and Honda Insight. A HEV is a vehicle that contains a small internal combustion engine and an electric motor. The electric motor is used to propel the vehicle at low speeds while the internal combustion engine is used at higher speeds. The electric motor also assists the internal combustion engine when additional power is needed. HEVs use regenerative braking to assist in recharging the battery. Lightweight materials and an aerodynamic body shape are used to minimize energy losses.

The Honda Insight is the most efficient of the hybrid vehicles available. It has US EPA mileage ratings of 61 mpg for city driving and 68 mpg for highway driving with a range of 700 miles/tank of fuel.[30] The Toyota Prius has US EPA ratings of 52 mpg for city driving and 45 miles for highway driving with a range of ~570 miles/tank of fuel.[31] Real world gasoline mileage for hybrids is reported to be 10–20 percent lower than US EPA ratings.

Most Americans have little interest in small vehicles with limited capabilities such as HEVs. It would be difficult or impossible to haul a big load or pull a bass boat/large trailer with a HEV, reasons why Americans have large vehicles. HEVs still use gasoline or diesel fuel but use it more efficiently than most internal combustion engine vehicles on the market today. Assuming the price of oil rises significantly in the future, there may be more interest in HEVs in coming years.

High Efficiency Diesel Powered Vehicles

With all the excitement concerning hybrid vehicles, the American public may have the impression that hybrids are the most fuel-efficient vehicles available but that is not the case. The Volkswagen Lupo gets ~90 mpg and it's not a hybrid.[32] The Lupo is a small 4-passenger car that uses an ultra-clean burning diesel engine. It was introduced in Europe during the fall of 1998, but has not been sold in the U.S.

In the Lupo's engine, the fuel and air are directly injected into the cylinders, improving fuel efficiency and lowering emissions. Emissions are further lowered with a catalyst. The Lupo complies with all European Community auto-emission regulations.

The Lupo is a bare-bones vehicle. It has no power steering, power brakes and air conditioning. To reduce weight, it has a light-weight suspension and light-weight seats. It's not a vehicle that would probably be too popular in the U.S.

Diesel powered cars are expected to capture ~40 percent of the European auto market in 2003.[33] When oil prices get sufficiently high, there may be demand in the U.S. for high efficiency diesel powered cars. Europeans have an incentive to purchase fuel-efficient vehicles because taxes raise the price of fuel in Europe to $3–5/gallon. Even with such high fuel prices, a much lower per capita oil consumption level and an impressive mass transit system, Western Europe still consumes a lot of oil, ~15 mb/d.[34]

The Lure of Oil Shale

The U.S. has truly enormous amounts of a resource termed "oil shale." Oil shale is actually a promotional term used to lure investors into investing in oil shale projects with the expectation that they will reap huge financial returns. Oil shale is more properly termed "organic marlstone," which is a mixture of an organic substance called kerogen, as well as clay and calcium carbonate. The U.S. may have 5 trillion or more barrels of oil contained in oil shale, but up to now essentially none of those 5 trillion barrels have been produced in spite of extensive efforts.[35]

Oil shale was created in shallow marine embayments or in lakes, ponds and swamps where organic matter, mainly plants, collected over time. The organic material was ultimately converted to kerogen. Deposits can range from a few gallons of oil per ton of shale to as much as 100 gallons/ton, but the average is typically less than 40 gallons/ton.[36] In the U.S., there are large oil shale deposits in the Piceance Basin of western Colorado, the Uinta Basin of eastern Utah and the Green River Basin of southern Wyoming.

As early as the 14th century, oil shale in Austria and Switzerland was heated to produce rock oil. In the U.S., native Americans and pioneers used pieces of oil shale in campfires. Prior to Edwin Drake's oil discovery in western Pennsylvania, there were people converting oil shale into fuel oil in the Atlantic states.

The first attempt in the U.S. to demonstrate the feasibility of large-scale oil production from oil shale started in 1946 with a U.S. Bureau of Mines project at Anvil Points, Colorado. The project was an outgrowth of the Synthetic Liquid Fuels Act of 1944. Apparently what the project demonstrated was the difficulty in large-scale production of oil from oil shale in the western U.S.

Due to the oil crises during the 1970s, oil companies put forth a major effort to develop oil shale in the western U.S., with encouragement from the U.S. government. The major oil shale projects were,

1. Exxon Corporation's Colony Oil Shale Project
2. Occidental Oil Shale Corporation's Cathedral Bluffs and Logan, Washington oil shale projects
3. Unocal Corporation's Long Ridge Project
4. The White River Oil Shale Project involving Phillips Petroleum, Sohio and Sunoco.

The largest of the above projects was Exxon's Colony Project. Exxon Corporation planned to spend more than $5 billion over several decades to create huge strip mines and 150 extraction plants.[37] After about 2 years of work on the project, Exxon terminated the project on Sunday May 2, 1982, better known to people in Colorado as Black Sunday. By 1991, all of the shale oil projects had met ignominious deaths. The last project to die was Unocal Oil Company's Long Ridge Project. A $650 million shale oil plant still remains as a testament to the endeavor.[38]

There are several major problems with converting oil shale to oil. First, in the western U.S., the quality of the oil shale varies greatly within short vertical distances so that the average quality is relatively low. Layers of 50 gallons/ton can be located within a few feet of layers that are less than 5 gallons/ton.[39] That means that the oil shale can't be mined efficiently. Also, most of the oil shale is so deep that it has to be mined using underground methods, which are more expensive.

After extracting the oil shale, the shale has to be hauled to a processing plant where the shale is crushed and heated to ~900°F. The liquid obtained must be further processed to produce a low-grade oil. For making refined products such as gasoline, the oil must be hydrogenated. Essentially every step in the process of obtaining usable oil is energy intensive. The energy profit ratio for oil derived from shale appears at best to be only slightly greater than 1.[40]

The western U.S. is a region that has very little water. Processing of oil shale requires large quantities of water. Long distance importation of water into the region would probably be prohibitively expensive. There is also the problem of dealing with the waste shale. In processing, the shale expands creating a larger volume of waste than the original volume of oil shale. If large quantities of oil were produced from oil shale, it would create huge quantities of waste shale that would need to be put somewhere, and put there so it wouldn't create future problems.

Considering all the problems with oil shale, it's questionable whether large-scale production of oil will ever take place.

Ethanol as a Replacement for Oil

The idea of using ethanol as a replacement for imported oil seems to be popular in the U.S. In reality, without subsidies ethanol would never be used as a transportation fuel and that highlights some underlying problems with ethanol use as a fuel.

Government subsidies for ethanol production started in the late 1970s in response to the energy crises of the 1970s. Ethanol was promoted as a substitute for oil and for its environmental benefits. It currently receives 2 subsidies: a tax credit for companies that blend ethanol and an exemption from federal excise taxes at the gasoline pump.[41]

The beliefs that ethanol can largely replace oil and that its use has major environmental benefits are appealing, but according to a 1990 General Accounting Office report the benefits of ethanol use are minuscule at best. On reducing petroleum imports, the GAO states, "Ethanol tax incentives have not significantly enhanced U.S. energy security." Ethanol use as a fuel reduces U.S. gasoline consumption by less than 1 percent. In terms of the environmental benefits of ethanol, the GAO states, "Available evidence suggests that the ethanol program has little effect on the environment."[42] The GAO further concluded that increasing ethanol production would greatly increase tax subsidy expenditures for ethanol production.

Several energy profit ratio studies have been performed on ethanol production from corn, the most efficient source of ethanol in the U.S. According to David Pimentel, Cornell University, the energy costs of corn production and its conversion to ethanol requires 131,000 BTU to make 1 gallon of ethanol while that 1 gallon of ethanol has an energy content of 77,000 BTU.[43] That would make the energy profit ratio 0.59. According to Hosein Shapouri and James Duffield, U.S. Department of Agriculture, and Michael Wang, Center for Transportation Research of Argonne National Laboratory, ethanol from corn has an energy profit ratio of 1.34.[44] Whatever the actual value is, it is very low relative to oil.

According to Pimentel, the average U.S. motor vehicle traveling 10,000 miles a year would require about 852 gallons of pure ethanol. Assuming a net production of 50 gallons of ethanol/acre of corn, and that all personal motor vehicles in the U.S. were fueled with ethanol, a total of approximately 2 billion acres of cropland would be required to provide the corn feedstock. That is 5 times greater than all the cropland actually and potentially available in the U.S.[45]

Considering the low energy profit ratio and the large land area needed to produce corn for significant ethanol production, it appears unlikely that ethanol would ever be more than a minor source of transportation fuel in the U.S.

The Oil from Coal Solution

Germany was the pioneer in the conversion of coal to oil for the obvious reason that Germany was not endowed with significant domestic sources of conventional oil. In 1913, the German chemist Friedrich Bergius was the first person to successfully convert coal into oil by hydrogenating the coal at high temperature and pressure in the presence of a catalyst. The product was a high-grade liquid fuel that could be used for aviation purposes.

A second process, known as the Fischer-Tropsch Process, was developed in Germany in the 1920s. The process involves using steam to break down coal into hydrogen and carbon monoxide and then reacting the two together to form synthetic oil. The Bergius process was determined to be the better of the two methods because it created higher quality oil.

In 1927, the German chemical company I.G. Farben built a pilot plant using the Bergius process. As a sidenote, Friedrich Bergius and Carl Bosch, of I.G. Farben, shared the 1931 Nobel Prize for chemistry based upon their work in coal hydrogenation. By 1931, I.G. Farben was producing oil at a rate of 2,000 b/d, but the company was in deep financial trouble because development was proving to be more difficult and expensive than anticipated.

At the time, the price of 1 liter of synthetic fuel was about 10 times more expensive than the price of a gallon of gasoline produced in the U.S., or about 38 times at constant volume.[46] With the benefit of huge government subsidies, production continued. By the early 1930s, Adolf Hitler had taken over the leadership of Germany and was keenly aware of the importance of having a secure source of oil, especially for war.

On September 1, 1939, Germany invaded Poland to start World War II. Germany had 14 hydrogenation plants in full operation, with 6 more under construction. In 1940, synthetic fuel production had increased to 72,000 b/d, accounting for 46 percent of Germany's oil supply and 95 percent of the aviation fuel supply.[47]

By the middle of 1943, Germany had been defeated in Russia and North Africa. Several of the strategic targets Hitler wanted were the oil fields around Baku, by the Caspian Sea, and fields in the Middle East. Without oil from those sources, Germany had to rely heavily on synthetic fuel production.

The Germans worked furiously to increase synthetic fuel production during the war and by 1943, production had increased to 124,000 b/d. It was aided greatly by the use of slave and "free" labor. According to one estimate, by 1944 one-third of the total work force in the German synthetic fuel industry was slave labor.[48]

On May 12, 1944, the Allies started bombing Germany's synthetic fuel plants and that proved to be a decisive factor in the war. In May, synthetic fuel production averaged 92,000 b/d. By September, production had declined to 5,000 b/d.[49] This proved to be a fatal blow to the Luftwaffe because there was virtually no fuel to power planes for defending Germany or even to train pilots.

Synthetic fuel from coal has also been produced in South Africa by a government created company called Sasol. The objective of synthetic fuel production was to help reduce South Africa's dependence on imported oil. The first synthetic fuel plant, called Sasol 1, was built in 1956 but it no longer produces fuel. In the 1970s, a second synthetic fuel plant was built at Secunda. That facility uses the Fischer-Tropsch process to make hydrocarbons that range from gasoline to tar. In 1996, the Secunda facility underwent an upgrade and expansion that included the addition of a ninth synthetic fuel reactor. Sasol now has a production capacity of ~150,000 b/d.[50]

In early 2000, Sasol began a feasibility study for feedstock conversion from coal to natural gas. Based upon the study, Sasol will convert the feedstock at the Secunda facility to natural gas starting in 2004.[51]

Another government created company, PetroSA (formerly Mossgas), uses natural gas and condensate to produce petroleum products. PetroSA has a capacity of ~50,000 b/d.[52] Both Sasol and PetroSA are aided by significant government subsidies.

There doesn't appear to be any push to produce synthetic oil from coal in the U.S. Maybe the high level of government subsidies necessary makes it politically unfeasible.

An important aspect of coal liquefaction is the huge amounts of coal that would be necessary to produce a significant amount of liquid fuel. Based upon the Sasol experience, it takes about 3.5 units of coal energy to make one unit of oil energy.[53] If 10 mb/d of oil were made from coal, it would take nearly 3 billion tons of coal/year to produce the oil. That is about 3 times more than the amount of coal that is presently produced in the U.S. Conversion of coal to oil is an effective way to rapidly accelerate the depletion of coal.

Natural Gas and Propane Vehicles

Natural gas and propane vehicles are available in the U.S. There is nothing particularly noteworthy about the vehicles other than they have limited ranges relative to gasoline and diesel powered vehicles and that they have relatively large fuel tanks.

Considering the inability of natural gas producers in North America to increase production and the likelihood that the situation will get worse, it doesn't appear that natural gas and propane vehicles will have a significant impact on the motor vehicle market in the U.S. unless large quantities of imported LNG are used.

Conclusion

It's reasonable to expect that all of the alternatives to conventional oil discussed above will be tried when a future oil crisis occurs. None of the alternatives will be as appealing as conventional oil for either economic and/or practical reasons.

Assuming hybrid and high efficiency diesel vehicles are used more extensively in the future, an ever-increasing number of vehicles would largely counteract their higher fuel mileage in terms of reducing oil demand, both in the U.S. and globally. That is assuming that an increasing number of people would be able to afford vehicles and fuel in the future.

11

Conclusions

One objective of writing this book is to provide the best available oil production data at the field, national, regional and global levels. It is hoped that the data provide a strong basis for believing that global oil production will peak in ~2010. There should be further growth in natural gas and natural gas liquids production after the oil production peak. That should ameliorate the problems associated with declining oil production for a short time. If the prediction by Colin Campbell and Jean Laherrere is in the ballpark, global natural gas production will peak around 2020. The decline of global natural gas production would aggravate the problems associated with declining oil production. It's reasonable to expect serious consequences due to the decline of global oil and gas production. Below are some possible problems that may be encountered in the future.

First, military conflicts over remaining conventional oil resources are possible. The most obvious possible conflict would involve the U.S. and China. The U.S. imports ~11 mb/d of TLHs and imports are expected to grow significantly in the future. Because oil production is declining in an increasing number of countries, the U.S. will have to rely more heavily on Middle East oil in the future. China is industrializing at breakneck speed and oil demand is increasing rapidly. By 2010, China will likely be importing well over half of its TLHs consumption, most of it coming from the Middle East. As both the U.S. and China rely more heavily on Middle East oil, military conflict is possible as the limits of the oil resources in the region become evident. Conflicts over oil between other nations are also possible.

As oil resources become tighter, prices will rise. We are now experiencing early signs of oil resource problems as the average oil price in 2003 was \$27.54/barrel and in the first 8 months of 2004 it was \$40.56/barrel. Even with elevated oil prices, supplies are still tight. As the price of oil increases, it's reasonable to expect that the impact will be felt most heavily by people in poor and developing countries, people who can't easily afford paying higher prices. Gradually people in those countries will be squeezed out of the market, to the detriment of their increasing expectations.

In wealthy countries, people can absorb higher prices up to a point. In the U.S., there have been complaints in the last few years over higher gasoline and heating fuel prices, but most people can handle the increased costs. In time, price increases will seriously impact the majority of Americans. During the oil crises of the 1970s, shootings occurred in gas lines as tempers flared. Any cutoff of oil supplies or dramatic increase in prices could result in a repeat of such behavior.

Assuming that the price of oil increases significantly in coming years, there will be a concerted effort to produce the world's remaining conventional oil as rapidly as possible. In the early 1980s, the price of oil increased to ~$35/barrel from ~$3/barrel in the early 1970s. Due to the price increase, the number of drilling rigs in the U.S. increased dramatically, but oil production in the lower 48 states barely increased. The same situation is likely to occur globally in coming years and the economic impacts could be severe. Back in the late 1970s and early 1980s, there were undeveloped conventional sources of oil globally that could be brought on-line, ultimately leading to higher production and a decline in the price of oil. There will be few undeveloped sources of conventional oil globally after ~2010.

Economists argue that declining conventional oil production will stimulate the production of unconventional oil resources, and that is true. There is further latitude to increase oil production from the Orinoco Oil Belt and Athabasca Oil Sands, but production from those sources can only be increased slowly relative to conventional oil. Most of the world's oil shale may never prove to be economically or practically viable. As well as the slow production rate increases from unconventional oil resources, the maximum possible production levels and low energy profit ratios are problems.

The alternatives to conventional oil discussed in Chapter 10 will be tried, but probably with limited success. The advantages of oil for transportation and heavy equipment use are substantial. There are no alternatives on the horizon that come close to the advantages of oil.

Increasing efforts at conservation and energy efficiency will occur as oil supplies tighten. In the U.S., urban sprawl has made much of the population dependent on motor vehicles. Americans will buy more fuel efficient vehicles in the future when oil prices get high enough, but it would not be easy to restructure urban areas so that people wouldn't need to rely on motor vehicles. U.S. motor vehicle manufacturers are dependent upon large fuel inefficient vehicles such as SUV's and light trucks to make profits.

Those manufacturers could develop serious financial problems if higher oil prices lead a large part of the population now buying SUV's and light trucks to buy higher efficiency motor vehicles. Manufacturer's problems would be more serious if a significant portion of the population couldn't afford motor vehicles due to high oil prices.

Although the U.S. population is quite wealthy relative to much of the world, it is ill prepared for large oil price increases. The U.S. economy is heavily dependent on cheap oil and many industries depend upon it: construction, agriculture, logging, air transportation, trucking, motor vehicle manufacturing, etc. Those industries could experience serious financial problems if the price of oil rises dramatically. The home building boom in the U.S. is predicated on the belief that cheap oil will last forever. Modern industrial agriculture has been termed a process of converting oil into food. Dramatically higher oil prices would greatly increase food prices over what they are today.

If terrorist attacks target oil pipelines and refineries in the Middle East causing a sudden cut-off of oil supply from that region, it could have a devastating impact upon the world economy. The impact would be even more serious in the future as the world relies more heavily on the Middle East for its oil supply.

Appendix A

Production Graphs for U.S. States

Appendix A contains production graphs for U.S. states that have produced at least 10 million barrels of oil. Data through 1998 for all states except Alaska are from the American Petroleum Institute (API). Data after 1998 are from the U.S. DOE/EIA except for Texas, Louisiana and California. Production data after 1998 for Louisiana and California are from *Oil & Gas Journal* because the journal includes oil production from federal offshore waters adjacent to those states, while U.S. DOE/EIA data do not. Production data for Texas after 1998 are from the Railroad Commission of Texas. Alaskan data are from the Alaska Department of Revenue. Production data are in barrels/day, b/d, or million barrels/day, mb/d.

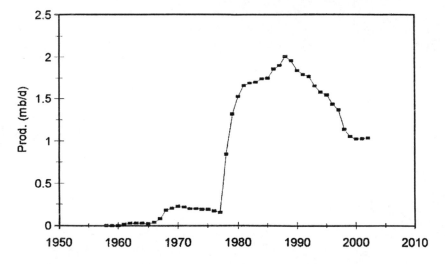

Alaska oil production Maximum production — 2.02 mb/d in 1988; Year 2002 production — 1.03 mb/d.

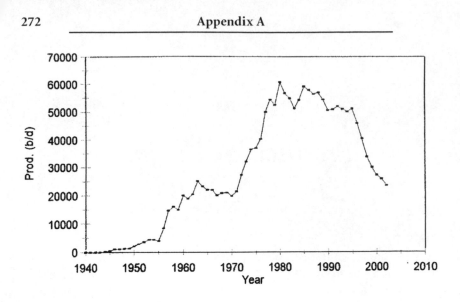

Alabama oil production; Maximum production — 60,693 b/d in 1980; Year 2002 production — 23,647 b/d.

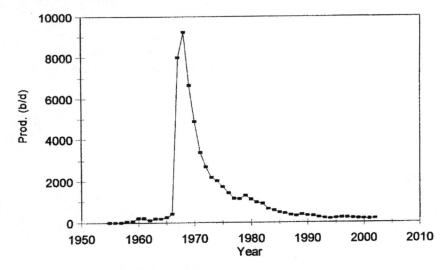

Arizona oil production; Maximum production — 9,233 b/d in 1968; Year 2002 production — 173 b/d.

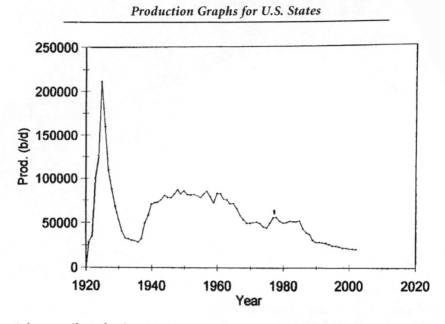

Arkansas oil production; Maximum production — 212,049 b/d; Year 2002 production — 20,121 b/d.

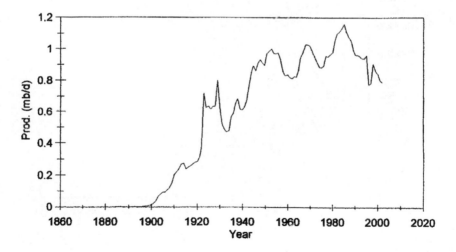

California oil production; Maximum production —1.16 mb/d in 1985; Year 2002 production —0.788 mb/d.

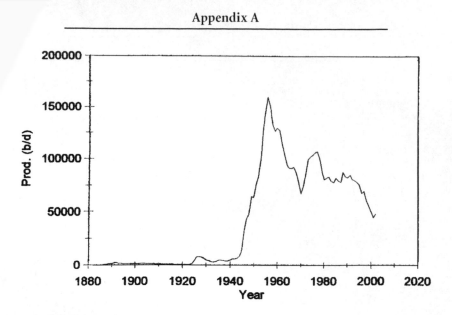

Colorado oil production; Maximum production — 160,318 b/d in 1956; Year 2002 production — 48,586 b/d.

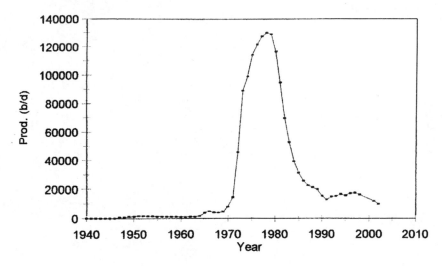

Florida oil production; Maximum production — 130,236 b/d in 1978; Year 2002 production — 10,016 b/d.

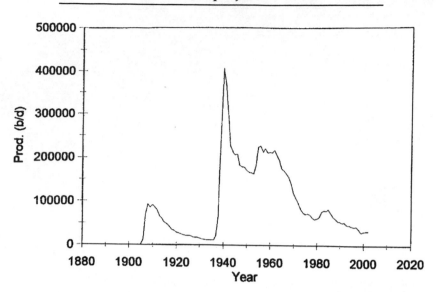

Illinois oil production; Maximum production — 404,512 b/d in 1940; Year 2002 production — 33,016 b/d.

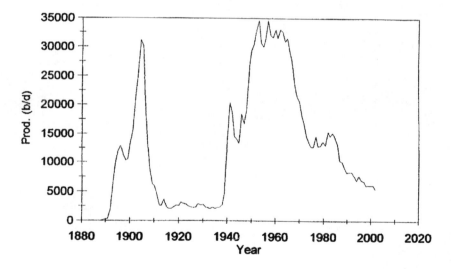

Indiana oil production; Maximum production — 404,512 b/d in 1940; Year 2002 production — 33,016 b/d.

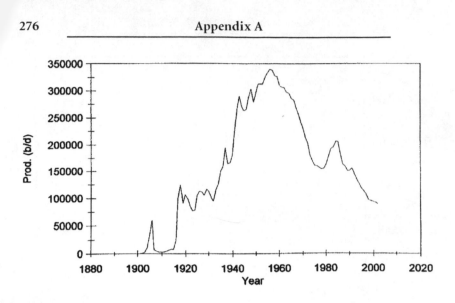

Kansas oil production; Maximum production — 340,285 b/d in 1956; Year 2002 production — 89,647 b/d.

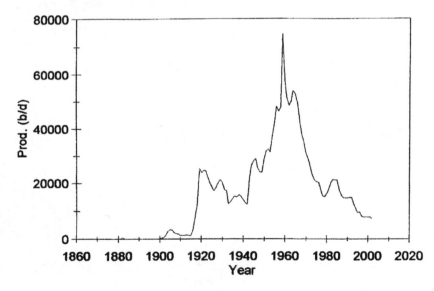

Kentucky oil production; Maximum production — 74,718 b/d in 1959; Year 2002 production — 7,340 b/d.

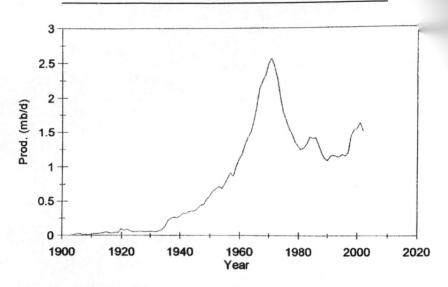

Louisiana oil production; Maximum production — 2.56 mb/d in 1971; Year 2002 production — 1.50 mb/d.

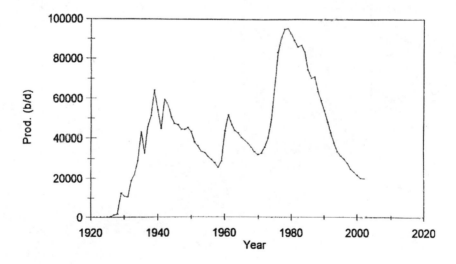

Michigan oil production; Maximum production — 95,512 b/d in 1979; Year 2002 production — 19,778 b/d.

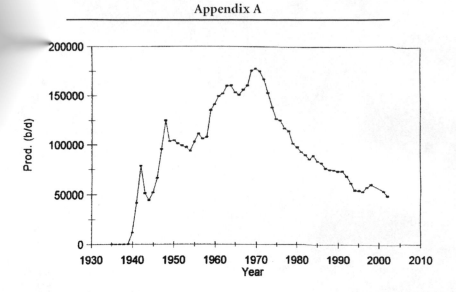

Mississippi oil production; Maximum production — 174,408 b/d in 1970; Year 2002 production — 49,356 b/d.

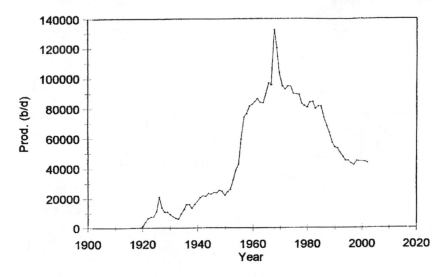

Montana oil production; Maximum production — 132,767 b/d in 1968; Year 2002 production — 46,178 b/d.

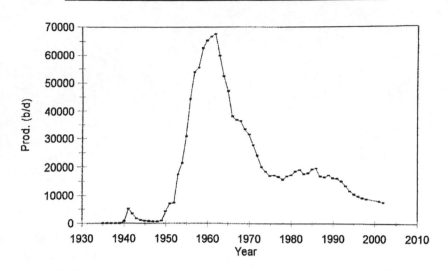

Nebraska oil production; Maximum production — 67,655 b/d in 1962; Year 2002 production — 7,614 b/d.

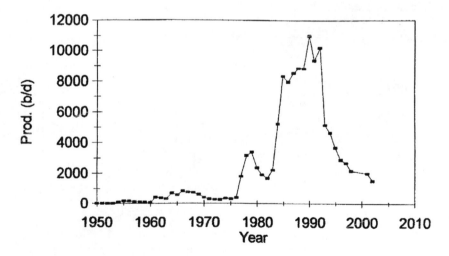

Nevada oil production; Maximum production —10,992 b/d in 1990; Year 2002 production —1,515 b/d.

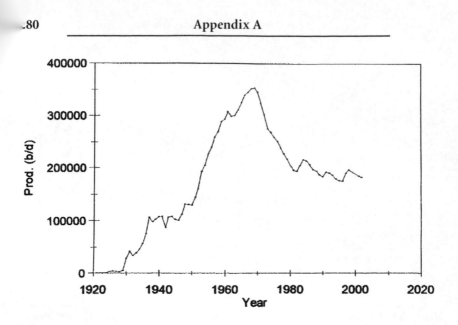

New Mexico oil production; Maximum production — 354,047 b/d in 1969; Year 2002 production — 183,674 b/d.

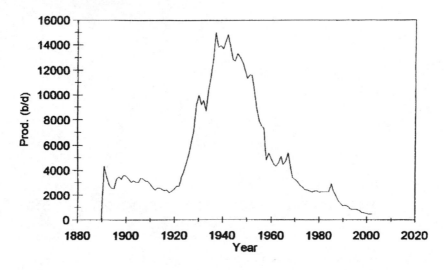

New York oil production; Maximum production — 15,008 b/d in 1937; Year 2002 production — 452 b/d.

Production Graphs for U.S. States

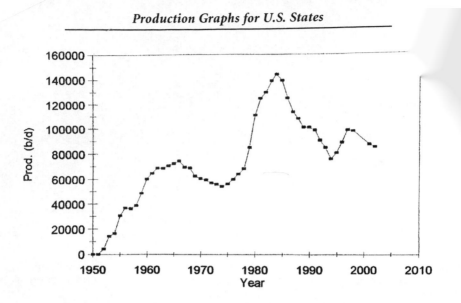

North Dakota oil production; Maximum production — 144,252 b/d in 1984; Year 2002 production — 84,912 b/d.

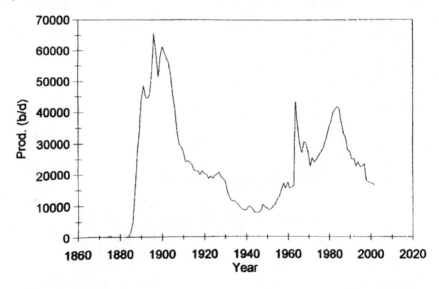

Ohio oil production; Maximum production — 65,592 b/d in 1896; Year 2002 production — 16,449 b/d.

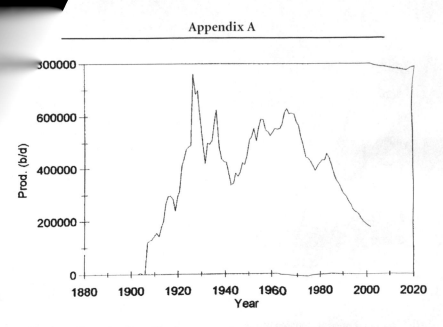

Oklahoma oil production; Maximum production — 761,027 b/d in 1927; Year 2002 production — 182,581 b/d.

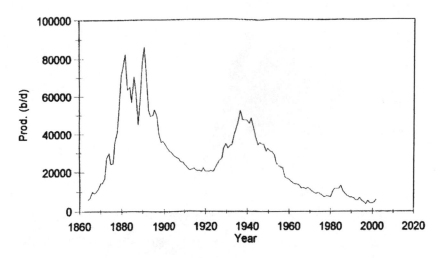

Pennsylvania oil production; Maximum production — 86,093 b/d in 1891; Year 2002 production — 6,118 b/d.

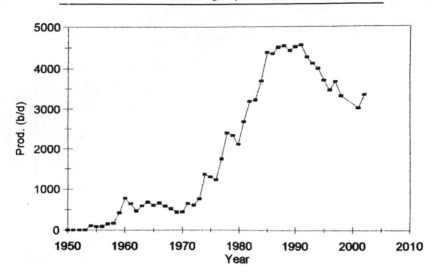

South Dakota oil production; Maximum production — 4,556 b/d in 1991; Year 2002 production — 3,326 b/d.

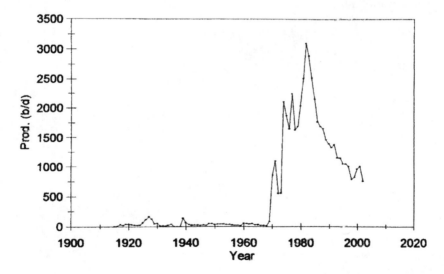

Tennessee oil production; Maximum production — 3,101 b/d in 1982; Year 2002 production — 753 b/d.

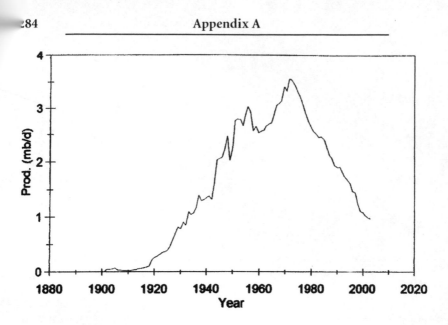

Texas oil production; Maximum production — 3.57 mb/d in 1972; Year 2003 production — 0.985 mb/d.

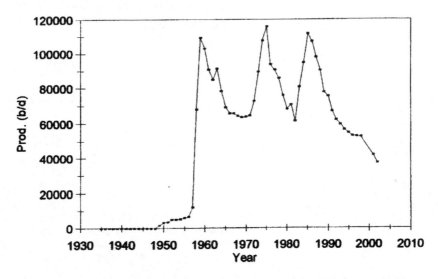

Utah oil production; Maximum production — 115,893 b/d in 1975; Year 2002 production — 37,468 b/d.

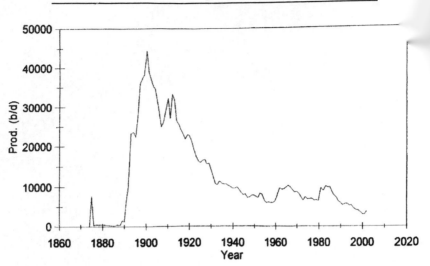

West Virginia oil production; Maximum production — 44,373 b/d in 1900; Year 2002 production — 3,786 b/d.

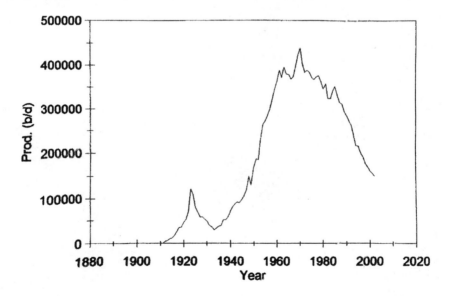

Wyoming oil production; Maximum production — 439,301 b/d in 1970; Year 2002 production — 149,910 b/d.

Appendix B

Production Data for U.S. States

Appendix B contains cumulative production data for U.S. states that have produced at least 10 million barrels of oil. Data are through 2001 and are given in Gigabarrels, Gb. Cumulative U.S. production at the end of 2001 from the states below was 183.43 Gb. Production from federal offshore waters is included in cumulative production data for adjacent states. Oil production/well is also given for 2001 for each state.

State	Cumulative Production (Gb)	Production per Well in 2001
Alaska	14.32	492.22
Alabama	0.64	31.11
Arizona	0.02	6.56
Arkansas	1.77	2.88
California	26.10	18.57
Colorado	1.87	7.08
Florida	0.59	170.79
Illinois	3.56	1.46
Indiana	0.55	1.12
Kansas	6.08	2.16
Kentucky	0.77	0.28
Louisiana	28.49	52.82
Michigan	1.23	5.75
Mississippi	2.29	35.98
Montana	1.50	14.07
Nebraska	0.49	6.82
Nevada	0.05	23.34
New Mexico	5.14	10.55
New York	0.21	0.12
North Dakota	1.40	26.39
Ohio	1.09	0.57
Oklahoma	14.47	2.23
Pennsylvania	1.37	0.28
South Dakota	0.04	21.76
Tennessee	0.02	1.63
Texas	60.81	8.68
Utah	1.24	21.59
West Virginia	0.58	2.76
Wyoming	6.74	15.89

Notes

Introduction

1. In the Dec. 22, 2003 issue of *Oil & Gas Journal,* global oil reserves are reported to be 1266 Gb, as of Jan. 1, 2003.

2. US DOE/EIA oil production data for Louisiana can be found at http://www.eia.doe .gov/oil_gas/petroleum/info_glance/crudeoil. html

3. *Oil & Gas Journal* data is from the Dec. 22, 2003 issue.

4. International Petroleum Production Data, US DOE/EIA, http://www.eia.doe.gov/ emeu/international/petroleu.html#IntlProduction.

5. "Global oil, gas fields, sizes tallied, analyzed," L.F. Ivanhoe and G G. Leckie, *Oil and Gas Journal,* Feb. 15, 1993, pp. 87–91.

6. "The World's Giant Oilfields," Simmons & Company International, 2001.

7. Country Assessment — Saudi Arabia, The Association for the Study of Peak Oil, Newsletter No. 21, September 2002, http:/ /www.asponews.org/ASPO.newsletter.021.php #99.

8. List of Oil Fields, Wikipedia — The Free Encyclopedia, http://en.wikipedia.org/wiki/ List_of_oil_fields.

9. Beyond Oil: The Threat of Food and Fuel in the Coming Decades, J. Gever; R.K. Kaufmann; D. Skole and C. Vorosmarty, 1991.

10. Geodestinies, Walter Youngquist, 1997.

11. Data from the US DOE/EIA, http:// www.eia.doe.gov/.

12. *Ibid.*

13. *Ibid.*

14 .Annual Energy Outlook 2003, US DOE/EIA, http://www.eia.doe.gov/oiaf/forecasting.html.

15. International Energy Outlook 2003, US DOE/EIA, http://www.eia.doe.gov/oiaf/forecasting.html.

16. *Ibid.*

17. Data from the US DOE/EIA, http:// www.eia.doe.gov/.

18. *Ibid.*

19. Country Analysis Brief — Caspian Sea, US DOE/EIA, 2001.

20. "Nuclear Energy and the Fossil Fuels," M.K. Hubbert, Presented at the spring meeting of the Southern District Division of Production, American Petroleum Institute, March 1956.

21. "The World's Evolving Energy System," M.K. Hubbert, *American Journal of Physics,* 49 (1981).

22. The 1990–2003 data are from Jean Laherrere.

23. World Petroleum Assessment 2000, United States Geological Survey, http://pubs. usgs.gov/dds/dds-060/.

24. International Energy Outlook 2001, US DOE/EIA, http://www.eia.doe.gov/oiaf/forecasting.html.

25. International Energy Outlook 2003, US DOE/EIA, http://www.eia.doe.gov/oiaf/forecasting.html.

26. International Energy Outlook 2001, US DOE/EIA, http://www.eia.doe.gov/oiaf/forecasting.html.

27. Data from the US DOE/EIA, http:// www.eia.doe.gov/.

28. International Energy Outlook 2003, US DOE/EIA, http://www.eia.doe.gov/oiaf/forecasting.html.

Chapter 1

1. Based upon production data from the American Petroleum Institute.

2. Based upon oil production data from the American Petroleum Institute and US DOE/EIA data for U.S. states, http://www.eia.

287

doe.gov/oil_gas/petroleum/info_glance/crude oil.html.

3. See note 1.

4. *Ibid.*

5. Oil production data for U.S. states, http://www.eia.doe.gov/oil_gas/petroleum/info_glance/crudeoil.html.

6. Daniel Yergin, *The Prize: The Epic Quest of Oil, Money, and Power*, 1991.

7. *Ibid.*

8. The Railroad Commission of Texas, http://www.rrc.state.tx.us/divisions/og/information-data/oginfo.html.

9. See note 1.

10. See note 8.

11. See note 1.

12. See note 5.

13. See note 1.

14. Based upon data from *Oil & Gas Journal*, 2nd December issues, 1971–2003.

15. International Petroleum Production Information, US DOE/EIA, http://www.eia.doe.gov/emeu/international/petroleu.html#ProductionQ.

16. See note 1.

17. See note 5.

18. See note 1.

19. See note 5.

20. See note 15.

21. Minerals Management Service, http://www.gomr.mms.gov/homepg/offshore/deepwatr/summary.asp.

22. M.K. Hubbert, "Nuclear Energy and the Fossil Fuels," presented at the spring meeting of the Southern District Division of Production, American Petroleum Institute, March 1956.

23. M.K. Hubbert, "The World's Evolving Energy System," *American Journal of Physics*, 49 (1981).

24. 1961 U.S. Oil & Gas Assessment, USGS, 1961.

25. U.S. Oil & Gas Assessments through the 1960s, USGS, 1962–1969.

26. Data obtained from personal correspondence with the Minerals Management Service.

27. See note 17.

28. See note 5.

29. See note 26.

30. See note 5.

31. Minerals Management Service, http://www.gomr.mms.gov/homepg/offshore/deepwtr.html.

32. Outer Continental Shelf Petroleum Assessment, 2000, Minerals Management Service, 2000, http://www.gomr.mms.gov/homepg/offshore/deepwatr/summary.asp.

33. Based upon personal correspondence.

34. See note 31.

35. Annual Energy Outlook 2003, US DOE/EIA, 2003, http://www.eia.doe.gov/oiaf/aeo/index.html.

36. Oil Market Report, International Energy Agency, July 2003, http://omrpublic.iea.org/.

37. Alaska Department of Revenue, http://www.tax.state.ak.us/programs/oil/production/index.asp.

38. Alaska Department of Natural Resources, http://www.dog.dnr.state.ak.us/oil/.

39. See note 37.

40. *Ibid.*

41. *Ibid.*

42. *Ibid.*

43. *Ibid.*

44. *Ibid.*

45. See note 35.

46. See note 38.

47. See note 6.

48. Based upon the 1995 National Assessment of United States Oil and Gas Resources, United States Geological Survey, 1995, http://www.usgs.gov/.

49. Arctic National Wildlife Refuge, 1002 Area, Petroleum Assessment, 1998, Including Economic Analysis, United States Geological Survey, 1998, http://www.usgs.gov/.

50. Potential Oil Production from the Coastal Plain of the Arctic National Wildlife Refuge: Updated Assessment, May 2000, U.S. DOE/EIA, http://www.eia.doe.gov/.

51. See note 35.

52. Future Oil Production for the Alaska North Slope, May 2001, U.S. DOE/EIA, http://www.eia.doe.gov/.

53. See note 15.

54. See note 32.

55. Minerals Management Service, http://www.mms.gov/.

56. International Petroleum Consumption Information, US DOE/EIA, http://www.eia.doe.gov/emeu/international/petroleu.html#ConsumptionQ.

57. *Ibid.*

58. *Ibid.*

59. See note 35.

Chapter 2

1. International Petroleum Production Data, Energy Information Administration, U.S. Department of Energy, http://www.eia.doe.gov/emeu/international/contents.html.

2. *Oil & Gas Journal*, last December issues from 1976–2001.

3. *Ibid.*

4. See note 1.

5. C.D. Masters, E.D. Attanasi, and D.H. Root, "World Petroleum Assessment and Analysis," U.S. Geological Survey, 14th World Petroleum Congress, 1994.

6. International Energy Outlook 2003, Energy Information Administration, U.S. Department of Energy, http://www.eia.doe.gov/oiaf/ieo/index.html.

7. International Energy Outlook 2001, Energy Information Administration, U.S. Department of Energy.

8. See note 2.

9. Norwegian Petroleum Directorate Annual Report, 2002, http://www.npd.no/English/Frontpage.htm.

10. Based upon projected production by Saga Petroleum in the late 1990s. Saga Petroleum is no longer in existence.

11. See note 1.

12. Norwegian Petroleum Directorate, http://www.npd.no/engelsk/cwi/pbl/en/index.htm.

13. *Ibid.*

14. See note 1.

15. See note 6.

16. *Ibid.*

17. See note 1.

18. Danish Energy Authority, 2003, http://www.ens.dk/sw479.asp.

19. *Ibid.*

20. Original Data, Association for the Study of Peak Oil, http://www.asponews.org/.

21. See note 18.

22. Countries include Austria, Belgium, Bosnia and Herzegovina, Croatia, Faroe Islands, Finland, Former Yugoslavia, France, Germany, Gibraltar, Greece, Iceland, Ireland, Italy, Luxembourg, Macedonia, Malta, Netherlands, Portugal, Slovenia, Spain, Sweden, Switzerland and Turkey.

23. See note 1.

24. *Ibid.*

25. *Ibid.*

Chapter 3

1. International Petroleum Production Information, US DOE/EIA, http://www.eia.doe.gov/emeu/international/contents.html.

2. Daniel Yergin, *The Prize: The Epic Quest of Oil, Money, and Power*, 1991.

3. *Ibid.*

4. *Ibid.*

5. *Ibid.*

6. See note 1.

7. Worldwide Production, *Oil & Gas Journal*, Dec. 22, 2003.

8. "A Primer on Oil & Gas in Mexico," Simmons & Company International, 2003.

9. *Ibid.*

10. Worldwide Production, *Oil & Gas Journal*, last December issue from 1971–2003.

11. See note 7.

12. "Politics Cloud Mexico's Promises," Oct. 2004, http://www.aapg.org/explorer/2004/10oct/mexico.cfm.

13. Alaska Department of Revenue, http://www.tax.state.ak.us/programs/oil/production/index.asp.

14. Norwegian Petroleum Directorate, http://www.npd.no/engelsk/cwi/pbl/en/index.htm.

15. See note 8.

16. See note 10.

17. See note 8.

18. Based upon personal correspondence.

19. See note 10.

20. *Ibid.*

21. *Ibid.*

22. *Ibid.*

23. See note 8.

24. Country Analysis Brief—Mexico, Feb. 2003, US DOE/EIA, http://www.eia.doe.gov/emeu/cabs/mexico.html.

25. David Shields, "Pemex Sets Sights on New Offshore Oil Projects," *The News Columnist*, August 28, 2002.

26. See note 8.

27. *Ibid.*

28. International Energy Outlook 2003, US DOE/EIA, http://www.eia.doe.gov/oiaf/ieo/index.html.

29. World Petroleum Assessment 2000, United States Geological Survey, http://pubs.usgs.gov/dds/dds-060/.

30. Original Data, Association for the Study of Peak Oil, http://www.asponews.org/.

31. See note 10.

32. Duncan's forecasts are at http://dieoff.org/42Countries/42Countries.htm.

33. See note 1.

34. See note 30.

35. See note 1.

36. In April 1999, as a result of the largest Aboriginal land claim settlement in Canadian history, legislation was passed renaming the easternmost 1.9 million square kilometer area of the Northwest Territories of Canada the territory of Nunavut.

37. See note 10.

38. "Alberta Oilsands Produce 25% More Than Conventional Oil Reserves," *Alexander's Gas & Oil Connections*, Vol. 8, issue #3, June 26, 2003.

39. Scott Haggert, "Oh, How the Patch Has Changed: Technology, Finances Revamp Landscape," *Calgary Herald*, 8/2/2003.

40. See note 10.

41. *Ibid.*

Ibid.

. Country Analysis Brief — Canada, Jan.
4, US DOE/EIA, http://www.eia.doe.gov/
eu/cabs/canada.html.

44. See note 29.

45. The Newfoundland & Labrador Statistics Agency, http://www.economics.gov.nf.ca
/indOIL.asp.

46. About Hibernia, http://www.hibernia.ca
/html/about_hibernia/index.html.

47. See note 45.

48. See note 43.

49. See note 45.

50. See note 43.

51. What is Terra Nova?, http://www.terranovaproject.com/html/what_is_terra_nova/
field_profile.html.

52. See note 43.

53. See note 45.

54. See note 43.

55. See note 10.

56. Alberta Energy and Utilities Board,
http://www.eub.gov.ab.ca.

57. See note 43.

58. Gal Luft, "Can Canadian Sands Replace
Arabia's?" http://www.energypulse.net/centers/article/article_display.cfm?a_id=421, July
31, 03.

59. L.F. Ivanhoe, "Canada's Future Oil Production: Projection 2000–2020," *Hubbert Center Newsletter*, 2002/2.

60. See note 7.

61. Walter Youngquist, *Geodestinies*, 1997.

62. See note 59.

63. US DOE/EIA, http://www.eia.doe.gov/
oil_gas/natural_gas/info_glance/natural_gas.
html.

64. Patrick Brethour, "Alberta Mulls Nuclear Plants to Power Oil Sands Extraction,"
Toronto Globe and Mail, Jan. 29, 2003.

65. James Stevenson, "Bitumen Recovery
at Risk in Northern Alberta: Conoco," James
Stevenson, *The Canadian Press*, August 2,
2003.

66. *Ibid.*

67. *Ibid.*

68. Patrick Brethour, "Soaring Costs
Plague Oil Sands," *The Toronto Globe and Mail*, May 20, 2003.

69. Patrick Brethour, "Syncrude Trust Battered as Investors Dump Stock," *The Toronto Globe and Mail*, March 6, 2004.

70. See note 43.

71. L.F. Ivanhoe, "The Petroleum Positions
of Canada and Mexico," *Hubbert Center Newsletter*, 1998/1.

72. See note 1.

73. See note 10.

74. *Ibid.*

75. See note 28.

76. See note 10.

77. See note 32.

78. See note 30.

79. See note 10.

80. See note 30.

Chapter 4

1. International Petroleum Production Information, US DOE/EIA, http://www.eia.doe.
gov/emeu/international/petroleu.html#Intl-Production.

2. *Ibid.*

3. *Ibid.*

4. "Petroleum Positions of Brazil and
Venezuela,," L.F. Ivanhoe, M.K. Hubbert Center, http://hubbert.mines.edu/news/Ivanhoe_
93–3.pdf.

5. *Ibid.*

6. See note 1.

7. See note 7.

8. See note 1http://www.eia.doe.gov/emeu
/international/petroleu.html — IntlProduction.

9. Country Analysis Brief-Venezuela, US
DOE/EIA, http://www.eia.doe.gov/emeu/cabs
/venez.html.

10. "PDVSA to Outsource Maintenance
Contracts," *Alexander's Gas & Oil Connections*,
vol. 8, issue #14, July 10, 2003.

11. *Ibid.*

12. "Higher Water Cuts Seen in Venezuela
Maracaibo Oil," Matthew Robinson, Reuters
News Service, July 2003.

13. See note 10.

14. *Ibid.*

15. "PDVSA to Invest up to US$45 Billion
through 2010," BNAmericas, July 21, 2003.

16. *Ibid.*

17. *Ibid.*

18. Oil Market Report, International Energy
Agency, July 2003, http://omrpublic.iea.org/.

19. See note 9.

20. *Ibid.*

21. International Energy Outlook 2003, US
DOE/EIA, http://www.eia.doe.gov/oiaf/ieo/
index.html.

22. See note 1.

23. http://dieoff.org/42Countries/42Countries.htm.

24. Original Data, Association for the
Study of Peak Oil, http://www.asponews.org/.

25. See note 7.

26. Petrobras, http://www2.petrobras.com
.br/ingles/index.asp.

27. Country Assessment Series-Brazil, Association for the Study of Peak Oil, Newsletter #26, Feb. 2003.

28. See note 26.

29. *Ibid.*

30. Production data for the Marlim field were obtained from Jean Laherrere.

31. See note 1.

32. World Petroleum Assessment 2000, United States Geological Survey, http://pubs.usgs.gov/dds/dds-060/.

33. "Wood Mackenzie Believes Deepwater Brazil Stands at the Crossroads," http://www.woodmac.com/news_e_30.htm.

34. See note 21.

35. Country Analysis Brief-Brazil, US DOE/EIA, http://www.eia.doe.gov/emeu/cabs/brazil.html.

36. *Ibid.*

37. See note 23.

38. See note 24.

39. See note 7.

40. *Ibid.*

41. See note 1.

42. http://www.oogc.com/world_oper/latin_america/over_colo.htm.

43. See note 7.

44. http://www.theworld.com/~habib/the-garden//uwa/uwarep.doc.

45. See note 7.

46. *Ibid.*

47. See note 1.

48. See note 18.

49. See note 21.

50. International Energy Outlook 2001, US DOE/EIA.

51. "Dangerous Colombia Fails to Lure Oil Explorers," Reuters News Service, July 24, 2003.

52. Country Analysis Brief-Colombia, US DOE/EIA, http://www.eia.doe.gov/emeu/cabs/colombia.html.

53. *Ibid.*

54. See note 23.

55. See note 1.

56. See note 24.

57. See note 7.

58. See note 24.

59. See note 1.

60. Country Assessment Series-Argentina, Association for the Study of Peak Oil, Newsletter #33, September 2003, http://www.asponews.org/ASPO.newsletter.033.php#243.

61. See note 21.

62. See note 1.

63. See note 18.

64. Platts Global Energy, http://www.platts/features/LatinAmericancrude/argentina.shtml.

65. See note 23.

66. See note 1.

67. See note 24.

68. See note 7.

69. *Ibid.*

70. Country Analysis-Ecuador, *Alexander. Gas & Oil Connections*, vol. 8, issue #4, February 20, 2003, http://www.gasandoil.com/goc/news/ntl30864.htm.

71. Country Analysis Brief-Ecuador, US DOE/EIA, http://www.eia.doe.gov/emeu/cabs/ecuador.html.

72. See note 1.

73. See note 21.

74. "Gutierrez: Output Not Enough to Fill OCP," BNAmericas, July 9, 2003.

75. *Ibid.*

76. See note 71.

77. See note 74.

78. See note 1.

79. See note 18.

80. See note 71.

81. See note 32.

82. See note 23.

83. See note 24.

84. See note 7.

85. See note 1.http://www.eia.doe.gov/emeu/international/petroleu.html — IntlProduction.

86. See note 32.

87. "Falkland Islands: the last frontier," *Alexander's Gas & Oil Connections*, vol. 3, issue #11, 3/4/1998, http://www.gasandoil.com/goc/news/ntl81460.htm.

88. See note 32.

89. See note 1.

90. See note 21.

91. See note 23.

92. See note 24.

Chapter 5

1. International Petroleum Production Information, US DOE/EIA, http://www.eia.doe.gov/emeu/international/petroleu.html#ProductionA.

2. *Ibid.*

3. See note 3.

4. International Petroleum Consumption Information, US DOE/EIA, http://www.eia.doe.gov/emeu/international/petroleu.html#IntlConsumption.

5. "Oil and Australia," Brian Fleay, Hubbert Center Newsletter, 2000/3, http://hubbert.mines.edu/.

6. "Country Assessment-Australia," ASPO Newsletter, Association for the Study of Peak Oil, #28, 4/2003, http://www.asponews.org/ASPO.newsletter.028.php#174.

7. See note 3.

8. "Australian Oil and Gas," http://www.istp.murdoch.edu.au/publications/projects/oilfleay/06australian.html.

9. Northern Territory Oil & Gas Fact Sheet, http://www.dme.nt.gov.au/dmemain/energy/facts_figures/Fact_Sheets/laminaria.html.

10. See note 1.

11. See note 3.

12. "Woodside's Laminaria Oil field Development Starts On Time," On-Line Pravda, 6/13/02, http://english.pravda.ru/comp/2002/06/13/30245.html.

13. See note 1.

14. International Energy Outlook 2003, US DOE/EIA, http://www.eia.doe.gov/oiaf/ieo/index.html.

15. See note 1.

16. http://dieoff.org/42Countries/42Countries.htm.

17. See note 1.

18. Original Data, Association for the Study of Peak Oil, http://www.asponews.org/.

19. See note 3.

20. Welcome to PetroChina, http://www.petrochina.com.cn/english/gsjs/zyyw_1_5_1.htm.

21. "Daqing oil field reports on crude output," Alexander's Gas & Oil Connections, vol. 8, issue 16, 8/21/2003.

22. See note 3.

23. Ibid.

24. See note 21.

25. See note 3.

26. China's Petroleum Industry, http://www.vitrade.com/china/chinanews_brieing_oil_industry.htm.

27. See note 20.

28. See note 3.

29. Ibid.

30. Ibid.

31. See note 20.

32. See note 3.

33. See note 26.

34. Country Analysis Brief-China, US DOE/EIA, http://www.eia.doe.gov/emeu/cabs/china.html.

35. See note 3.

36. World Petroleum Assessment 2000, United States Geological Survey, http://pubs.usgs.gov/dds/dds-060/.

37. "China's Tarim Basin: Gushing with Oil or Just Hype?," Reuter's, 12/09/03.

38. Ibid.

39. Ibid.

40. See note 3.

41. See note 34.

42. See note 1.

43. Oil Market Report, International Energy Agency, 1/2004, http://omrpublic.iea.org/.

44. See note 14.

45. See note 16.

46. See note 18.

47. See note 3.

48. See note 1.

49. See note 4.

50. See note 14.

51. "China becomes world-class oil buyer," Alexander's Gas & Oil Connections, vol. 8, issue 16, 8,21,2003.

52. See note 3.

53. See note 1.

54. See note 3.

55. Ibid.

56. Ibid.

57. http://www.projectsmonitor.com/detailnews.asp?newsid=2930.

58. See note 3.

59. Ibid.

60. "India can triple oil production in 10 years," rediff.com, 03/25/03, http://www.rediff.com/money/2003/mar/25oil.htm.

61. See note 14.

62. See note 16.

63. See note 1.

64. See note 18.

65. See note 3.

66. Ibid.

67. ChevronTexaco, http://www.chevronTexaco.com/.

68. "The EOR System in Duri: Comparison Between Conventional and Non-Conventional Systems," A.N. Lasman and M.D. Isnaeni, http://www.iaea.or.at/inis/aws/htgr/fulltext/29026696.pdf.

69. See note 67.

70. See note 68.

71. See note 67.

72. Ibid.

73. Ibid.

74. See note 3.

75. Ibid.

76. See note 1.

77. See note 3.

78. Country Analysis Brief-Indonesia, US DOE/EIA, http://www.eia.doe.gov/emeu/cabs/indonesa.html.

79. "Oil field mega projects 2004," Chris Skrebowski, Petroleum Review, Jan. 2004.

80. See note 14.

81. See note 16.

82. See note 1.

83. See note 18.

84. See note 3.

85. See note 1.

86. See note 4.

87. See note 1.

88. See note 3.

89. See note 1.

90. "Petronas goes global as reserves at home dwindle," Business Times, http://www.btimes.co.za/96/1117/world/world.htm.

91. Country Analysis Brief-Malaysia, US

DOE/EIA, http://www.eia.doe.gov/emeu/cabs/malaysia.html.

92. "ExxonMobil Maximizes Production from Malaysian Fields," Rigzone.com, 12/10/2001, http://www.rigzone.com/news/article.asp?a_id=2168.

93. "Petronas Announces Angsi's First Oil and Gas," 12/21/2001, http://www.petronas.com.my.

94. Malaysia Sector Summaries: Oil, Gas, Refining and Petrochemicals, http://www.britain.org.my/trade/sector_summary/oil&gas.htm.

95. See note 91

96. See note 14.

97. See note 1.

98. See note 16.

99. See note 18.

100. See note 3.

101. See note 4.

102. See note 1.

103. *Ibid.*

104. Country Analysis Brief-Vietnam, US DOE/EIA, http://www.eia.doe.gov/emeu/cabs/vietnam.html.

105. See note 14.

106. See note 36.

107. See note 16.

108. See note 18.

109. See note 3.

110. *Ibid.*

111. See note 1.

112. See note 43.

113. *Ibid.*

114. See note 14.

115. See note 16.

116. See note 18.

Chapter 6

1. International Petroleum Production Information, US DOE/EIA, http://www.eia.doe.gov/emeu/international/petroleu.html#Intl-Production.

2. *Ibid.*

3. *Ibid.*

4. Daniel Yergin, *The Prize: The Epic Quest of Oil, Money, and Power*, 1991.

5. Country Assessment — Saudi Arabia, Association for the Study of Peak Oil, Newsletter No 21, September 2002, http://www.asponews.org/ASPO.newsletter.021.php#99.

6. See note 1.

7. See note 5.

8. Country Analysis Brief — Saudi Arabia, US DOE/EIA, http://www.eia.doe.gov/emeu/cabs/saudi.html

9. "The World's Giant Oilfields," Simmons & Company International, 2001.

10. Based upon data from *Oil & G* nal, 2nd December issues, 1971–2003.

11. See note 9.

12. See note 5.

13. Wikipedia-The Free Encyclopedia, ht //en.wikipedia.org/wiki/List_of_oil_fields.

14. The Saudi Arabian Oil Miracle, Matthew Simmons, 2004, http://www.simmonsco-intl.com/research.aspx?Type=researchspeeches.

15. See note 10.

16. See note 13.

17. See note 9.

18. See note 10.

19. See note 9.

20. See note 13.

21. See note 10.

22. See note 9.

23. See note 13.

24. See note 9.

25. See note 13.

26. See note 5.

27. http://dieoff.org/42Countries/42Countries.htm.

28. Original Data, Association for the Study of Peak Oil, http://www.asponews.org/.

29. See note 10.

30. See note 13.

31. Country Analysis Brief — Kuwait, US DOE/EIA, March 2003, http://www.eia.doe.gov/emeu/cabs/kuwait.html.

32. See note 10.

33. See note 31.

34. http://www.icckw.com/iccindex.html.

35. See note 31.

36. See note 10.

37. See note 34.

38. See note 31.

39. *Ibid.*

40. *Ibid.*

41. See note 1.

42. See note 34.

43. See note 28.

44. See note 27.

45. See note 28.

46. See note 10.

47. *Ibid.*

48. *Ibid.*

49. See note 9.

50. See note 10.

51. See note 28.

52. See note 10.

53. *Ibid.*

54. See note 1.

55. Country Analysis Brief — Iran, US DOE/EIA, November 2003, http://www.eia.doe.gov/emeu/cabs/iran.html.

56. See note 10.

57. *Ibid.*

58. See note 9.

ee note 55.
Country Assessment — Iran, Associa-
or the Study of Peak Oil, Newsletter No
August 2003, http://www.asponews.org/
PO.newsletter.032.php#219.
61. See note 55.
62. *Ibid.*
63. *Ibid.*
64. See note 60.
65. See note 55.
66. See note 28.
67. See note 27.
68. See note 28.
69. See note 10.
70. Country Assessment — Iraq, Association for the Study of Peak Oil, Newsletter No
24, December 2002, http://www.asponews.org
/ASPO.newsletter.024.php#118.
71. *Ibid.*
72. World Petroleum Assessment 2000,
United States Geological Survey, http://pubs.
usgs.gov/dds/dds-060/.
73. Country Analysis Brief — Iraq, US
DOE/EIA, March 2004, http://www.eia.doe.
gov/emeu/cabs/iraq.html.
74. *Ibid.*
75. *Ibid.*
76. See note 10.
77. See note 70.
78. See note 27.
79. See note 70.
80. See note 10.
81. *Ibid.*
82. See note 9.
83. Country Analysis Brief — United Arab
Emirates, February 2004, http://www.eia.doe.
gov/emeu/cabs/uae.html.
84. See note 10.
85. See note 9.
86. See note 10.
87. See note 9.
88. See note 10.
89. See note 83.
90. See note 1.
91. See note 83.
92. See note 28.
93. See note 27.
94. See note 28.
95. See note 10.
96. *Ibid.*
97. *Ibid.*
98. Country Analysis Brief — Qatar, US
DOE/EIA, November 2003, http://www.eia.
doe.gov/emeu/cabs/uae.html.
99. See note 10.
100. *Ibid.*
101. Country Analysis Brief — Qatar, US
DOE/EIA, 1997.
102. See note 10.
103. International Energy Outlook 2003,

US DOE/EIA, http://www.eia.doe.gov/oiaf
/forecasting.html.
104. See note 27.
105. See note 28.
106. See note 10.
107. *Ibid.*
108. Country Analysis Brief — Oman, US
DOE/EIA, October 2003, http://www.eia.doe
.gov/emeu/cabs/oman.html.
109. See note 1.
110. See note 108.
111. *Ibid.*
112. See note 103.
113. See note 27.
114. See note 28.
115. See note 10.
116. See note 1.
117. Country Analysis Brief — Yemen, US
DOE/EIA, May 2003, http://www.eia.doe.gov
/emeu/cabs/yemen.html.
118. See note 103.
119. See note 27.
120. See note 28.
121. See note 10.
122. See note 117.
123. Monthly Country Assessment — Syria,
Association for the Study of Peak Oil, Newsletter No 17, May 2002, http://www.asponews.
org/ASPO.newsletter.017.php#57.
124. See note 1.
125. See note 103.
126. See note 27.
127. See note 28.
128. See note 10.
129. See note 103.
130. See note 27.
131. See note 28.

Chapter 7

1. International Petroleum Production
Data, US DOE/EIA, http://www.eia.doe.gov
/emeu/international/petroleu.html#Produc-
tionA.
2. Daniel Yergin, *The Prize: The Epic
Quest of Oil, Money, and Power*, 1991.
3. *Ibid.*
4. *Ibid.*
5. See note 1.
6. *Ibid.*
7. Country Analysis Brief-Russia, US
DOE/EIA, September 2003, http://www.eia.
doe.gov/emeu/cabs/russia.html.
8. "Largest West Siberia Oil and Gas Bearing Basin: Giant and Unique Petroleum Systems," Vilen Gavura and Alla Rovenskaya,
http://aapg.confex.com/aapg/hu2002/tech-
program/paper-46622.htm.

9. "Majors Return to Russian Oil Fields," http://www.geotimes.org/apr03/resources.html.

10. See note 8.

11. *Ibid.*

12. Data from Jean Laherrere.

13. See note 9.

14. "The World's Giant Oilfields," Simmons & Company International, 2001.

15. "Oil and Gas Resources in North-West Russia," http://arcticcentre.urova.fi/barents info/economic/02/03.html.

16. *Ibid.*

17. "Sakhalin Island Still Attracts Oil Companies," *On-Line Pravda*, July 24 ,2002, http://english.pravda.ru/comp/2002/07/24/33087.html.

18. "Sakhalin Island Optimistic about Oil Projects," *Alexander's Gas & Oil Connections*, Vol. 8, issue #6, March 20, 2003.

19. See note 17.

20. "Country Assessment-Russia," Association for the Study of Peak Oil, Newsletter #31, July 2003, http://www.asponews.org/ASPO. newsletter.031.php#212.

21. Country Analysis Brief-Caspian Sea Region, US DOE/EIA, 2001.

22. http://www.divineandvital.net/oil-gas_reserve.htm.

23. See note 21.

24. "Caspian: Sea's Oil Reserves Estimate Revised Downward," Michael Lelyveld, Radio Free Europe Radio Liberty, April 10, 2002, http://www.rferl.org/features/2002/04/10042 002090808.asp.

25. Country Analysis Brief-Kazakhstan, US DOE/EIA, July, 2003, http://www.eia.doe.gov /emeu/cabs/kazak.html.

26. *Ibid.*

27. *Ibid.*

28. *Ibid.*

29. *Ibid.*

30. Country Analysis Brief-Azerbaijan, US DOE/EIA, June, 2003, http://www.eia.doe.gov /emeu/cabs/azerbjan.html.

31. *Ibid.*

32. International Energy Outlook 2003, US DOE/EIA, http://www.eia.doe.gov/oiaf/ieo/ index.html.

33. http://dieoff.org/42Countries/42Countries.htm.

34. Original Data, Association for the Study of Peak Oil, http://www.asponews.org/.

35. Personal correspondence.

36. See note 34.

Chapter 8

1. International Petroleum Production Information, US DOE/EIA, http://www.eia.doe. gov/emeu/international/petroleu.html#Intr Production.

2. *Ibid.*

3. Based upon data from *Oil & Gas Journal*, 2nd December issues, 1971–2003.

4. *Ibid.*

5. *Ibid.*

6. Country Analysis Brief—Algeria, US DOE/EIA, Feb. 2004, http://www.eia.doe.gov /emeu/cabs/algeria.html.

7. *Ibid.*

8. *Ibid.*

9. *Ibid.*

10. International Energy Outlook 2003, US DOE/EIA, http://www.eia.doe.gov/oiaf/ieo/ index.html.

11. http://dieoff.org/42Countries/42Countries.htm.

12. Original Data, Association for the Study of Peak Oil, http://www.asponews.org/.

13. Country Assessment—Angola, Association for the Study of Peak Oil, Newsletter No 36, Dec. 2003, http://www.asponews.org /HTML/Newsletter36.html#286.

14. See note 1.

15. See note 3.

16. Norwegian Petroleum Directorate Annual Report, 2002, http://www.npd.no/English/Frontpage.htm.

17. MBendi: Information for Africa, http://www.mbendi.co.za/proj/p08h.htm.

18. Country Analysis Brief—Angola, US DOE/EIA, Feb. 2004, http://www.eia.doe.gov/ emeu/cabs/angola.html.

19. See note 3.

20. See note 17.

21. See note 3.

22. See note 18.

23. See note 10.

24. See note 11.

25. See note 1.

26. See note 12.

27. See note 3.

28. *Ibid.*

29. Country Analysis Brief—Congo, US DOE/EIA, July 2003, http://www.eia.doe.gov /emeu/cabs/congo.html.

30. See note 10.

31. See note 11.

32. See note 12.

33. See note 3.

34. Country Assessment—Egypt, Association for the Study of Peak Oil, Newsletter No 30 June 2003, http://www.asponews.org/ ASPO.newsletter.030.php#199.

35. See note 12.

36. See note 1.

37. Country Analysis Brief—Egypt, US DOE/EIA, Feb. 2004, http://www.eia.doe. gov/emeu/cabs/egypt.html.

38. See note 3.
39. *Ibid.*
40. See note 10.
41. See note 11.
42. See note 12.
43. See note 3.
44. See note 1.
45. Country Analysis Brief — Gabon, US DOE/EIA, Oct. 2003, http://www.eia.doe.gov /emeu/cabs/gabon.html.
46. *Ibid.*
47. See note 10.
48. See note 11.
49. See note 12.
50. See note 3.
51. See note 1.
52. Country Analysis Brief — Libya, US DOE/EIA, Jan. 2004, http://www.eia.doe.gov /emeu/cabs/libya.html.
53. See note 10.
54. See note 11.
55. See note 12.
56. See note 3.
57. Country Analysis Brief — Nigeria, US DOE/EIA, March 2003, http://www.eia.doe. gov/emeu/cabs/nigeria.html.
58. *Ibid.*
59. See note 1.
60. See note 10.
61. *Ibid.*
62. See note 11.
63. See note 1.
64. Country Assessment — Nigeria, Association for the Study of Peak Oil, Newsletter No 27, March 2003, http://www.asponews. org/ASPO.newsletter.027.php#159.
65. See note 3.
66. Country Analysis Brief — Sudan, US DOE/EIA, Jan. 2003, http://www.eia.doe.gov /emeu/cabs/sudan.html.
67. *Ibid.*
68. See note 10.
69. See note 1.
70. See note 12.
71. See note 3.
72. See note 1.
73. *Ibid.*
74. See note 10.
75. Duncan does not have an oil + NGLs forecast for Sudan.
76. See note 10.
77. See note 12.

Chapter 9

1. US DOE/EIA International Energy Outlook 2003, http://www.eia.doe.gov/oiaf/ ieo/index.html.
2. US DOE/EIA, http://www.eia.doe.gov /emeu/international/petroleu.html#IntlPro- duction.
3. Based upon cumulative oil production data in *Oil & Gas Journal* at the end of 1992 and US DOE/EIA annual production totals since then.
4. World Petroleum Assessment 2000, United States Geological Survey, http://pubs. usgs.gov/dds/dds-060/.
5. http://dieoff.org/42Countries/42Coun- tries.htm.
6. Data from the Association for the Study of Peak Oil, http://www.peakoil.net/.
7. See note 2.
8. *Ibid.*
9. *Ibid.*
10. See note 1.
11. See note 2.
12. "Russian oil output growth may slow down," Gulf News on-line edition, Dec. 5, 2003, http://www.gulf-news.com/articles/ news.asp?articleID=104611.
13. See note 1.
14. "Oil field mega projects 2004," Chris Skrebowski, *Petroleum Review*, Jan. 2004.
15. *Ibid.*
16. *Ibid.*
17. *Ibid.*
18. Short-Term Energy Outlook- December 2002, US DOE/EIA, http://www. eia.doe.gov/emeu/steo/pub/outlook.html.
19. Country Analysis Brief — Angola, US DOE/EIA, Feb. 2004, http://www.eia.doe.gov /emeu/cabs/angola.html.
20. Based upon data from *Oil & Gas Jour- nal*, 2nd December issues, 1971–2003.
21. Country Analysis Brief — Congo, US DOE/EIA, July 2003, http://www.eia.doe.gov /emeu/cabs/congo.html.
22. See note 14.
23. *Ibid.*
24. See note 2.

Chapter 10

1. "Trucking," Jerry Flint, *Forbes*, vol. 162, issue 13, 12/14/1998.
2. US DOE/EIA, http://www.eia.doe. gov/.
3. "Why the U.S. Is Running Out of Gas," Donald Bartlett and James Steele, *Time* mag- azine, July 21, 2003.
4. PEM Fuel Cells, http://fuelcells.si.edu/ pem/pemmain.htm#1.
5. http://science.howstuffworks.com/ news-item10.htm
6. Thomas Spiro and William Stignati,

Chemistry and the Environment, Second Edition, 2003.

7. The Future of Fuel Cells, http://www.benwiens.com/energy4.html.

8. "Running on Fumes," Richard Monastersky, *The Chronicle of Higher Education*, vol. 50, number 7, Oct. 10, 2003.

9. "Hydrogen: The Fuel of the Future?," Joan Ogden, *Physics Today*, April 2002.

10. See note 8.

11. "Comparative Assessment of Fuel Cell Cars," Malcolm Weiss; John Heywood; Andreas Schafer; and Vinod Natarajan, Massachusetts Institute of Technology, Laboratory for Energy and the Environment, Feb. 2003.

12. "Is Hydrogen Sustainable," Oliver Sylvester-Bradley, *EV World*, July 19, 2003, http://evworld.com/view.cfm?section=article&storyid=550.

13. See note 4.

14. See note 8.

15. See note 12.

16. *Ibid.*

17. "The Hydrogen Hallucination," Mark Sardella, http://www.solaraccess.com/news/story?storyid=5497, Nov. 2003.

18. See note 11.

19. "Two Hundred Hours," Bill Moore, Report One on the SAE Fuel Cell/Hydrogen Workshop in Sacramento, Feb. 18–19, 2004, http://groups.yahoo.com/group/energyresources/message/52194.

20. See note 9.

21. See note 8.

22. "Hydrogen: clean, safer than in the past and popular with politicians but will it be the cheap fuel of the future," http://www.scientific-alliance.com/news_archives/transport/hydrogencleansafer.htm.

23. See note 8.

24. History of Electric Vehicles, http://avt.inel/gov/evhl.html.

25. *Ibid.*

26. *Ibid.*

27. *Ibid.*

28. *Ibid.*

29. http://www.evworld.com/archives/reports/ford_eKa.html.

30. http://www.hondacars.com/models/model_overview.asp?ModelName=&bhcp=1&BrowserDetected=True.

31. http://www.toyota.com/prius/.

32. "Minicars make their mark outside U.S.," Bobbi Nodell, MSNBC, http://www.msnbc.com/news/586472.asp?pne=msn&cp=1.

33. http://www.indiacar.com/index2.asp?pagename=http://www.indiacar.com/infobank/ageofdiesels.htm.

34. See note 2.

35. "Oil Shale — The Elusive Energy," Walter Youngquist, *Hubbert Center Newsletter* # 98/4.

36. *Ibid.*

37. Today in Technology History, The Center for the Study of Technology and Society, http://www.tecsoc.org/pubs/history/2001/may2.htm.

38. See note 35.

39. *Ibid.*

40. Walter Youngquist, *Geodestinies*,1997.

41. "Push Ethanol off the Dole," Stephen Moore, Cato Institute, July 10, 1997, http://www.cato.org/dailys/7–10–97.html.

42. *Ibid.*

43. "Ethanol for Fuel Fundamentally Uneconomic," *University Science News*, http://unisci.com/stories/20013/0813012.htm.

44. "Estimating the Net Energy Balance of Corn Ethanol," Hosein Shapouri et al., US Department of Agriculture, Economic Research Service, Office of Energy and New Uses, Agricultural Economic Report No. 721, July 1995.

45. "Energy and Dollar Costs of Ethanol Production with Corn," David Pimentel, *Hubbert Center Newsletter* # 98/2.

46. Daniel Yergin, *The Prize: The Epic Quest of Oil, Money, and Power*, 1991.

47. *Ibid.*

48. *Ibid.*

49. *Ibid.*

50. Country Analysis Brief — South Africa, US DOE/EIA, http://www.eia.doe.gov/emeu/cabs/safrica.html.

51. *Ibid.*

52. *Ibid.*

53. See note 40.

Bibliography

"About Hibernia." http://www.hibernia.ca/html/about_hibernia/index.html.

Alaska Department of Natural Resources. http://www.dog.dnr.state.ak.us/oil/.

Alaska Department of Revenue. http://www.tax.state.ak.us/programs/oil/production/index.asp.

Alberta Energy and Utilities Board. http://www.eub.gov.ab.ca.

"Alberta Oilsands Produce 25% More Than Conventional Oil Reserves." *Alexander's Gas & Oil Connections*, Vol. 8, issue 3, June 26, 2003.

American Petroleum Institute. http://api-ec.api.org/intro/index_noflash.htm.

"Annual Energy Outlook 2003." US DOE/EIA. http://www.eia.doe.gov/oiaf/forecasting.html.

"Arctic National Wildlife Refuge, 1002 Area, Petroleum Assessment, 1998, Including Economic Analysis." United States Geological Survey, 1998. http://www.usgs.gov/.

Association for the Study of Peak Oil. http://www.asponews.org/.

"Australian Oil and Gas." http://wwwistp.murdoch.edu.au/publications/projects/oilfleay/06australian.html.

Bartlett, Donald, and Steele, James. "Why the U.S. Is Running Out of Gas." *Time*, July 21, 2003.

Brethour, Patrick. "Alberta Mulls Nuclear Plants to Power Oil Sands Extraction." *Toronto Globe and Mail*, Jan. 29, 2003.

_____. "Soaring Costs Plague Oil Sands." *Toronto Globe and Mail*, May 20, 2003.

_____. "Syncrude Trust Battered as Investors Dump Stock." *Toronto Globe and Mail*, March 6, 2004.

Campbell, C. J. "The Imminent Peak of World Oil Production." A presentation to the House of Commons All-Party Committee, July 7, 1999. http://www.hubbertpeak.com/campbell/commmons.htm.

ChevronTexaco. http://www.chevronTexaco.com/.

"China Becomes World-Class Oil Buyer." *Alexander's Gas & Oil Connections*, vol. 8, issue 16, August 21, 2003.

"China's Petroleum Industry." http://www.vitrade.com/china/chinanews_brieing_oil_industry.htm.

"China's Tarim Basin: Gushing with Oil or Just Hype?" Reuters News Report, Dec. 9, 2003.

"Country Analysis—Ecuador." *Alexander's Gas & Oil Connections*, vol. 8, issue 4, February 20, 2003. http://www.gasandoil.com/goc/news/ntl30864.htm.

"Country Analysis Brief—Algeria." US DOE/EIA, Feb. 2004. http://www.eia.doe.gov/emeu/cabs/algeria.html.

"Country Analysis Brief — Angola." US DOE/EIA, Feb. 2004. http://www.eia.doe.gov /emeu/cabs/angola.html.

"Country Analysis Brief — Azerbaijan." US DOE/EIA, June 2003. http://www.eia.doe. gov/emeu/cabs/azerbjan.html.

"Country Analysis Brief — Brazil." US DOE/EIA. http://www.eia.doe.gov/emeu/cabs/ brazil.html.

"Country Analysis Brief — Canada." US DOE/EIA, Jan. 2004, http://www.eia.doe.gov/ emeu/cabs/canada.html.

"Country Analysis Brief — Caspian Sea Region." US DOE/EIA, August 2003. http:// www.eia.doe.gov/emeu/cabs/caspian.html.

"Country Analysis Brief — Caspian Sea." US DOE/EIA, 2001. http://www.eia.doe.gov/ emeu/cabs/contents.html.

"Country Analysis Brief — China." US DOE/EIA, http://www.eia.doe.gov/emeu/cabs/ china.html.

"Country Analysis Brief — Colombia." US DOE/EIA. http://www.eia.doe.gov/emeu/ cabs/colombia.html.

"Country Analysis Brief — Congo." US DOE/EIA, July 2003. http://www.eia.doe.gov/ emeu/cabs/congo.html.

"Country Analysis Brief — Ecuador." US DOE/EIA. http://www.eia.doe.gov/emeu/ cabs/ecuador.html.

"Country Analysis Brief — Egypt." US DOE/EIA," Feb. 2004. http://www.eia.doe.gov/ emeu/cabs/egypt.html.

"Country Analysis Brief — Gabon." US DOE/EIA, Oct. 2003. http://www.eia.doe.gov/ emeu/cabs/gabon.html.

"Country Analysis Brief — Indonesia." US DOE/EIA. http://www.eia.doe.gov/emeu /cabs/indonesa.html.

"Country Analysis Brief — Iran." US DOE/EIA, Nov. 2003. http://www.eia.doe.gov/ emeu/cabs/iran.html.

"Country Analysis Brief — Iraq." US DOE/EIA, March 2004. http://www.eia.doe.gov/ emeu/cabs/iraq.html.

"Country Analysis Brief — Kazakhstan." US DOE/EIA, July 2003. http://www.eia.doe. gov/emeu/cabs/kazak.html.

"Country Analysis Brief — Kuwait." US DOE/EIA, March 2003. http://www.eia.doe. gov/emeu/cabs/kuwait.html.

"Country Analysis Brief — Libya." US DOE/EIA, Jan. 2004. http://www.eia.doe.gov/ emeu/cabs/libya.html.

"Country Analysis Brief — Malaysia." US DOE/EIA. http://www.eia.doe.gov/emeu /cabs/malaysia.html.

"Country Analysis Brief — Mexico." US DOE/EIA. Feb. 2003. http://www.eia.doe.gov/ emeu/cabs/mexico.html.

"Country Analysis Brief — Nigeria." US DOE/EIA, March 2003. http://www.eia.doe. gov/emeu/cabs/nigeria.html.

"Country Analysis Brief — Oman." US DOE/EIA, October 2003. http://www.eia.doe. gov/emeu/cabs/oman.html.

"Country Analysis Brief — Qatar." US DOE/EIA, 1997. http://www.eia.doe.gov/emeu /cabs/contents.html.

"Country Analysis Brief — Qatar." US DOE/EIA, Nov. 2003. http://www.eia.doe.gov/ emeu/cabs/uae.html.

"Country Analysis Brief — Russia." US DOE/EIA, Sept. 2003. http://www.eia.doe.gov/ emeu/cabs/russia.html.

"Country Analysis Brief — Saudi Arabia." US DOE/EIA. http://www.eia.doe.gov/emeu /cabs/saudi.html.

"Country Analysis Brief — South Africa." US DOE/EIA. http://www.eia.doe.gov/emeu/cabs/safrica.html.

"Country Analysis Brief — Sudan." US DOE/EIA, Jan. 2003. http://www.eia.doe.gov/emeu/cabs/sudan.html.

"Country Analysis Brief — United Arab Emirates." US DOE/EIA, February 2004. http://www.eia.doe.gov/emeu/cabs/uae.html.

"Country Analysis Brief — Venezuela." US DOE/EIA. http://www.eia.doe.gov/emeu/cabs/venez.html.

"Country Analysis Brief — Vietnam." US DOE/EIA. http://www.eia.doe.gov/emeu/cabs/vietnam.html.

"Country Analysis Brief — Yemen." US DOE/EIA, May 2003. http://www.eia.doe.gov/emeu/cabs/yemen.html.

"Country Assessment Series — Angola." Association for the Study of Peak Oil, Newsletter no. 36, Dec. 2003. http://www.asponews.org/HTML/Newsletter36.html#286.

"Country Assessment Series — Argentina." Association for the Study of Peak Oil, Newsletter no. 33, Sept. 2003. http://www.asponews.org/ASPO.newsletter.033.php#243.

"Country Assessment Series — Australia." Association for the Study of Peak Oil, Newsletter no. 28, April 2003. http://www.asponews.org/ASPO.newsletter.028.php#174

"Country Assessment Series — Brazil." Association for the Study of Peak Oil, Newsletter no. 26, Feb. 2003. http://www.peakoil.ie/newsletters/147.

"Country Assessment Series — Egypt." Association for the Study of Peak Oil, Newsletter no. 30, June 2003. http://www.asponews.org/ASPO.newsletter.030.php#199.

"Country Assessment Series — Iran." Association for the Study of Peak Oil, Newsletter no. 32, August 2003. http://www.asponews.org/ASPO.newsletter.032.php#219.

"Country Assessment Series — Iraq." Association for the Study of Peak Oil, Newsletter no. 24, December 2002. http://www.asponews.org/ASPO.newsletter.024.php#118.

"Country Assessment Series — Nigeria." Association for the Study of Peak Oil, Newsletter no. 27, March 2003. http://www.asponews.org/ASPO.newsletter.027.php#159.

"Country Assessment Series — Russia." Association for the Study of Peak Oil, Newsletter no. 31, July 2003. http://www.asponews.org/ASPO.newsletter.031.php#212.

"Country Assessment Series — Saudi Arabia." The Association for the Study of Peak Oil, Newsletter no. 21, September 2002. http://www.asponews.org/ASPO.newsletter.021.php#99.

"Country Assessment Series — Syria." Association for the Study of Peak Oil, Newsletter no. 17, May 2002. http://www.asponews.org/ASPO.newsletter.017.php#57.

"Dangerous Colombia Fails to Lure Oil Explorers." Reuters News Service, July 24, 2003.

Danish Energy Authority. 2003. http://www.ens.dk/sw479.asp.

"Daqing Oil Field Reports on Crude Output." *Alexander's Gas & Oil Connections*, vol. 8, issue 16, August 21, 2003.

Duncan, Richard. Country production forecasts at http://dieoff.org/42Countries/42Countries.htm.

"Ethanol for Fuel Fundamentally Uneconomic." *University Science News*, http://unisci.com/stories/20013/0813012.htm.

"ExxonMobil Maximizes Production from Malaysian Fields." Rigzone.com, Dec. 10, 2001. http://www.rigzone.com/news/article.asp?a_id=2168.

"Falkland Islands: The Last Frontier." *Alexander's Gas & Oil Connections*, vol. 3, issue 11, March 4, 1998, http://www.gasandoil.com/goc/news/ntl81460.htm.

Fleay, Brian. "Oil and Australia." *Hubbert Center Newsletter*, 2000/3, http://hubbert.mines.edu/.

Flint, Jerry. "Trucking." *Forbes*, vol. 162, issue 13, December 14, 1998.

"Future Oil Production for the Alaska North Slope." U.S. DOE/EIA, May 2001. http://www.eia.doe.gov/.

Gavura, Vien, and Rovenskaya, Alla. "Largest West Siberia Oil and Gas Bearing Basin: Giant and Unique Petroleum Systems." http://aapg.confex.com/aapg/hu2002/tech-program/paper-46622.htm.

Gever, J.; Kaufmann, R.K.; Skole, D.; and Vorosmarty, C. *Beyond Oil: The Threat of Food and Fuel in the Coming Decades.* Third Edition. Boulder: University Press of Colorado, 1991.

"Gutierrez: Output Not Enough to Fill OCP," BNAmericas, July 9, 2003, http://www.bnamericas.com/, http://www.bnamericas.com/.

Haggert, Scott. "Oh, How the Patch Has Changed: Technology, Finances Revamp Landscape." *Calgary Herald*, August 2, 2003.

History of Electric Vehicles, http://avt.inel/gov/evhl.html.

http://science.howstuffworks.com/news-item10.htm.

http://www.divineandvital.net/oilgas_reserve.htm.

http://www.evworld.com/archives/reports/ford_eKa.html.

http://www.hondacars.com/models/model_overview.asp?ModelName=Insight&bhcp =1&BrowserDetected=True.

http://www.icckw.com/iccindex.html.

http://www.indiacar.com/index2.asp?pagename=http://www.indiacar.com/infobank/a geofdiesels.htm.

http://www.oogc.com/world_oper/latin_america/over_colo.htm.

http://www.projectsmonitor.com/detailnews.asp?newsid=2930.

http://www.theworld.com/~habib/thegarden//uwa/uwarep.doc.

http://www.toyota.com/prius/.

Hubbert, M. K. "Nuclear Energy and the Fossil Fuels." Presented at the spring meeting of the Southern District Division of Production, American Petroleum Institute, March 1956.

_____. "The World's Evolving Energy System." *American Journal of Physics*, 49.

"Hydrogen: Clean, Safer Than in the Past and Popular With Politicians, But Will It Be the Cheap Fuel of the Future?" http://www.scientific-alliance.com/news_archives /transport/hydrogencleansafer.htm.

"India Can Triple Oil Production in 10 Years." rediff.com, March 25, 2003, http://www.rediff.com/money/2003/mar/25oil.htm.

"International Energy Outlook 2001." US DOE/EIA. http://www.eia.doe.gov/oiaf/fore-casting.html.

"International Energy Outlook 2003." US DOE/EIA. http://www.eia.doe.gov/oiaf/fore-casting.html.

"International Petroleum Consumption Information." US DOE/EIA. http://www.eia. doe.gov/emeu/international/petroleu.html#ConsumptionQ.

"International Petroleum Production Information." US DOE/EIA. http://www.eia.doe. gov/emeu/international/petroleu.html#ProductionQ.

Ivanhoe, L. F. "Petroleum Positions of Brazil and Venezuela." Hubbert Center. http:/ /hubbert.mines.edu/news/Ivanhoe_93-3.pdf.

_____. "Canada's Future Oil Production: Projection 2000–2020." *Hubbert Center Newsletter*, 2002/2.

_____. "Get Ready for Another Oil Shock." *The Futurist*, Jan./Feb. 1997.

_____. "The Petroleum Positions of Canada and Mexico." *Hubbert Center Newsletter*, 1998/1, http://hubbert.mines.edu/.

_____, and Leckie, G. G. "Global Oil, Gas Fields, Sizes Tallied, Analyzed." *Oil and Gas Journal*, Feb. 15, 1993, pp. 87–91.

Lasman, A. N., and Isnaeni, M. D. "The EOR System in Duri: Comparison Between Conventional and Non-Conventional Systems." http://www.iaea.or.at/inis/aws/htgr/fulltext/29026696.pdf.

Lelyveld, Michael. "Caspian: Sea's Oil Reserves Estimate Revised Downward." Radio Free Europe Radio Liberty, April 10, 2002. http://www.rferl.org/features/2002/04/10042002090808.asp.

Luft, Gal. "Can Canadian Sands Replace Arabia's?" http://www.energypulse.net/centers/article/article_display.cfm?a_id=421, 7/31/03.

Mackenzie, James J. "Oil as a Finite Resource: When Is Global Production Likely to Peak?" World Resources Institute, March 1996, updated March 2000.

"Majors Return to Russian Oil Fields." http://www.geotimes.org/apr03/resources.html.

"Malaysia Sector Summaries." http://www.britain.org.my/trade/sector_summary/oil&gas.htm.

Masters, C. D.; Attanasi, E. D.; and Root, D. H. "World Petroleum Assessment and Analysis." U.S. Geological Survey, 14th World Petroleum Congress, 1994.

"MBendi: Information for Africa." http://www.mbendi.co.za/proj/p08h.htm.

Minerals Management Service. http://www.gomr.mms.gov/homepg/offshore/deepwatr/summary.asp.

Monastersky, Richard. "Running on Fumes." *The Chronicle of Higher Education*, vol. 50, no. 7, Oct. 10, 2003.

Moore, Bill. "Two Hundred Hours." Report One on the SAE Fuel Cell/Hydrogen Workshop in Sacramento, Feb. 18–19, 2004. http://groups.yahoo.com/group/energyresources/message/52194.

Moore, Stephen. "Push Ethanol Off the Dole." Cato Institute, July 10, 1997. http://www.cato.org/dailys/7-10-97.html.

"National Assessment of United States Oil and Gas Resources—1995." United States Geological Survey, 1995. http://www.usgs.gov/.

Newfoundland & Labrador Statistics Agency. http://www.economics.gov.nf.ca/ind OIL.asp.

Nodell, Bobbi. "Minicars Make Their Mark Outside the U.S." MSNBC. http://www.msnbc.com/news/586472.asp?pne=msn&cp1=1.

"Northern Territory Oil & Gas Fact Sheet." http://www.dme.nt.gov.au/dmemain/energy/facts_figures/Fact_Sheets/laminaria.html.

Norwegian Petroleum Directorate. http://www.npd.no/engelsk/cwi/pbl/en/index.htm.

"Norwegian Petroleum Directorate Annual Report, 2002." http://www.npd.no/English/Frontpage.htm.

Ogden, Joan. "Hydrogen: The Fuel of the Future?" *Physics Today*, April 2002.

"Oil and Gas Resources in North-West Russia." http://arcticcentre.urova.fi/barentsinfo/economic/02/03.html.

"Oil Market Report." International Energy Agency, Jan. 2004. http://omrpublic.iea.org/.

"Oil Market Report." International Energy Agency, July 2003. http://omrpublic.iea.org/.

"Outer Continental Shelf Petroleum Assessment, 2000." Minerals Management Service, 2000. http://www.gomr.mms.gov/homepg/offshore/deepwatr/summary.asp.

"PDVSA to Invest Up to US$45 Billion through 2010." BNAmericas, July 21, 2003. http://www.bnamericas.com/.

"PDVSA to Outsource Maintenance Contracts." *Alexander's Gas & Oil Connections*, vol. 8, issue 14, July 10, 2003.

"PEM Fuel Cells." http://fuelcells.si.edu/pem/pemmain.htm#1.

Petrobras. http://www2.petrobras.com.br/ingles/index.asp.

"Petronas Announces Angsi's First Oil and Gas." Dec. 21, 2001. http://www.petronas.com.my.

"Petronas Goes Global as Reserves at Home Dwindle." *Business Times.* http://www. btimes.co.za/96/1117/world/world.htm.

Petrucci, Ralph, et al. *General Chemistry: Principles and Modern Applications.* Eighth Edition. Englewood Cliffs, N. J.: Prentice Hall, 2001.

Pimentel, David. "Energy and Dollar Costs of Ethanol Production with Corn." *Hubbert Center Newsletter* no. 98/2, http://hubbert.mines.edu/.

Platts Global Energy. http://www.platts/features/LatinAmericancrude/argentina.shtml.

"Politics Cloud Mexico's Promises." Oct. 2004. http://www.aapg.org/explorer/2004/ 10oct/mexico.cfm.

"Potential Oil Production from the Coastal Plain of the Arctic National Wildlife Refuge: Updated Assessment, May 2000." U.S. DOE/EIA, http://www.eia.doe.gov/.

"A Primer on Oil & Gas in Mexico." Simmons & Company International, June 6, 2003. http://www.simmonsco-intl.com/SearchResult.aspx?ID=800.

Railroad Commission of Texas. http://www.rrc.state.tx.us/divisions/og/information-data/oginfo.html.

Robinson, Matthew. "Higher Water Cuts Seen in Venezuela Maracaibo Oil." Reuters News Service, July 2003. http://today.reuters.com/rss/newsrss.aspx.

"Russian Oil Output Growth May Slow Down," Gulf News on-line edition, Dec. 5, 2003. http://www.gulf-news.com/articles/news.asp?articleID=104611.

"Sakhalin Island Optimistic about Oil Projects." *Alexander's Gas & Oil Connections,* Vol. 8, issue 6, March 20, 2003.

"Sakhalin Island Still Attracts Oil Companies." *On-Line Pravda,* July 24, 2002. http://english.pravda.ru/comp/2002/07/24/33087.html.

Sardella, Mark. "The Hydrogen Hallucination." Nov. 2003. http://www.solaraccess. com/news/story?storyid=5497.

Shapouri, Hosein, et al. "Estimating the Net Energy Balance of Corn Ethanol." U.S. Department of Agriculture, Economic Research Service, Office of Energy and New Uses, Agricultural Economic Report No. 721, July 1995.

Shields, David. "Pemex Sets Sights on New Offshore Oil Projects." *The News Columnist,* August 28, 2002.

"Short-Term Energy Outlook — December 2002." US DOE/EIA, http://www.eia. doe.gov/emeu/steo/pub/outlook.html.

Simmons, Matthew. "The Saudi Arabian Oil Miracle." Simmons & Company International, 2004. http://www.simmonsco-intl.com/research.aspx?Type=research speeches.

_____. "The World's Giant Oilfields: How Many Exist? How Much Do They Produce? How Fast Are They Declining?" Simmons & Company International, 2001. http:// www.simmonsco-intl.com/Research.aspx?Type=MSSpeechArchives.

Skrebowski, Chris. "Oil Field Mega Projects 2004." *Petroleum Review,* Jan. 2004.

Spiro, Thomas, and Stigiani, William. *Chemistry and the Environment.* Second Edition. Englewood Cliffs, N. J.: Prentice Hall, 2003.

Stevenson, James. "Bitumen Recovery at Risk in Northern Alberta: Conoco." *The Canadian Press,* August 2, 2003. http://www.cp.org/english/hp.htm.

Sylvester-Bradley, Oliver. "Is Hydrogen Sustainable?" *EV World,* July 19, 2003. http://evworld.com/view.cfm?section=article&storyid=550.

"The Future of Fuel Cells." http://www.benwiens.com/energy4.html.

"Today in Technology History." The Center for the Study of Technology and Society. http://www.tecsoc.org/pubs/history/2001/may2.htm.

United States Department of Energy/Energy Information Administration (DOE/EIA). Useful sites for oil and gas production and consumption data include: http://www.eia.doe.gov/

http://www.eia.doe.gov/emeu/international/petroleu.html#IntlProduction
http://www.eia.doe.gov/oil_gas/natural_gas/info_glance/natural_gas.html.
http://www.eia.doe.gov/oil_gas/petroleum/info_glance/crudeoil.html
United States Geological Survey. U.S. Oil & Gas Assessments, 1961–1969. http://
www.usgs.gov/.
Weiss, Malcolm; Heywood, John; Schafer, Andreas; and Natarajan, Vinod. "Comparative Assessment of Fuel Cell Cars." Massachusetts Institute of Technology, Laboratory for Energy and the Environment, Feb. 2003.
"Welcome to PetroChina." http://www.petrochina.com.cn/english/gsjs/zyyw_1_5_
1.htm.
"What Is Terra Nova?" http://www.terranovaproject.com/html/what_is_terra_nova/
field_profile.html.
"Wood Mackenzie Believes Deepwater Brazil Stands at the Crossroads." http://www.
woodmac.com/news_e_30.htm.
"Woodside's Laminaria Oil field Development Starts On Time." *On-Line Pravda*, June
13, 2002. http://english.pravda.ru/comp/2002/06/13/30245.html.
"World Petroleum Assessment 2000." United States Geological Survey, http://pubs.
usgs.gov/dds/dds-060/.
"Worldwide Production." *Oil & Gas Journal*. Found in the last December issue of each
year.
Yergin, Daniel. *The Prize: The Epic Quest for Oil, Money and Power*. New York: Free
Press, 1991.
Youngquist, Walter. *Geodestinies: The Inevitable Control of Earth Resources over Nations
and Individuals*. National Book Company, 1997.
_____. "Oil Shale — The Elusive Energy." *Hubbert Center Newsletter* 98/4. http://hubbert.mines.edu/.

Index